The Fading Light of Advaita Ācārya

AAR RELIGION IN TRANSLATION

SERIES EDITOR
Mark Csikszentmihalyi, University of Wisconsin-Madison
A Publication Series of
The American Academy of Religion
and
Oxford University Press

EXPLAINING RELIGION
Criticism and Theory from Bodin to Freud

J. Samuel Preus

DIALECTIC
or, The Art of Doing Philosophy
A Study Edition of the 1811 Notes

Friedrich D. E. Schleiermacher
Translated with Introduction and Notes by
Terence N. Tice

RELIGION OF REASON
Out of the Sources of Judaism

Hermann Cohen
Translated, with an Introduction
by Simon Kaplan
Introductory essays by Leo Strauss
Introductory essays for the second edition by
Steven S. Schwarzchild and Kenneth Seeskin

DURKHEIM ON RELIGION
Émile Durkheim
Edited by W. S. F. Pickering

ON THE *GLAUBENSLEHRE*
Two Letters to Dr. Lücke

Friedrich D. E. Schleiermacher
Translated by James Duke and
Francis Fiorenza

HERMENEUTICS
The Handwritten Manuscripts

Friedrich D. E. Schleiermacher
Edited by Heina Kimmerle
Translated by James Duke and Jack Forstman

THE STUDY OF STOLEN LOVE
Translated by David C. Buck and
K. Paramasivam

THE DAOIST MONASTIC MANUAL
A Translation of the *Fengdao Kejie*

Livia Kohn

SACRED AND PROFANE BEAUTY
The Holy in Art

Garardus van der Leeuw
Preface by Mircea Eliade
Translated by David E. Green
With a new introduction and bibliography by
Diane Apostolos-Cappadona

THE HISTORY OF THE BUDDHA's RELIC SHRINE
A Translation of the Sinhala Thūpavamsa

Stephen C. Berkwitz

DAMASCIUS' *PROBLEMS AND SOLUTIONS CONCERNING FIRST PRINCIPLES*

Translated by Sara Ahbel-Rappe
Introduction and Notes by Sara Ahbel-Rappe

THE SECRET GARLAND
Āṇṭāḷ's *Tiruppāvai* and *Nācciyār Tirumoḻi*

Translated with Introduction and Commentary by
Archana Venkatesan

PRELUDE TO THE MODERNIST CRISIS
The "Firmin" Articles of Alfred Loisy

Edited by Charles Talar
Translated by Christine Thirlway

DEBATING THE DASAM GRANTH

Robin Rinehart

THE FADING LIGHT OF ADVAITA ĀCĀRYA
Three Hagiographies

Rebecca J. Manring

The Fading Light of Advaita Ācārya

Three Hagiographies

REBECCA J. MANRING

OXFORD
UNIVERSITY PRESS

OXFORD
UNIVERSITY PRESS

Oxford University Press, Inc., publishes works that further
Oxford University's objective of excellence
in research, scholarship, and education.

Oxford New York
Auckland Cape Town Dar es Salaam Hong Kong Karachi
Kuala Lumpur Madrid Melbourne Mexico City Nairobi
New Delhi Shanghai Taipei Toronto

With offices in
Argentina Austria Brazil Chile Czech Republic France Greece
Guatemala Hungary Italy Japan Poland Portugal Singapore
South Korea Switzerland Thailand Turkey Ukraine Vietnam

Published by Oxford University Press, Inc.
198 Madison Avenue, New York, New York 10016

www.oup.com

Library of Congress Cataloging-in-Publication Data
The fading light of Advaita Acarya : three hagiographies / Rebecca J. Manring.
p. cm.—(AAR religion in translation)
Includes translations from Bengali and from Sanskrit.
Includes bibliographical references and index.
ISBN 978-0-19-973646-1 (hardcover : alk. paper)—ISBN 978-0-19-973647-8 (pbk. : alk. paper)
1. Advaita Acarya, 15th century. 2. Vaishnavites—Biography. I. Manring, Rebecca J. (Rebecca Jane), 1951– II. Haricarana Dasa. Advaita mangala. English. III. Laudiya Krsnadasa. Balyalilasutra. English. IV. Isana Nagara, 1865-1954. Advaita prakasa. English.
BL1175.A187F33 2011
294.5'512092—dc22
[B]
2010042382

1 3 5 7 9 8 6 4 2

Printed in the United States of America
on acid-free paper

for Mary Naomi Wilson Peyton
1883–1968

CONTENTS

FOREWORD

Advaita Ācārya, a learned Vārendra brahmin, was the forerunner of the Vaiṣṇava *bhakti* movement in Bengal in the sixteenth century. At a time when the Vaiṣṇavas of Bengal were misunderstood and exposed to banter and ridicule, Advaita Ācārya boldly championed their cause and unified them against their brahminical detractors. He prepared the ground for the emergence of Caitanya as the charismatic leader of the *bhakti* movement. So great was Advaita Ācārya's importance that he was honored as the god Śiva and the god Mahāviṣṇu incarnate. He labored very hard to mobilize a large section of the brahmins of the towns of Shantipur and Navadvīpa behind Caitanya's essentially radical movement. His noncommunal frame of mind was revealed in his fraternization with Brahmā Haridāsa, who was a Muslim.

Advaita Ācārya's activities are delineated in some detail in the biographies of Caitanya, who was born in 1486 when Advaita was, in all probability, fifty or fifty-two years of age. Advaita Ācārya's early life and career are steeped in mystery. It is said that he was born in far Śrīhaṭṭa in eastern Bengal, that he came to Shantipur with his parents at the age of twelve, that he was a disciple of a saint named Mādhavendra Purī, that he married the two daughters of a Vārendra brahmin named Nṛsiṃha Bhāḍurī, and that he was the father of six sons. He was probably a Vedāntic monist, a traveler on the path of knowledge (*jñāna*), who later developed a marked preference for Vaiṣṇava *bhakti*. According to traditional accounts, he considered himself a servant (*dāsa*) of Kṛṣṇa/Caitanya. He played the leading role in the apotheosis of Caitanya during a Vaiṣṇava festival in Purī. In some Vaiṣṇava lyrics he is described as a handsome but potbellied old man who walked in a peculiar manner.

The Vaiṣṇava gurus of the lineage of Advaita Ācārya are well known for their adherence to brahminical norms. Advaita Ācārya evidently did not hold any brief for the so-called *madhura bhāva*, or the "erotic mood," which was later interpreted as the fundamental point of Gauḍīya Vaiṣṇavism. Although the old savant disliked Nityānanda Avadhūta's uncommon emotional conduct, he shared his *dāsya bhāva*, or 'the mood of servility.' The Gauḍīya Vaiṣṇavas did not consider it advisable to write the biography of Nityānanda. One Haricaraṇa Dāsa wrote a biography of Advaita Ācārya in the seventeenth century. Its title is *Advaita Maṅgala*. It has been published twice. He was probably a disciple of Advaita Ācārya's son Acyutānanda. As the work does not conform to the facts given in the biographies of Caitanya written by Murāri Gupta, Kavi Karṇapūra, and Vṛndāvana Dāsa, it is considered to be an unauthoritative version of Advaita Ācārya's role in the Vaiṣṇava *bhakti* movement. The significance of Advaita Ācārya consisted in the fact that as an accountable brahmin householder, he represented those staid Vaiṣṇavas who supported the ethical norms of *bhakti* and repudiated questionable principles.

It should be noted that in Kṛṣṇadāsa Kavirāja's *Caitanya Caritāmṛta*, Nityānanda Avadhūta has been given precedence over Advaita Ācārya, particularly in the chapters of the *Ādi Līlā* of the work where the *tattva*s, or principles, which they were supposed to represent are explained. Kṛṣṇadāsa Kavirāja also records the precedence of Nityānanda Avadhūta over Advaita Ācārya in his account of the *śākha*s, or "branches" of the *bhakti* movement of Caitanya. It is presumable that Advaita Ācārya's importance gradually waned after his death, the reasons for which are not far to seek. There was hardly any cohesion among his followers. Some of them were led by Sītā Devī, Advaita Ācārya's principle wife. Another group followed his son Acyutānanda, who was recognized by Kṛṣṇadāsa Kavirāja as the real spiritual heir of the great Vaiṣṇava savant. A third group was led by a man named Kāmadeva Nāgara. It is said that Īśāna Nāgara, who is supposed to be the author of the *Advaita Prakāśa*, and another Vaiṣṇava named Jānu Rāya ultimately succeeded in bringing about a compromise between Sītā Devī and Acyutānanda. The group led by Kāmadeva Nāgara did not recognize Caitanya's divine status.

The descendants of Advaita Ācārya followed the brahminical norms. They admitted into their community only brahmins, vaidyas, and the so-called pure śūdras. The suborder of Advaita Ācārya was always controlled by a dominant minority. The Vaiṣṇavas who belonged to it believed that only Advaita Ācārya's interpretation of the theology of the *bhakti* movement of Caitanya was correct. Their view was that, since Kṛṣṇa and Caitanya were not differentiable, only a single set of mantras was required for their worship. On this point the difference between the so-called Advaitānanda *gosvāmīs* of Shantipur and the Vaiṣṇavas of Navadvīpa grew very sharp toward the end of the nineteenth century.

This was the historical background of Acyutacaraṇa Caudhurī Tattvanidhi's discovery of the manuscripts of Lauḍīya Kṛṣṇadāsa's Sanskrit work titled *Bālya-Līlā-Sūtra* and Īśāna Nāgara's *Advaita Prakāśa*. Īśāna Nāgara was a servant of Advaita Ācārya. After his master's demise he became a guru in his own right, married at the age of seventy, raised a family, and spread the faith successfully in some villages of Mānikgañja subdivision of Dhaka District. It is indeed very remarkable that a biography of Caitanya, written by one Govinda Karmakāra of Bardhamāna, who was supposed to be Caitanya's servant, and a biography of Advaita Ācārya, written by his servant Īśāna Nāgara, were suddenly discovered toward the end of the nineteenth century. These works were considered apocryphal by a number of scholars for a variety of reasons which have been critically studied by Dr. Rebecca J. Manring and Dr. Tony K. Stewart in an essay titled "In the Name of Devotion: Acyutacaraṇa Caudhurī and the Hagiographies of Advaitācārya" (*Journal of Vaiṣṇava Studies* 5, no. 1 [Winter 1996–97]: 103–26).

It should, however, be noted that in studying the history of Gauḍīya Vaiṣṇavism one has to take into account all sorts of evidence, sacred and profane. Some of the evidence is gleaned from the "holy" authoritative sources, and some from apocryphal and even highly deviant accounts. For a scholar it would not be proper to ignore any relevant work in which a particular viewpoint is manifest.

Īśāna Nāgara's *Advaita Prakāśa* is no longer easily accessible. Dr. Manring's translation of the work is admirably lucid. The work has the basic structure of a standard Vaiṣṇava hagiography. Its language and style are premodern. The only modern (and dubious) component in this curious work is a noticeable concern for exact chronology. The constant emphasis on the supernatural events and traits of such historical persons as Advaita Ācārya and Caitanya is a medievality that lends a great charm to this work and helps it gain a place by the side of other such hagiographical writings. The person who composed it (presumably in modern times) was a master hagiographer, who was fully conversant with the tools, rules, and technique of writing the biography of a godlike medieval saint. Dr. Manring's introduction is remarkable for its exactitude. No praise is sufficient for the high quality of her research. I heartily commend the publication of this work.

Ramakanta Chakrabarty
Professor of History
University of Burdwan (retired)

ACKNOWLEDGMENTS

This book's seeds were planted nearly two decades ago now, and I owe much gratitude to far too many than I can thank here. Fortunately, most were thanked in the acknowledgments to my earlier book, *Reconstructing Tradition*, and though I will not repeat myself here, I continue to be grateful to all the scholars, librarians, officials, and friends in India and Bangladesh without whose help neither book could have been written.

Discussions with a number of colleagues over the years have helped me sharpen the way I think about translation. Here at Indiana University these include David Haberman, Paul Losensky, Rosemarie McGerr, Breon Mitchell, Jan Nattier (no longer at Indiana), and Leah Shopkow. Conversations with colleagues (and with students) who do not do translation have forced me to articulate just what translation is, and why we bother, especially, as some tell me (but I do not believe), when "we have machines to do that."

Nicole Willock read a number of Tibetan hagiographies with me and discussed the Advaita corpus and my approach to hagiography over the course of a semester; her insights have been very helpful to my thinking. Similarly, conversations with other students over the past decade have shed light on various aspects of this project. Richa Pauranik helped me visualize one of the standard gestures of respectful submission mentioned so often in the texts that had me stumped; Amy "Zeri" Ort and David Bolter reminded me of the sheer delight of linguistic play. Others whose questions and conversation have proved useful include Ashlee Andrews, Kristin Francoeur, Aimee Hamilton, Nicole Karapanagiotis, Deonnie Moody, Rowena Potts, and Alexis Saba. My Sanskrit students over the years have provided more intellectual sustenance than they can possibly realize; in addition to those already named, I am grateful to Rhonda Baird, Carole Barnsley, Joy Brennan, Patton Burchett, Abby Crisman, Jenny Dubeansky, Kailash Hemachandra, Michael Luurtsema, Arti Mehta, Caitlyn Odya, and Dheepa Sundaram.

Two people with whom I began this project will not see its completion. Dr. Carol Salomon's work appears, as I said at the Madison panel in her honor in October

2009, between the lines of the curriculum vita of every one of her many students. Carol first introduced me to the Bengali language in 1983 and continued to be a helpful resource until her death in March 2009. Professor Subhadra Kumar Sen also died suddenly in 2009. He opened his father's rich manuscript collection to me nearly twenty years ago in Barddhaman, and we became fast friends; his flat on Raja Rajkissen Street remains my first stop on every visit to Kolkata, though his chair now sits empty. Son Sunandan ("Som") is now the third generation of his family to join the Department of Linguistics of Calcutta University; daughter Sunṛtāvalī ("Nupur") is also an academic and shares her father and grandfather's love of pulp fiction. Their mother, Mrs. Krishnā Sen, continues to be the backbone of the family, and I am grateful for their friendship over these years.

Professor Ramakanta Chakrabarty graciously wrote the foreword to this book. We spent many hours together, in the early stages of this project, working through Gauḍīya Vaiṣṇava politics and their implications. I am honored that a scholar of his reputation and considerable accomplishments had a part in my *Fading Light*.

Recent work in language pedagogy has given me a different perspective on translation than is possible through philological work alone, and conversations with colleagues in that field have also helped sharpen my own translation skills. I served my first teaching assistantship at the University of Washington under Professor Michael C. Shapiro, a master pedagogue and fellow grammar aficionado, and I continue to appreciate his dedication to our field as well as his sometimes unexpected humor. The teachers, students, and staff of the Bangla Language Institute in Dhaka, Bangladesh, with whom I worked closely for two summers, amazed and inspired me with their commitment and enthusiasm. I thank them for showing me a side of Bengali culture I might otherwise have missed.

Anne Monius, series editor for this Texts in Translation series, and Cynthia Read, editor, both of Oxford University Press, have been a pleasure to work with. Their thoughtful suggestions have certainly improved this book. Rachel Meyer, production editor, led a team of able professionals including Charlotte Steinhardt (editorial assistant) and Michael "Philo" Philoantonie (project manager). I have particularly appreciated Philo's careful attention to detail, for this is no small task when it involves all the diacritical marking of South Asian transliteration.

Heartfelt gratitude must always go to my mentor, Professor Tony K. Stewart of North Carolina State University. Tony first suggested the Advaita corpus as a dissertation topic and has been a tireless conversation partner ever since. His own meticulous work is something to which I can only aspire.

Closer to home I am grateful to my friends, colleagues, and family for their ongoing emotional support. Rose, Lily, Camelia, Ann, and Keith Manring; Bea and Nick Manring; Donetta Cothran, Gretchen Horlacher, and Ann Mongoven; Rita Agarwal and Susama Nayak; David Brakke; Julie Bloom; Purnima Bose, Ellen Dwyer, and Leah Shopkow; Radhika Parameswaran, Susan Seizer, and Pravina Shukla; Michael Dodson; Tim Callahan; and the man from Almora District whose model of remaining calm in the midst of every storm I keep trying to emulate. And to my own peaceful warrior, whose patience especially in the final months of this project made it possible for me to meet my deadlines. Thank you, Timothy M. Bagwell.

My career trajectory did not begin with a clear plan, but its inspiration has always been apparent to me. Shortly after the First World War, Mary Naomi Wilson made her way, alone, from the wheat fields of eastern Washington across the ocean to China, where she would spend the next several decades as a teacher and eventually became the principal of the Peking American School. World War II brought internment in Shantung Province and eventual repatriation to the United States. Back in small-town eastern Washington she continued, nearly to the end of her life, to tutor the young new readers she loved so much. When I was growing up, Grammy's wonderful bedtime stories and songs instilled in me the idea that the world did not have to be a dangerous place and was out there to be explored and enjoyed; and, that all the people in that world are important, and we can learn much from them. Eventually, her stories sent me to India. This book is dedicated to her, in memory of her wisdom, beauty, and courage.

NOTES ON TRANSLATION AND TRANSLITERATION

Translation is both an art and a science. Every language has its own culture-bound repertoires of terms and concepts. Some of the special issues with Bengali include three registers of the second-person pronoun, reflecting degree of intimacy and respect, and the lack of gender marking in the pronominal system. Add to that the extreme state of flux of Bengali morphology in the precolonial period, and you have dazzling levels of ambiguity for the unwary in every text. Bringing a nineteenth-century text written in the Middle Bengali of the sixteenth century for a conservative Vaiṣṇava audience in colonial India to twenty-first-century American students presents a wide range of challenges. Such a task requires finding English equivalents for many terms that could remain untranslated for an English-speaking Indian audience, or for an audience already familiar with the theological issues at stake. It requires moving away from a literal word-for-word translation, for such an exercise would have yielded a product unrecognizable as English. And yet relying on footnotes would have indicated a failure of translation. Even writing styles themselves offer challenges. For example, South Asian languages generally favor the use of the passive voice, which we in English consider (in most cases) poor form. And indirect speech is rare. My goal has been to remain as true to the text as possible in producing a translation that students like those I teach at Indiana University can read and make sense of. I have often translated quotations as indirect discourse, and avoid the English passive unless using it gives a more natural English reading.

In some cases, translating a term would have been less precise or helpful than leaving it in the original language. Many of these will be familiar—guru, dharma, karma—but I have included others in the glossary. These include technical theological terms and a few administrative titles. I use the spelling "brahmin" when referring to members of the priestly caste.

Every edition of the *Advaita Prakāśa* is published with chapter divisions, which I preserve; the verses are not numbered. This has allowed a bit more freedom to the translator, as very often a single thought continues for several lines, and

I usually choose to follow content over syntax. Ravīndranātha Maiti's *Advaita Maṅgala* has five books, each subdivided into chapters; again, individual verses are not numbered except as noted. I have followed the Bengali publishers' leads and have not numbered the verses in this translation. Most of these two texts are in the Bengali *payāra* meter, a two-line meter of fourteen syllables per line, with the caesura coming after the eighth syllable. The two lines that constitute each verse, rhyme. Both poets occasionally switch to the *tripadī* meter. Each verse in *tripadī* consists of two halves containing three feet each. The first two feet are of eight (or sometimes seven) syllables each, and the third, ten. Each *tripadī* section has ten verses. In some of the earliest Bengali poetry, *tripadī* "was considered to be the fit metre by the poets of old school for giving expression to feelings of mourning or of any dire loss."[1] Haricaraṇa switches to *tripadī* five times. The first time, he lays out his dedication to and motivation for the project he is about to undertake with his composition, and the fourth time, he reiterates that intention. The other three times describe visions or meditative visualizations, that is, the speaker is functioning outside normal reality. While the shift of verse does not conform to the classical purpose of signaling grief, it does consistently herald a change of locus in some sense.

The *Bālya-Līlā-Sūtra* is a Sanskrit text. Translating this work presented additional difficulties as in many places, as Acyutacaraṇa Caudhurī Tattvanidhi indicated in his introduction to the sole published edition, the text is corrupt. Whether composed by someone whose Sanskrit was flawed, or simply the victim of scribal error, the *Bālya-Līlā-Sūtra* contains many examples of both metrical and grammatical infelicities. These require the translator to make some editorial decisions, and in every case I did so relying first on the meter to provide clues, and then on context. The author used a remarkable variety of meters in his composition, and reproducing them in some appropriate English format is both well beyond my abilities and not necessary for my purposes, and so I have chosen to translate into English prose.

Extant in a sole published edition, the text is neatly divided into eight chapters with numbered verses. I have retained that numbering in the translation. Occasionally it made sense to translate several verses together, and I have indicated this in my own text.

In no case have I attempted to reproduce an author's versification or to render his work in English verse. Rather, I have chosen prose translation as the best means to transmit what these authors have to say, to my contemporary readers.

The Fading Light of Advaita Ācārya is intended to serve as a resource for students of hagiography regardless of their background in South Asian languages or religious history. I have used the Standard Academic Transliteration system in use for Sanskrit throughout the book. This may cause the Bengali purists some

[1] Dinesh Chandra Sen, *History of Bengali Language and Literature*, 815.

consternation as it does not consistently reflect the Bengali phonology, but it will make words and names transparent to a broader audience. I have not used diacritics or italics with Indic words current in English (e.g., dharma, pandit), nor with familiar toponyms, nor with names of scholars who frequently publish in English. I have used the English spellings that South Asian writers use for their own names.

Passages in the *Advaita Prakāśa* translation marked with square brackets are found in the sole extant manuscript of that text, but not in any of the published editions. Similarly, square brackets mark verses in the *Advaita Maṅgala* not found in every version of the text.

Names in the index are alphabetized according to Bengali style, that is, by first name, unless the author published the work cited in English.

The Fading Light of Advaita Ācārya

A Case Study in Hagiography

Introduction

This book complements my *Reconstructing Tradition: Advaita Ācārya and Gauḍīya Vaiṣṇavism at the Cusp of the Twentieth Century*. We had planned to publish these two volumes together, but a change in one publisher's profile, and my own recognition of the importance of presenting all three of Advaita Ācārya's major hagiographies together, resulted in a delay of several years for this volume with its translations of those texts treating the life of Advaita[1] Ācārya.[2]

The original manuscript of this book included only the *Advaita Prakāśa*. Once I realized that that text was a very recent composition I became fascinated with the notion of hagiography as a process with a set of goals quite beyond that of simply setting out the details of a life. It soon became apparent that publishing the *Advaita Maṅgala* alongside the *Advaita Prakāśa* would give readers something to compare the later text to, so that they could see what a more contemporary (to its protagonist) hagiography might look like, and notice differences between the two. And then as long as we were presenting the two full hagiographies, it was only reasonable to include the relatively short *Bālya-Līlā-Sūtra*, treating only Advaita's childhood.

This book is above all the translations. I have dealt elsewhere in detail with the history of each of these, and other, texts treating Advaita Ācārya. Other scholars[3] have treated the Caitanya corpus and the theology of the *gosvāmīs*. Because their excellent work is readily available, I have given only enough background to allow readers of these particular hagiographies to make sense of them.

The *Advaita Maṅgala* is the earliest extant full hagiography treating Advaita Ācārya. Haricaraṇa Dāsa appears to have completed this composition in the early seventeenth century, and it circulated widely enough that Ravīndranātha Maiti

[1] The name literally means "nondual," or "without a second," and is often interpreted as "nondifferent (from Kṛṣṇa)."

[2] "Master." Thus his official title may be translated "Master of Nondualism."

[3] Edward C. Dimock Jr.; Tony K. Stewart; S. K. De; Rāmakānta Chakrabarty; David L. Haberman, to name but a few.

was able to consult six different manuscripts as he produced his critical edition, published in 1966. The provenance of the *Bālya-Līlā-Sūtra* is unclear. The sometimes awkward Sanskrit and many metrical flaws give the impression that what we have (in only one published edition and no extant manuscripts) is a sort of draft, a project outline its author never completed. Finally, our third text is the *Advaita Prakāśa*, a text that suddenly appeared for the first time in 1898. These hagiographies reflect changing political and social, as well as theological, concerns. Written over a span of centuries, these works can provide a useful index of the evolution of Advaita Ācārya's position within Gauḍīya Vaiṣṇavism, as the construction of biographical images and subsequent changes in those images can serve as indices to the place and fortunes of the group creating them.

Advaita Prakāśa,[4] a text in Middle Bengali, was purportedly written by Īśāna Nāgara in 1568. In actuality the text is a late nineteenth-century composition most likely produced by the Bengali scholar and patriot Acyutacaraṇa Caudhurī Tattvanidhi.[5] Who was Advaita Ācārya, and why would someone want to tell his life story three centuries after the fact and yet rather than claim authorship, announce he had just discovered two very old texts? In this essay I will reiterate several issues elaborated upon in *Reconstructing Tradition* and discuss some of the rhetorical strategies hagiographers use, with specific attention to Īśāna Nāgara, the identity Acyutacaraṇa Caudhurī Tattvanidhi assumes to produce his life of Advaita Ācārya.

Let us begin in the abstract by first considering how to approach religious biography, before embarking on the specific texts treating Advaita Ācārya.

How to Read Hagiography

Hagiography (religious biography) poses a number of challenges to unwary readers. This genre, like its cousin biography, treats the lives of its subjects, and so normally proceeds from the births of those individuals through their lives to their deaths. Often at least some of the story is historical in the sense that it is verifiable through outside, that is, nonsectarian, sources. But hagiography is above all political. I use the word "political" not in reference to any government or to public affairs but rather in its secondary sense of the opinions and principles by which people order their participation in larger groups, and the strategizing such participation may entail. These works are written, or commissioned, to convey a specific message or image of their subjects, and to do specific work, else why bother to produce them.

[4] The title is wonderfully multivalent. We could translate it "The Light That Was Advaita"; "The Revelation about Nondualism"; "Advaita's Revelation"; and that does not exhaust the possibilities. Even more delightful is the probability that the author intends all of these simultaneously.

[5] Tattvanidhi (storehouse of wisdom) is a title that Caudhurī earned at some point in his illustrious career, and not part of his proper name. Nonetheless, Bengalis never refer to him without it.

These texts are several levels deep. At the surface we find the presentation of a life and set of teachings associated with that life. As we dig deeper we notice that a given author will emphasize particular aspects of that life and/or teachings. With the Advaita Ācārya corpus we have several treatments of the same historical figure that differ in key respects, and those differences intrigue us as scholars.

Devotion does not occur in a vacuum; devotees live in a world affected by such circumstances as family and popular attitudes to their behavior and piety; rulers' attitudes to their own and others' religious practices; concerns about the future—the continuity—of the tradition; and so forth. Thus a writer may be laying out the life story of his beloved guru or setting out a new theology, on the one hand, and at the same time responding to his political and social environment. Piety does not preclude farsightedness, wisdom, or any other motive. As Eric Hobsbawm and Terence Ranger have observed, "All invented traditions . . . use history as a legitimator of action and cement of group cohesion."[6] And what tradition in human society is *not* an "invented" one? Hagiographers often intend their works to serve as foci for community formation by providing a common history around which people will unite. Their works are also literary, and so we can borrow tools from literature scholars to help us make sense of them.

Hayden White brought literary criticism to bear on historiography, departing dramatically from the disciplinary tension among nineteenth-century scholars of history, art, and science. He knew we must not read historical writing for its face value alone:

> A historical narrative is thus necessarily a mixture of adequately and inadequately explained events, a congeries of established and inferred facts, at once a representation that is an interpretation and an interpretation that passes for an explanation of the whole process mirrored in the narrative.[7]

The same may be said of the variety of history writing known as hagiography. We read the material skeptically so that we ask many questions of it: What is the author trying to tell us, and what metaphorical ax, if any, does that author have to grind? Do the events recounted, and the way in which they are recounted, recall any other hagiographies? What important figures, other than the protagonist, are mentioned, how are they described, and how much textual space do they occupy?

This type of material can be very frustrating if one is hoping to document the "facts" of the person's life. Over time, the myths that arise around such persons blur with the remembered or documented empirical events of their lives, to the point that people can no longer separate "fact" from "fiction." But as scholars, we

[6] Hobsbawm and Ranger, *The Invention of Tradition*, 12.

[7] White, *Tropics of Discourse*, 51.

are less interested in the true historical events of the life of a religious founder—even if we could discover them—for hagiography is not historical biography in the sense in which we may be accustomed to thinking.

"There is no way to get past texts in order to apprehend 'real' history directly," according to Edward Said, for "texts are worldly, to some degree they are events, and, even when they appear to deny it, they are nevertheless a part of the social world, human life, and of course the historical moments in which they are located and interpreted."[8]

Hagiographers also make many fantastic assertions about their protagonists that stretch and often even defy credibility. Pious exaggeration, a term I do not use pejoratively, is not unique to the Vaiṣṇavas; stories of the lives of saints in any tradition often require great faith and the suspension of rationality on the part of the authors' intended readers. These authors are not attempting to mislead their audiences with any Devīous or malicious intent, but rather are acting in the name of devotion to further an agenda they understand to have been propounded by the individual whose life story they relate, or that they themselves want to advance. They are writing several levels deep.

We can of course simply accept hagiography as wonderful stories, but if we ponder these works in their larger context and keep in mind some of the questions suggested previously, our reading will prove much richer.

Throughout this essay when I refer to events described in the hagiographies, the reader should recognize that I am merely reporting from the hagiographies, and should not understand my statements as uncritically historical. There is no way to determine how much of a given text is hyperbole, as mentioned earlier, and how much historical truth has intruded into the narrative. But more important, a hagiographical corpus can serve as a record of a group's views of the person under consideration. Those views may change over time as the group's political status alters, or as the passage of time calls for more details of the subject's life to be "remembered," and so we find different accounts of the same individual's life.

Individual authorship is a relatively insignificant concept in South Asia, even in the early modern period. Authors might pay homage to another by mimicking the latter's style and then claiming that they had found an undiscovered poem by that earlier writer, rather than claiming it as their own. "Borrowing" from other writers and their compositions constitutes high praise and/or philosophical agreement and does not carry the ethical stigma it has for us today. This trend was so dominant that quite regularly authors wanting to emphasize a particular idea claim it was legitimate by pointing to it in some earlier, established, authoritative text. And if they cannot find the needed reference, they might just make it up to produce a citation that the alleged source author could have intended to say but never did, or at least could credibly have produced. Vaiṣṇava material is riddled

[8] Said, *The World, the Text, and the Critic*, 4.

with just this sort of made-up citation, and a lot of "real" ones, too. The goal, after all, is to propagate devotion, and nothing that accomplishes that goal (which ultimately results in liberation from *saṃsāra*) is problematic.

So what, intellectually speaking, can one do with this sort of a document? After all, even a novel, Dominick LaCapra[9] claims, documents something of its historical mode of production; what, then, can a hagiography like the *Advaita Prakāśa*, which seems to have appeared suddenly out of nowhere, and left us no trail in the process, be said to document? What sort of second-order history can we use it do to? And why should we be interested?

One way to study the *Advaita Prakāśa* and the *Advaita Maṅgala* is to compare the stories their authors tell with stories about the same people and events in other Gauḍīya Vaiṣṇava literature. This comparison is not a popularity contest in which the version that appears the most often will be deemed the One True Story. Rather, we want to discover how the stories differ, and then see what those differences suggest. Some are quite familiar to members of the community, but others appear nowhere else. What are those new stories doing here, and why should we take them seriously? We will examine a few of these later in this essay.

Obviously, to some extent, we take them seriously because they are there. The author wants us to hear those stories because they tell us things about Advaita that we will not find elsewhere, that he feels are important for us to know. They reveal, among other things, Advaita's true identity (in the eyes of his followers) as God—as Kṛṣṇa—something no one else asserts in the same way.

Authors sometimes make claims about a protagonist metaphorically, sometimes even somewhat covertly, through the miraculous events they portray. For example, in Gauḍīya literature an individual who has had a religious revelation of some sort is often rewarded by a vision of the Lord. Whenever Advaita grants someone a vision of his true form, he does so as a recompense for their new level of understanding. Unusually, Advaita's future wives Sītā and Śrī, and their father, are allowed to see Advaita in his majestic form on their first meeting, and that signals us that they already possessed some degree of realization even prior to that meeting.

We might expect that a document concocted by a late nineteenth-century author who had been exposed to Western rationalism would report fewer, not more, miracles than genuinely earlier texts. But Caudhurī is working very hard to establish his spiritual ancestor's divinity. His concurrent claim that this is a sixteenth-century text gives him the opportunity to write in great detail in the style of the much earlier *purāṇas*, that vast body of mythological literature in which we find the stories of the gods. Hagiography in South Asia, and certainly hagiography whose producers want to demonstrate their subjects' "true" identities as divine, takes much inspiration from the vast body of *purāṇas* and *mahātmyas* that both

[9] In his *Rethinking Intellectual History* in particular.

tell the stories of the gods and extol their virtues. Myth is simply one means of cultural communication, "a message system coexisting with other cultural message systems and exhibiting the same structures."[10] This is why myth "works": it differs only in content from other sorts of cultural communication.

Myths "must be understood primarily as texts in context, specific acts of communication between specified individuals, at specific points in time and space, about specifiable subjects."[11] Myth constitutes a "distinctive dimension of human thought"[12] and serves "not to present an objective vision of the world, but to present man's true understanding of himself in the world in which he lives."[13] Myths accomplish this through the use of rhetorical and literary strategies to build an aesthetically coherent story. And myths have authors. In some cases the authors are myriad, adding, changing emphasis, and removing material over time, but always for a reason.

As readers of myth, and particularly as outsider readers of myth, we must always bear this authorial intentionality in mind. J. Z. Smith wrote often of how scholars should read other people's myths. Most to the present point, he said, "The claimed ahistorical character of myth is a product of the scholar's gaze and not of some native world-view, be it of a literate or non-literate culture. It robs the "other" of indigenous capacity for thought with respect to the hard work of cultural creation."[14] In reading the three works translated in this book, keep in mind this hard work on the part of their authors, and what sort of "cultural creation" they had in mind as they labored over their hagiographies.

One of the places we see this intentional creation is in hagiographers' treatment of the end of their subject's life. How they handle death can be as telling as what they say about birth. In some cases, they avoid the subject altogether, using what at first glance appears to be a euphemism ("disappeared") but in fact is to be taken quite literally. Locana Dāsa's *Caitanya Maṅgala*[15] ends with Caitanya's apparent merging into the temple image of Jagannātha, Lord of the Universe. Locana Dāsa uses the word "disappeared" for a distinct theological purpose. God, who for this tradition has an eternal existence and location, cannot die. He merely changes venues, in this case returning to the eternal Vraja, out of sight of us ordinary mortals. That notion is not surprising. One must wonder, then, whether a human embodiment of God is also immortal. Although this sort of thing is well beyond the experience of most of us, logic would seem to indicate that a divine being even here on earth must by definition also be deathless. And so many of the Vaiṣṇavas claim.

[10] Worthen, *The Myth of Replacement*, 14.

[11] Smith, *Imagining Religion*, xiii.

[12] Rasmussen, *Mythic-Symbolic Language*, 21.

[13] Ibid., 10.

[14] Smith, *Drudgery Divine*, 109.

[15] Jayānanda Miśra composed a different text with the same title.

Vṛndāvana Dāsa, writing shortly after Caitanya's death, and Kṛṣṇadāsa Kavirāja, authors of the most popular of the Caitanya hagiographies, do not mention Caitanya's death at all, nor does Haricaraṇa Dāsa mention his protagonist's death in his *Advaita Maṅgala*. He ends with the account of the "three lords"—Caitanya, Advaita, and Nityānanda—enacting the *dāna līlā* at the Gaṅgā in Shantipur. It is a gloriously ecstatic moment that this author uses to highlight, one last time, Advaita's theological identity.

Īśāna, however, in his *Advaita Prakāśa* describes Advaita Ācārya's disappearance in much the same way as does Locana. The word "death" does not appear in the text. Rather, Advaita enters the Madana Gopāla temple in Shantipur, and the doors slam shut behind him. No one can force the doors to open. When the doors finally do open, of their own accord, Advaita is nowhere to be found. Īśāna assumes Advaita has been absorbed by his beloved Madana Gopāla, than whom he is no different, "*a-dvaita*." Advaita, like Caitanya, simply disappeared without a trace. An ordinary man would have left his body for others to find, but a divine body is not subject to the laws of physics or biology, and so we are to understand both men as divine.

Gauḍīya Vaiṣṇavism Situated

One of the most enduring, and certainly the most far-reaching, religious streams to flow through and eventually out of Bengal is that of Gauḍīya Vaiṣṇavism. "Gauḍa" and its adjective "Gauḍīya" referred originally to the northern and western sections of that part of the world known as Bengal.[16] The term is now used to refer to the modern Indian state of West Bengal and the nation of Bangladesh. And the term "Vaiṣṇavism" indicates some connection to the god Viṣṇu, one of South Asia's most widely worshiped gods. Viṣṇu's followers believe, as Kṛṣṇa tells Arjuna in *Bhagavad Gītā* IV.7–8, that Viṣṇu takes birth on earth in times of abject chaos and unrighteousness to restore the world to order and righteousness. Different groups around the South Asian subcontinent have formed around worship of various of these earthly descents[17] of Viṣṇu. One of these, Rāma, is a favorite object of Vaiṣṇava devotion in both North and South India. Rāma was born into a royal family, and his reign is affectionately "remembered" as a golden age of Hinduism.[18] Rāma and his queen Sītā are still the model many newlyweds are encouraged to emulate in their mutual devotion.

[16] Originally the southern and eastern areas were known as "Vaṅga."

[17] *Avatāra*, sometimes mistranslated "incarnation," literally connotes a crossing downward and always refers to a god who has moved from his or her heavenly abode to appear on earth among us mortals. Because the form we see is understood as divine, there is no question of assuming mortal flesh.

[18] And, perhaps not surprisingly, much of his story has been adopted by some contemporary politicians for their own ends.

Equally important is Kṛṣṇa, who gains in popularity as one moves farther east. Kṛṣṇa is the main object of worship in places associated with the events of his life, like Mathurā and Vṛndāvana, both a part of the region known as Vraja, located near the city of Agra just a three hours' train ride south of India's capital city of New Delhi. Vraja is a pastoral region, and according to legend Kṛṣṇa, born a prince, was fostered in a cow-herding family there. A vast mythology about Kṛṣṇa has arisen over the centuries, with the stories of his childhood and adolescence the most popular. His devotees can name all of his childhood playmates, tell stories of his teasing the local girls, and know his every demon-vanquishing adventure.

Believers hold not only that Kṛṣṇa lived in ancient history but also that he has an eternal existence in Vraja with his foster family and their entire community, including the landscape. Kṛṣṇa's followers hope to cultivate such a strong personal relationship with him that they will join those eternal activities after death as a part of Kṛṣṇa's community of friends and relatives.

The Bengali Vaiṣṇavas claim that this entire eternal Vraja, normally imperceptible to our mortal eyes, occasionally coexists with the earth we know. This, they say, is just what happened in 1486 with the birth of Viśvambhara Miśra (1486–1533), later known as Kṛṣṇa Caitanya, in the small town of Navadvīpa, some ninety kilometers north of present-day Kolkata in West Bengal. Viśvambhara was very early recognized as Kṛṣṇa himself,[19] born as one of the previously described *avatāras* of Viṣṇu to remedy the chaos that human beings had made of life on earth, and to restore humanity to its natural state of righteousness. Kṛṣṇa, *Svayaṃ Bhagavān*, the Lord Himself, incarnated serially, sending portions of himself, and his parents and other elder relatives, ahead to begin to pave the way for his own advent. Kamalākānta (Kamalākṣa)[20] Bhaṭṭācārya, later known as Advaita Ācārya, was among the first to arrive, some fifty years ahead of the *avatāra* himself.

What is this larger religious movement Caitanya introduced? What were its early proponents reacting to, and how did they propose to rescue people from *saṃsāra*, the seemingly endless cycle of birth, disease, old age, death, and birth again? Many Americans have encountered one strain of Gauḍīya Vaiṣṇavism through its friendly members distributing flowers and books in airports. The movement spread as far afield as Europe and the United States in the mid-1960s when A. C. Bhaktivedānta Swāmī Prabhupāda brought his International Society for Kṛṣṇa Consciousness (ISKCON, whose members are perhaps more familiarly known as the Hare Kṛṣṇas) to New York. In its homeland ISKCON is a very small presence, only one of several Vaiṣṇava schools, but it has achieved remarkable success in Europe and the Americas. In recent years, ISKCON temples, once the

[19] And later, as the dual embodiment of Kṛṣṇa and his favorite girlfriend, Rādhā.

[20] *Kamalā* (lotus) is an epithet for the goddess Lakṣmī, consort of Viṣṇu; *kānta* means "beloved of." Thus Kamalākānta is an epithet of Viṣṇu. *Akṣa* means "eye," so Kamalākṣa is the Lotus-Eyed One, an attractive name.

preserve of Western devotees, have begun to serve as community centers for ethnic Hindus[21] in the United States.

The goal of life for followers of those religious traditions that fall under the broad umbrella of Hinduism is to escape *saṃsāra*. Throughout history thinkers have prescribed various ways to accomplish this. For Caitanya, the key was to cultivate a personal relationship with the divine that one could continue after death in the eternal Vraja. In this respect his philosophy was decidedly dualistic, although Caitanya conceived of a god who was both transcendent, existing in the timeless eternal Vraja, and imminent, capable of simultaneously adopting human forms on earth, both partially and completely, without any diminution of that eternal existence or his powers. This seemingly oxymoronic theology came to be known as *acintya bhedābheda*, "inconceivable difference and nondifference," in recognition of how difficult it is for us to wrap our minds around it.

This theology represented a dramatic shift in religious thought in Bengal. First of all, liberation does not constitute the old monistic notion of merging into Oneness, but rather the establishment of an eternal dualistic relationship with one's object of worship. Second, this movement's writers produced a tremendous body of literature, mostly in the vernacular languages that were accessible to the general populace. Up until then, high religion had been the exclusive province of the priestly brahmin caste,[22] and scriptures had been composed in Vedic or Classical Sanskrit, languages that had long ago ceased to be the common parlance. At least in theory, release from the cycle of birth and death was now available to anyone at all.

By the nineteenth century Europeans were also firmly established in the region. Many educated South Asians, and Bengalis in particular, were now searching for ways to assert their own intellectual integrity in the midst of all the new models then appearing. To this end South Asian scholars began to concern themselves with regional history and the formulation of vernacular literary canons. Bengalis in particular took up this cause. Until 1912 Calcutta was the capital of British India, giving Calcuttans a very close look at colonialism as well as some of its perks. But Bengal had also been partitioned in 1905, after lengthy and ongoing discussions, in what many viewed as a strike against growing nationalism in that region. Some Hindus saw the move as a plan to cultivate Bengali Muslims independently, and most Muslims supported it, for now they were in the majority in East Bengal. In any case, the move was unpopular and did drive a wedge between the East (mostly Muslim) and the West (mostly Hindu) Bengalis and launched a furor of anti-British reactions. It also left East Bengali Hindus stranded. Much of Acyutacaraṇa Caudhurī Tattvanidhi's historical writing seems motivated by his

[21] To paraphrase Jan Nattier.

[22] Numerous movements had arisen throughout history to challenge the brahminical hegemony. The most durable of these are Buddhism and Jainism. Buddhism was at one time the majority religion in South Asia, but it eventually faded in its homeland.

concern that his region of Sylhet was being overlooked, and particularly its Hindu history. Both Caitanya's and Advaita's families had immigrated to Nadīyā from the region, and Caitanya returned to Sylhet on his fund-raising tour. But now few Hindus remained in the area to carry on the memory of their illustrious ancestors. And West Bengali intellectuals were by and large ignoring their East Bengali counterparts, Hindu or Muslim. Acyutacaraṇa Caudhurī Tattvanidhi and his school of Gauḍīya Vaiṣṇavism may well have anticipated their own fade from memory, if not outright demise, while branches centered in the West continued to thrive. At the same time, given the presence of other groups, the Vaiṣṇava theologians and other writers needed to make very clear statements about how they differed from the others, and why what they had to offer was more likely to guarantee soteriological success. Their agenda in the late nineteenth century was thus quite different from their agenda centuries previously when the Gauḍīya Vaiṣṇavas were simply trying to gain a foothold.

Early Gauḍīya Vaiṣṇava History

Advaita Ācārya predates the airport book distributors by several centuries. How do the Gauḍīya Vaiṣṇavas understand him?[23] All branches of this eventually fragmented tradition assert that he brought Kṛṣṇa, that is, Caitanya, to earth, but how did he manage to do this? Numerous authors report that Advaita had long felt that the world was rapidly degenerating, and in his despair, beseeched Kṛṣṇa to come rectify the situation as he had promised in the *Bhagavad Gītā*. Advaita performed prayers, rituals, and arduous austerities for years, demanding heavenly attention. All the authors who describe this portion of Advaita's life also describe the ferocious "roaring" with which he stormed heaven, shouting out the mystical syllable *hum*. Various signs and portents had shown him where the miracle of divine advent would occur, and so he kept a close watch on the couple he had determined would become Kṛṣṇa's parents. Meanwhile, he ran a traditional school for brahmin boys in the community and continued to fulfill all his more mundane responsibilities.

When Caitanya was born, all accounts report,[24] Advaita recognized signs in the infant indicating that his prayers had been answered. After Caitanya grew to adulthood, Advaita became a primary disciple of the younger man, serving at his right hand and often providing financial backing to the new group.

[23] As yet we have no complete history of Vaiṣṇavism in Bengal, but the works of Edward C. Dimock Jr., Tony K. Stewart, B. B. Majumdar, Rāmakānta Chakrabarty, and S. K. De are very useful.

[24] Everything we "know" about Caitanya, we find in his eight hagiographies and other sectarian sources. The authors of these works are not entirely in agreement about the life of their protagonist, but aside from a few passing references in other groups' literature, we have no nonsectarian sources from which to draw.

As the fifteenth century gave way to the sixteenth, Caitanya was propounding some very unorthodox notions. Among these was the idea that anyone at all could aspire to liberation in this lifetime; that a person did not have to be born a brahmin, and male, and study Sanskrit for twelve years in order to learn scriptures (all of which were written in that ancient language) to be able to achieve the goal of freedom from the seemingly endless cycle of birth, death, and rebirth. Fundamental to Gauḍīya Vaiṣṇavism is the idea of a deep personal relationship between worshiper and worshiped, a relationship that functions reciprocally. Kṛṣṇa responds to his worshipers' desires and comes when he is summoned in a form and manner to match the desire. Caitanya was possessed of a vision that in these degenerate times, Kṛṣṇa (that is to say, the Supreme Reality) in his mercy (and this God is not only male, he is the *only* male in the Vaiṣṇava community) had decreed that he would rescue anyone who simply called out to him with loving devotion, the way, for example, a mother might call her child, or a friend might call a friend, or a lover, a lover. The worshiper had only to repeat the Lord's name to be guaranteed eternal freedom from *saṃsāra*.

These concepts were not unique to Caitanya's theology. We find them throughout the writings of the poets and theologians of the various devotional movements that began in South India and had begun to appear in the North by the twelfth century. Devotion had long been practiced among the nonelite masses, and only now were those at the top of the social hierarchy becoming interested. For the brahmin community in Bengal, then, these notions of universal accessibility to god and the possibility of escape from *saṃsāra* were quite new and needed to be carefully framed in order to gain acceptance among their often very conservative numbers.

Caitanya would lead groups of young men through the streets of his hometown of Navadvīpa at all hours of the day and night, singing Kṛṣṇa's praises to the accompaniment of drums and other musical instruments. This was not normal behavior for men of Caitanya's class, and while this brand of devotion certainly attracted a huge following, it may also have annoyed many citizens who would rather have been sleeping. The presence of the staid, elderly pillar of the community Advaita Ācārya at the head of the crowd gave the group their much-needed respectability in those early days.

Eventually Caitanya decided to leave his family to live the life of a renunciate, a move he believed would provide a better example to his followers of unalloyed devotion to Kṛṣṇa. Were he to continue to live as a householder, his attention to family responsibilities would both distract him and confuse his audience. At that point he moved to Purī, on the Bay of Bengal, site of the enormous Jagannātha Temple complex and thus a major pilgrimage center. There Caitanya came into contact with a greater number of potential converts. As time passed, his focus turned increasingly away from the physical world and toward the eternal Vraja. In his later years Caitanya adopted more and more of the behavior of the cowherd maid Rādhā, pining away for love of the absent Kṛṣṇa. And one day, according Locana Dāsa's *Caitanya Maṅgala* (4.15.15–39), as mentioned earlier, Caitanya simply disappeared, apparently by merging into the Jagannātha image in the great temple.[25]

The Literature of Gauḍīya Vaiṣṇavism

Any new religious movement with aspirations to change society must demonstrate why people should take it seriously. Quite often, in India, new movements do this by producing literature outlining their theology and connecting that theology to the Vedas, ultimate source of all knowledge and authority. Another strategy, usually combined with the first, is to demonstrate that one's founder is divine.

When these theologians codified the new movement's doctrines, they wrote in Sanskrit. Their choice of the ancient language of many earlier religious texts in itself helped to legitimate their compositions simply because Sanskrit has often been considered sacred, and hence the appropriate language choice for this type of writing. Meanwhile, poets and musicians, writing in the vernacular languages, created countless short devotional lyrics[26] based on the tales of their lord Kṛṣṇa as child and adolescent, as well as on the Bengali figure said to be the contemporary embodiment of Kṛṣṇa.

Caitanya's followers began worshiping their leader as a divine incarnation even during his lifetime, although he seems not to have encouraged such adulation. "Biographies" of Caitanya began to appear shortly after his death at the juncture of the sixteenth and seventeenth centuries.[27] These works pay Advaita the homage due to the forerunner of their founder but have little to say about Advaita's life before Caitanya entered it, or after Caitanya's passing. By that time, several factions had formed among Caitanya's followers, led by such devotees as Nityānanda, Advaita, Narahari Sarakāra, and the six *gosvāmī*s who had earlier been sent to Vṛndāvana to continue the tasks of recovering lost sites of Kṛṣṇa *līlā* and systematizing Caitanya's theology.

These hagiographical works are some of the last devotional compositions to appear in Bengal. Writers of earlier literary genres, in Bengal and elsewhere, were far more prolific. Beginning in the South as early as the eighth century, short poems of passionate love for the Divine were among the first to appear. In North India, Kṛṣṇa devotion most often focuses on either the very naughty child Kṛṣṇa, born a

[25] The most likely cause of Caitanya's death was infection, a scenario which Jayānanda Miśra presents in his own *Caitanya Maṅgala*. This view is of course the least popular among Caitanya's followers.

[26] The non-Bengali-speaking reader will find Baru Caṇḍīdāsa's very early *Śrī Kṛṣṇa Kīrtana*, translated by Mimi Klaiman, and the collaborative translation of Edward C. Dimock Jr. and Denise Levertov, *In Praise of Kṛṣṇa*, of interest. Much similar literature from other parts of India, composed in other vernacular languages, is now appearing in English translation.

[27] The most comprehensive treatment of the Caitanya corpus to date is Stewart's *Final Word*.

prince but raised by foster parents in a cow-herding community, or on the adolescent charmer. Kṛṣṇa and his playmates are forever alternately stealing dairy products from the village women and fighting off threatening demons. When Kṛṣṇa reaches adolescence he becomes quite the ladies' man, irresistible to any woman of any age he meets. The most famous story of this phase of his life features the *rāsa līlā*, a dance in a large open field under the full moon with 160,000 cowherd maidens (the *gopīs*), each of whom believes she and she alone is partnered by Kṛṣṇa. The ninth-century South Indian Sanskrit composition *Bhāgavata Purāṇa*, in its Tenth Book, features these exploits of Kṛṣṇa and the *gopīs*, and many subsequent writers have written short lyrical poems on various events in the *līlā*, as well as longer works like Jayadeva's masterful Sanskrit *Gīta Govinda*, in which the erotic activities of Kṛṣṇa and his favorite partner, Rādhā, are related in joyous detail.

Poetry, the theological treatises, and the Caitanya hagiographies have been copied repeatedly and circulated widely. Manuscripts of these texts are held in libraries from Vṛndāvana in the west to Comilla and Sylhet in the east, a clear indication of their importance and popularity. Further, the tradition is notoriously self-referential, a trait that conveniently yields still more clues to literary value.

Citation constitutes endorsement and praise. Conversely, a work that no other author cites was ignored either because the larger community did not accept its message or because it did not yet exist. In composing his *Caitanya Caritāmṛta*, the "final word," as Tony Stewart has demonstrated, on the life and teachings of Caitanya, Kṛṣṇadāsa Kavirāja used citations from earlier works both to bolster his own message and to lend those works a stamp of authenticity. Works he did not cite are not part of the standard Gauḍīya Vaiṣṇava canon. Haricaraṇa Dāsa, author of the *Advaita Maṅgala*, similarly cites *purāṇa*s and various writings that support and legitimate what he is saying about Advaita Ācārya. Haricaraṇa was writing the very first treatment of the life of the father of his guru Acyutānanda, Advaita's eldest son. He would no doubt have been familiar with Locana Dāsa's *Caitanya Maṅgala*, finished within a few years of Kavi Karṇapūra's *Caitanya Candrodaya Nāṭaka*, which he also cites. But he had not seen Kṛṣṇadāsa Kavirājā's massive and thorough *Caitanya Caritāmṛta*; that text had not yet reached Bengal. The *Advaita Maṅgala* and the *Caitanya Caritāmṛta* were probably completed around the same time, but Kṛṣṇadāsa was writing in Vṛndāvana, and Haricaraṇa was in Bengal.

No one at all,[28] outside of Advaita's school, cites any of the Advaita hagiographies. Not only do no other authorities cite Īśāna Nāgara's work, but the only manuscript version of the *Advaita Prakāśa* is very recent. The rest of the Advaita Ācārya corpus fares little better, though six extant manuscripts of the *Advaita Maṅgala* were enough to allow Ravīndranātha Maiti to produce a critical edition of that text, in 1966. Why is there so little material on Caitanya's forerunner (his John the Baptist, as one Gauḍīya Vaiṣṇava told me)? For that matter, why did the

[28] With the exception of Nityānanda Dāsa in his *Premavilāsa*, an extremely problematic text.

other authors *not* cite Īśāna's work? They did not cite the *Advaita Prakāśa* because they had not seen it.

The *Advaita Prakāśa* is one of the last pieces of hagiography to treat Advaita Ācārya, not (as its colophon[29] proclaims) the first, and so seals the corpus on the life and teachings of its subject. This text provides us with many examples of polemic about Vaiṣṇavism in general, but also more specifically about Advaita and his importance to the group. Many of the stories all three of our authors tell are so miraculous in nature that even the novice scholar of religion will readily grasp their rhetorical points, usually so shallowly embedded in the narrative that we can easily extricate them for our own examination and, in so doing, come to understand the many uses of hagiography as a religious literary genre. Further, the first section of the *Advaita Prakāśa* is a vernacular elaboration on a short Sanskrit text, the *Bālyā-Līlā-Sūtra*, and we will investigate the relationship between these two works later in this introduction. Let us turn now to Advaita Ācārya himself.

Who Was Advaita Ācārya, and Why Should We Care?

Advaita Ācārya was born Kamalākṣa (in the *Advaita Prakāśa*) or Kamalākānta (in the *Advaita Maṅgala*) Bhaṭṭācārya in the village of Navagrāma, twenty miles up the Surma River from Sunamganj, in what is now Sylhet District of Bangladesh.[30] Providing a good example of hagiographical hyperbole, Īśāna tells us Advaita lived from 1434 to 1559; Haricaraṇa provides no such dating. In describing the life spans of figures who lived a very long time, South Asian hagiographers routinely claim their subjects lived 125 years.[31] A 125-year life span is just beyond credibility but effectively makes the point that Advaita Ācārya lived a remarkably long time. His life bracketed that of Caitanya. At the age of twelve he relocated to Shantipur, about ninety kilometers north of Kolkata in what is now West Bengal, to complete his education. Such an imposing individual must be matched with a suitable life partner, and Īśāna assures us that that is the case. Īśāna describes Advaita Ācārya's romance with his wives in chapter 8.[32] Up until this point in the narrative, Advaita

[29] The section at the end of a manuscript that provides information about its production, such as the date and place of copying and the name of the scribe, as well as the names of the text and its author. The *Bālya-Līlā-Sūtra* purports to be earlier but because it treats only the childhood of Advaita Ācārya, it is not a complete hagiography.

[30] As previously stated, we find "information" on the events of Advaita Ācārya's life only in the hagiographical literature, and so the reader is warned against reading this section as empirical history. In April 1994 I was shown what the local priests swore was the exact location of Advaita's birth in the Bangladeshi village of Navagrāma.

[31] Rāmānuja, the eleventh-century South Indian theologian credited with developing the *Viśiṣṭādvaita* (qualified nondualism) school of Vaiṣṇavism, is another such example.

[32] Prior to the passage of the Hindu Marriage Act in 1957, polygamy and the marriage of sisters to a single man were not unusual among the wealthy.

had never demonstrated any interest in family life. Now, however, his elders have commanded him to marry so that he could produce progeny, thereby generating a lineage to carry on his work as well as to perform the requisite funeral rites after his death. Further, a good wife would be able to take care of him properly, alleviating many of his domestic burdens.

By the time Advaita does marry, he is no longer young, and yet the two young sisters, Sītā and Śrī, fall hopelessly in love with him the moment they first see him at the river. When he invites the girls and their father into his home, he reveals his majestic *aiśvarya* nature to them, transforming his house into a palace and appearing seated on a crystal throne. Īśāna and to a lesser extent Haricaraṇa present this scene in some detail, and the picture we see is reminiscent of visualization instructions given to tantric practitioners who strive first to mentally see, and then to become, their object of devotion. The marriage occurred late in Advaita's life and produced six sons. Advaita lived the remainder of his life in Shantipur.

Although a much younger man is generally recognized as the founder of Gauḍīya Vaiṣṇavism, most adherents of the school would probably consider their movement's history to have begun with Advaita. His pedigree among the highest ranks of Bengali brahmins and his classical Sanskrit philosophical education made him the anchor of respectability for the young Gauḍīya Vaiṣṇava tradition. But most important, Advaita is said to have been responsible for the advent of Kṛṣṇa Caitanya himself, the movement's founder and leading early exponent. Caitanya's followers understood him to be either Kṛṣṇa or the androgynous dual embodiment of Kṛṣṇa and Rādhā.[33]

Advaita Ācārya's Primary Role: The Advent of Viśvambhara Miśra

Advaita not only heralded Caitanya's advent but also outlived the younger man by at least two decades. By the time of Caitanya's birth Advaita seems to have already acquired a following through his teaching and orthodox Vedāntic erudition.[34] Once Caitanya came of age as a religious leader, Advaita Ācārya aligned himself closely with Caitanya's new movement, apparently shifting his own philosophical orientation to bring it into harmony with the dualistic devotion beginning to sweep the region. Advaita brought most of his own students along with him, and this group became an important school of Gauḍīya Vaiṣṇavism, and still continues today.[35]

[33] I will return to the dual nature of divinity—this androgyny—later in this introductory chapter.

[34] Literally, "the end of the Vedas," Vedānta refers collectively to the Upanishads and the scholastic and commentatorial literature treating them. This material appeared in the second half of the first millennium BCE and is overwhelmingly monistic, a view that will be at odds with medieval Vaiṣṇava theology.

[35] The movement split into a number of factions. A second lineage formed under the leadership of Nityānanda, known as an *avadhūta*, who had the reputation of a wild man given to ecstatic excesses and probably behavioral excesses as well. His followers were, and are, far more numerous than Advaita's.

Gauḍīya writers unanimously acknowledge Advaita's role as the herald of the new age of devotionalism in Bengal through his summoning of Kṛṣṇa to earth. Īśāna Nāgara goes considerably further than other Vaiṣṇava authors in attributing Caitanya's advent to Advaita. For Īśāna this is no mere statement to highlight Advaita's constant storming of heaven—something of which anyone would have been capable—but rather a lengthy series of illustrations of Advaita's own divinity and, in a sense, his paternity of the *avatāra* of the age. Nowhere is this clearer than in chapter 10 of the *Advaita Prakāśa*, where Īśāna presents the story of the birth of Caitanya.[36]

The chapter opens with Advaita performing his usual morning worship in the Ganges River, or Gaṅgā as it is known in India, wondering aloud, as he so frequently did, when the Lord would come to earth to restore righteousness. One of the flowers he has offered to Kṛṣṇa suddenly begins to float upstream, and immediately recognizing this anomaly as Kṛṣṇa's work, Advaita follows it for fifteen miles, all the way to Navadvīpa, where a young pregnant woman, Śacī Miśra, is bathing. Two hard-held folk beliefs enter the narrative at this point: first, that it is inauspicious for offering remnants to adhere to a person's body; and two, that no mortal fetus can withstand the homage of a brahmin.

Since the flowers he had offered to Kṛṣṇa have adhered to Śacī's belly, Advaita recognizes this woman as the future mother of the embodiment of Kṛṣṇa for this degenerate Kali Age and, hoping that her very visible pregnancy is that embodiment, bows before her. She miscarries instantly.

This series of events is repeated a number of times, and Śacī suffers many miscarriages. She begins to despair of ever producing a living child to continue her husband's lineage and to care for the couple in their old age and beyond. Desperate, the couple approach Advaita, asking him to leave them in peace. He reassures them that they will not only have a son, but a most remarkable son. When once again his offerings begin to float upstream, Advaita knows Śacī is pregnant and that his long-awaited savior is on his way. Once again he bows to her, but this time she retains the fetus in her womb, a sure sign that her child is divine. And indeed first Viśvarūpa, who is never heard from in the narrative again, and then after a subsequent pregnancy Viśvambhara, who will later be known as Kṛṣṇa Caitanya, is born.

If the image of the flower floating upstream against the current and adhering to Śacī's body is not sufficiently semen-like to carry the message that it is Advaita who is truly responsible for Caitanya's birth, Īśāna continues to highlight this connection as the advent story unfolds. Advaita and Sītā live in Shantipur, about fifteen miles downstream from Navadvīpa.[37] Advaita senses Viśvambhara's arrival

[36] I am indebted to Tony K. Stewart for the development of this deconstruction.

[37] Due to the river's changing course in subsequent monsoon seasons, Shantipur is no longer situated on the riverbank.

and quickly goes to the Miśra home. Śacī is in seclusion in the childbirth hut, as is traditional, where she will remain with the baby for forty days. Only the midwife and immediate family members are permitted contact with the new mother and child during this important time of family bonding. Yet Advaita, who is not related to either parent, enters unchallenged to see the infant. Śacī, understandably upset to see him, given her childbearing history, tells him that the child will not nurse. Advaita asks her to step aside while he investigates the matter, and takes the baby in his arms—something again only the parents are permitted to do. The baby speaks to Advaita, telling him that the problem is simply that his mother has not been properly initiated with the Hare Kṛṣṇa mantra.[38] Until that initiation takes place, he cannot drink her milk.

Advaita returns the baby to his mother, now sitting outdoors at the base of a neem tree,[39] and initiates her with the requisite mantra. He puts the child in her arms as a midwife puts a newborn into its mother's arms, thus further signaling his delivery of the *avatāra* of the age to his human parents.

In none of the other biographies, in either the Advaita or the Caitanya corpus, is this responsibility for Caitanya's advent attributed to Advaita so clearly and in such a detailed manner. Caitanya's biographers give Advaita credit for recognizing the need for a new *avatāra* to come solve the contemporary world's problems; some talk about his fervent prayers to Kṛṣṇa for that to happen. But Īśāna all but tells us Advaita is the father of Caitanya, conferring on him far more importance than the Gauḍīya tradition had previously granted him. Even the episode's location in chapter 10 (of twenty-two) makes it central to Īśāna's message.

Haricaraṇa Dāsa places Caitanya's birth much later in his work, waiting until V.4 to describe Caitanya's advent. We have flower buds floating against the current, as in the *Advaita Prakāśa*, but here they come from some mysterious source *to* Advaita, and do not proceed *from* him. In a scene reminiscent of countless similar tales from Indian history the old sage feeds one bud to each wife (Śacī Miśra, wife of Jagannātha, and Advaita's own wife Sītā), both of whom bear sons shortly thereafter. The episode is an important one, but not central to Haricaraṇa's main purpose.

Haricaraṇa tells us the same story Īśāna uses to explain why Saci's infant would not nurse (his mother had not been properly initiated with the Kṛṣṇa-mantra). His theological point is that Advaita is Kṛṣṇa's *svarūpa*, his true form. But so is Caitanya! That means that when Caitanya was born, that *svarūpa* resided in two separate bodies. Haricaraṇa's Caitanya repeatedly stresses that no one can get him without Advaita; both are essential to attaining Vaiṣṇava salvation.

[38] The basic prayer of the Gauḍīyas, *Hare Kṛṣṇa, Hare Kṛṣṇa, Kṛṣṇa, Kṛṣṇa, Hare Hare; Hare Rāma, Hare Rāma, Rāma Rāma, Hare Hare.*

[39] Also unlikely; this soon after delivery the mother would normally still be in seclusion. This tree is the basis for Caitanya's nickname of Nimāi.

Caitanya's hagiographical material indicates that he was first exposed to devotionalism while on pilgrimage following his father's death, when he met Rāmānanda Rāya. Advaita's biographies, however, give Advaita, and not Caitanya, credit for bringing devotionalism from the south back to Bengal by having him meet Mādhavendra Purī at Madhva's hermitage[40] long before Caitanya is born. Advaita subsequently brings Mādhavendra Purī's teachings—among them most notably a mysterious text called the *Ananta Saṃhitā*—back to Bengal. Advaita summons the *avatāra* for the age onto the ground that he has prepared, thanks to his discussions with Mādhavendra Purī.

The Theology and Theophany of Advaita Ācārya

The name "Advaita Ācārya" literally means "master of nondualism," an etymological inconvenience for the dualistic Gauḍīya Vaiṣṇavas, and their writers often take pains to explain what his name "really" means. Īśāna and a number of others interpret Advaita Ācārya's name to mean "no different from" Kṛṣṇa, an interpretation that allows Advaita to actually *be* Kṛṣṇa, but a Kṛṣṇa less complete than Caitanya. In this section we will explore how it is that both Advaita and Caitanya can be Kṛṣṇa.

Our authors make use of three different theological frameworks as they describe Advaita's role in Gauḍīya history. De, Dimock, and Stewart all discuss these models in great detail; here we simply provide a brief overview. First, the *vyūha* (emanation) doctrine from the old Vaiṣṇava *pāñcarātra*[41] system holds that divinity projects itself serially into creation and then maintains that creation. Vāsudeva emanates himself serially into the world, followed by Saṃkarṣaṇa, then Pradyumna, and finally Aniruddha. Rūpa Gosvāmī, one of Gauḍīya Vaiṣṇavism's major theologians, asserts that Vāsudeva is only an aspect of Kṛṣṇa, and that Kṛṣṇa is the greater. Īśāna asserts both Caitanya's elder brother Viśvarūpa and Nityānanda's son Vīracandra as Saṃkarṣaṇa but does not use the rest of the scheme. Haricaraṇa, however, has Advaita as Vāsudeva, Nityānanda as Saṃkarṣaṇa, and Advaita's sons, Acyutānanda as Pradyumna and Balarāma as Aniruddha. Thus Advaita begins the divine expansion into creation as its first evolute, and his sons finish it, with only one non-family member in the configuration. While in this scheme Advaita is the first divine evolute, he is not its source. This *vyūha* system is the earliest model in play.

The second scheme is that of *aṃśī*, the source of all descents, and its *aṃśa*s, or portions. Stewart describes *aṃśa* as "a reduced portion of divinity contained

[40] The pro forma association of the Gauḍīya *Sampradāya* (school) with Madhva's much older group is an interesting and controversial story but is not germane to the present discussion. For details, see Hardy, "Madhavendra Puri."

[41] An earlier form of Vaiṣṇavism, also known as the Bhāgavata sect, popular as early as the sixth century CE. For more on *pāñcarātra*, see Matsubara, Gonda, and Jaiswal.

within a worldly operable figure in order to achieve a specified worldly goal."[42] As the Supreme, Kṛṣṇa is in no way diminished when he sends a part of Himself to earth. He can thus simultaneously exist as both a portion of divinity and the source of all the parts. Haricaraṇa repeatedly states that the Whole is in the Parts and the Parts are in the Whole as he describes the relationship of the three lords Advaita, Caitanya, and Nityānanda.

As the *aṃśī* he is his own fullest, most complete form, *Pūrṇatama*, the Kṛṣṇa of the Vraja *līlā* and the playfully romantic exploits with the cowherd maidens. Kṛṣṇa's *Pūrṇa* "complete" form also appears in Vraja, in the person of his elder brother Balarāma. And finally Kṛṣṇa has a "fuller" form, *Pūrṇatara*, as in his activities in Mathurā, where he defeats the evil King Kaṃśa.

Followers of earlier theistic schools in Bengal worshiped an all-powerful, almost unapproachable god, focusing their devotion on a quality they called "majesty," or *aiśvarya*. That is, God, like the king, required a certain distance and decorum from those who sought to stay in his favor. But the various medieval Vaiṣṇava schools began to speak of a god with whom one could have a personal relationship, and the theologians had a great deal to say about the range of possible relationships one could develop with Kṛṣṇa.

In Bengal Kṛṣṇa became not merely one of the many *avatāra*s of Viṣṇu but the source of all *avatāra*s himself. The Bengali community developed a very sophisticated theology based on the ancient Sanskrit system of aesthetics, or *rasa*, by which the devotee learned to cultivate an ever-closer relationship to the object of devotion.[43] In this theology the eternal Kṛṣṇa of Vraja descends to earth serially, first sending lesser forms of himself, and his parents and friends, and finally appearing fully in all his glory after the others have set the stage for him. Advaita is the main component of the first wave of that descent of the eternal Vraja.

Advaita's hagiographers describe him[44] as an embodiment of Mahāviṣṇu, in most Vaiṣṇava traditions the Supreme Being who from time to time takes birth to save the world. One of those periodic appearances was as the Kṛṣṇa of Vraja and the *Bhagavad Gītā*. In Gauḍīya theology, however, Kṛṣṇa is the Ultimate Reality and Mahāviṣṇu is a part of Kṛṣṇa, but in either case Mahāviṣṇu represents the *aiśvarya* aspect of divinity: the awesome, in its original sense. Advaita is also sometimes described as a joint incarnation of Mahāviṣṇu and Sadāśiva,[45] a Śiva who like Mahāviṣṇu is described in different ways by different people. Sadāśiva, judging by contemporary seals, was the tutelary god of the Sena dynasty, who ruled the region from the late eleventh century into the thirteenth

[42] Stewart, *The Final Word*, 110.

[43] See David Haberman's translation of *The Bhaktirasāmṛtasindhu of Rūpa Gosvāmin*, as well as his earlier *Acting as a Way of Salvation*.

[44] See appendix 1 for a list of Advaita Ācārya's theological equivalences.

[45] Advaita's hagiographers use the names Sadāśiva and Śiva interchangeably.

century.[46] His worship came to the fore under the Palas, who ruled in the three centuries immediately before the Senas.[47] But the inclusion of Śiva at all here constitutes an acknowledgment that Viṣṇu was not at the core of all Bengali religious expression at the time, and an attempt to bring the local Śaivites into the Vaiṣṇava fold. I will discuss competition among religious groups in a later section.

Conceptions of Caitanya's divinity began with the view of him as partial incarnation (*aṃśa*) of Kṛṣṇa, in Murāri Gupta's early biography the *Kṛṣṇa Caitanya Caritāmṛta*, to *avatāra* and even *avatāra* for the age in the same work, all of which conceptions emphasize the distant, awe-inspiring (*aiśvarya*) aspects of Kṛṣṇa.

Theologically, Advaita stands symbolically on one end of a continuum of devotional attitudes and models for his followers the steady movement toward Kṛṣṇa.[48] These attitudes are very human, beginning with the most distant sort of relationship that can still go by that name, *aiśvarya*, progressing to that most intimate of all human relationships, the erotic, *mādhurya*. Thus one might begin to approach divinity as a very distant deity before whom one stands in complete awe. Gradually the relationship would become more personal, as the devotee progressed to *sakhya*, or friendship with the deity; then to *vatsalya*, or feelings of parental love toward the object of devotion; and finally reach *mādhurya*, in which the devotee approaches the divine as lover, with each attitude encompassing all those that precede it. *Mādhurya* is, according to the Gauḍīya Vaiṣṇavas, the most desirable attitude to cultivate in one's religious life because it represents the most intimate of all possible human relationships. That is, one cannot possibly get closer to God, or anyone else, than through the erotic mode. One would do this largely through meditative visualization practices in which the aspirant viewed himself as one of Kṛṣṇa's adoring *gopīs* (milkmaids) or some other, usually female, member of Kṛṣṇa's inner circle who aided the divine couple in their love play.

By the time of Kṛṣṇadāsa Kavirāja's *Caitanya Caritāmṛta*, completed between 1600 and 1612, *aiśvarya* has been completely supplanted by the intimacy of the *mādhurya* mode, and the Gauḍīyas understand Caitanya as a dual incarnation of Rādhā and Kṛṣṇa, and as *Svayaṃ Bhagavān*, "God himself."[49] The notions of divine

aiśvarya	*śānta*	*dāsya*	*sakhya*	*vatsalya*	*mādhurya*
majesty	peacefulness	servitude	friendship	parental love	sweetness
Advaita Ācārya					Caitanya

Figure 1 Continuum of divinity

[46] Chatterjee, *Religion in Bengal*, 138.
[47] Ibid., 147.
[48] Please see Figure 1.
[49] *Caitanya Caritāmṛta* 2.20.209; 2.24.54.

hermaphroditism and of dual embodiment are not new in South Asia, as is evident from the many sculptures of Śiva as Ardhanarīśvara (the lord who is half woman) found throughout the region.

As the text progresses, we will see Advaita move from that *aiśvarya* mode along the continuum of devotion, until he finally reaches *mādhurya*, as is foreshadowed in chapter 2 with his childhood encounter with the goddess in the temple in Lauḍa. Īśāna has constructed this progression in his literary narrative as a template for devotional progress. The pinnacle of devotional expression could come only in *mādhurya*, as modeled by the cowherd women of Vraja. Though they were married, the moment they heard the sound of Kṛṣṇa's flute, they would drop everything and run to him. Pots were left bubbling on stoves, children were left untended, and clothes were only half donned, all in the women's haste. This was *parakīyā* love, the love for someone committed to another. Each meeting with such a lover may be the last. Discovery of the affair will mean utter disgrace and the loss of social standing and even family. The elements of high risk and desperation render the love much more intense, and so much sweeter. *Svakīyā* love, the love for one's own partner, is predictable and routine, conditioned by social obligation. Stewart translates an obscure text, Manohara Dāsa's *Dīnamaṇicandrodaya*: "As the pinnacle of experience, *madhura* was best experienced by the *parakīyā* love of the *gopīs* in Vraja, a love devoid of any ignorance, pride or lust . . . and was totally selfless."[50] *Svakīyā* is selfish, undertaken for one's own satisfaction; the goal of *parakīyā* is the partner's gratification.[51] The Advaita Ācārya of the *Advaita Maṅgala* is a *parakīyā* practitioner. He initiates his wives into *parakīyā* ritual shortly after their wedding. Vaiṣṇavas argued endlessly over whether these practices were to be carried out mentally, through visualizations, or physically. Īśāna does not discuss *parakīyā* at all. He has set out a more straightforward model for devotional progress. That is, this is a rhetorical strategy designed to evoke the same movement in the readers, for we, too, should likewise (in the view of the author of the text) be cultivating a close personal relationship with Kṛṣṇa. It is further a literary and aesthetic strategy overlaying the entire text as the author allows us, the readers, to savor the many flavors (*rasa*) of devotion.

Religious Competition

Kṛṣṇa devotion is a relative newcomer to Bengal. Other and older strong regional traditions included Śāktism (goddess worship), Śaivism (worship of the god Śiva), and the various less clearly definable movements of the *sahajiyās*, advocates of the so-called natural religion that uses sexual ritual to attain the divine. No one can say how old any of these strands is, although their sudden literary profusion suggests that the *sahajiyās* attached themselves to Vaiṣṇavism in the seventeenth

[50] Stewart, *The Final Word*, 344.

[51] Edward C. Dimock discusses *parakīyā* love at length in his *Place of the Hidden Moon*, 210–21.

century. Various forms of Buddhism had also enjoyed a long presence in the area, as we know from both the monastic ruins that scatter the landscape and such literature as the mystical Buddhist *Caryāgīti* of the late first millennium. And Islam was making serious inroads, bringing new people in to settle previously unpopulated areas in the east. In this section we will discuss the competing forces briefly, then provide examples from the texts of how the main authors, Īśāna and Haricaraṇa, addressed these threats.

Śāktism and Śaivism dominated the local religious landscape prior to Caitanya's introduction of his new brand of Vaiṣṇavism. The cult of the goddess was indigenous to Bengal, long preceding the arrival of Aryan Vedic religion with its male focus. Although Śāktism and Śaivism are quite different, local brahmins sought to harmonize them through the notion of the divine marriage of male and female principles. The brahmins began equating all female divinity with Śakti as Śiva's counterpart. Further, the priests tried to draw the cults of those goddesses celebrated in the Middle Bengali epics known as *maṅgala-kāvya* into their own Śaivite orthodoxy by putting them into relationship with Śiva, with varying degrees of success. Brahmin Śaiva priests retained control of the temples and the rituals conducted in those temples. Much of their clientele, however, belonged to the lower ranks of society and followed the old goddess cults, now, at least in the minds of the priests, absorbed into orthodox Śaivism.

The new Vaiṣṇava movement cut into that client base with its emphasis on devotion over (brahmin-controlled) ritual.[52] It purported to have no need for the sacerdotal intermediary, as salvation was available to anyone who called on Kṛṣṇa. And so much of the Śākta and Śaiva orthodoxy resisted the very real threat of the Vaiṣṇavas. They were not ignoring them, however, for by the time Rāmaprasāda (1718–75) was writing his Śākta devotional lyrics, according to McDermott, "Śākta Tantras were being written with the express intention of bringing the Vaiṣṇava experience under the Śākta religious umbrella."[53]

The new threat could take a different approach. Because Advaita, representing traditional brahminical religion in its many forms, is the instrumental cause for the advent of Caitanya, the Gauḍīya Vaiṣṇavas claim that Caitanya's mode of ecstatic and very personal devotion is the natural development, the next step upward, from the older traditions, and that the older ideas are very much a part of the newer form. The Gauḍīyas have very easily and neatly absorbed their potential competition, marked that competition as "no different from us," and rehierarchized their theology to produce one seamless whole—all without any overt antagonism, either with other Vaiṣṇavas or, they hoped, with other religious groups. I will examine an example of this phenomenon later. Richard Eaton cites William Smith in his discussion of the pre-Muslim religious scene in Bengal, in

[52] Eaton, *The Rise of Islam and the Bengal Frontier*, 111.

[53] McDermott, *Mother of My Heart*, 78.

which Śiva was "the hub around which the Bengali divine hierarchy revolves."[54] The ruling family in Nadīyā, for example, was Śākta,[55] and the goddess is often associated with royalty.

Zamindars[56] had historically supported the construction of mosques, temples, and so forth, and patronized scholars and artists of all religious persuasions.[57] With the institution of Indo-Turkish rule, however, such patronage dried up.[58] Under Husain Shah (r. 1494–1519) and his immediate successors, however, Vaiṣṇavas (but not Śāktas) did receive generous patronage, at least until Mughal rule reached Bengal in 1583.

In Advaita's lifetime Bengal was under Muslim rule with authority centralized in Delhi that left local areas under varying degrees and modes of control. Imperial officials were not local, nor did they permanently settle in Bengal,[59] and so they were not only not Vaiṣṇava but also not Bengali. But they often provided patronage to Hindu intellectual institutions. We see little evidence in the literature of Caitanya's time of chronic hostilities between Muslims and Vaiṣṇavas,[60] and some evidence to suggest that the two groups sometimes united against the local Śāktas and Śaivas, whose practices the former groups considered debased. But by the late nineteenth century the line between Hindu and Muslim had become less permeable than it had been in Advaita's lifetime, and it seemed to be more important to know on which side of that line one sat.

Cynthia Talbot argues convincingly in a recent article that nationalism, or perhaps the sense of a "supralocal" identity, did not appear for the first time in the nineteenth century. She suggests "that supralocal identities were articulated with increasing force by regional political elites after A.D. 1000 and that historical traditions played a critical role in this process of identity formation. One possible stimulus for the growth of a historical consciousness was the Muslim presence in the subcontinent, and not only because Islamic tradition provided models for historical writing."[61]

Any power shift triggers changes in other aspects of society. The more conservative brahmins may have felt threatened by the increasing Muslim presence in Bengal, but Śāktism and tantra seem to have done quite well.[62]

[54] Smith, *The One-Eyed Goddess*, 134; Eaton, *The Rise of Islam and the Bengal Frontier*, 104.

[55] McDermott, *Mother of My Heart*, 29.

[56] Ray, *Change in Bengal Agrarian Society c. 1760–1850*, 14–21. The *zamindars* were large landholders who maintained law and order, also served as local leaders, and in turn paid tribute to the administration in Delhi.

[57] McDermott, *Mother of My Heart*, 29.

[58] Eaton, *The Rise of Islam and the Bengal Frontier*, 104.

[59] Van Schendel, *A History of Bangladesh*, 52–53.

[60] The *Caitanya Caritāmṛta* does contain a few examples of unfriendly communal interaction, usually when small groups meet unexpectedly on the road. These episodes, while clearly uncomfortable for all concerned, come nowhere near the large-scale wholesale violence of the modern world.

[61] Talbot, "The Story of Prataparudra," 284.

[62] Bhattacharya, *History of the Śākta Religion*, 127.

Bengal was not religiously homogeneous, and so people developed methods of coping with religious diversity. In chapter 1, to cite just one (as promised earlier), Advaita's pregnant mother-to-be, Lābhā, has a vision of Mahāviṣṇu and Sadāśiva merging into a single being in her womb. She had already lost many sons at or shortly after birth and so was particularly anxious that this pregnancy come to fruition.[63] Her dream first of all establishes Advaita Ācārya as an important, indeed divine, person. More significantly, though, the dream also indicates authorial desire to enfold other forms of devotionalism into the new Kṛṣṇa *bhakti* (devotion), which it obliquely suggests is supreme.

Throughout their compositions all three authors remind us that Advaita is himself divine. Others will address him as "Sadāśiva" or use an epithet suggesting another aspect of divinity. These names tell us in effect that even the mighty god Śiva, object of worship of a competing school, worships Kṛṣṇa! Īśāna plays with these sorts of images throughout his composition. For example, in chapter 15 of the *Advaita Prakāśa* in a humorous anecdote about a feast Advaita shared with Caitanya and his other main associate, Nityānanda, Caitanya identifies Advaita as Śiva, and a few lines later Nityānanda refers to Advaita as a four-handed dwarf,[64] alluding to one of the earlier *avatāra*s of Viṣṇu. Advaita then declares Nityānanda to be Ananta, the cosmic serpent on whom Mahāviṣṇu rests between periods of creation, also associated with Kṛṣṇa's elder brother Balarāma though the two were not related; Nityānanda was approximately twelve years older than Caitanya. Both men are staking out their theological territory, and each other's at the same time. Nityānanda is teasing Advaita about his physical appearance while giving us yet another divine identity for his friend, and Advaita, in using the standard equation of Nityānanda as Ananta, is perhaps a bit kinder than Nityānanda was to him, for Advaita is saying that Nityānanda is the support of the entire movement. But this is not the way Īśāna usually portrays Nityānanda, and later in the same chapter he will cut Nityānanda out of the picture entirely. Many authors describe him as the Balarāma for Kali Yuga and use such appropriate epithets as Ananta and Saṃkarṣaṇa for him. But Gauḍīya writers often hinted at a long-standing quarrel between Nityānanda, something of a wild man, and the staid, proper Advaita.

Most of the Gauḍīya writers describe Nityānanda as a man who has little interest in propriety and ritual purity. The contrast between him and Advaita Ācārya is usually made quite dramatic. Much of the literature strongly suggests that those two leaders quarreled frequently. Yet Īśāna describes a Nityānanda from a good brahmin family who is respectful of the opinions of his elders, particularly when it comes time for his marriage, and is quite honorable in the eyes of society. Although Īśāna does not speak ill of the man, he also, aside from the single

[63] Note the parallels with Caitanya's advent story.

[64] Some of the short lyric poems known as *padāvalī* describe Advaita as a short, potbellied old man.

instant mentioned earlier, has Advaita Ācārya usurp the role usually assigned to Nityānanda as the *dhāman*, the site, for Kṛṣṇa's birth in Kali Yuga.

Both Haricaraṇa and Īśāna, in contrast to most of the other Gauḍīya Vaiṣṇava hagiographers, do not use the usual Gauḍīya epithets to refer to Nityānanda (except at the feast described previously). They thus cut Nityānanda out of the power structure of the first generation, and do so without a harsh partisan word. Later, in chapter 15 of the *Advaita Prakāśa*, when Caitanya and his closest associates are reenacting Kṛṣṇa's water play in the river, we find Advaita taking over the Ananta role as he floats on his back and holds Caitanya on his chest to portray Mahāviṣṇu lying on his serpent bed waiting for the next cycle of creation to begin. Nityānanda is not present and does not take part in this activity at all. In V.9 of the *Advaita Maṅgala* all three "lords" participate in the reenactment of the *dāna līlā*, but Nityānanda does not have a role to play beyond his presence.

Īśāna devotes one chapter, chapter 20, to Nityānanda and his deeds, choosing to focus on the story of Nityānanda's marriage to two sisters, Vasudhā and Jāhnavī. Haricaraṇa tells Nityānanda's birth story in V.3 but does not mention his marriage. Other Gauḍīya materials report that Jāhnavī played a leading role for her husband's disciples after Nityānanda's death and was every bit as active and significant as Sītā Devī was for Advaita's disciples. Īśāna, however, downplays her importance, and Haricaraṇa never mentions her at all. First Īśāna tells us that Vasudhā, and not Jāhnavī, was Nityānanda's primary wife. The two were sisters, and their father was initially reluctant to marry his daughters to this man who had simply appeared one day, because he knew nothing about Nityānanda's family and background. Only later, when Nityānanda manages to revive the apparently dead Vasudhā, is the marriage allowed to take place. And then Jāhnavī comes along as her sister's dowry. This may have been common at the time, but Śrī does not accompany her sister Sītā as dowry but as a full co-wife when she enters Advaita's household. Jāhnavī is merely an afterthought in Nityānanda's marriage negotiations.

Further, Vasudhā is the mother of Nityānanda's son and heir Vīrabhadra.[65] While Kṛṣṇa Miśra is Sītā's son passed off out of kindness as Śrī's,[66] and is the heir to his father's temple image and responsibilities, Vīrabhadra is not the son of the wife who will come to lead his father's group. Īśāna is casting oblique aspersions on the legitimacy of Nityānanda's successors, whom Haricaraṇa does not mention at all.

And last, in *Advaita Prakāśa* chapter 22, Vīrabhadra turns not to his father's group for mantra initiation but to Advaita Ācārya, in a move Īśāna uses to indicate Vīrabhadra's acknowledgment of the supremacy of the Advaita lineage. Advaita refuses to initiate the young man, sending him back to his own mother, Jāhnavī, but Jāhnavī does not confer the mantra herself. Instead, she sends Vīrabhadra to

[65] Also called Vīracandra.

[66] Details below.

"some scholar" for his spiritual instruction. Advaita behaved properly by sending Vīrabhadra back to his own lineage, but Jāhnavī does not consider herself qualified to do the job. She turns not to anyone we recognize as important in Gauḍīya Vaiṣṇavism but to a person whose name the author does not consider worth mentioning.

Īśāna's treatment of Advaita Ācārya's main competition offers an example of how a skilled hagiographer can rewrite previously accepted sectarian views of history. Nityānanda's group of Vaiṣṇavas has always been larger than Advaita's group. Although Advaita's school shrank steadily over the years, its members always prided themselves in their origins at the top of Bengali society and in their maintenance of brahminical purity in the face of increasing pressures to relax standards. Īśāna reminds us constantly of these two issues and how they distinguish Advaita Ācārya from his contemporary Gauḍīyas.

Īśāna does give Nityānanda a significant place in that first generation but denies him any lasting importance in sectarian history. He shows Nityānanda's family as insignificant, unable to bestow mantras and thus incapable of assuming leadership for the future of Nityānanda's branch of Gauḍīya Vaiṣṇavism.

Haricaraṇa takes a different approach to Nityānanda. At several points almost in passing he mentions Nityānanda as one of the three lords, "to be equally revered" along with Advaita and Caitanya. In V.3, the chapter preceding that covering Caitanya's birth, Haricaraṇa tells the story of Nityānanda's birth. He states clearly that Nityānanda is Kṛṣṇa's elder brother Balarāma, and his parents, Rohiṇī and Vasudeva; he is also Ananta, the cosmic serpent and Saṃkarṣaṇa.

The infant's father cannot come up with a name for his son, so he takes him to Shantipur to see Advaita, who proclaims him no ordinary child, but Īśvara himself! Advaita names him "Nityānanda," eternal bliss.

The only other episode in Haricaraṇa's work in which Nityānanda features prominently is in the same chapter. It is an odd story in which Nityānanda saves the soul of a brahmin-hating demon and sends him to Advaita to repent and die beside the Gaṅgā.

Later, in V.5, Haricaraṇa tells us, in *tripadī* meter so we know this is important, that Kṛṣṇa walks the earth as all three lords Caitanya, Advaita, and Nityānanda. In verse 9 of this poem he says, "Nityānanda is his [Kṛṣṇa's] *svarūpa*."

In V.8 the author describes yet another of Sītā's exquisite banquets, where Nityānanda is present and indulging his fondness for sweets. This is not the humorous tale found in the *Advaita Prakāśa*, but one of miracles and reverential awe for Sītā, who is its focus. Here Sītā replicates herself so that each guest thinks she is waiting on him alone—and Nityānanda and Advaita point out to Caitanya the parallel with Kṛṣṇa's doing the same with the *gopī*s in his *rāsa līlā*.

Finally, Nityānanda is present in the culminating episode of the *Advaita Maṅgala*, the reenactment of the *dāna līlā*, bragging to Advaita about something unspecified. But he has no role in the play! Haricaraṇa meticulously lists ten others, besides Advaita and Caitanya, who played specific roles, but Nityānanda is not among them. But he is present, for at the end of the play, "the three began to regain consciousness, embracing, unable to speak," and Nityānanda and Caitanya dance ecstatically.

Īśāna has much to say about Advaita's successors and writes of a family that remains active and vibrant. Sītā Devī confers mantra initiation on at least one of her sons and a daughter-in-law, and while three of Advaita's sons were particularly close to Caitanya, the others, too, are leaders in the community (though they have not always seen eye-to-eye with their father). Haricaraṇa tells us that all six sons are great Vaiṣṇavas and gives no hint of the splits that were history by the late nineteenth century.

As should be apparent by now, both the *Advaita Maṅgala* and the *Advaita Prakāśa* are rich in metaphorical imagery. Paying close attention to the entailments in that imagery will allow us to look beneath the surface of the narrative to ascertain what an author is really trying to tell us. Advaita, Īśāna tells us, is the joint embodiment of Śiva and Mahāviṣṇu. His wives are embodiments of the goddess Lakṣmī, consort of Mahāviṣṇu, and so clearly appropriate mates for this man. For Haricaraṇa, though, Advaita is Kṛṣṇa himself who has come to make Rādhā and Kṛṣṇa appear in one individual. For him, it is all Kṛṣṇa. He uses *pāñcarātra vyūha* language to help explain how that is possible. Thus not only does the *dhāma* arrive serially, but it also sends forth serial emanations. According to *pāñcarātra*, Vāsudeva emanates portions of himself out into the world, and Saṃkarṣaṇa is the first of those evolutes.

Master of Nondualism?

The concern about Advaita Ācārya's sectarian history and allegiance, and the extent to which he embraced monistic philosophy, is echoed in frequent passages in the text where key actors debate the path of intellectual knowledge (*jñāna*, usually understood as monistic) versus the path of devotion (*bhakti*, usually, and always among the Gauḍīyas, conceived as dualistic). It is very likely that Advaita was indeed originally trained as the master of nondualism his name connotes. In fact, the last philosophical movement to sweep South Asia with similar force was Śaṅkara's monism,[67] and many subsequent schools of thought built on what Śaṅkara had begun. We do know[68] that Advaita had received the traditional brahminical education, which would have included instruction in the Vedas and Upanishads, the various grammatical and astrological treatises, and material from the six classical schools of philosophy. Advaita had set up his own traditional

[67] In the eighth century.

[68] Again the reader is cautioned to remember how it is that we "know" about Advaita's education. Given his family's wealth and status, it is very likely that he was actually educated as described, but we have no high school transcripts or similar documents with which to verify these claims.

school for brahmin boys in Navadvīpa so as to be near at hand when Kṛṣṇa did finally arrive, and we must only presume that he provided his students with the standard curriculum.

That school is then ready for Caitanya when he and his close friend Gadādhara come to Advaita to study. By this time the young men had already worked with several other accomplished scholars. Advaita was Caitanya's last formal teacher, and therefore the best of all of them, since he put the finishing touches on Caitanya's education. And from all indications, Caitanya's education too was quite traditional, including that final portion he received from Advaita. We know[69] that Caitanya himself founded a school shortly after completing his education but began losing students after he became too absorbed in his devotion to Kṛṣṇa to teach coherently.

Finally, Īśāna uses Mādhavendra Purī as a literary device to highlight another important doctrinal innovation, that of *yugala sevā*, or worship of the divine couple, Rādhā and Kṛṣṇa, as a unit. Up until the time of Caitanya, worshipers of Kṛṣṇa worshiped the single image of Kṛṣṇa. Haricaraṇa uses Mādhavendra Purī somewhat differently. In the *Advaita Maṅgala*, Mādhavendra Purī introduces the notions of *parakīyā* and the mutual dependence of Rādhā and Kṛṣṇa. He launches Kamalākānta, as he is still known, on his life's work, which is not only to bring Kṛṣṇa to earth but to use Kṛṣṇa's name as the vehicle by which people will be saved. Mādhavendra Purī describes Advaita as *bhaktāvatāra*, but in the same verse, recognizes him as *both* Kṛṣṇa and his consort Rādhā! No other author makes such a bold assertion about Advaita, and it is never repeated, but is nonetheless striking. Mādhavendra Purī is the *dīkṣā*-guru who initiates Advaita with the Hare Kṛṣṇa mantra through which he will save the world. The guru mentions that as a celibate renunciate Kamalākānta's desires to propagate devotion can only go so far. He takes the hint and understands that he must eventually marry and start his own lineage to keep the teachings going. We do not hear of Mādhavendra Purī outside this section of the *Advaita Maṅgala*.

Īśāna Nāgara plays with the notion of joint worship in interesting ways prior to introducing Rādhā-Kṛṣṇa worship specifically. The child in Lābhā's womb who will be born as Kamalākānta, and will come to be known as Advaita Ācārya, he tells us, is an amalgam, the joint incarnation of Mahāviṣṇu himself and Sadāśiva. This merger represents the conjunction of the most majestic elements of divinity then imaginable. Further, it constitutes the first appearance on the scene of Kṛṣṇa *līlā*, as Viṣṇu begins to set the stage for the other performers.

That joint embodiment of Mahāviṣṇu and Śiva then in turn unearths (literally) two very important items: the image of Madana Gopāla outside Vraja, and the picture of Kṛṣṇa that Viśākhā painted for the distraught Rādhā, suffering from separation from her divine lover Kṛṣṇa. Mādhavendra Purī appears at that point

[69] See previous note.

in the narrative (chapter 5) to instruct Advaita to return to Shantipur and install the two images in his own temple, and worship them as a unit.

If we step back from the story for a moment, we can see that Īśāna is constructing a framework in which the great gods Mahāviṣṇu and Śiva are themselves worshiping the loving couple Rādhā and Kṛṣṇa. If even the gods worship Rādhā and Kṛṣṇa, then clearly the divine couple represents the ultimate in power and divinity, and mere mortals should worship them, too. In other words, Īśāna is "proving" that the worship of Kṛṣṇa and Rādhā is superior to the older worship of Śiva and Mahāviṣṇu. Throughout *Advaita Prakāśa*, Īśāna Nāgara has very cleverly embedded such messages in episodes recounted nowhere else in the corpus.

The Puṣṭi Mārgīs[70] tell a very similar story in which Mādhavendra Purī discovers the image, and perhaps Haricaraṇa Dāsa used that story as his source in his *Advaita Maṅgala*. Kṛṣṇadāsa Kavirāja recounts the same story at 2.4.104–68 of his *Caitanya Caritāmṛta*. But in Haricaraṇa Dāsa's version of the story, Advaita, and not Mādhavendra Purī, uncovers the image of Madana Gopāla. The story is basically the same as in the *Caitanya Caritāmṛta* and the *Advaita Prakāśa*, but its hero and the disposition of his prize change. Earlier, in I.2, Vijaya Purī has an encounter in Vṛndāvana with the same Madana Gopāla.

Haricaraṇa has much more to say about this bleedthrough from the eternal Vraja than does Īśāna, and Īśāna expands the tale into Advaita Ācārya's present and takes it to Shantipur, signaling at every step of the way that this new religion introduced by Advaita Ācārya and propagated by Kṛṣṇa Caitanya both subsumes all others and is more effective, and hence worthwhile, than its predecessors.

In chapter 2 Īśāna had already shown that what Advaita has to say is more important than goddess worship, and has even made a mighty Śākta king convert to Vaiṣṇavism. Here he takes on Śaivites and *pāñcarātra* worshipers as well, and later he will attack the Muslims. Īśāna's Advaita Ācārya outwits local Śāktas in a series of events also described in chapters 5 and 6 of the *Bālya-Līlā-Sūtra* (BLS). In the BLS version in particular we see all goddesses deliberately conflated in a strategy that first diminishes each separately identified goddess and, second, reiterates the divinity of Advaita Ācārya in very conventional terms. The goddess in the temple is named repeatedly and inconsistently, that is, using various names, and nearly every name is labeled as Advaita's consort. Gods must be partnered.

Lauḍīya Kṛṣṇadāsa calls this goddess Caṇḍī, Kālī, Śarvāṇī, Lakṣmī, Bhavānī, Katyāyanī, and Śakti; all but Lakṣmī can serve as names of Śiva's consort, and Lakṣmī is of course the consort of Mahāviṣṇu. Not only are all goddesses to be understood as one, but Kamalākṣa, we are repeatedly reminded, is to be understood as both Viṣṇu and Śiva. The author uses so many names to make his theological point that Kamalākṣa is her—whatever we call "her"—eternal

[70] Another group prominent in the Vṛndāvana area. Vallabhācārya is the putative founder of this group, most of whose members are from the western region of Gujarat.

husband. Lauḍīya Kṛṣṇadāsa establishes Kamalākṣa as Śiva while at the same time associating him with Viṣṇu.

He also calls her "Māyā." Literally "illusion," Māyā is Viṣṇu's magical potency who always precedes his own descent into the world, and that pattern is consistent throughout the Advaita Ācārya corpus. Simply by his choice of names for the goddess Lauḍīya Kṛṣṇadāsa demonstrates that Śiva has temporal priority over Viṣṇu, and that Śiva worships Viṣṇu.

In these episodes, young Kamalākṣa refuses to bow before the image of the goddess on her festival day. And if such disrespect is not bad enough, he responds to a reprimand from his friend the king's son with such a ferocious roar that the prince collapses, unconscious.

When Kamalākṣa finally does bow to the goddess, on a subsequent occasion, as an act of filial piety, her behavior makes his reluctance clear. No good South Asian wife would expect her husband to bow before her or to humble himself in any way. She finds this behavior on his part so outrageous that she simply cannot tolerate it, and leaves in a blaze of light.

Lābhā's lament for her missing son in chapter 7 continues this conflation as it dawns on her that she may have behaved inappropriately with the boy she now realizes must be divine. She refers to him as Śiva, but a Śiva who is an aspect of Kṛṣṇa devoted to his own followers. She recalls Kamalākṣa's early childhood in imagery familiar to all who know the stories of the mischievous toddler Kṛṣṇa with his love of sweets. And then she recalls, mortified, how she, just like Kṛṣṇa's foster mother, Yaśodā, tied him up to keep him out of mischief. Finally, when the parents are at last reunited with their son, they send him to study with a scholar named Śānta, whom Kubera describes as having the same qualities as Kṛṣṇa's tutor Sāndīpani.

Why do both Īśāna and Lauḍīya Kṛṣṇadāsa use two discrete installments to tell this story? We have first Kamalākṣa's refusal to subjugate himself before the goddess with such ferocity that his friend collapses in a faint, and then the subsequent restoration of the boy to consciousness. Second, Kamalākṣa and his father debate the merits of Śāktism, with the son eventually capitulating only out of respect for his father, and then the temple image shatters. The first episode demonstrates Kamalākṣa's power and majesty, while the second, explicitly in Īśāna's telling, allows us to see our protagonist in his future *mādhurya* mode united with the goddess. Advaita has moved all the way through the devotional continuum in the space of a single chapter (in Īśāna's work). Keeping these two episodes separate creates the impression that Kamalākṣa regularly encountered the goddess, and never, until their final confrontation, publicly acknowledged her.

Haricaraṇa Dāsa tells the story in two separate episodes, one in I.4 and the other in II.1. The explosion of the goddess's image is simply further proof of the child Kamalākānta's true identity, and functions to convince the local ruler that Śāktism is no longer the only game in town. The child instructs him in Kṛṣṇa worship, driving home the point that the goddess—here called, significantly, Māyā—is merely Kṛṣṇa's servant. And then the child takes his parents and leaves, in disgust, for Shantipur.

Kamalākānta's playmate the king's son does not feature at all in that episode, as he does in Īśāna's version. But in the previous chapter Kamalākānta grows annoyed with his friend's teasing him for always saying "Hari Bol!" and finally snaps. And disappears. This particular day happens to be his birthday, and his parents have been home all day getting ready for the party, and now begin to worry when their son has not come home. They eventually find him in a cave, in a mud enclosure, and his mother Lābhā pulls him out screaming. As Tony Stewart has most recently pointed out, "rebirth from the womb of the earth" was "the standard literary or mythic device for signifying radical change found so commonly in hero mythologies."[71]

Caitanya has a similar experience—emergence from a cave transformed—but not until he is on pilgrimage following the death of his father. Kamalākānta's experience, on the other hand, comes when he is only five or six years old. Haricaraṇa Dāsa and Īśāna Nāgara want us to know that their protagonist came into himself much earlier in life than did Caitanya, the figure he worked so hard to invoke. And Advaita would outlive Caitanya by several decades.

Family and Succession

Sometime after her husband's "disappearance," Sītā Devī became a sectarian leader in her own right. The two hagiographical works dedicated to her, as well as the considerable space Īśāna devotes to her in his *Advaita Prakāśa*, support her leadership. But religious authority is not something that one can simply claim and expect to be accepted. Rather, one has to be able to demonstrate the right to hold a position of authority, a right that could be very difficult for a woman to defend in the sixteenth century. Realizing this, Īśāna takes pains to proclaim her virtues.

Īśāna introduces Sītā and Śrī in chapter 8, then interrupts his narrative to recount the story of Sītā's birth and tell a few anecdotes from her childhood. He uses this chapter to demonstrate first who Sītā actually is (Mahālakṣmī, consort of Mahāviṣṇu[72]) and then to provide "proof" of her divinity by supplying examples from throughout her life. Īśāna gives his reader the impression that he has selected but a few of many instances in which Sītā revealed her divinity, a technique that further serves to bolster his claims about her.

In chapter 8 we find a remarkable example of hagiographical license in Īśāna's borrowing of a motif not from another South Asian source but from the Christians

[71] Stewart, *The Final Word*, 50–51.

[72] *Mahā* is "great." When used with the name of a god, the prefix conveys the idea that this is the ultimate version or manifestation of that god.

who had educated his alter ego, Acyutacaraṇa Tattvanidhi Caudhurī. In this episode Nṛsiṃha Bhāduri plans to take his daughters to a festival on the other side of the river. When they reach the boat dock, a storm is developing, and fearing the crossing would be too rough for the girls, their father leaves them behind with a servant. Sītā and Śrī, not willing to miss out on the fun, simply use their yogic abilities to walk across the river, to the amazement of their father and everyone else who sees them do so. Īśāna injects a little humor at this point when he describes what happens when some "wicked foreigners"[73] try to follow suit and nearly drown. They lack the young girls' spiritual development and so remain bound by the laws of nature.

In chapter 15 of the *Advaita Prakāśa* we see Sītā conferring *mantra* initiation on her son Kṛṣṇa Miśra and his wife, even while her husband still lived. Mantra initiation marks the beginning of an individual's formal religious practice and is taken very seriously, and so must be conferred by a suitable guru for the initiation creates an indissoluble bond between guru and disciple. The implication is that Sītā had her husband's confidence, as well as his permission, to initiate their son and daughter-in-law.

Both Haricaraṇa and Īśāna ignore Jāhnavī, the wife of Nityānanda, another wife who became a Vaiṣṇava leader following her husband's death. By saying nothing about Jāhnavī, the authors use a common Vaiṣṇava literary strategy to discredit her and, by extension, Nityānanda's branch of the movement. The Gauḍīya Vaiṣṇavas, notoriously self-referential, did not discuss those individuals and ideas to which they gave neither credence nor support. Sītā then remains (at least by implication) the only woman in the movement, at least in its second generation, to take a leadership role.

Sītā slipped into a leadership position without any apparent forethought on the part of her husband. When it came to the succession of the next generation, however, Īśāna reports that Advaita Ācārya had very definite plans. The eldest of Advaita's six sons, Acyuta, refused to marry, but the second, Kṛṣṇa Miśra, did marry. Advaita, concerned about the continuation of both his physical and his spiritual lineages, bypassed his eldest son and passed the responsibility for maintaining the family temple and its Madana Gopāla image to Kṛṣṇa Miśra. Acyuta, Īśāna tells us, consented to this rather unusual situation, and the third son, Gopāla Dāsa, also agreed to the plan. The fourth and fifth sons, Balarāma and Jagadīśa (and presumably Jagadīśa's twin Svarūpa, as well), resented this and set up their own Kṛṣṇa images elsewhere. Today the town of Shantipur is dotted with Vaiṣṇava temples, most of which are maintained by direct descendants of Advaita Ācārya, all of whom bear the surname "Gosvāmī."[74] The temple of Madana Gopāla Jiu, in the Madana Gopāla temple

[73] Perhaps Muslims, they may or may not have actually been foreigners at this point.

[74] As do Nityānanda's descendants.

precinct, is presently tended by Mañjulikā Gosvāmī and her son Rañju, whose late father, a direct descendant of Kṛṣṇa Miśra, was the heir to the name and responsibility for Advaita's own image. The ravages of time have since forced the replacement of that original image, and it is no longer in use for regular worship.

Haricaraṇa Dāsa devotes much less space to the problem of succession. In V.6 he tells us that Advaita Ācārya bequeathed his *Bhāgavata Purāṇa* (did a copy of his monistic commentary manage to survive, we wonder) to his son Balarāma, identified as Sītā's second son, and his painting of Madana Gopāla to Śrī's son Kṛṣṇa Miśra. The eldest son, Acyutānanda, he tells us was an *aṃśa* of Caitanya; the two were very close in age, born after their respective mothers had eaten the tulasī buds that had floated upriver to Advaita in Shantipur. And Balarāma, captivated by Kṛṣṇa's flute, was the fourth evolute of Vāsudeva, Aniruddha, and used the *sādhanā* identity of Venu (the flute) Mañjarī. Haricaraṇa repeatedly tells us that all six sons are important lineage-bearers and worthy disciples of their father.

Kṛṣṇa Miśra, the heir, is generally believed to be the only son of Śrī (as Haricaraṇa states), Sītā's co-wife and younger sister, while all the rest of Advaita's sons were born to Sītā. However, in chapter 11 Īśāna tells the very poignant story that Sītā, for the second time, and Śrī, for the first time, were about to deliver children on the same day. Sītā was delivered of a healthy boy, but Śrī's son was stillborn. Śrī was beside herself with grief, so the ever-noble Sītā quietly approached their husband and asked permission to give her own son to Śrī, since Sītā already had one healthy son (Acyuta). Advaita agreed that Sītā's plan was kind and wise, and so history records Kṛṣṇa Miśra as Śrī's son, but we fortunate readers know the real story, this "deep secret," as Īśāna calls it.

The story of Kṛṣṇa Miśra's true maternity is more than a simple account of sisterly devotion. The implications for Advaita's school of Gauḍīya Vaiṣṇavism are tremendous. First of all, Īśāna has already demonstrated that Advaita, as the embodiment of Mahāviṣṇu and Śiva, is divine. He has also shown that Sītā, like Rāma's Sītā not born from a mortal womb, is Lakṣmī herself, the lotus-born goddess, whereas Śrī was born in the usual manner and is entirely human. While Haricaraṇa has much to say about the miracles Sītā performed, he tells us nothing about her origins. Thus we now know that Kṛṣṇa Miśra's parentage is entirely divine as well, and so he is truly the proper heir to his father's mantle. Since Īśāna will tell us in chapter 21 that Kṛṣṇa Miśra, rather than the eldest son, Acyuta, will inherit the sectarian mantle, he has to have already demonstrated why Kṛṣṇa Miśra is the most appropriate choice. He further must show that the entire family, especially Acyuta, supports his action. And since we are privy to the secret held by Advaita Ācārya and his wives alone, we know why Kṛṣṇa Miśra is indeed the right choice.

Membership Eligibility

Once the issues of leadership and succession have been resolved, Īśāna can turn to the question of eligibility for membership in Advaita's school. Most members of Advaita's group were brahmin, though the Gauḍīyas officially decried the injustices that seemed by then an inherent part of the caste system, and partially redefined the term "brahmin" to mean "Vaiṣṇava." That is, anyone who professed Vaiṣṇavism became not merely equal to, but better than, a brahmin. The Gauḍīyas insisted that birth has nothing to do with social position, that instead individuals are responsible for their own position through their deeds and their attitude toward Kṛṣṇa. They nonetheless retain the caste distinctions, for they never claim that devotees *become* brahmins but merely that they become *like* brahmins.

However noble this assertion may sound, it is difficult to ascertain the extent to which it was followed in practice, because the leaders of the community were all brahmins, and we have so little mention of prominent non-brahmins among the Gauḍīya Vaiṣṇavas. One exception is Brahmā Haridāsa, a close associate of Advaita Ācārya. Haridāsa, a Muslim, is so much an exception that his presence in the community requires explanation. Haricaraṇa provides that explanation in two parts in IV.2. First, the gods petition Brahmā, fearing that all the austerities Advaita is performing will render him capable of displacing them. Brahmā dismisses their concerns and instead announces that they will all take birth on earth to worship and serve him. Brahmā himself chooses a low-caste home where he refused all solid food. At the age of five, orphaned, he finds himself at Advaita Ācārya's house. He tries to maintain the segregation required of the difference in their respective social statuses, but Advaita will have none of it. Advaita explains to the child that he had once been one of Kṛṣṇa's childhood playmates. In the middle of one of the boys' milk-stealing rampages through town, Haridāsa scolded Kṛṣṇa and swore at him. His punishment was subsequent birth in a low-caste family.

Īśāna provides a different tale in chapter 7 of *Advaita Prakāśa*. He uses a popular story from the *Bhāgavata Purāṇa* (X.13–14) to account for this apparent anomaly and at the same time to explain why "Brahmā" is part of his name.

In this story the god Brahmā carries off the calves and cowherd boys of Vraja so that he can enjoy watching the child Kṛṣṇa and the play of his magic in private. Kṛṣṇa, omniscient, realizes who has taken his companions and why, and to please Brahmā and to keep his friends' mothers happy, he makes himself appear as all those boys and calves who had been abducted.

Brahmā has to be punished for his failure to recognize Kṛṣṇa's power, and so is eventually born into a Muslim family. However, we read, he would drink only milk, never accepting the solid food his Muslim mother prepared, because since she was not Hindu, it would have been, from a Vaiṣṇava viewpoint, impure.

Īśāna's account differs not only from Haricaraṇa's. When we compare Īśāna's account of Haridāsa with those of other Gauḍīya writers, like Kṛṣṇadāsa Kavirāja in his defining hagiography of Caitanya, the *Caitanya Caritāmṛta*, we find very different stories. Kṛṣṇadāsa Kavirāja[75] simply glosses over Haridāsa. Haridāsa is present in Kṛṣṇadāsa's narrative but does not play a major role, and the emphasis in the *Caitanya Caritāmṛta* is on Brahmā's realization of Kṛṣṇa as supreme and himself as relatively insignificant. In Īśāna's story the point is rather to correlate the folly of the Brahmā of the *Bhāgavata Purāṇa* with the anomalous Muslim in the Vaiṣṇavas' midst. Īśāna, like Kṛṣṇadāsa, has used a basic story already familiar to his readers. Īśāna's overlaid story of Brahmā passing through successive gates, guarded by Brahmās with successively more heads, further highlights Brahmā's growing understanding of himself, and the other gods, as of no significance next to Kṛṣṇa. Every gate through which he passes, that is, every universe—and there are an infinite number of universes—has its own Brahmā, Śiva, and Indra, and the deities of each are ignorant of their counterparts elsewhere. They are limited. Kṛṣṇa alone is unique, omniscient, and omnipresent.

Īśāna has given the story a new emphasis to highlight something no one else has discussed. In Īśāna's work, Haridāsa is a very important actor. He is even present with Advaita when Caitanya is born. Why? In thinking about this and many of the issues the *Advaita Prakāśa* raises, I find Gabrielle Spiegel's work useful. She talks about texts occupying "determinate social spaces, both as products of the social world of authors and as textual agents at work in that world.... Texts both mirror and generate social realities, which they may sustain, resist, contest, or seek to transform, depending on the case at hand."[76] This of course is one of the functions of literature writ large.

Although Caitanya apparently insisted that anyone who loved Kṛṣṇa was as good as a brahmin, the presence of significant figures who exemplified that assertion still required explanation. The *Bhāgavata Purāṇa* story fit their purposes perfectly. It gave the Gauḍīya leaders a framework to explain why a non-brahmin would be attracted to, and accepted into, Gauḍīya Vaiṣṇavism. Haridāsa could then be explained to be Brahmā atoning for his past arrogance (a notion that also conveniently described Vaiṣṇava perceptions of Muslims, without their having to malign their neighbors directly). Then his Vaiṣṇava practices[77] erase all the sins of his unfortunate (in Vaiṣṇava eyes) birth and restore him to his proper place in the world as a member of the community of devotees of Kṛṣṇa. Most likely he was always Muslim and had simply added some Vaiṣṇava practices to his religious habits. This is less unusual than it may

[75] *Caitanya Caritāmṛta* 2.21.43–72.

[76] Spiegel, *The Past as Text*, 24.

[77] Some secondary sources, but (to my knowledge) no primary source, refer to Haridāsa's "conversion." We have no reason to believe he ever renounced his Muslim identity.

seem at first glance. Many American Jews and Christians today practice yoga. Their having found something in yoga they consider valuable does not change the fact that they are Christian or Jewish.

One must still wonder why Haridāsa seems to present no problem for most of the Gauḍīya hagiographers, but does for Advaita's hagiographers. He probably is a historical figure, as his name (at least) appears widely throughout the literature. But the designations "Muslim" and "Hindu" were not widely used by South Asians themselves until well into the colonial period, and the idea that one must pick one religion exclusively is foreign to precolonial South Asia, where at least in terms of religion, the law of the excluded middle does not apply. This universe is not constructed of opposed binaries but rather of overlapping elements. Thus individuals do not choose to be either "Hindu" or "Muslim," concepts whose manifestations in fifteenth- and sixteenth-century Bengal probably did not differ much anyway, but may be both. A person born into a "Hindu" family could adopt "Muslim" practices just as a Muslim like Haridāsa could adopt "Hindu," or specifically Vaiṣṇava, practices. Even today one can see Muslim children in Kolkata enjoying the Dūrga Pūjā festivities and counting the number of Dūrgās they have seen, with the same excitement as their Hindu classmates (and, for that matter, visiting American academics). However, the children know they are "Hindu" or "Muslim."

But four hundred years ago, these distinctions were much less clear, or even significant. The fact that Īśāna finds it necessary to tell us so much about Haridāsa and his history reflects a nineteenth-century sensibility imported by the British colonial rulers. Īśāna makes very skillful use of the *Bhāgavata Purāṇa* story outlined earlier to make his point, but it is a point Kṛṣṇadāsa Kavirāja and his predecessors felt no compulsion at all to make. This is one of the issues that point to the late nineteenth-century date of composition of the *Advaita Prakāśa*.

Īśāna uses one more technique to demonstrate that Vaiṣṇavism is truly an easy path, available to all, requiring little or nothing in the way of technical knowledge to follow and find success. He makes repeated mention of the seemingly superficial detail of the importance of the proper dress for worshiping Kṛṣṇa. In chapter 7 we learn that the prostitute's hypocritical dress and worship of Kṛṣṇa still "counted," simply because she had donned the proper costume. We read in *Bhāgavata Purāṇa* 6.2.14 that "even if done in confusion, ridicule, as an interjection or in contempt ... taking the Name [of Viṣṇu/Kṛṣṇa] removes countless sins."

In chapter 14 Īśāna describes Caitanya's appearance immediately after his formal renunciation, including all the marks he had put on his body. Later in that same chapter he tells us that even the demoness Pūtanā attained liberation in Kṛṣṇa, for in her disguise as wet nurse she looked the part of a person committed to Kṛṣṇa. Wearing the proper costume, with the proper markings on the body, is very simple, and this uncomplicated behavior, even performed deceptively, still carries the sin-erasing benefits of deliberately devotional acts, and in fact is the best means of doing so in our degenerate Kali Yuga.

Authorship of the Texts

Who is this Īśāna Nāgara who says he composed the *Advaita Prakāśa*? I have elsewhere[78] demonstrated that Īśāna is merely the identity Acyutacaraṇa Caudhurī Tattvanidhi assumes to produce the *Advaita Prakāśa* as an act of devotion to his own guru and to his ancestor, Advaita Ācārya. If that is the case, who is this character Acyutacaraṇa created?

Our author, Īśāna Nāgara, has described himself as a young brahmin orphan, a servant in Advaita's household and therefore someone who participated in the daily life of the family; he was intimately positioned to observe and report on what went on there. Immediately we see that Advaita's family life centered around the various rules and regulations governing issues of purity and pollution. Those rules dictate that one take cooked food and water only from the hands of someone on the same rung, or a higher one, in the caste hierarchy, and Īśāna fits those requirements. Īśāna tells, in the *Advaita Prakāśa*, of such daily occurrences as Sītā's preparing of lavish feasts for her husband's pupils, of her careful attention to her daily worship, and of Advaita's religious observances.

Īśāna's hagiographical colleagues Haricaraṇa and Lauḍīya Kṛṣṇadāsa also occupied intimate positions vis-à-vis their subject that they reveal. Their roles as eyewitnesses grant them credibility and authority. None states his relationship to Advaita Ācārya more clearly, or more frequently, than does Īśāna Nāgara. Not coincidentally, we find far more miracles attributed to Advaita in the *Advaita Prakāśa* than in his earlier hagiographies. From summoning the subcontinent's sacred waters for his mother, to causing a temple image to shatter, to his ability to summon Caitanya[79] from a great distance, Advaita performs many feats that defy the laws of nature. Clearly this is not an ordinary man, nor even a mortal man. We would hardly believe these accounts, Īśāna expects, were we not hearing them from a reliable witness. The author uses his omniscient position first to tell us that his protagonist is a joint embodiment of Mahāviṣṇu and Śiva, and then to give us evidence of that divinity through scenes of the miraculous—and this in a text that appeared in the late nineteenth century, when Western rationalism was exerting a strong influence on intellectual activity even in the "colonies."

"Īśāna" reveals his identity bit by bit throughout the text. He tells us that Advaita's eldest son, Acyuta, asked him to write his father's life story. Īśāna himself met Advaita at the age of five, when his widowed mother, an impoverished brahmin, approached the very wealthy Advaita for help. Advaita and Sītā took the mother and child into their household as servants, and Īśāna became the family's water bearer. As a member of the household, Īśāna was thus well positioned to

[78] Manring, *Reconstructing Tradition*.

[79] Credited with founding the Gauḍīya Vaiṣṇava movement, this ecstatic devotee apparently left no writings of his own but inspired many. More about Caitanya later in this introductory chapter.

observe, and later to comment upon, the doings of the various members of the family. He would know the intimate and mundane details of the family's life—things to which few others would have had access. He tells readers that everything he wrote is based on either his own eyewitness testimony, or his reading, or the word of such senior and reputable Vaiṣṇavas as Padmanābha, Śyāmadāsa, and Advaita Ācārya's own sons Acyuta and Kṛṣṇadāsa. Īśāna reports that after Advaita's death, Sītā asked him to return to both families' home region of Lauḍa, in what is now Sylhet, in northeastern Bangladesh, to marry and start a family of his own. Īśāna expresses skepticism over the wisdom of her suggestion, as he is now over seventy years of age, but Sītā reassures him that one of the other Vaiṣṇavas will see to it that he finds a suitable bride, and indeed, we read, that is what happens. Finally, Īśāna reports that he finished composing his *Advaita Prakāśa* in the east (i.e., east of Shantipur, and probably an allusion to the Sylhet area) in the year 1568 CE.

That date, 1568 CE, would make *Advaita Prakāśa* an earlier composition than either Vṛndāvana Dāsa's popular *Caitanya Bhāgavata* (c. 1570) or Kṛṣṇadāsa Kavirāja's monumental *Caitanya Caritāmṛta*, the final word[80] on the life of Kṛṣṇa Caitanya. Given the liberal name-dropping so typical of the Bengali Vaiṣṇava authors, one would expect citations from such an early text to appear in later works, but none of the other hagiographies (outside the Advaita corpus) or theological treatises mentions Īśāna's work, or even his name.[81] Further, one would expect to find manuscripts of such an early text throughout the important libraries of the region, and yet the only extant manuscript is a very recent one in the possession of Dhaka University. Also very remarkable is the text's apparent discovery in the late nineteenth century by Acyutacaraṇa Caudhurī Tattvanidhi, a leading literary and historical scholar from Sylhet. Acyutacaraṇa's most significant work is his hefty history of Sylhet, but his bibliography credits him with twenty-eight monographs and countless scholarly articles. If we look at his literary output, then, we quickly see that he was a scholar, and very proud of his homeland and his heritage.

The Gauḍīyas produced a number of biographies of Caitanya, about which much has been written elsewhere.[82] As for other prominent early Vaiṣṇavas, Advaita's disciples were the first to follow suit, and Haricaraṇa Dāsa's *Advaita Maṅgala* seems to have appeared sometime in the late sixteenth or early seventeenth century. We hear nothing from the Advaita lineage for nearly three hundred

[80] To quote from Tony K. Stewart.

[81] With one exception, which I discuss later. Kṛṣṇadāsa Kavirāja does mention two different Īśānas in his *Caitanya Caritāmṛta*, one the servant of Sanātana (2.20.16–35) and the other a member of Caitanya's Gauḍīya lineage (1.10.108), but we have no reason to believe that either of these is the Īśāna who served as Advaita's servant until after Advaita's death.

[82] Most notably in Edward C. Dimock Jr. and Tony L. Stewart's translation and commentary on *Caitanya Caritāmṛta* of Kṛṣṇadāsa Kavirāja. See also Stewart, *The Final Word*.

years after that, until suddenly in the late nineteenth century, two works treating Advaita and one on his primary wife, Sītā Devī, mysteriously crop up, all discovered by the previously mentioned prolific Sylheti writer Acyutacaraṇa Caudhurī Tattvanidhi. *Advaita Prakāśa* and a putatively even earlier work, Lauḍīya Kṛṣṇadāsa's Sanskrit composition *Bālya-Līlā-Sūtra*, cover those portions of Advaita's life in which Caitanya played no immediate part. The *Bālya-Līlā-Sūtra* is a short Sanskrit work treating Advaita's family history and childhood. Lokanātha Dāsa's *Sītā Caritra* is a hagiographical treatment, in both Sanskrit and Middle Bengali, of Sītā Devī; and Īśāna Nāgara's *Advaita Prakāśa* is a lengthy Middle Bengali treatment of Advaita's entire life.

As it turns out, Acyutacaraṇa is a direct descendant of Advaita Ācārya, and it is more than likely that he himself composed some of these works. I believe that he is the author of the *Advaita Prakāśa* and of those portions of the *Sītā Caritra* that appear in the published editions but in none of the extant manuscripts. Acyutacaraṇa produced these materials as an act of devotion[83] to his own guru, who may have requested him to do so,[84] and to his lineage, which by the late nineteenth century had shrunk significantly.

We find no manuscripts of Īśāna's text in any of the libraries in the region, nor do other authors refer to Īśāna or to the *Advaita Prakāśa*. These three factors alone are suspicious, even though to the uninitiated it may appear that this is a dangerous argument from silence. But in this part of the world, the lack of something, either in physical form or through citation, is significant. As mentioned earlier, texts that were important were copied and circulated widely. If we find few copies of a text, and those few not widely distributed, we know that the text never garnered much attention, that it was never taken very seriously, or possibly that it presented a viewpoint unacceptable to the larger community. And if we find no artifacts whatsoever, material or otherwise, it is very likely that the text did not exist. If we find no artifacts whatsoever of a text in which we find startling claims of the sort that should have merited some reaction, we can be quite certain that the text had no prior existence. Why, then, pretend that it did? What would the author and the group he represents gain by this apparent subterfuge?

Spiegel urges us to "seek to locate texts within specific social sites that themselves disclose the political, economic and social pressures that condition a culture's discourse at any given moment."[85] She writes about medieval French historiography, but her advice applies to the Indian situation as well. What axes of power enter into the discourse, and when, to trigger the production of a text like the *Advaita Prakāśa*?

[83] For more on this phenomenon, see Manring and Stewart, "In the Name of Devotion."

[84] Remember that "Īśāna" writes that Advaita Ācārya's son Acyuta had asked him to write about Advaita Ācārya. Gauḍīya Vaiṣṇava hagiographers often claim that they write at the request of the guru.

[85] Spiegel, *The Past as Text*, 27.

In late nineteenth-century Bengal, when the Indian Nationalist Movement was gaining momentum, Bengali intellectuals were also trying to define their own regional history and even formulate a Bengali literary canon in the face of a colonial power on record for stating that "the entire native literature of India and Arabia" is not worth "a single shelf of a good European library."[86] Indian intellectuals generally, and Bengali intellectuals particularly, were giving a great deal of thought to who they were and the implications of that identity. We find a range of responses in the literature to emerge from this period.

By the end of the nineteenth century, Advaita's own school had dwindled almost to the point of disappearance, and while his role as forerunner of Caitanya would never be overlooked, people remembered little else about him. No text exists in a vacuum, and I tend to agree with LaCapra that a text "is situated in a fully relational network."[87] Here the network includes the descendants, spiritual and biological, of Advaita; the larger Gauḍīya movement; scholars who had only recently become interested in regional history; and the entire Gauḍīya literary corpus to date. LaCapra posits six useful contexts to assist us in considering the precise nature of these complex relations: "intentions, motivations, society, culture, the corpus, and structure."[88] I have already discussed most of these ideas and their role in hagiography and even community formation. Let us now take a second look.

Īśāna's intentions are of course very difficult to determine. On the surface, Īśāna wants to provide us with his, and Advaita's, credentials: Īśāna's reliability as a witness, and Advaita's as a staunchly conservative brahmin householder, the true torchbearer of Caitanya's message. Īśāna wants to record those events of Advaita's life that have not been discussed in the Caitanya corpus, he also tells us, and does so from the eyewitness testimony of other elders in the community, and himself. Fair enough. But most of those events include some element of the miraculous, and even a number of theophanies; few are widely witnessed; and no other accounts have such remarkable things to say about Advaita Ācārya.

So Īśāna claims that his motivation is simply to correct the absence of such data in the public record. I contend that his motivation is as he states, but on a deeper level, not only to remedy the lack of empirical information (as if we could have such a thing) but to provide incontrovertible "evidence" that Advaita is not only the appropriate herald of Caitanya's new age of devotionalism, but that with his adherence to ritual purity in the face of all sorts of temptations and other sectarian pressures, remains the sole suitable and true vessel for Caitanya's teachings. Caudhurī-as-Īśāna was writing long after most of the Gauḍīya Vaiṣṇava literature had been produced. He had the advantage of having all of it before him so he could see the big picture of the whole movement, as well as what had become

[86] Thomas Babington Macaulay, Minute of 2 February 1835 on Indian education.

[87] LaCapra, *Rethinking Intellectual History*, 44.

[88] Ibid., 36.

of the schools led by the three key members of the first generation. He knew all Caitanya's hagiographies very well and could draw inspiration and material from them at will.

As we are now beginning to see, "context" poses a different set of questions in premodern South Asia than it might elsewhere. Thus Haridāsa is described as having overcome the "handicap"—a term unlikely to be used earlier—of his Muslim birth, and further, Īśāna has Advaita Ācārya tell us, those who behave properly are like true brahmins, regardless of birth.

Despite the late discovery of the text in terms of the group's history, and despite skepticism about its "authenticity," the *Advaita Prakāśa* is now a part of the canon of Advaita's subschool. Its late appearance is unproblematic, for like the gods its protagonist embodies, the *Advaita Prakāśa* is, for Advaita's followers, timeless. And so today if one visits any of the Shantipur temples for the festivities of Advaita's birthday, and joins the crowd in the *maṇḍapa*, in between the exuberant singing of *kīrtana* one hears recitation of the *Advaita Prakāśa*. That tells us that that group of people finds it useful; they think it important. It gives them something they needed when the text appeared. How does it do that? As LaCapra says, "To the extent that a text is not a mere document, it supplements existing reality, often by pointing out the weaknesses of prevailing definitions of it.... texts may function to shore up norms and values that are threatened but still experienced as viable."[89]

With these lines LaCapra perfectly summarizes the situation with the *Advaita Prakāśa*: it functions "to shore up norms and values that are threatened but still experienced as viable."[90] The intertextuality among Caudhurī's works, including the *Advaita Prakāśa*, lies in their all furthering many of the same goals, in very broad terms: to make sure a geographic region did not fail to be included in the Bengali nationalist agenda; to ensure that one of its favorite sons was not allowed to fade into historical obscurity; and at the same time, to strike a blow for brahminical purity and supremacy—the religious right of its day.

This last is not insignificant. We must not underestimate the role of the changing social hierarchy in this matter. In the words of Karl Mannheim, "So long as [the intellectual] was the only accredited interpreter of the world he could claim in it a significant role,"[91] where we understand "intellectual" as "brahmin." Mannheim continues: "The pundit's faith in his own mission... lasts only so long as he holds the key to the secrets of the universe, so long as he is the thinking organ of the other strata. His presumptuousness ends when he encounters the commanding world view of another group."[92]

[89] Ibid., 48.

[90] Ibid.

[91] Mannheim, *Essays on the Sociology of Culture*, 102.

[92] Ibid.

The values that Īśāna's Advaita embodies are values of the past that many feel are slipping away with ever-increasing colonial presence in the region, and with the inevitable loosening of standards that comes with the passage of time. The Gauḍīya Vaiṣṇava community was becoming more inclusive and Advaita's group within it, small and marginalized (and Nityānanda's branch remained large), while education now had become the provenance of the British rulers and was no longer exclusively in brahmin hands. Īśāna, however, and of course Advaita feel that their conservative brahminical standards are timeless and should be shored up by the culture.

The *Advaita Prakāśa* is not written in the modern Bengali language of the late nineteenth century but in its fifteenth-century precursor. Acyutacaraṇa Caudhurī Tattvanidhi had mastered the Middle Bengali that would make the text sound authentic, and that is no small feat. This was a language very much in flux, with grammatical categories loosely defined and inflectional morphology both optional and varied. Caudhurī reproduces this language seamlessly, with none of the linguistic or historical anachronisms that marred the fabrications of some of his contemporaries.

"Reconstructing tradition," or parts of it, was a thriving enterprise at the time, with scholars using their linguistic and literary skills in the service of devotion. Some did so more successfully than others. The "discovery" of *Govindadāsa's Notebook*, which purported to be the record of Caitanya's journey to South India in the words of his servant Govindadāsa, is perhaps the best known of these. Although many suspected that it was spurious (no previous record of a Govindadāsa accompanying Caitanya on this trip existed), the work was convincing enough to fool a number of reputable scholars.

Bepin Vihari Dasgupta, in his 1937 book unfortunately titled *Govinda's Kadcha: A Black Forgery*, persuasively argues that the text must be a late composition. Dasgupta published in the midst of what he calls "a heated controversy." The manuscript of *Govinda's Notebook* appeared at the end of the nineteenth century, and the text was first published in 1895, and again in 1926. The version that came to light was a very recent copy, allegedly, of a two- to three-hundred-year-old manuscript, which no scholars ever saw and which seems to have disappeared entirely. Dasgupta reports, "The story that Kālīdas Nath one day brought several books to Joygopal Gosvāmī among which were two manuscripts—'Govindadas's Kadcha' and 'Adwaitaprakash,' was an absolutely got-up one."[93]

The great literary scholar Dinesh Chandra Sen, who accepted the *Notebook* as a genuine sixteenth-century text, explains in a 1925 article that Joygopal Gosvāmī was a direct descendant of Advaita Ācārya and lived in Shantipur.[94] Sen cites

[93] Dasgupta, *Govinda's Kadcha*, 11.

[94] Sen, "The *Karchā* by Govindadas," 569.

Joygopal's son, Banwari Lal Gosvāmī, who claims that the Advaita work in question was Haricaraṇa Dāsa's *Advaita Maṅgala*.[95]

The pages of Bengal's literary journals were full of this debate, and occasionally it became vituperative and ad hominem. Scholars expressed outrage that such a fraud as this had been perpetuated, while those of the opposing view, equally outraged, could not believe their reputations were being so slandered.

Dasgupta seems to have had the final word in the dispute, and did so not through determining which party was the most trustworthy (an obviously impossible task) but by painstaking examination of the text itself. Unfortunately, both Jadunath Sarkar, in his foreword, and Dasgupta himself cast aspersions on the character and intellectual acumen of D. C. Sen, when to my mind the scholar was quite innocently deceived by a clever forgery. Dasgupta identified toponymic anachronism, historical error, and plagiarism (citing its various sources) and very convincingly used this and more internal evidence to clearly demonstrate the modernity of *Govindadāsa's Notebook*.

Other clues that *Govindadāsa's Notebook* might not have been the early composition its discoverers claimed were its existence in a sole exemplar that disappeared mysteriously, and the lack of citations from this work in other texts. As discussed early in this essay, authors would frequently quote from the works of their contemporaries, as well as from earlier writers, to support their own arguments and theology. Sometimes these citations are specifically identified, and sometimes they are introduced with a vague reference like "as the *gosvāmī* said." And sometimes even these citations are fabricated to make a point! The *Padma Purāṇa* is one such frequently quoted text whose vastness seems to permit invention. The text[96] is so voluminous that locating a citation in it can be difficult, and some authors have taken advantage of this situation by making statements similar to what one might reasonably expect to find in the *Padma Purāṇa* and spuriously claiming that text as their source.

The complete absence of citations from *Govindadāsa's Notebook* elsewhere in Gauḍīya Vaiṣṇava literature suggests either that the larger tradition did not accept the message it conveyed (and so chose not to give it the attention of a citation) or that the text was not yet available. Since surely an eyewitness account of Caitanya's journey would have contained a wealth of detail about the man, and we have no evidence of its being mined for use in other Gauḍīya Vaiṣṇava literature, in addition to the clues mentioned earlier, all evidence points to its very late composition.

The only extant manuscript of the *Advaita Prakāśa* is in the library of Dhaka University,[97] and both the handwriting and the paper itself reveal that it is less

[95] Ibid., 576.

[96] Actually there are at least two texts by this name, but one is a Śākta treatise, a very different piece entirely.

[97] Manuscript No. 4683.

than one hundred years old. That manuscript[98] shows words crossed out and changed, usually to metrically equivalent synonyms. Jatindramohan Bhattacharjee listed no other manuscripts of the text, and his work is remarkably thorough.

The only text in which we find mention of the *Advaita Prakāśa* is the *Prema Vilāsa*, a text that expanded over the years from the earliest attested eighteen-chapter version to one that eventually contained twenty-four chapters. We find a lengthy discussion of Advaita Ācārya and specific reference to the *Advaita Prakāśa* in that twenty-fourth chapter, a chapter that seems not to have existed prior to the twentieth century.

We have clear evidence from the manuscript repositories that texts that were deemed important received wide circulation throughout the Bengali-speaking area. We have equally clear evidence through intertextuality of what texts a given tradition's writers valued and promoted.

One rather jarring feature of the *Advaita Prakāśa* is the profusion of specific dates we find therein. It is one thing to find a day and month, and quite another to see the addition of a year (in the Śaka dating system, which begins with the year 78 CE). Astrological dates of birth are very important for such purposes as coordinating horoscopes when arranging marriages, but until the late modern era we rarely find years recorded, if at all, in anything other than a very local dating system. And yet Īśāna lists the precise dates of birth of Advaita, Haridāsa, Nityānanda, Caitanya, and each of Advaita's sons. None of the authors of any other Gauḍīya Vaiṣṇava hagiographies reports so many dates with this degree of precision. This in fact seems to be a modern, not a sixteenth-century, concern.

It would then appear that only on linguistic grounds can Īśāna Dāsa's *Advaita Prakāśa* be called a Middle Bengali composition.

Like Advaita, Acyutacaraṇa Caudhurī Tattvanidhi lived in a time when hallowed brahminical purity was under assault from without (by foreigners) and from within, as people fell away from their old practices in the face of encroaching modernity. By the late nineteenth century the British Raj was firmly established, with its capital in the new city of Calcutta,[99] now capital of the state of West Bengal. Christianity had become a presence to be reckoned with, the missionaries at Serampore running a thriving publishing industry and others already long-established even in the remote areas of the northeast. By now also elite Bengalis were being educated in English-medium, usually missionary-run, schools, with a view to becoming civil servants in the British government. Consequently, many educated Bengalis were very familiar with the Christian Bible, an intimacy that allowed occasional borrowing, as we saw earlier.

[98] Which I examined in 1994.

[99] The city has recently reverted to its older name of Kolkata. Independent India has a history of changing colonial city names back to their original, pre-British-era names. Bombay is now Mumbai, Poona is Pune, and Madras, Chennai.

Meanwhile, the majority faction of the Gauḍīya Vaiṣṇavas had reorganized themselves into the formally structured Gauḍīya Maṭha, modeled on European monastic organizations, in response to the very present influence of institutional Christianity in the region. This formal structure left little room for sectarian offshoots, and Advaita's followers had already dwindled considerably. Clearly those few remaining saw the end at hand and wanted to ensure that their founder's name and importance, if not his lineage, would not be lost to history. Acyutacaraṇa's work ensures that Advaita's name lives on in Bengali religious and literary history. Thus the *Advaita Prakāśa* is a piece of religious literature that does significant political and sociological work. Haricaraṇa Dāsa wrote some decades, not centuries, after the death of Advaita Ācārya. His composition then reflects concerns of Advaita's lineage within a generation or two. It certainly makes assertions about Advaita's divinity but has much to say about praxis. Haricaraṇa's Advaita Ācārya is generally at the *aiśvarya* end of the scale, though in his practices he adopts other attitudes. The theophanies he grants are majestic, four-armed. Haricaraṇa is not concerned with foreign incursions or even loss of memory of his protagonist; he is simply setting out the life of an important, perhaps the most important, and certainly the first of the Gauḍīyas.

Sources for Composing the *Advaita Prakāśa*

Just as the *Caitanya Caritāmṛta* seals the hagiographical tradition on Caitanya, so *Advaita Prakāśa* is the final work on the life of Advaita Ācārya. In many respects the latter work is modeled on the former. The authors of the entire Caitanya corpus always portray Advaita Ācārya in relation to Caitanya. Therefore, in order to understand Advaita Ācārya's biographical image, one must first understand Caitanya's place in Gauḍīya Vaiṣṇavism.

Advaita Ācārya was unquestionably a well-respected leader in his own right, who dedicated his entire life to Kṛṣṇa/Caitanya. Prior to Caitanya's birth, Advaita performed extensive austerities and prayers designed to force Kṛṣṇa to appear on earth. Once Caitanya had been born, Advaita's life revolved around that of Caitanya. Like Caitanya's hagiographers, Advaita's hagiographers perceived their subject as a divine embodiment, but (in most of his biographies) to a lesser degree than the younger man. Whereas Caitanya was identified as the Ultimate Reality, Kṛṣṇa, Advaita was identified as Mahāviṣṇu and/or Sadāśiva. As such, Advaita represented the majestic, powerful aspect of divinity while Caitanya embodied the divine sweetness portrayed by the relationship between Rādhā and Kṛṣṇa.

Let us return now to see how the author of the *Advaita Prakāśa* used the *Caitanya Caritāmṛta* as his template. Kṛṣṇadāsa Kavirāja had one agenda, and Īśāna Nāgara had quite another. Nonetheless, Kṛṣṇadāsa in his masterful work had established standards for what would thereafter be expected of a person who embodied the divine. These included the usual sorts of signs[100] and portents at key points in the individual's life, but also certain activities he would perform. Īśāna borrowed, and often elaborated upon, events in Caitanya's life as recounted in the *Caitanya Caritāmṛta*. He also to a great extent borrowed the linguistic format and the style of that text. Kṛṣṇadāsa Kavirāja begins each chapter of his work with a Sanskrit verse mined from the works of previous authors, and sprinkles such Sanskrit verses throughout the body of his text. The Bengali portions that constitute the bulk of the *Caitanya Caritāmṛta* are then elaborations and commentary on those Sanskrit verses. One could read those Sanskrit verses alone as an outline of the entire work,[101] so that they could be viewed as one coherent text.

Īśāna tells us that he drew material on Advaita Ācārya's childhood from Lauḍīya Kṛṣṇadāsa's *Bālya-Līlā-Sūtra*, a short (eight-chapter) Sanskrit text. The provenance of the *Bālya-Līlā-Sūtra*[102] is even murkier than that of the *Advaita Prakāśa*. The *Bālya-Līlā-Sūtra* was published only once, and there are no extant manuscripts. It appears to have reached Acyutacaraṇa Caudhurī Tattvanidhi via a very circuitous route. The putative author, Lauḍīya Kṛṣṇadāsa (Kṛṣṇa's servant from Lauḍa), was the king in whose court Advaita Ācārya's father Kubera worked.

Chapters 3 through 8 of the text are rather sketchy, but the first two chapters present Advaita Ācārya's family history in great detail. The author traces Advaita's lineage all the way back to the god Brahmā and tells us that one of Advaita's ancestors, Harṣa, was one of the five ritually pure brahmins whom King Ādiśūra brought to Bengal at some uncertain point between the eighth and eleventh centuries[103] when he deemed all the local brahmins too contaminated to perform the various rituals he needed. Lauḍīya Kṛṣṇadāsa provides explanation of the various rankings among the highest of Bengali Vārendra[104] brahmins—*kulīna*s at the top, and *siddha-śrotriya*,[105] *sacchrotriya*, and *kaṣṭātmaka-śrotriya*s.

Advaita Ācārya's paternal grandfather Nṛsiṃha was the fourteenth-century Rāja Ganeśa's secretary of state, according to this text. At this point the family is *siddha-śrotriya*, a rank King Vallāla Sena conferred on them some six generations prior. Nṛsiṃha decides to elevate their status by marrying his daughter to a *kulīna*. This hypergamy is a permissible move but would probably not have been the

[100] For example, personae in the devotional literature often manifest one or more of the official symptoms of devotion, laid out in various texts. The eight most frequently mentioned are paralysis, tears, perspiration, change of color, fainting, horripilation, trembling, and stammering.

[101] I am grateful to Tony K. Stewart for the many private conversations which led me to this realization.

[102] See chapter 5 of my *Reconstructing Tradition*.

[103] Scholars disagree widely on when this occurred, but Bengali historians do accept that ritual brahmins were at some time in their history deliberately imported. See the works of R. C. Majumdar, Mahimacandra Majumdara, and T. K. and B. R. Raychaudhurī for more on this issue.

[104] Bengali brahmins are divided into the Vārendra (in the north) and RāṚhi (in the southwest) groups. Each of these two further divides brahmins slightly differently.

[105] The word *śrotriya* connotes a Vedic priest, and among Vārendras there are three *śrotriya* ranks.

preference of the *kulīna* groom's family, and so to ensure his success Nṛsiṃha uses a clever trick to force the intended groom to agree to the marriage.

In order to support his claims regarding Advaita Ācārya's brahminical purity, Īśāna wants to demonstrate that Advaita comes from a long line of ritually observant high-ranking brahmins. Marriage is perhaps the most important of the ten sacraments (*saṃskāras*) marking life passages for Hindus in all traditions. Ronald Inden's early work focused on Bengali marriage and social rank:

> One of the specific purposes of marriage was to provide a caste and its clans with children, and especially sons, embodying the coded substance of their parents' caste and clan. Only children having the same substance and code as their parents were considered capable of taking up the caste's particular livelihood.[106]

Children of mixed marriages "invariably acquired the rank of the father,"[107] so that Kullojvalā's marriage to Madhumaitreya would guarantee *kulīna* children. By marriage a woman was transformed "into her husband's half body," "sharing the coded bodily substance not only of her husband but of his clan (*kula*) as well."[108] Since Narasiṃha's clan was at the top of the *śrotriya* brahmin ranking, his daughter was legally eligible to become the bride of a top-ranking *kulīna* brahmin.[109] Men at this rank typically married women who, like Kulojjvalā, were *siddha-śrotriyas*.

Marriage into a *kulīna* family could elevate the status of the bride's family: "where the daughter is given, there is one's rank."[110] Once Nṛsiṃha has succeeded in marrying his daughter Kulojjvalā into the *kulīna* ranks, his whole family is in effect promoted. Subsequently, when his now-*kulīna* son Kubera similarly takes a bride from the rank immediately below his own to marry the *sacchrotriya* Lābhā, she skips a rank and in turn becomes *kulīna*, and of course all of the children of Kubera and Lābhā will be *kulīna*. Lauḍīya Kṛṣṇadāsa has cleverly woven *kulīna* history into Advaita Ācārya's family history to make his point that his protagonist is from the highest rank of society. Lacking independent corroboration, we can neither confirm nor refute his claim, but that does not matter. What matters is that Lauḍīya Kṛṣṇadāsa wants us to know this "history," and why.

This author not only has drawn Advaita Ācārya as *kulīna*, a ranking that Vallāla Sena is credited with devising in the twelfth century, but also has drawn his parentage from two of the five Kānyakubja brahmins imported into Bengal for ritual purposes at a time when the local brahmins had in some unspecified way lost their

106 Inden, *Marriage and Rank in Bengali Culture*, 92–93.

107 Ibid., 94.

108 Ibid., 96.

109 Ibid., 97.

110 Ibid., 103, citing Vasu.

ritual purity. The only way this pedigree could possibly be further enhanced is through a claim of divinity, which of course we also have.

The rest of the *Bālya-Līlā-Sūtra* describes events on which Īśāna Nāgara elaborates in his own composition. Perhaps Acyutacaraṇa Caudhurī Tattvanidhi came across the *Bālya-Līlā-Sūtra* at a pivotal moment in his own thinking, when he was concerned that his ancestor Advaita Ācārya was not being recognized as the pure vessel of divine truth his followers believe him to be. As a Vaiṣṇava of scholarly inclinations, Acyutacaraṇa would be very familiar with the *Caitanya Caritāmṛta* and its structure and organization. The chance encounter with the *Bālya-Līlā-Sūtra* may well have inspired him to use that text as the outline for his own life of Advaita Ācārya, which he in turn patterned on the *Caitanya Caritāmṛta*.

Conclusion

Kṛṣṇadāsa Kavirāja brought into his work the writings of the theologians, as well as the stories of Rādhā and Kṛṣṇa that allowed him to make his points about Caitanya as the androgynous, dual incarnation of the divine couple. Īśāna, on the other hand, is writing about Advaita, the man all who mention credit with summoning that incarnation into the world. But Advaita never had the kind of following Caitanya did, and his branch of the Gauḍīya tree shrank significantly over the years.

Īśāna/Caudhurī seems to have suffered from a nostalgia for what he imagined as the "good old days" when everyone knew their place and brahmins, especially *kulīna* brahmins, were worshiped by all and revered as the embodiments of divine truth and law. The *Caitanya Caritāmṛta* provided "Īśāna" with a convenient template to use. By the late nineteenth century the *Caitanya Caritāmṛta* was widely known in the region, and so the use of the same events with different protagonists would have triggered the desired associations in the minds of readers of the *Advaita Prakāśa*. What would then emerge were the points where the two works diverged, and Īśāna/Acyutacaraṇa uses these points to show how Advaita Ācārya was even more appropriate than Caitanya to herald the new age of Kṛṣṇa devotion.

Shortly after the death of his father, Caitanya sets out on pilgrimage. During his travels he is converted to Vaiṣṇavism. And shortly after the deaths of *his* parents, Advaita undertakes a similar voyage. But Advaita's pilgrimage is not the simple series of visits an average devotee might make, because Advaita is after all Mahāviṣṇu and Sadāśiva in one. He visits sites connected with those two gods and, interestingly, does not visit the various Śākta *pīṭhas* in the same areas. However, Advaita is doing this about half a century before Caitanya did, and Īśāna does not have him convert to Vaiṣṇavism en route but rather has a leading Vaiṣṇava recognize Advaita's already active deep devotion when he finds him unconscious at "Madhva Ācārya's place."

In the *Caitanya Caritāmṛta*, Mādhavendra Purī discovers the image of Kṛṣṇa in Vṛndāvana through a series of dreams; in the *Advaita Prakāśa*, Advaita makes this discovery, and Mādhavendra Purī, who had become his guru earlier when Advaita Ācārya was traveling through South India, comes to Shantipur some time later, in chapter 5. In that chapter Īśāna has Mādhavendra Purī visit Advaita in Shantipur en route to Purī to obtain sandal paste for Gopāla. Mādhavendra at that time instructs Advaita to worship the divine couple and to marry. Kṛṣṇadāsa Kavirāja tells this same story in his work at II.4. He does have Mādhavendra stop at Advaita's place in Shantipur but places no emphasis on this visit. In Īśāna's version Advaita Ācārya is telling his own devotees Mādhavendra's story, including their personal connection. In the *Caitanya Caritāmṛta*, Caitanya is telling the story but had had no personal connection with Mādhavendra. Īśāna/Acyutacaraṇa does not have to diminish Caitanya to tell us that Advaita has the stronger claim as the bearer of Gauḍīya Vaiṣṇavism. Īśāna is very subtly telling us that actually Advaita, not Caitanya, first brought devotionalism to Bengal, and that as Caitanya's teacher, Advaita was responsible for inculcating the younger man with these new ideas so that he could go on to spread them throughout the countryside.

Borders between traditions in Bengal have always been quite fluid. A given tradition will not claim to have the One True Path to ultimate liberation, nor claim that all other traditions are false. Rather, one group will assert that its neighbors are quite correct but are only lacking one tiny piece of the picture, which they can provide. This history of accommodation and adaptation has allowed for a great diversity in belief and praxis to flourish, in relative harmony. We do have clear guru lineages, but a guru may draw his or her teachings from any number of sources.

Despite this apparent harmony, the orthodox upholders of the tradition, its clerics, must always insist that their way is the only way. And in *Advaita Prakāśa*, perhaps anachronistically, we see a great deal of anti-Muslim polemic, especially in chapter 9. Chapter 2 presents us with a stunning piece of anti-Śākta polemic, when Advaita refuses to bow to the image of the goddess Kālī until filial piety forces him to do so, at which point the image shatters dramatically. Kālī has recognized Advaita as her husband Śiva, and no proper wife can accept the worship of her husband under any circumstances, and certainly not in public. Later, Advaita Ācārya defeats Śāktism when King Divyasiṃha of Lauḍa, last of a long lineage of Śākta rulers, converts to Vaiṣṇavism.

These ongoing battles between religious groups for members, with Advaita's group consistently winning, provide some of the more obvious examples of hagiographical authorial intent. We cannot read hagiographical work like *Advaita Prakāśa* literally because its author, like all hagiographers, has a particular agenda, resulting from his own biases, conscious or otherwise, which are in turn colored by his own specific social circumstances (male, brahmin,

South Asian, etc.). The author is writing at his guru's behest (or at least claims to be doing so) and reflects the views of that person as well. The Gauḍīya Vaiṣṇava biographies thus constitute some of the few examples in which one can actually know, at least to some degree, authorial intent, because merely by virtue of their survival the writings do actually reflect their author's (or that author's guru's) intent. Īśāna makes it very clear that while Advaita Ācārya brought an entirely new mode of religion to Bengal, he is no social nonconformist. At every stage in his life Advaita behaves appropriately, performing the proper rituals at the right times.

Until very recently, and still today in much of rural India, the life cycle was entirely predictable, with every act in a person's life governed by prescribed rites and rituals. Everyone married, usually at quite a young age, although marriages were not usually consummated until both parties had reached an appropriate age. After the parents' deaths the eldest son was responsible for carrying out the funeral rites and making sure the proper offerings were made each year in the parents' and other ancestors' honor. Thus we find Advaita Ācārya, like Caitanya, traveling to the holy city of Gayā, the nearest major center of pilgrimage, to offer the requisite rice balls for his parents shortly after their simultaneous deaths.

Advaita has little interest in marriage and has to be reminded of the importance of maintaining his lineage before he will consider setting aside his devotional practices to start a family. He marries quite late in life but, once he has married, wastes no time in producing six sons. After their births, Advaita arranges for all the usual and indispensable life-cycle rituals for his sons: their naming ceremonies, performed very shortly after birth; the ceremonies at which a child is given its first solid food, when the child is between six and nine months of age; the ritual in which chalk is first placed in the child's hand, usually around age five, indicating readiness to begin the education process.

Īśāna's mention of all these events tells us that Advaita Ācārya and his family were responsible members of the community who conformed fully to social and religious expectations. This conformity is a large part of what makes them reliable sources of knowledge for that community and, it follows, for us.

As with any religious account, the historical authenticity of *Advaita Prakāśa*, and particularly of the more fantastic elements of the text, is of far less importance than the believers' views of those elements. That is, if believers accept the miracles as true, then the accounts must be accepted as legitimate statements of sectarian belief, and examined with that perspective in mind.

We as scholars are not interested in the validity of any apparent truth claims an author makes, but in why and how the author makes them. Community formation and definition, establishing or supplanting canon, providing aesthetic enjoyment to an audience—are all concerns for us to consider and weigh.

What are the most important points Īśāna Nāgara, or Acyutacaraṇa Caudhurī Tattvanidhi, wants us to learn from the *Advaita Prakāśa*? First, that Advaita Ācārya is the forerunner of the entire Gauḍīya movement. Advaita was the individual responsible for bringing *bhakti* across the Vindhya Mountains and east into Bengal. Advaita introduced the new practice of *yugala sevā*, worship of the divine couple. And, most important, Advaita brought Kṛṣṇa himself, in the form of Caitanya, and his entire Vraja *līlā* to Bengal in the late fifteenth century.

Haricaraṇa Dāsa's *Advaita Maṅgala*

Book 1

Chapter 1

Lord Kṛṣṇa's Līlā and Its Replication in Bengal

(Invocation)
Homage to Sarasvatī. Homage to Bhagavadvādarāyaṇa. Homage to the most glorious guru. May Rādhā and Kṛṣṇa be victorious! Homage to the moons Caitanya, Nityānanda, and Advaita. Homage to Vāsudeva. I praise (text missing) love incarnate whose consciousness is delighted by Krsna.

Homage to that Rādhikā (text missing).

I praise the boy with eyes soft as lotus petals, dear as life to the cowherd maidens. Let us worship him, the ground of Vraja, along with Rādhā.

I praise Lord Caitanya who brings delight to the world, who has come to earth in Kali Yuga.

Salutations to that lord, a great ocean of eternal bliss, whose soul is sunk in bliss and divine love, who is dear to Kṛṣṇa.

I praise the glorious Lord Advaita, eternal locus of Gaura, sunk in the love of Rādhā and Kṛṣṇa, like a drunken lion here on earth.

I praise Gaura's two devotees who are Caitanya's very life, my lords Advaita and Nityānanda; may their grace be (text missing)

I praise that lord-guru who shines in his eternal locus; there is no doubt that the tiniest drop of his mercy fulfills our fate.

1. I placed the lotus feet of the glorious guru on my heart, as the measure by which I write. Salutations to that image of love, Kṛṣṇa's life's breath; I await the command from his glorious mouth.
2. I write what he showed me from beginning to end, only because of his command, with his blessing. He charged me to reveal my lord's activities in an *Advaita Maṅgala*, and now I begin its first section.

3. Kṛṣṇa appeared in Vraja; the Part and the Whole as one; we see this in the purāṇas and *Āgamas*. The Vedas and the purāṇas testify to Kṛṣṇa's inconceivable activities which no one can understand.
4. How can a miserable wretch describe this? I am obeying Acyutānanda's command, and that of all my lord's sons, disciples, etc. but still I am an arrogant fool to even try.
5. I raise the dust from Lord Advaita's feet to my head and place his lotus feet on my heart. My lord saw what Svarūpa had previously written and gave me my instructions.
6. Vṛndāvana is the eternal abode, the playground of the lady Rādhikā alone; its name is full of eternal bliss. Lord Kṛṣṇa, the complete Bhagavān, is called Pūrṇatama; he is the sweetheart of the lady Rādhikā, her lover.
7. There are four degrees of *bhāva* in Vraja. Pūrṇatama reigns there, and creates the delightful Vraja-līlā. There is nothing greater than Vraja; the favorite place we see, with the Kālindī [Gaṅgā] and the Yamunā Rivers gliding through.
8. Day and night Nandīśvara plays his many games at Govardhana, and his *rāsa līlā* in Vṛndāvana. He takes the lady Rādhikā's girlfriends to a secluded grove where he fulfills their hearts' desires.
9. The Pūrṇa and the Pūrṇatama—the two—and their male and female companions, play within the holy site of Vraja. The mysterious *līlā* of Vraja, the Part and its Source, shine forth, as the Vedas and *purāṇas* explain.
10. They worshiped the rich Vraja *līlā* in that holy place, describing it as divine energy.

As the *sakhas* and *sakhīs* reveal the best *līlā* and serve the true form of Rādhā-Kṛṣṇa.

(Next verse appears only in Baṅgīya Sāhitya Pariṣat MS 2639)

And as it says in the Vedas:

And all the *avatāras* have many aspects. The Vraja *līlā* is the one to contemplate because there is none higher.

And in the *Viṣṇu Purāṇa*:

"Vāsudeva appeared like a flash of lightning in that house after Nanda's daughter had been absorbed into the Universal Spirit. He looked just like Vasudeva."

And in another purāṇa:

"Nanda's wife Yaśodā had a beautiful girl and a boy called Govinda; the little girl went to Mathurā."

Kṛṣṇa Pūrṇatama entered Yaśodā's womb as Yogamāyā and appeared in Vraja.

Pūrṇatara, Vāsudeva, was born from Devakī's womb in Vasudeva's house. Under the constellation Rohiṇī, Kaṃśa feared Vasudeva and imprisoned him.

The Source and its Part were one and the same, but took on different bodies just for fun.

We know the eldest brother as the Full Pūrṇa Form, Saṃkarṣaṇa; he appeared as Rohiṇī's own son. The activities in Vraja are out of this world—no one can quite grasp it, but they believe in it by Rādhikā's grace. For ten years, six months, and five days, the ecstasy of the eternal *līlā* manifested as the Vraja *līlā*. Kṛṣṇa played in places like Mathurā as Pūrṇatara, where his *līlā* brought unparalleled delight.

While he was playing in Dvarakā Kṛṣṇa cursed the brahmins. The Vedas proclaim this his unmanifest *līlā*. He told the whole story from beginning to end. He taught Uddhava his whole yoga. "Countless demons are weighing down the earth, and when I saw people's suffering, I came down. I will have innumerable devotees in Kali Yuga; anyone born in Kali Yuga will be in luck."

And with regard to Ekādaśī, in the dialogue with Nimi and the king:

> With regard to the various ages, O King, (your) subjects want to be born in the Kali Age. Indeed in the Kali Age they will be devoted to Nārāyaṇa. (*Bhāgavata Purāṇa* 11.5.38)

He revealed both manifest and unmanifest to society. He slew the demon Dantavaktra as he played in Vraja. He made everyone come who had been with him in Vraja: the devotees, his parents and companions, all his beloved servants. They all delighted in his many exploits. He duly sent every portion of himself to Deva Purī, city of the gods. He did everything a god does, granting those eternal companions endless pleasure. He replicated his eternal abode, his eternal play, his eternal activities. He replicated his every eternal sport—unparalleled bliss. Everyone witnessed his manifest amorous activities, all the eternal devotees witnessed that eternal *līlā*. Infancy, childhood, youth: his eternal sports; with regard to his eternal companions, this time was identical to that.

As it says in *Sanatkumāra* (*Tantra*):

> Servants, companions, parents, and those dear to Hari; all are the best of eternal sages, like him, storehouses of virtue. (*Padma Purāṇa* Pātālakhaṇḍa 52. 3)

I learned something of his eternal *līlā*. I've written about his eternal *līlā*, telling a bit.

All those eternal companions and parents appeared here at the dawn of the Kali Age.

Vasudeva and Devakī were the first created, and they came down and appeared first of all.

The eternal entourage hear all this philosophy devotedly, following the rules for worship.

Haricaraṇa Dāsa, whose hopes are at the lotus feet of the Lord of Shantipur, recites the *Advaita Maṅgala*.

This is the description of the guru, etc. from the first chapter in the *Advaita Maṅgala*, called "Lord Kṛṣṇa's *Līlā*."

Chapter 2

Arrival of Vijaya Purī

I fondly praise my lord Advaita's lotus feet. Everyone knows that he is Śrī Caitanya's guru.
The lord of Shantipur is identical to Caitanya, as is Nityānanda the *avadhauta*.

Please, devotees of all three masters, have pity on me. I praise all their feet with joined hands. One is the great lord, "Mahāprabhu," and the other two are *prabhus*, "Lords." I am describing a bit of Advaita's biography.

Kavi Karṇapūra described Lord Caitanya's *līlā*, in which is a tremendous *rasa*, the *līlā* of eternal bliss. I will describe some of Advaita's *līlā* from beginning to end, start to finish. The five phases of Advaita's *līlā* are infancy, childhood, adolescence, youth, and old age. The "infancy" phase, book 1, begins with the story of his birth. Everyone listen carefully as I recite.

He came to Shantipur as a child, and I'll describe that in book 2. His pilgrimage journey, coming to Vṛndāvana, and the appearance of the Gopāla image occurred during the "adolescence" phase. His victory over the Digvijayī, the widely renowned scholar, in *bhakti* scriptures, grammar, et cetera, and how he acquired the name "Advaita" are in the same section. In book 3 I cover his trip to Vṛndāvana as an adolescent. I reveal many *līlās* of his youth: his performing austerities and the like; his settling in Shantipur. In book 4 I will discuss how people are sanctified in the month of Śrāvana. I will write about his old age: his marriage to Sītā, and making Nityānanda and Caitanya descend to earth. The *līlā* of these three *prabhus* took place in Shantipur. They generated unparalleled bliss with their disciples. Advaita's disciples, starting with Acyutānanda, Balarāma, Gopāla, Kṛṣṇa Miśra, Jagadīśa, and Svarūpa, number in the thousands.

I will describe the five phases of his *līlā* in chronological order. My lord's sons and his entire school insisted that I do this. I am my lord's servant, at his command, so I write enthusiastically at his feet. I know I'm not a poet and I can't write well, so I simply write the story with love. I meditate on my lord's lotus feet in the lotus of my heart as I narrate the verses of book 1.

Scriptures testify to the *avatāras* for every age. Brahmā himself became aware of the troubles of the world. Brahmā went to the shore of the cosmic ocean and proclaimed that the lord would soon descend to earth in human form. He observed that Dvāpara Yuga was at an end, and now, at now the beginning of the Kali Yuga, the Pūrṇatama lord appears. And then he heard a divine voice from the sky proclaiming that Kṛṣṇa was ready. He dispatched the *vyūha* part as doorkeeper; all this you'll learn from the *Vāraha Purāṇa*.

Kṛṣṇa gathered his entire entourage and urged them to go uproot sin on earth. They all passionately desired to try to experience Rādhikā's emotions, and Svayaṃ Bhagavān commanded them to take birth beside the Gaṅgā as his devotees. Vāsudeva drew Nanda to appear and ordered everyone to follow him to earth.

"After your parents are born then you take birth, and take Saṃkarṣaṇa. When you shout for me, I will come; this is your charge. You will satisfy every heart's desire. Every age has its own weapons and tools, wars and strife; the name of the weapon for the Kali Age is *prasāda*. Brahmā and all the gods are at your command. When you summon them, they will obey. All the ascetics and sages are your *aṃśa*s, portions of you. Rest assured that I am at your command."

His *icchāśakti*—power of desire—abides in Kṛṣṇa, as that desire, so through that heart's desire his true form (came) to earth.

As,

> In this sin-beset age, the Lord's mere name embodies the eternal *līlā* with all its components/pleasures. My inspired true devotee will shout out that name. (unattested)

I have written the verses of book 1 right here, and will now proceed with the birth story.

Seven years[1] before Mahāprabhu, Advaita came and woke everyone from their slumber. Meditating with my lord's foot upon my heart, I will tell about his advent as if I had witnessed it. My lord brought in his sons and his servants and all his retainers. Among them was one named Vijaya Purī, an elderly renunciate with Kṛṣṇa's name on his lips. He had a golden complexion that glowed with divine splendor.

Advaita stood up respectfully to greet him, then fell at his feet. Vijaya Purī lifted my lord back up and embraced him. My lord Advaita smiled and seated him at his side.

Purī said, "Kamalākānta, you are here! Now I know I've reached Vaikuṇṭha! I've wandered all over, but nowhere did I find the pure love of devotion to Kṛṣṇa. I have come to you to hear the *Bhāgavata Purāṇa*. Please expound the interpretation that you've been teaching throughout the land. Goloka, Vaikuṇṭha, all merge in you. Please instruct me. You have descended to earth to preach love of God; do not

[1] A controversial number; the Baṅgīya Sāhitya Pariṣat manuscript says seven hundred years! Advaitācārya was actually just over fifty years older than Caitanya.

deprive me further! While I was in Kāśī I met a number of renunciates, but since they do not know you, they know nothing. I spent quite a while in Mathurā on the banks of the Yamunā! I saw Vṛndāvana and roamed its forests. I sat in a cave at the Twelve Adityas landing, where I worshiped the image of Śrī Madana Gopāla for so long! That image stayed there three nights, fasting on fruits and roots, leaving Vṛndāvana desolate.

"Madana Gopāla said, 'Feed me some fruit. Why are you making me suffer fasting?'

"I replied that I had come to see Kṛṣṇa appear, that as a devotee I wanted to hear all about him, but Madana Gopāla ordered me back to Advaita Ācārya's place. He told me not to worry about my body. 'The lord himself has been born as the one named Kamalākānta. He has come as a partial descent of Īśvara Bhagavān, and has appeared in the east with his retinue. At the moment he is sitting beneath a banyan tree concentrating on the rice-balls to offer for his parents' funerals. I am here by his command. You will hear about his activities there; I cannot talk about them, but know for certain that he is the *bhaktāvatāra*, the divine model devotee.'

"Nephew, Madana Gopāla told me that he is yours. Now please tell me what to do, don't toy with me."

Kamalākānta replied, "Listen, Uncle, stay a few days, and then we'll go to Shantipur. I'll take good care of you."

He built a house in a secluded place to stay in, and Śyāmadāsa and Īśāna both served him. Kamalākānta took great pains to take care of him, and Purī was pleased with this hospitality.

I've written as enjoined about Vijaya Purī's arrival. Now listen carefully, everyone, to their previous conversations.

Haricaraṇa Dāsa, whose hope is at the lotus feet of the Lord of Shantipur, recites the *Advaita Maṅgala*.

This is chapter 2, "The Arrival of Vijaya Purī," with a verse from book 5, in book 1 in the *Advaita Maṅgala*.

Chapter 3

The Conversation with Vijaya Purī

I praise Advaita, lord of Sītā's life, who brought in Mahāprabhu, the lord of Goloka.
I praise my lord's sons Acyutānanda, Balarāma, and Kṛṣṇa Miśra and the rest.
At your command I write carefully of the conversation with Vijaya Purī. Listen carefully:

Vijaya Purī was a disciple of the same teacher as Mādhavendra Purī. My lord revered him and became attached to him. At dawn, after Purī had performed his ablutions, he went to my lord and sat next to the tulasī planter where my lord was teaching. All the disciples were seated around the tulasī plant as my lord recited the *Bhāgavata Purāṇa*, explaining devotion.

The *Bhāgavata Purāṇa*, beginning, middle, and end, is the ultimate definitive text on devotion and divine love. They had worked through book 9 of the text, and now as they listened to the tenth, they were floating on the nectar of divine love.

My lord stood on the riverbank, as we listened, and told us how Saṃkarṣaṇa, who had been born in Rohiṇī's womb, is now that stream of the nectar of love called Nityānanda, born in HāṚāi Pandit's house.

"Vasudeva's son Kṛṣṇa was born in prison.[2] Brahmā and the other gods came to praise him. At dawn, when Kaṃśa was supposed to kill everyone, Kṛṣṇa said, 'Vasudeva, take me to Gokula! Put me in Yaśodā's arms. In time I will return to your house.' The newborn child said all this and more. Vasudeva took his son to Gokula, to Nanda's house. There his son Kṛṣṇa and his daughter Yogamāyā met, and Kṛṣṇa stayed, protected by Yogamāyā." And as my lord said: (text missing)

And in the *Padma Purāṇa*: (text missing)

And in *Yamalā*: (text missing)

And from book 10 of the *Bhāgavata Purāṇa*:

> That goddess immediately disappeared into thin air, Viṣṇu's invisible elder sister with her eight great arms. (*Bhāgavata Purāṇa* X. 4. 9)

"From across the room Vasudeva watched Kṛṣṇa in his wife's lap. Vasudeva could not see that in him the Part and the Whole were one."

At this point, Purī objected that the presence of two Kṛṣṇas at the same time would be a huge disaster.

My lord said, "Don't worry; I'll explain it to you. The Pūrṇatama Kṛṣṇa is in Gokula, and his emanation went to Mathurā. Both came at the same time for fun; the Part and its Source came together in Kṛṣṇacandra. In the *Bhāgavata Purāṇa* we find the story of his birth in Vasudeva's house, and I've already mentioned his birth in Nanda's house. And as Śukadeva says:

> When his son was born high-minded Nanda was delighted. After he had bathed and was properly dressed he summoned brahmin soothsayers. (*Bhāgavata Purāṇa* X. 5. 1)

"And Brahmā's words on the same subject:

[2] The evil king Kaṃśa imprisoned his sister Devakī and her husband Vasudeva, the rightful king, hoping to avoid the prophecy that the couple's eighth child would be his death. Inexplicably Kaṃśa threw them both in the same cell, and of course children ensued. As each subsequent child was born, he dashed it against the stone walls of the prison, and killed six infants.

I worship and praise you, your garments like lightning in a cloud, your face lit up by the peacock feather and your garland of flowers, adorned with wildflowers, with your flute, horn, reed, mouthful, and other emblems, your tender feet, the son of a cowherd. (*Bhāgavata Purāṇa* X. 14. 1)

And in another (part of that) Purāṇa:" (text missing)

Relaxing, Purī then asked my lord to tell him about the joys of that lifetime. As they spoke about those who had appeared in Gokula and played, even greater divine love arose in the two men. When Vijaya Purī heard about the slaying of the demon, he cried out, "Kill him! Kill him!" and "Hari! Hari!"

My lord said, "Settle down and listen, you Durvāsa! This isn't a battle. Behave yourself!"

Chastened, Purī sat back down, and he described the *rāsa līlā* himself: "The sound of Kṛṣṇa's flute stopped the gopīs in their tracks. They dropped everything and came to Vṛndāvana. They abandoned all propriety and duty as their passion grew, running down the path of love. We find Kṛṣṇa, darling lord of Vraja, on the path of love—Kṛṣṇa experiencing Vraja with Rādhikā. Kṛṣṇa left the *rāsa līlā* with Rādhā." Kamalākānta's eyes rolled back in his head as he cried, "Rādhā! Rādhā!"

For several minutes my lord stayed focused on the play in the bower he was envisioning: Kṛṣṇacandra was making love with Rādhā in the bower, and my lord and the *sakhīs* waited on them.

1. In his meditative state my lord took all the *sakhīs* along to serve the couple. Śrī Rūpa Mañjarī and the great Lavaṅgā Mañjarī—they all waited on them with great delight.
2. Hey *Sakhī*! Kṛṣṇa is the great king of cleverness. He left the *rāsa līlā* to please Rādhikā, and the two went off to delight in each other alone. Their attendants worked hard to indulge the couple's every whim.
3. They fanned them from time to time with a jeweled fan, filled their mouths with betel, brought fragrant blossoms raining down on the couple; the pair are enacting the mood of mirth.
4. Noticing the couple start to tire, a *sakhī* massaged their bodies with Malay sandalpaste. The love play resumed, the two hearts an ocean of happiness.
5. All the *sakhīs* served the couple tirelessly. Kṛṣṇa glanced at them and said, "Look, Rādhikā, all your *sakhīs*—what can I say about how they're serving us!"
6. Sitting on the flower-bedecked throne, their hands entwined, they tease each other. Lavaṅgā brings them a pomegranate and another takes it; this is the story of their clever give-and-take.
7. As their clothing and ornaments get disarrayed, the *sakhīs* straighten them up. The *sakhīs* take the flowers from their hands and get them dressed again; the *sakhīs* watch the whole affair.

8. Kṛṣṇa wipes his face with the hem of his garment. What a marvelous story! They watch Kṛṣṇa bring his hand to his chin and fall into sweet sleep.
9. "Oh, I'm dying!" Rāi bites him again. Rādhā wants those curved brows. Kṛṣṇa's happiness doubles when he sees her face. Their ardor is well-matched.
10. Rādhā sees him wearing her flower garland. Kṛṣṇa has put on her clothes! When they realized that Rādhikā's clothes were all torn and disarrayed, the *sakhīs* lovingly straightened her sari.
11. When Kṛṣṇa realized the (other) women of Vraja were anxious, he returned to comfort them, rejoining the *līlā*. He is nothing if not dependent on the cowherd maidens with their simple faith in him.

My lord's very dear friend Śyāmadāsa spoke about Kṛṣṇa publicly and privately. Kṛṣṇa spoke repeatedly about his dependence on the gopīs. Śyāmadāsa recited the verses about the *rāsa līlā* constantly.

As:

> No matter how long I live, with impeccable behavior, I cannot reciprocate your blameless love; you have cut the unbreakable chains of marital propriety to worship me. May your sacrifice of that propriety be repaid. (*Bhāgavata Purāṇa* X. 32. 22)

My lord assured Śyāmadāsa privately that Kṛṣṇa could not resist the love of the gopīs. Grasping my Lord's feet, Śyāmadāsa said, "Tell me in detail about Rādhikā's love."

Advaita slapped Śyāmadāsa playfully and told him to "serve the (divine) couple, not me. There's no use in all this talking! Later on I'll tell you about their overwhelming devotion. For now, listen to Purī Gosvāmī's teachings." My lord continued in a different place in the text.

Starting with the slaying of (the demon) Keśī, he told it all, up to the arrival of Akrura. Kṛṣṇa had bathed before Akrura reached Mathurā. He took pity on Akrura and showed him full hospitality. Pūrṇatama Kṛṣṇa who amused himself in Vraja went to the city of Mathurā as Pūrṇatara.

"Durvāsa" got agitated at that. "O, you playboy of Mathurā! You have explained it. While I was in Goloka I heard that you are Kṛṣṇa in the flesh. Now please explain your basic theology."

My lord said, "Listen carefully. Kṛṣṇa explained three gradations of his *bhakta* (forms):

" 'Pūrṇatama' the Fullest is the Kṛṣṇa in Vraja, where his associates share that Pūrṇatama nature. Pūrṇatara, Fuller, Mathurā; Pūrṇa, Full, the land of Dvarakā. Kṛṣṇa finally took them both, along with his Icchāśakti, to Vraja, where he made known his Vraja Pūrṇatama Fullest *līlā*.

"I tell you unequivocably, I have come to taste the love of Rādhā for Kṛṣṇa. I am here with the heart of a devotee, for I saw the whole world completely lacking in devotion. Kṛṣṇa took on the mood of a devotee to experience the devotion of his followers. That's why I've come here: there's absolutely no devotion anywhere. And so I invoked him, Kṛṣṇa the playboy of Vraja, and eagerly gave him the most attractive name of Kṛṣṇa Caitanya. He was born in Navadvīpa in Jagannātha's house, from the blessed womb of his wife Śacī. Now I'm going to show you his childhood activities. As he commanded me, I've taken on the mood of devotion."

Then he revealed his true form, with its four arms, right before Purī Gosvāmī's eyes. Gradually he contracted it all back in to reveal the two-armed form with the flute at his lips.

Purī fell down flat at his feet. Each time he tried to get up, he fell back down, and finally he fainted.

My lord said, "You are the best of sages, perfected through your practices. Nothing of me is beyond your grasp."

Purī said, "Why did Gopāla send me here? I've seen all this by your grace. In three days I'll go back to see the city of Mathurā, with your permission."

Then Govinda Vaidya kept Advaita's students company. "Show us Kṛṣṇa Caitanya, or we'll leave. Please kindly bless us and fulfill our hearts' desires!"

Along with Purī, Govinda, Mādhava, Haridāsa, and the others—these five undertook the completion of the task. My lord went with them to see to Purī Mahārāja.

He bowed, said "Nārāyaṇa!" and embraced the Vaiṣṇava renunciate.

Govinda laid out the whole story. My lord said "I've heard that Purī has come."

Purī said, "Mādhavendra and I are classmates, and Advaita Ācārya is Mādhavendra's student. If you listen to him you can learn everything you need to know. He can give you the power and intellectual strength to see."

Mahāprabhu said, "Listen, you are most worshipful. What the Ācārya has so respectfully said is true. The Ācārya is a great devotee and a great human being. Whatever command he is given, he obeys. I am the object of his affection, he has mercy on me. Whatever you have said, I will report to him."

Then Purī said, "The Ācārya has confirmed that you are who you are; my salutation." He got up respectfully and bowed. In the guise of a child, Mahāprabhu played children's games.

Then Govinda Mādhava affectionately conducted Purī to Shantipur, and when they arrived there, told the whole story. He grasped the feet of all the devotees, and spoke, and described the lord's birth, by their grace. Again, he spent several days in Shantipur, filling up on the heavenly flavors of Sītā's cooking. After they ate he sat in solitude in the house, and then joyfully began his tale.

Haricaraṇa Dāsa, whose hope is at the lotus feet of the lord of Shantipur, recites the *Advaita Maṅgala*.

This was chapter 3, the conversation with Vijaya Purī, in book 1 of the *Advaita Maṅgala*.

Chapter 4

The Story of His Birth

I praise Śrī Advaita, lord of my life, most important of Caitanya's associates.
I carefully praise Sītā's lotus feet, and those of Acyuta, Balarāma, and all her sons.
I praise lord Vijaya Purī, laying my head at his lotus feet.
I learned my lord's birth story from the sage "Durvāsa" who had come here.

"Everyone, listen carefully to the story of my lord's nativity," Purī began to speak:
"My lord's sons Acyuta, Balarāma, Kṛṣṇa Miśra; Śyāmadāsa, Vasudeva, Murāri, Govinda; and his disciples, Haridāsa and Mādhava Dāsa, so devoted to my lord; everyone listen carefully to my lord's plans," and Purī began to speak, following the cues my lord gave.

"There is a place called Navagrāma in the Sylhet area, a holy, pure, spiritual place. We know Bharadvāja Muṇi's lineage is a family of scholars always virtuous and wise. Vasudeva Ācārya was born into that very lineage and was given the name Kubera Ācārya. He studied Agnihotra the fire sacrifice, *yajñā*, the Brāhmaṇas, the Vedas. There was a sudden uproar across the earth and cries of 'Victory! Victory!' resounded when Vasudeva came to earth.

"At the time the astrologers decreed his name 'Kubera'; in time Kubera reached adolescence. In the same village there was a wise brahmin, Mahānanda, who had a strikingly beautiful daughter who looked just like Devakī in every respect. Her father had named the radiant girl Lābhā. Kubera's parents sent the marriage broker with a proposal for her. She was married to Kubera Ācārya, and the whole village considered itself blessed.

"I lived in that very village; I took my vows there. The priest Mahānanda, my guru, was like a father to me, and everyone called me Lābhā Devī's brother, so I thought of her as my sister. And so I called my lord Ācārya, 'Uncle.' My first and last responsibility is to him."

Let's settle down, and everybody listen carefully. Now you'll hear all about Advaita's birth.

The eternal Goloka *vyūha* is in Vṛndāvana, and Pūrṇatama the Fullest came there, as Vāsudeva. He heard *Bhāgavata Purāṇa* from the holy mouth of Advaita. He was born in Vasudeva's house in Goloka, and lived happily. Advaita told them to destroy his commentary, but didn't say why. He tore it apart at Akrura Landing when he went to that region. Nanda's darling Kṛṣṇa had commanded Advaita to hide his divine purpose when he appeared.

The eternal locus, his parents, his entire entourage: he commanded them all to go to earth. Vasudeva appeared as Kubera, and Devakī became Lābhā in the entourage. Eventually Lābhā had six sons, and a daughter born after them: Lakṣmikānta, Śrīkānta, Hariharānanda, Sadāśiva, Kuśala, and Kīrtīcandra. Four of the sons became renunciates and went off on pilgrimage, never returning home. Two sons remained at home and married; their descendants are in the east.

Kubera and Lābhā eventually moved to Shantipur to live on the bank of the Gaṅgā. Kubera Ācārya missed his sons terribly, and that was when the *avatāra*'s plan presented itself. An effulgent spirit penetrated his heart, and then a beautiful woman appeared before him. Up to his knees in the Gaṅgā, Kubera was dumbstruck when he saw Lakṣmī herself in her awesome majesty. "Your difficult times are over. I command you to take your wife and return home. You will have a son, indeed, he is my husband! Your heart's desire and all your efforts will be fulfilled."

Lakṣmī's words broke his meditative concentration. It seemed like a dream, and he couldn't make any sense of it. He returned home and told Lābhā the whole story, and shortly thereafter she conceived. As she began to glow with the pregnancy, the Ācārya realized that her womb held the Supreme Lord. The couple remained in Shantipur a while longer, then returned to Navagrāma, and in time that radiant essence was ready to appear.

"You'll have a son on the bank of the Gaṅgā," everyone had proclaimed, "who will bring us all great wealth." At the auspicious moment the earth learned the good news, and you were born on the seventh day of Mākara. With the sounds of musical instruments "Hare Kṛṣṇa!" resounded as all creatures took their dip on that auspicious day. That particular ritual was very important in that region. Huge multitudes made grand preparations.

When he saw he had a son, Kubera summoned the astrologer, whose calculations revealed that this child was Īśvara the Lord.

"Regardless of who he is, may the boy have a very long life," people proclaimed throughout the world.

Six months later they held his *annaprāśana*, the ritual for his first solid food, and settled on a name based on his horoscope. The wise old priest was an astrologer who could tell men's fates, a learned scholar in the lineage of the sage Śāṇḍilya. He asked what name he should give the newborn, so Kubera told him what had happened before the child was born.

"While I was performing my austerities on the bank of the Gaṅgā, in Shantipur, the goddess came and spoke to me, saying that her husband would come as our son. She promised that my heart's desire been granted and sent me back home. That goddess was Lakṣmī herself. Now tell me who you think this lovely child is."

The priest replied, "I am well-versed in astrology, yet I hesitate to say these words. He is the husband of lotus-born Lakṣmī, so you should name him Kamalākānta. All the scriptures say he is no different from Bhagavān; he will be famous as 'Advaita,' He Who Is No Different (from the lord).

"[That Vāsudeva who was once born in Vasudeva's house, is now to be known as Kamalākānta.]

"In a previous birth he appeared as Vāsudeva, and now we'll know him by the name of Kamalākānta."

When Lābhā heard about her son, she rejoiced. She and her husband gave the brahmins particularly generous gifts. Everyone placed hands on the infant's head in blessing, amazed to behold his radiance.

But he wouldn't drink from his mother's breast and only cried "Hari! Hari!" to his devoted mother. If he'd hear "Hare Kṛṣṇa," he'd stop crying. What a marvel, the story of his boyhood!

Every morning, Lābhā cooked food to offer the goddess, but could not put any food in her own mouth. At midday she prepared lunch for the *śālagrāma*; she managed to eat a little but left most of it.

When he'd speak at all, he'd tell everyone "Say 'Kṛṣṇa.'" The only sound he'd make was to tell everyone to say "Kṛṣṇa." He'd say "Kṛṣṇa Hari" when he'd play with the other boys, so they called him "Śrī Kṛṣṇa."

When he was five, they put chalk in his hand and he started studying; how quickly he learned! If we asked Kamalākānta what he was studying, he would not say a word. His parents, in their affection, didn't say anything. He just did whatever came into his mind.

His boyhood was wonderful. These are just a few words about it. It's been a long time now since that wise man died. I'm barely clinging to life myself, and won't last much longer.

Listen everyone, to what happened on Kamalākānta's birthday. A party had been planned. They got oil, turmeric, etc. ready; the priest was meticulously reciting the Vedas. Kamalākānta had gone out to play and had not yet come home.

The king's son was making fun of him."Where does this 'saying Kṛṣṇa' business come from? Does anyone around here know where it's from?"

Kamalākānta got angry and sat down in a huff. Meanwhile his parents were looking for him, in vain. The day was nearly done and he still hadn't come home. They went to the prince's house, only to discover that the prince had collapsed and looked dead. A great tumult broke out in the village. How had this happened? No one knew! The king asked everyone, and they said, timidly, "He was playing with Kubera Ācārya's son, and made some insinuations about him that made the boy angry. And then the prince just collapsed like this."

And so the king summoned Kamalākānta's father the Ācārya to inform him.

The Ācārya said, "His birthday party's about to begin. We've looked everywhere but can't find our son."

The prince suggested they search the cave where they'd been playing, so the king and queen and Kamalākānta's parents set off for the cave, and there they found him, sitting in a mud enclosure, silently, like an ascetic. His mother took his hand and pulled him, wailing, out of the cave. She took him in her arms and comforted him, and they all returned to the Ācārya's house. His parents sat him down for a scolding.

"Today's your birthday party and we've put a lot of effort into it. Why have you worried everyone like this?"

They bathed him with oil and turmeric and then performed the *pūjā* with the proper Vedic mantras. She fed her child and held him in her lap, and very affectionately told him what the king had said. The queen fell at his feet, until Lābhā Devī asked her to get up.

Smiling, Kamalākānta said, "Listen, Mother. Her son said some mean things to me, and I got mad."

The queen covered her head with her garment and praised him. She did her best to cheer his parents, telling the child, "Listen, Kamalākānta, this is how it is in our land. This *pūjā* is for all of us. Boys do all sorts of things when they're playing! All this happened because you got angry."

The others chimed in, "In your place we'd be offended, too. The prince is mortified, so he stayed home. Seriously, why should anyone get upset with what kids say when they're playing?"

Lābhā Devī covered him with kisses. "You made us worry so much!" When he realized how worried his mother was, he felt badly, and shouted at everyone to go home. "Please just think of me as an ordinary boy. Let's go ahead and feed the brahmins as planned."

And so the king and queen prostrated themselves before him and left, and Kamalākānta's parents gave the brahmins the feast themselves. He suddenly became a boy, like before, and enjoyed the party with everyone else.

Remember this story of mine which I've told so carefully. And how many more *līlās* he did as a boy! How could I possibly remember them all! I've told only a little of his exploits as an infant, and now I will describe as much as I can of the next stage of his life, his boyhood.

His parents enjoyed their child. What I have related above constitutes the most important parts of that first phase. I've written only what Purī Gosvāmī told me; I can't tell the difference between true and false myself.

Haricaraṇa Dāsa, whose hope is at the lotus feet of the lord of Shantipur, recites the *Advaita Maṅgala*.

This is chapter 4, the Birth Story, in Vijaya Purī's speech in book 1—*Bālya Līlā*—in the *Advaita Maṅgala*.

Book 2

Chapter 1

The King's Submission

I praise the glorious Advaita, lord of Sītā's life, who drew Caitanya to earth by his thunderous roar.

I praise the glorious brothers Acyutānanda, Balarāma, Kṛṣṇa Miśra, Gopāla, Jagadīśa, and Rūpa.

By the kindness of all you who have gathered, I will write something of the second phase of the celebrated Advaita's life.

My lord's childhood activities are an endless delight, but who can possibly describe them all? Among his childhood activities is Divyasiṃha's conversion. And there was quite the spectacle when Kamalākānta came to Shantipur. He took his parents to live beside the Gaṅgā, and there his assiduous study of scripture proved his wisdom. This book 2 covers my lord's childhood. I've put it in verse; listen now to what transpired.

Then Vijaya Purī said, "Listen, Everyone! Nārāyaṇa himself had come to Shantipur. He played a trick on the king to teach him a lesson. Let's go to Shantipur! The scholars are training the boy; he's learned the Kalāpa grammar in a very short time. Those scholars just sit among themselves, studying. They look at each other, laughing. At the end of the day they say, 'Victory to Kṛṣṇa!' and tie up their manuscripts and head home, and at last the boys are free to play. Kamalākānta tells the (other) boys to repeat Kṛṣṇa's name, for the only reason to study scripture is Hari's name. A lot of the boys take his advice, but the haughty atheists have their (own) opinions. He gives lessons to most of the other boys in the scholars' community.

"All those egotistical people feel ashamed. They cause the king a lot of grief with all their complaining."

Divyasiṃha the "Divine Lion" was the king of that region, and a great devotee of the goddess. Kamalākānta had struck down his son for his abusive speech. My lord restored the boy's life when the king begged him to. That misbehaving prince was always envious of others, and didn't know a thing about God's majesty. He made fun of Kamalākānta's saying "Kṛṣṇa," but when Kamalākānta began to glow like the radiant sun, everyone was terrified. The king said, "Everything arises from Śakti. Boy, how can you give up Śakti for Kṛṣṇa?"

Kamalākānta angrily replied, "Look at your goddess! She's right in front of me but *I'm* supposed to serve *her*? There's a large gold flag atop the Devī's temple, flapping gently, all bejeweled. The fearsome goddess stays inside her big, tall temple eating sacrificed goats."

Kamalākānta and the king approached the goddess. When she saw Kamalākānta, the goddess turned her face away. She averted her face! And when Kamalākānta smiled at her, the goddess exploded. Everyone was horrified, king and courtiers alike. The king fell to the ground, stunned.

Kamalakānta, nonplussed, went home and told his parents in no uncertain terms, "Let's not stay here, let's go to Shantipur. That's where I belong, on the bank of the Gaṅgā. Since the king is a nonbeliever, his kingdom will be destroyed. Let's not stay here, things are going to get difficult. You are both old, and I solemnly promise to take care of you, body and soul."

Everyone went to tell the king that the family was leaving Navagrāma. King Divyasiṃha and his entire retinue approached the Ācārya with joined hands. They covered their heads with their garments and fell at his lotus feet. Kamalākānta said, "Father, I can't stay here another second!"

Kubera Ācārya was a very clever noble man. He revered the king and fulfilled his responsibilities. "Listen, O Great King: your majesty is formidable. Build a great temple for the passionate goddess, and by her grace your kingdom will last forever. My son's order is a very good one. You won't accrue any sin for the offenses you committed in ignorance. I'll take him with me to Shantipur."

The king replied, "Listen, O Wise Ācārya. He's not an ordinary boy; your son is Īśvara in the flesh! I didn't know that, and kept offending him. I don't know what will come of that carelessness! My crown is no excuse! That boy, Śrīdhara-Viṣṇu who holds the goddess on his lap, tamed that goddess. The only way for me to stay in power is if your son takes pity on me. I've realized that he is definitely Viṣṇu's *avatāra*, for who else could subdue the goddess Māyā?"

Joining his hands, covering his head with his garment, the king praised Kamalākānta, but the boy said nothing. Despairing, the king continued, "You are Lord Nārāyaṇa, I am a senile old man. In my ignorance, I insulted you. Please take pity on me! I take refuge in you. I am caught up in your magic, but you are omniscient. Please release me altogether from Māyā! I know that creation, preservation and destruction arise from you. I'm just a miserable creature caught up in it." Divyasiṃha praised him in every way.

Delighted, the child replied, "I am Kṛṣṇa's servant in human form. These praises of yours are entirely inappropriate. You have committed an enormous offense against Kṛṣṇa, so he cannot even look at you! If anyone in the kingdom rejects Kṛṣṇa, the kingdom will be destroyed and everything that person does falls apart. You are the great king in this kingdom. Who am I to punish you? Go back home, O King, with all your courtiers and companions. I am a brahmin beggar, roaming from place to place. My parents are old, and I'm only a child. I'll take them to the shelter of the Gaṅgā and look after them there. You're a devotee of the goddess, so worship her. Make another image of the goddess just like the first one. But the goddess will forsake you if you insult Kṛṣṇa again—she won't tolerate that! Everyone knows that Māyā is the servant of an *avatāra* of even the tiniest part of Krsna.

"There are three types of Māyā according to the three qualities of nature: *sattva*, *rajas*, and *tamas*. Māyā is Kṛṣṇa's servant in each, so that goddess deserves to be worshiped by everyone! She won't eat anything unless it has first been offered to Kṛṣṇa. Kṛṣṇa's people are quite familiar with this, as it is a Vaiṣṇava practice. The *rajas* goddess accepts the king's worship. She roams around filling her belly. She terrorizes people if they don't provide her with food, and devours them in front of everyone. Kṛṣṇa does not hate that goddess, because that's just the way *rajas* people are.

"The *tamas* goddess lives in an awful place. She's a hunter who eats lowly creatures. That's the form in your temple. You should always be devoted to her. You know the goddess will protect your kingdom and all you hold dear. Worship the goddess carefully with all due protocol in *rajas* and *tamas guṇas*. So long as there are no flaws in the worship she will be pleased and grant you a boon that will make you very happy. Ten days of ease and comfort with her are really suffering. And then you go to hell; it's very subtle. If you make the slightest mistake, then she'll devour you and all your sons and companions. So worship that goddess you've chosen! But she cannot bear to hear Kṛṣṇa maligned. I made no mistake in standing before her. And then that goddess of yours shattered; what could I do? Go back home. That will please her. Hurry up!"

The king threw himself at Kamalākānta's feet and proclaimed, "I abandon my entire kingdom to take refuge in you. I'm renouncing the kingdom I served for so long. The moment I saw you, it vanished. After everything you said, I realized that you, the one whose maidservant is Māyā, have come. When she saw you angry she could not run away from you, so she turned her face and cracked, and now is far away. Now you have mercy on me permanently. I was the king, and I know who you are."

My lord said, "The evidence shows that I'm a child. You're making a mistake; why all this fuss?"

The king replied, "Īśvara has appeared as a child time after time. As a child, he lifted the entire Mt. Govardhana, and he managed to slay great demons like Pūtanā, Triṇavartā, and others. As Vāmana he tricked Bali. You are that same child, born now. Have mercy on me, save me from the ocean of existence, reveal the name of the savior of the fallen, O Ocean of Mercy! I've been worshiping the goddess my whole life and she has deceived me. I renounce her absolutely."

Lord Kamalākānta smiled and said, "Make up your mind here," but the king took refuge with his body, mind, and speech and placed his head on Kamalākānta's feet. Compassionately, Kamalākānta instructed him to recite Kṛṣṇa's name, sing Kṛṣṇa's *bhajanas*, sing his virtues.

"Worship Kṛṣṇa with thought, word, and deed. When you see another Kṛṣṇa devotee, join your hands in salutation. Serve brahmins and Vaiṣṇavas attentively, and you will know Kṛṣṇa's mercy eternally, the scriptures say. Build a temple to Kṛṣṇa and make an image to put in it. Learn how to worship Vaiṣṇavas and brahmins. Purify the equipment and offer meals, and eat Kṛṣṇa's *prasāda* with the congregation. Go on pilgrimage and organize great festivals as much as you can. Fulfill all your duties and enjoy your kingdom. After you've ruled a while longer, and tasted devotion, give the kingdom to your son and become a renunciate; we'll meet again in Shantipur, where I'll give you further instructions."

The king fell full length at those lotus feet, asking, "Please stay here another ten days; that would completely fulfill my heart's desires."

But my lord replied that he would return to Shantipur, to his home on the bank of the Gaṅgā. And so the king took his leave and returned to his own home, and Kamalākānta, to Shantipur.

Haricaraṇa Dāsa, whose hope lies at the lotus feet of the lord of Shantipur, recites the *Advaita Maṅgala*.

Thus ends chapter 1, called "The King's Submission," in book 2, the *Pauganḍa Līlā*, of the *Advaita Maṅgala*.

Book 2

Chapter 2

The Arrival in Shantipur

Victory, victory to my Lord Advaita Ācārya! He fulfilled his duty by making Caitanya his guru.

Victory, victory to my lord's son, Sītā's darling! My life's treasure is meditation on your feet.

Victory, victory to the immortal Vijaya Purī, Durvāsa incarnate, famous throughout the world. With great devotion I praise the feet of him, the sound of whose voice set my lord's *līlā* in motion.

Purī resumed his tale: "Listen to something amazing! That same king became a consummate Vaiṣṇava. He constructed a temple with a great tower and served Kṛṣṇa meticulously. He employed a brahmin Vaiṣṇava for *pūjā* and scrubbed the temple (floor) with his own hands. He and his queen performed the duties, serving my lord's feet with every thought, word, and deed. He spread a feast of sanctified food fit for a king and served the Vaiṣṇavas, seated in ten rows. The Vaiṣṇavas ate, crying, 'Victory!' The king covered his head with his garment, again lost in rapture. At the end of the meal he offered everyone betel. He washed their feet and drank that water, and everyone departed. Then he ate the leftovers. This was the way he worshiped.

"He employed ten brahmins to sing Kṛṣṇa's name day and night. He held a festival for Kṛṣṇa's birthday in the month of Bhādra for the pleasure of the whole kingdom. When Dola Yātrā came, the villagers played musical instruments for two months. They put on a huge festival, putting Govinda on a swing to play. Calling Kamalākānta's name, he'd go blind with divine love. He never failed to carry out my lord Kamalākānta's every command.

"He obeyed those orders throughout his reign, and then with due ceremony abdicated his kingdom and turned it over to his son. Thereafter he kept his schedule of ritual worship and preached all about the lord. The king renounced worldly life and came to Shantipur, where my lord instructed him to preach about Kṛṣṇa. That foremost renunciate accepted the order. He grasped my lord's feet when Kamalākānta gave him the name 'Kṛṣṇadāsa.' Kṛṣṇadāsa took his leave and went to Vṛndāvana, where he attained bliss.[3]

"No one can understand Kṛṣṇa's will. Everyone, hear about the *paugaṇḍa līlā*, Kamalākānta's boyhood activities.

"The Vaiṣṇava community had a hard time in those places where nonbelievers ruled. When such people hear Kṛṣṇa's name, they make fun of it. That same Kṛṣṇa-name brings the tongue under control. He who once sat on the throne and wielded ultimate authority renounced it all and breathed his last in Vṛndāvana.

"I can't (begin to) describe Advaita Ācārya's mercy. With his mercy, what could *not* happen? I couldn't begin to understand all the dramas of his childhood were it not for his mercy. Now as you didn't know then the greatness of his mercy, listen as I tell you of my lord's teachings.

"Advaita came, with his parents, to Shantipur, where they lived in profound bliss, and he made studying scripture his priority. I left them and went on pilgrimage. I took my renunciate vows in Kāśī and stayed there for a long time.

"When Kubera Ācārya and Lābhā left this world, the Ācārya-lord went on pilgrimage, and we met again in Kāśī. He wasn't concerned about his physical needs; he was truly Īśvara. Śrī Madana Gopāla blessed me and revealed the lord who sported in Shantipur! Then he imparted to me this whole story. In seeing him my life's purpose was fulfilled."

With that, Purī embraced me. All of us gathered there fell at his feet. Now that we knew my lord's story, we all got back up and went to him. My lord rose to greet us. Purī covered his head with his garment and joined his hands. "I behaved like an affectionate friend with you. Please forgive me for all those offenses.[4] You write the Vedas and *purāṇa*s in every age. No one can fulfill his destiny without Īśvara's grace. I have already pledged devotion to your lotus feet and have gone on pilgrimage. Please tell me what to do now!"

My lord the Ācārya replied, "Kṛṣṇa, Kṛṣṇa! You are my guru! Why are you acting like the disciple? You are clearly Kṛṣṇa's companion Durvāsa. Moreover you are a renunciate, Nārāyaṇa's splendor. Second, since you are Purī Gosvāmī's

[3] That is to say, he died.

[4] Cf *Bhagavad Gītā* XI.41–42; this is exactly what Arjuna tells Kṛṣṇa by way of apology for having been too familiar.

godbrother, then you are a master worthy of my respect. Bless the work I've come here to do. Serving as Kṛṣṇa's guru will fulfill my heart's desire."

Purī said, "You have brought in the darling lord of Vraja. What greater heart's desire could anyone know? I knew what he would say; he didn't know. But the one you will grace, knew." With Kṛṣṇa's name on his lips, Purī horripilated. He left for Vṛndāvana. I've now related Purī's story.

Now you'll know the whole truth about Vijaya Purī. He who has listened attentively with devotion reaches Advaita's feet and enjoys his mercy. We can't get Caitanya/consciousness[5] without Advaita's grace. Glorify him, Brother, glorify Advaita Gosvāmī!

Now I turn to the *līlā* of my lord's studies, and what he studied at the home of the sage Śānta. In the village of Phullabāṭī, near Shantipur, lived the brahmin Śānta, in the glory of his scholarship. Seated on the bank of the Ganges, that scholar taught many students and revealed *bhakti* through his discussions. With both men and women Śānta displayed tremendous restraint. He remained unmarried, firm and poised.

One day my lord approached him, bowed, and sat on the riverbank. "Please instruct me, Master Śāntanu. You are like Sarasvatī the goddess of learning, a scholar to be listened to."

Master Śānta replied, "You are an extraordinary boy, and you glow like the sun. What can I possibly teach you?"

"What text are you teaching now? I'll listen. Teach me like that, and I'll work hard."

"What shall we read?" said the scholar. "I am teaching the Kalāpa grammar; listen respectfully. Tell me what you want me to teach you. If I teach you Kalāpa, you'll have some practice with that. Then you should work on astrology."

My lord said, "I humbly agree to whatever you want to teach me. By your grace I will learn the teachings and duties. Recite it to me once, Bhaṭṭācārya, and the second time, Master, explain what it means. Bhaṭṭācārya, please teach me all the scriptures—astrology, *alaṃkāra*, et cetera—in six months. Please also teach me the *Bhāgavata Purāṇa*, in which (we learn of) Kṛṣṇa's mercy to the whole world."

Śānta Ācārya said, "You are Īśvara descended among us. You are acting like a child to trick me. You have already explained whatever scriptures you studied. No one else can make any sense of them. Even at your young age the Vedas ring off your tongue, enchanting all the gods and sages. When the whole world hears your commentary on the *Bhāgavata Purāṇa*, their life purposes will be fulfilled. Whoever you are, if I instruct you in this theology it'll be like getting Kṛṣṇa the crestjewel of virtue in birth after birth. Please grant me devotion to Kṛṣṇa as my fee." My lord said, "By Kṛṣṇa's grace you are his witness."

[5] A pun, as Caitanya's name means "consciousness."

In this way he served his parents for a long time, practicing devotion among ordinary people, floating in bliss. Before long his parents passed away, and he performed their funeral rituals carefully.

Now I've recited the second phase of my lord's boyhood activities. The second phase of my lord's life is boundless, immense. I will write the entire piece you've heard.

Haricaraṇa Dāsa, whose hope is at the lotus feet of the lord of Shantipur, recites the *Advaita Maṅgala*.

Thus ends chapter 2, the description of his coming to Shantipur and studying with Śānta, from book 2, the *Paugaṇḍa Līlā*.

Book 3

Chapter 1

The Vision in Vṛndāvana

I praise Lord Advaita, lord of Sītā's life, who brought in Mahāprabhu Caitanya, known throughout the world.

I praise my lord's sons and the feet of those assembled, by whose mercy I describe the unfolding of Advaita's life.

I praise holy Shantipur with its assemblage of devotees, most of whom dwell beside the flowing Gaṅgā.

Now I will describe my lord's adolescence, which we'll call the third phase, book 3. In his adolescence we have my lord's trip to Holy Vṛndāvana, the consecration of the Gopāla image, and many other tales. I cannot fathom such endlessly intricate activities, (but) meditating on his holy feet, I'll write what I can. I heard all of this from holy Kṛṣṇadāsa himself. At that time I was working for Kṛṣṇadāsa, and so this came straight from his mouth. We discussed it, and then I wrote as he wished. Everyone pay attention, listen carefully.

Kamalākānta went to Gayā to perform his parents' funeral rites, moving majestically, shouting (the mystical syllable) HUM! My lord had Kṛṣṇa's name on his lips, his body shone, he was like a kadamba bud, and the hair on his body stood erect. After several days in Gayā, he went north and took all the brahmins with him. He offered rice balls at the demon Gayā's head, my lord performing all the rituals according to tradition. This behavior satisfied all the brahmins. Then he set out to the west.

He went to Kāśī, where he met the renunciate Vijaya Purī, and stayed three nights. He conveyed the news of his parents' deaths and told Purī he was going on pilgrimage. He bathed at Maṇikarṇika landing and visited the temple of Viśvanātha, Lord of the Universe. He spent three days and nights there, then moved on.

The bliss in my lord's heart when he went to Prayāga! He spent several days there at Triveṇī, the confluence of the three rivers. At Prayāga he visited the temple of Kṛṣṇa-Venimādhava. He bathed and offered water at the Triveṇī landing. He performed austerities at the pilgrimage spot at the confluence, spending several days at the river at Prayāga. There he saw Bhīma's indestructible mace and talked endlessly about the war with King Jarāsandha.

Bhīmasena fought a lengthy duel with maces. After twenty-one days he still had not won. Jarāsandha and Bhīma suspended the mace battle and switched to wrestling, but neither could defeat the other. Bhīma's strength began to gradually ebb, (but then) Kṛṣṇa transferred his own power to him and doubled it. Still Bhīma could not figure out how to kill Jarāsandha. Kṛṣṇa used a blade of grass to give him a clue, and Bhīma finally understood what to do: Bhīma dropped his mace and sliced Jarāsandha's body in two. A roar of laughter resounded through the town. All the people at court who heard this were amazed.

From there my lord went to the city of Mathurā and decided to make a pilgrimage tour there. Singing the praises of his parents' feet, he lost himself in divine love when he saw it all. He bathed at Viśrānti dock, and all his cares floated away. He bathed at each of the twenty-four landings in turn. He visited the temples of Śambhu, Bhūteśvara, Gokarṇa, and visited the temple of the goddess, Nanda's daughter, and the *sakhīs*. Then he asked about Kubjā's house, wanting to spend a few days there, and was happy to hear that there was supposed to be an image of Kubjā in Vṛndāvana.

My lord announced that he would recover that image in Vṛndāvana. The entire unmanifest *līlā* in Vraja remained hidden, so he went to Vṛndāvana and started to look around. Everywhere he turned in Vṛndāvana he saw something significant; when he saw Govardhana he was overcome with divine love. He bathed in Rādhā's Pond and Śyāma's Pond, and told the people there to praise the Lord of Vraja in those places. Then he went to Madhuvana,[6] Madhu's Forest, and bathed in the pool just as that honey-drinker Kṛṣṇa had played. When he went to Tālavana, the Palm Forest, his divine love bloomed, and he felt that everyone was his brother. For quite some time he circled the area, trotting around in divine bliss. He saw the sparkling beauty of the Kumuda Forest and went and put a garland around his neck, and then my lord went to the mighty Bahulā Forest.

When he saw Bahulā the cow he praised her. He bathed in the pond and went to Govardhana. He circumambulated Govardhana, and then, in a cave in that mountain, he unexpectedly got *darśana* of Harideva. He bowed full-length again and again, and purified his entire body with a mental bath in the Gaṅgā. He saw the Dāna landing, where Rādhā and her girlfriends had paid their "tax," and

[6] Our protagonist is embarking on the "journey through the twelve forests," sites of Kṛṣṇa's storied activities. See book 10 of the *Bhāgavata Purāṇa* and David Haberman's *Journey through the Twelve Forests*.

laughed in delight. One by one he saw every forest, and with each one he saw, my lord became more overwhelmed.

Next my lord went to Kāmya Forest. He took a holy bath in that spotless place. Then he saw the cowherds playing hide-and-seek and said, "Hey you Vraja-ites, play with me!" My lord Advaita Ācārya very enthusiastically took on the role of a *sakhī* and joined them. Playing hide-and-seek, running here and there; how much fun he had everywhere he turned in the forests of Vraja.

My lord said, "If I spend the night here, Kṛṣṇacandra might come play in the water with the girls." My lord's mood when he saw those playgrounds was unmistakable. On his third day there his love grew restless. Then he went to Vṛkabhanu's house in Barsāna, where he saw Kīrtīdā.

Roaming from house to house he saw them all. He bathed in Pāvana Lake, a deserted place. He went to Lord Nanda's palace, bowing to Yaśodā, bathing in Pāvana Lake, and spent the night there. He saw Khadira Forest and went to the village of Javat, and cleansed his body with a bath in the Kiśorī pond.

He went to Rāma's landing and saw the temple of the Śeṣaśāyi Lord Viṣṇu lying in the Ocean of Milk. He bowed at Balarāma's place. He saw the Gopī landing and said, "Here is my desire fulfilled!" He saw Akṣaya Vaṭa, the imperishable banyan tree, and immediately sat down beneath it. He saw the Chira landing, and sat at the foot of a kadamba tree for a moment to meditate. Then he moved on to the village of Bhadrā and meditated on the story of the abduction of Nanda. He crossed Bhadrā Forest and went into Bhandira Forest, where the cowherd boys like to play.

My lord said, "I'm playing that I've tamed a demon. I'll blind him and ride him off in triumph." He played in this way for some time. Rādhā came with her girlfriends on the way to Vṛndāvana. He talked like this and then proceeded to Loha Forest. He was very happy and went toward Mahāvana, the Great Forest. He saw the birthplaces of Arjuna and the twins. He saw Pūtanā's pit and the cowherds' well. When he saw the Brahmāṇḍa landing he ate its earth.[7] Happily, he saw Yaśodā there at Brahmāṇḍa. When he saw the *līlā* places in the forests he became ecstatic. He sat at the Yamunā landing and watched the current.

Meanwhile, Kṛṣṇadāsa, that chief brahmin, who now lived at Kāmya Forest and had (once) reviled (the path of) devotion, who had been associated with Advaita in Advaita's adolescence, bowed low to Advaita and sang his great praise."I will remain here as your servant, studying the devotional scriptures brought to light in your mind." My lord was pleased and embraced him who had become my lord's chief companion.

Then my lord circled clockwise around Govardhana, and that source of the *avatāras*[8] continued on to Mathurā. Early in the morning he entered Vṛndāvana,

[7] Like the baby Kṛṣṇa ate clay at the same spot.

[8] Here again Haricaraṇa asserts Advaita as *aṃśī*.

thrilled to see that land again. At every location in Vraja where my lord spent the night, people would look after him. They would cook the *prasāda* with their own hands, taking great care of my devout lord.

While he was in Vṛndāvana he spent three days in the Kuñja Forest, where he sat at the foot of a banyan tree to think.

1. My lord said, "O Supreme one! Listen, you are my very life." And Madana Gopāla appeared! "I went to Vṛndāvana at a very young age, staying to see the Yamunā *līlā*.
2. "O Supreme Being, listen to this whole story of mine. The shade of a young banyan tree comforted my body with the breeze from the waves on the Yamunā. The trees and vines in Vṛndāvana laughingly tell the whole story, aided by everyone.
3. "Vṛndāvana is desolate—the people of Vraja keep cattle—suddenly we hear their lowing. My thirsty eyes; I run from forest to forest so far, and then I faint.
4. "Day and night I am unaware and can hardly tell black from white, then I return to my senses. In the distance I see Śyāma. The place is like a vine-covered tree. I see Rādhikā at his left.
5. "Lalitā and all the other *sakhī*s look at me. Śrī Rādhā says, 'My friends, my life!' Śyāma's sweet laugh/smile, his charming flute at his lips, he stands in a lovely pose, bent in three places.
6. "Muralī plays the flute gently and ambrosia rains down. 'Go, Advaita, and find Gaura's abode; you are Visnu; we will all flourish when it comes!
7. 'You have seen me; I will arise like the light of the sun at a later date. Do not remain here! I tell you, go to Gaura's place.
8. 'All you have to do is think of me and I will appear. The people of Vraja will come as your disciples; the gopīs will come see me, too. I will make all the people of Vraja appear there.
9. 'I will make the unmanifest lord of Vraja live on the bank of the Yamunā, at the twelve Ādityas landing, in the Kuñja Forest. There will be no more strife. Everyone will find their way to you. Just do your *pūjā* in the morning.
10. 'Sprinkle some Yamunā water around and that will make your worship succeed.' Śyāma spoke like this and hid in the glade. Alas! Rādhā-Madana Mohana!"

He described the Vṛndāvana *darśana* to his disciples, telling them that Gopāla Mahārāja would appear in the morning.

Haricaraṇa Dāsa, whose hope is at the lotus feet of the lord of Shantipur, recites the *Advaita Maṅgala*.

This is chapter 1, "The Vision in Vṛndāvana," in book 3, the *Kaiśora Līlā*, in the *Advaita Maṅgala*.

Chapter 2

The Appearance of Madana Gopāla

I praise my lord Advaita, noblest in the world. Making Caitanya appear was his whole focus.
I praise my lord's disciples, those wells of the nectar of devotion. Rādhā made the world float in the nectar of divine love.

Then my lord opened his eyes and saw the forest. When he tried to look around, everything was out of focus. He saw ten women of Vraja before him and told them the whole story. "Madana Mohana was the deity of Vraja. Listen, everyone, I want to find him! Bring shovels and pickaxes from the village, and we'll hack an entrance into the grove."

The women raced to tell the townspeople, and they all returned at daybreak with machetes and other tools. He showed them the mound and they all started to hack away at its sides. They made the Muslim ruler's attendants flee in fear. Madana Mohana was disguised as Gopāla. Madana Mohana displayed the mood of early courtship. Listen, O Supreme One, for this image is my deity.

Meanwhile, the villagers kept on hacking at the boulders, and they managed to cut a way into the grove. They sprinkled Yamunā water all around, and then they noticed a stone shrine to one side. They placed Gopāla on its platform and consecrated it with water. They scrubbed and bathed it, making the dark image of the young Ghana Śyāma gleam. They worshiped him with fruit and flowers and offered food, performed *ārati*, and then distributed the *prasāda*.

The people of Vraja built a temple. They brought in a brahmin and charged him with the worship service. The image heard all this and called out Kṛṣṇa Miśra's name. Śrī's[9] son is such a storehouse of virtue!

The deity of Vraja called himself Gopāla. Everyone wanted to know how he came to be in Vraja. My lord said, "I'll tell you; listen carefully. This is Rādhā-Kṛṣṇa's eternal abode, it's eternally *parakīyā*. Eager to taste *parakīyā rasa*, the playboy of Vraja appeared. And so the *pūrvarāga* is the best. Pūrṇamāsī was the one who began to proclaim that emotional attitude.

"Kṛṣṇa and his friends were tending their cows when suddenly Pūrṇamāsī showed up. Kṛṣṇa fell at Pūrṇamāsī's feet. She whispered the two syllables of the name "Rādhā" in his ear, and Rādhā's name immediately agitated Kṛṣṇa. He cried 'Rādhā! Rādhā!' completely absorbed.

"He went back to his friends, his eyes darting around. When Śrīdhāma asked what was wrong, Ujjvala and Subala explained. 'Pūrṇamāsī's disciple Rādhā,

[9] One manuscript says "Sītā's son" here; cf. *Advaita Prakāśa*, chap. 11, for the significance of this variant reading.

daughter of Vṛkabhānu, Cidāma's elder sister—it's because of her beauty. If that jewel of a woman saw you, she'd get just as agitated!'

"Then Pūrṇamāsī went to Rādhikā. Everyone stood up respectfully, and a bit nervously. Rādhā fell completely prostrate at her feet. Pūrṇamāsī placed her hand on Rādhā's head to bless her. She whispered the *kāma gāyatrī* mantra in her ear and uttered the two syllables of 'Kṛṣṇa,' initiating her properly according to tradition.

"Those two syllables of Kṛṣṇa's name in her ear incited love, and Kṛṣṇa became her every thought and word. She burst out suddenly with 'Kṛṣṇa! Kṛṣṇa!' and from that day on, the two had profound mutual passion, and neither could sleep at night.

"By the time Kṛṣṇa returned home he was nearly out of his mind. Yaśodā was worried when she saw her son like this. Concerned, she took him to Pūrṇamāsī and threw herself at the old woman's feet, saying, 'You've always really frightened me.'

"Pūrṇamāsī said, 'Don't worry about a thing. I'll give your child a mantra and he'll be fine.' She whispered the mantra in Kṛṣṇa's ear. 'As soon as you've mastered the mantra, go, this very day, and look for Rādhā." Yaśodā was reassured by those delightful words. You are the son of a king; she, a beautiful girl. No one will be able to understand what will happen. God has ordained your secret love.' The same thing took place at her house, 'Now go to Vṛndāvana to graze the cattle; you will certainly meet Nārāyaṇa, your husband.'

"With that, she blessed Yaśodā. 'Your son will be fine,' she said, her work complete.

"[Rādhā's companions' eyes flowed with tears. But the elders cowered in fear.

"Lalitā and Viśākhā both discussed this, worried about how to get Kṛṣṇa.] Lalitā said, 'Girlfriend, I know him well. I'll bring him to you on some pretext. When Kṛṣṇa's eyes meet yours, he'll start moving in your direction.'

"Just then Pūrṇamāsī turned up. Everyone stood up to greet her, and she blessed them. 'You will meet Kṛṣṇa. All of you—this very day your heart's desire will be fulfilled! Lalitā, you are clever and wise, take all the girls to Vṛndāvana to worship the sun. Tell Jaṭilā that you want to worship the sun, and then you all can worship at the Gopeśvara Temple. Jaṭilā will come to see the image there; she's done a lot of *pūjā*. Ask her to teach you the right way to do it. Tell her 'Your prayers earned you Pārvatī as daughter-in-law. You will get tons of wealth and riches. It's Sunday, please teach us how to worship the sun now.' Lalitā, once you know what sun *pūjā* looks like, ask Jaṭilā to send her daughter-in-law with our friends.'

"Jaṭilā was very helpful, collected all the necessary materials, and sent her daughter-in-law along to worship the sun. Rādhā and her *sakhīs* went to Vṛndāvana, to the edge of the Yamunā on the pretext of doing sun *pūjā*.

"When Kṛṣṇa and Balarāma[10] heard all this, they said, 'Without Pūrṇamāsī *svakīyā* passion is just not the same.'

[10] We cannot tell from the context whether this comment is part of the narrative or of its frame. That is, are the Kṛṣṇa and Balarāma in question Advaita's sons, or the originals of those names, in Vraja? Both options fit the situation!

My lord said, "That same Pūrṇamāsī has come now, revealed as my guru, Mādhavendra Purī.

"So listen: I'll tell you something of Rādhā's state, which was also Kṛṣṇa's. Kṛṣṇa and his friends took their cows and went anxiously to the bank of the Yamunā. He took Subala to look for Rādhā, his eyes thirsting for a glimpse of her. Ujjvala and Subala were both trying to console him. Now then, everyone, hear about the state Rādhā was in.

"The young women came to Vṛndāvana to worship the sun. Sūrya Ghāṭa, the sun landing, was a very popular place. It has the cool shade of the trees, and the clear waters of the Yamunā flow past. Rādhā sat there dreaming of Kṛṣṇa. 'How is Kṛṣṇa? I want to see him. How will I see his moon-face? I cannot contain my heart, burning in my chest. What are the eyes on that sweet face like? I need to see them to survive. If I don't, I'll die!'

"Viśākhā drew a picture and showed it to Rādhā, but when she looked at the drawing, Rādhā's anguish only doubled in intensity. 'Alas, alas, Lord of my Life! Where do I have to go to find you? Oh, girlfriend, I'm going to drown myself in the Yamunā!' Not seeing the pupils of Kṛṣṇa's eyes, she fainted, bereft of Kṛṣṇa.

"Viśākhā wrote a letter using hibiscus juice and gave it to the *sakhī* Tulasī to deliver to Kṛṣṇa alone so that Cidāma and the other *sakha*s wouldn't find out.' Take my message straight to him. Once you see him, be nice. Everyone will tell you what state my friend is in. Tell him to come here by himself.'

"The *sakhī* took the letter and went into the forest, where the gentle breezes were blowing through the banyan trees. One *sakhī* mentioned having seen Kṛṣṇa on the bank of the Yamunā, chatting with Ujjvala and Subala. Tulasī found Kṛṣṇa unconscious there at the foot of a kadamba tree, babbling incoherently.

"When he took the letter, his heart was in Subala's hands, so Subala read it to him. As soon as he'd heard it, he wanted to know where Rādhā was, so he could go to her. He strung a garland of colorful flowers with his own hands and eagerly gave it to Tulasī. 'Hurry, give this garland to her. Don't let her try to drown herself!'

"Meanwhile, Rādhā was pacing up and down, impatiently awaiting her girlfriend's return. 'I'm going to run into the river and end my life. He's not letting me see his lotus eyes. What's the point of keeping this body?'

"Just then Tulasī returned with the garland. She handed it over to Viśākhā, who gave it to Rādhā and told her, 'Listen, dearest friend! Look at this garland that Kṛṣṇa made for you! Put it on.' Rādhā clutched at her heart and put the garland to her eyes, when Kṛṣṇa came out from behind a red hibiscus hedge.

"Their delight knew no bounds, until a *sakhī* warned them that Jaṭilā was on her way. The old woman stormed in and stood there, her face distorted with rage. Startled, the two returned to their respective houses. That very Kṛṣṇa is my Madana Gopāla. I've painted that Gopāla image and brought it here; you've seen the painting and my *Bhāgavata Purāṇa* at my place."

That is the whole story that my lord told when he told us about Madana Gopāla. Now that we've heard the tale of Madana Gopāla, we revere him. In life after life we get that Lord Hari of Vraja.

I've taken my lord Advaita's feet to my heart, and proclaim what I heard from his very mouth. Those whose all is the feet of the lords Caitanya, Nityānanda, and Advaita attain this wealth.

Haricaraṇa Dāsa, whose hope is at the lotus feet of the blessed lord of Shantipur, recites the *Advaita Maṅgala*.

This is chapter 2, "The Appearance of Śrī Madana Gopāla," in book 3, the *Kaiśora Līlā*, in the *Advaita Maṅgala*.

Chapter 3

The Conversation with Mādhavendra Purī and His Dīkṣā

Victory, victory to the glorious Advaita, lord of Sītā's life, who made Rādhā and Kṛṣṇa appear—the lord of Goloka!
Previously they were two, each with a separate body. In Kali Yuga the two are one, come in love.
Victory, victory to my lord's son, full of divine love, at whose command I am enjoined to write.
What he whispered in my ear entered my heart. He lovingly revealed it with his eyes and made me write it.

My lord offered tulasī and rice balls and then returned to Shantipur; he had such tremendous discipline. He would perform austerities in the daytime and preach at night, with his companion Kṛṣṇadāsa who lived beside that holy spot. That Kṛṣṇadāsa dwelled in Kāmya Forest. When he saw what my lord was doing, he came to help. He put out the water vessel and the grass mats himself, and came along with him to the holy site. That brahmin boy was so well-versed in scripture. He remained ever young in my lord's service, worshiping and preaching day and night for ten years. Then my lord, pleased, initiated him as a disciple.

Every day he got up an hour before sunrise and watered my lord's tulasī plant. He brought cool water from the Gaṅgā in the summer, and applied musk and sandal paste to its roots. He sat beneath the tulasī and recited the *Bhāgavata Purāṇa* to the hundreds of people sitting there.

That tulasī was ancient, from the Treta Yuga, but its leaves and blossoms were ever new. Worshiping the fragrant blossoms of that eternal tulasī, my lord served the Gaṅgā and the tulasī. He scattered the blossoms of his tulasī worship far, and a village named Phuliyā sprang up there.

The village of Shantipur became famous for miles. My lord said it was just like his eternal abode of Mathurā. Vaikuṇṭha's Virajā River flowed through Shantipur in three places. Whenever my lord would sit in the gentle current of the Gaṅgā, it was as if he were in the Ocean of Milk.[11]

My lord worshiped the Gaṅgā with fruit and flowers, and roared; Advaita was oblivious to everyone at those times. My lord's flower garden was the village of Phulbāṭī; his wisdom grew like the lilies Kṛṣṇadāsa brought his guru as tuition. My lord took them and offered them into the Gaṅgā one by one.

The splendor of Shantipur cannot be described. The women were Lakṣmī, the men, Viṣṇu, eternally situated there. The kadamba trees, coconuts, and peepul trees are like no others, and their reflections sparkle in the Gaṅgā. The oranges and other wild trees, the champa: people offered all these to my lord as they came before him.

My lord remained silent as he offered them all to the Gaṅgā, and everyone got the results they wanted.

My lord bathed in the Gaṅgā as a child, a youth, a young man, in all twelve months of the year. After his bath he would circumambulate the tulasī and then always bow prostrate before it. He passed many days in such austerities, and then suddenly one day he began to speak.

"Last night I had an interesting dream, that Mādhavendra had come and was sitting right in front of me. He had his servant prepare a place, and spoke immediately to those assembled: 'Offer one rice ball by itself,' Purī had said, 'and you will make me come that very day.'"

So at twilight my lord took his disciples and sat where they could see Purī coming up the road, and soon Mādhavendra Purī arrived. My lord got up to greet him. They embraced, saying, "Kṛṣṇa! Kṛṣṇa! Hari!" with the fitting discussion of divine love.

Purī asked after my lord's health, and my lord replied, "After a long time, I'm finally blessed. I went to Vṛndāvana and roamed around, but nowhere did I find you. I saw the house of a virtuous man at the edge of Govinda Kuṇḍa. His servant told me you had gone back home. But now you've been so compassionate as to come to me here. How long can you stay? Please speak of Kṛṣṇa!"

Purī said, "I had gone home to the south, and from there, came to Govardhana. Madana Gopāla's servant told me about you, so I came here to see you. The lord who lifted Mt. Govardhana appeared as Śrī Gopāla, the absolutely incomparable. In just the same way you revealed Madana Gopāla, Gopāla was revealed at your command. The Govardhanadhārī image of Kṛṣṇa lifting that mountain was installed in Vraja, and once he'd manifested, I promised to maintain his worship. I built Govardhana Temple and installed him in it, and the people of Vraja have been very lovingly worshiping him. He commanded me to bring him cream and sandal paste, hoping I could accomplish both tasks in the same trip."

[11] Viṣṇu reclines on the Cosmic Serpent, floating on the Ocean of Milk, in between cycles of creation.

When my lord heard that Gopāla had appeared, he drowned in bliss. The two men traded news.

Then Purī granted his wish: they sat up all night lost in divine love, meditating on Madana Gopāla's *līlā*. They arose at dawn to perform their morning rituals and sat by the Gaṅgā to discuss scripture.

My lord gave Purī sanctified food cooked with his own hands, and he was thrilled with that *prasāda*. The voracious Purī's usual fee was milk. He recognized my lord's true nature, as he had promised. Even though the practices of Kṛṣṇa devotion are strict about self-control, getting Kṛṣṇa's *prasāda* confers tremendous delight. As long as he remained in Shantipur he accepted food from my lord; elsewhere he would accept only milk.

The two sat by themselves answering each other, overwhelmed in Kṛṣṇa's divine love. My lord asked about Kṛṣṇa, Rādhā, and devotion—all of these, his bliss incomparable.

Purī expressed surprise that my lord, who was Īśvara, wanted him to tell my lord about Kṛṣṇa.

My lord asked that Purī reinitiate him with the proper mantra, and spell out the whole thing. He bestowed the mantra, explaining its meaning in detail. When he spoke of the true nature of Rādhā and Kṛṣṇa, they both saw the (divine) couple.

They spent three days and nights like this in that secluded place. Drunk on divine love, they worshiped Kṛṣṇa. When my lord slipped into Rādhā's *pūrvarāga* state of anticipating meeting her beloved, Purī comforted him.

My lord said, "Let me see Kṛṣṇa all the time! With your *prasāda*, Kṛṣṇa would grant that to everyone. I have a *sakhī*'s heart that you have given me. Your *darśana* tells me that Kṛṣṇa has graced me."

Purī said, "Your devotion will drive you mad. You will accomplish every task that comes your way. I see now that you are that very Kṛṣṇa, that very Rādhā his consort—you are the *avatāra* who epitomizes the (perfect) devotee."

My lord replied, "I have come to introduce Kṛṣṇa worship, because there was no Kṛṣṇa worship in the world. And so, sir, you will see: I will produce Lord Kṛṣṇa-Caitanya, and proclaim him. Then I will worship him, and serve him, and then my heart's desire will be fulfilled."

Purī said, "Īśvara, because of this desire of yours, you will never again cross into mortal birth. The source of all divine manifestations, you are its part; the part has become its source. From the moon you became a moonbeam, and the moonbeam became the moon. As a tree arises from its fruit, and the fruit from its tree, so Brahmā is the source of everything. Until he's 'ripe,' no one understands *bhedābheda*, this philosophy of the undifferentiated in the differentiated. Similarly, Rādhā's affection is strengthened through Kṛṣṇa. How can I speak of all your *līlā*s? You took birth in the Yadu clan, and built a home and a family. Now as a celibate scholar what do you think you can accomplish?"

My lord said, "If you ask me to, I'll get married. I will preach a while longer as an ascetic, and then will do as you wish wholeheartedly. At the end of this Dvāpara Yuga life is full of sin. I will use these austerities to bring in the lord of Vraja. I will rescue everyone with Kṛṣṇa's *saṅkīrtana*. When people hear Kṛṣṇa's name they will be liberated, floating in the Name. At your command Rādhā-Kṛṣṇa fulfilled my longing. Now command me, awaken the Vraja *rasa*! When I took refuge in you, the *rāsa līlā* happened. When I took refuge in you, Vraja appeared. When I took refuge in you, I became dependent on you. You who are self-dependent, disclosed *parakīyā*."

Purī said, "Listen, Kamalākānta-Kṛṣṇa! The path of Rādhikā's love is not self-dependent. Kṛṣṇa's name is Rādhikā's life-support. Kṛṣṇa's true form is identical to Rādhā's. They delight in each other's bodies. The *sakhīs* understand that each is the container of the other's delight. The delights of *rasa* are found in the *parakīyā* sensitivity, with another's woman. With Kṛṣṇa in *svakīyā* as one's own there is (only) the slightest hint of *rasa*. Kṛṣṇa is Svayaṃ Bhagavān, the darling lord of Vraja. Rādhikā is his Hlādinī Śakti, his pleasure-giving principle. If you make them both appear, your delight will be permanent. The (full) significance of the *līlā* lies in the *parakīyā* sensitivity of one who belongs to another. The sensitivities of mother, father, friends, servants—the *līlā* looks different depending on the devotee. In that, I have figured out your purpose. You will make it all appear—I've figured out your intention. In the Kali Yuga, the name is just as strong as sacrifice (used to be). You will proclaim this; I've figured out your whole plan."

My lord replied, "In this age the sixteen names—thirty-two syllables—are the salvation. You explained it in the *Brahmāṇḍa* and *Agni Purāṇas*—these two *purāṇas* prescribe Hari's name.

For,

> Hari's name, Hari's name, Hari's name alone. In Kali Yuga there is no, there is no, there is no other path at all." (*Caitanya Candrodaya Nāṭaka* 1. 73)

Purī replied, "You have revealed the name-sacrifice. I have no interest in leading a normal life with its various stages and responsibilities."

Meanwhile, Kṛṣṇadāsa was worshiping nearby, not saying a word. That devotee steeped in his pride as a servant did not understand; for him, there was no other work. Kṛṣṇadāsa wrote down all this secret material that Śrīnātha Ācārya gave him.

Śrīnātha Ācārya was my lord's best disciple, most assiduous in his scholarship, well-versed in scriptures. Śrīnātha showed mercy to me; I write based on what he taught me. I write now; this world is false and futile; I place my lord Acyutānanda's command upon my head.

Then Purī said, "I've been roaming the world for such a long time. Bid me farewell! I am entirely devoted to you."

My lord replied, "I am the embodied soul and you are Brahmā. You have sanctified me by telling me this mystery."

"Whatever happens," Purī told me, "devotion abides in you, as you wished."

Then my lord circulambulated Purī and touched his feet, saying, "Kṛṣṇa! Kṛṣṇa!" and Purī set off for the south.

Purī had spent two months with my lord. After bidding Purī farewell my lord sat with his rosary. Tradition holds that my lord received initiation at Mādhavendra's place. Thus the teachings were spread.

Whoever listens with devotion to this story worships Rādhā and Kṛṣṇa blissfully with the *dīkṣā* mantra. Take the conversation between Advaita Ācārya and Mādhavendra Purī to heart—this is a blessing.

Whoever places his hope at the lotus feet of Rādhā and Kṛṣṇa is worshiping the feet of his servant Advaita.

Whoever makes the feet of the lords Caitanya, Nityānanda, and Advaita their all will find the treasure of divine love.

A person who turns his back on Advaita cannot have Caitanya's grace; Nityānanda says, "I am no brother of his."

The One is in all three, the three are in the One—one single body.

Haricaraṇa Dāsa, whose hope is at the lotus feet of the lord of Shantipur, recites the *Advaita Maṅgala*.

This is chapter 3, "The Conversation with Mādhavendra Purī and His *dīkṣā*," in book 3, the *Kaiśora Līlā*, in the *Advaita Maṅgala*.

Chapter 4

The Revelation of the Name "Advaita" and the Defeat of the Digvijayī

Previously I praised the glorious lord Caitanya. Praise the glorious lord Nityānanda, his elder brother! I affectionately praise the lotus feet of Lord Advaita. Everyone knows he's no different from Caitanya. The three lords whose forms are (really) Vāsudeva, Saṃkarṣaṇa, and Śrī Kṛṣṇa, are one. This is the real point of the doctrine. One who worships the feet of Advaita with devotion knows the truth about the differences between these three.

I praise the feet of all the devotees listening. Listen, everyone, to "Advaita Revealed."

So much time passed like this, in austerities. The whole world worships at the lord's holy feet.

A southern brahmin came, from Tamil Nadu. He was a great scholar called a "Digvijayī," a conqueror in all directions, who had defeated scholars from all over, north, south, and west. He came to Kāśī, where all the wisest scholars and judges are found, reciting all the scriptures. The Digvijayī made his way to the Viśvanātha

Temple. When he had taken *darśana* of Viśvanātha he asked permission to make a request, and he debated with a pandit there.

The Digvijayī went to the place at Maṇikarṇikā landing where all the pandits were sitting. He sat there for three days and three nights, debating all the scholars in Kāśī. By Viśvanātha's command the Digvijayī won; he was deemed victorious.

After he'd conquered the city of Kāśī, he proceeded to Gauḍa and debated the scholars there. The great pandit got word of an ascetic renunciate and wanted to meet him. By repeated inquiries he found his way to Shantipur to test himself against him.

The midday sun had risen oppressively, but the great scholar Kamalakānta had not arrived. My lord completed his austerities first, then greeted him and sat at the base of the tulasī. Then he elaborated the praises of the tulasī. He described the Gaṅgā as the Pūrṇatara devotee of Kṛṣṇa.

That repugnant speech broke my lord's concentration. "The Gaṅgā is Brahmā in liquid form," he said.

The two men sat on the bench by the tulasī and debated. People said the Digvijayī was the son of Sarasvatī herself.

My lord said, "This Gaṅgā is liquid Brahmā. Nārāyaṇa became liquid to save the three worlds. In heaven it's the Mandākinī, in hell, the Bhogavatī. On earth, this Gaṅgā is actually a form of Viṣṇu. Whoever repeats the name 'Gaṅgā! Gaṅgā!' will be liberated. Say it; you are a natural devotee."

> Whoever says "Gaṅgā! Gaṅgā!" is liberated from all sins, even for thousands of years; he goes to Viṣṇu's heaven. (*Padma Purāṇa*, Uttarakhaṇḍa 22. 9)

My lord continued, "Whoever immerses himself in the Gaṅgā and drinks its water is Kṛṣṇa's devotee, according to scripture."

The Digvijayī rebutted that the formless Brahmā presents a problem. Bit by bit my lord built the case for an embodied god: "The formless Brahmā is no different from Kṛṣṇa. Kṛṣṇa does not see all the people devoted to Brahmā. Even the tiniest portion of his triple-natured soul makes creation occur. Svayaṃ Bhagavān Kṛṣṇa is the best of all. Whomever he shows his grace to, obtains Him. Whoever receives the blessings of Kṛṣṇa as his guru attains those feet."

> One should recognize the Master as me and never treat him disrespectfully nor take him to be a mortal; for the preceptor contains all the gods. (*Bhāgavata Purāṇa* 11. 17. 27)

The Digvijayī accepted his every interpretation, and my lord's deliberations defeated him. The debate had lasted for seven days and nights, and my lord never budged from his seat.

The Digvijayī felt embarrassed, and sadly spoke to Sarasvatī.

Sarasvatī replied in a voice from heaven, "Why are you debating with Lord Advaita?"

Hearing that, the Digvijayī fell at Advaita's feet, sobbing and crying, "Advaita! Advaita! It's true that your name is Kamalākānta, (but) the voice from heaven just called you Advaita Ācārya, Master of Nondualism."

Thus was the name "Advaita" revealed to the world. "You have conquered the world; I am defeated by you." The Digvijayī again made full prostration. My lord said, "You are the victor with regard to all the scriptures."

Such mercy my lord showed him! He placed his hand on his head and blessed him. The Digvijayī was a great, wise scholar. By my lord's grace, he was once again all that. He recognized my lord as Īśvara and praised him profusely. He wrapped his garment around his neck and joined his hands in prayer.

"I have worshiped Sarasvatī for a very long time, and have traveled the wide world three times. Again I sat on the bank of the Gomatī River fasting, performing austerities for seven full weeks. She was pleased and granted me *darśana*, appearing before me as an aged brahmin, and asked me, 'What are you killing yourself for? Study and you'll gain wisdom; think about it and see.'

"But I could not answer her, and fasted for another seven days. Then Sarasvatī appeared right in front of me, playing her *vīṇā*. As our eyes met, I gazed on her feet, absorbed, and fell at them. She placed her blessed hand on my head and said, 'Hey, Brahmin! You will now be a master of every scripture. You—my dear son—will be the victor everywhere, I tell you.' Then I saluted her and fell at her feet, and Sarasvatī then returned to her realm. From that day on, I've roamed at will, debating scripture. I defeated all comers. In Tamil Nadu one scholar was the embodiment of the four Vedas. I admired him, and defeated him. In the city of Avantī one Vyāsa, a renunciate, was on pilgrimage, performing a *vrata*. I spent two whole months debating with him. When he was defeated he signed a statement declaring me the victor. Then I came to Kāśī to debate, and stayed at the Viśvanātha Temple. I worshiped Viśvanātha and prayed for his instructions. I gave him the letter that renunciate I'd defeated had written. Look at these three testimonials you hold before you. I come before you, defeated. Now I realize that you are Nārāyaṇa. Who else could defeat a son of Sarasvatī? Please be so kind as to let me see your true form, and my doubts will be forever dispelled."

My lord replied, "Why say 'Kṛṣṇa' like that; this way everyone knows you are Sarasvatī's son. You took pride in Sarasvatī's boon, and so Nārāyaṇa has broken that pride. I am a renunciate, a brahmin ascetic, who has taken refuge on the bank of the Gaṅgā and settled there. You, the four Vedas incarnate, bless me. The Gaṅgā has shown me mercy and granted (me) devotion to Kṛṣṇa."

The Digvijayī circumambulated[12] my lord repeatedly, making full prostrations and bowing to him. "Listen, Lord Advaita Ācārya! You are truly Nārāyaṇa,

[12] A ritual act of devotion.

I've figured out your purpose. Creation, maintenance and dissolution occur at your command. The eternal cosmic egg comes from you. The luminous Brahmā is your radiance. I have figured it all out, for certain. You came and appeared in the Yadu lineage. You have destroyed evil and rescued creation. I realize that you are that very lord who descends to earth in every age. Sarasvatī spoke to me as a voice from heaven. If you do not grant me *darśana*, I will die right now."

My lord said, "You are no longer proud. You are a scholar, look closely at the devotional texts."

The Digvijayī said, "Command your servant! Take pity on this blind man and deal with (me)."

Then Advaita revealed his four-armed form to him. Fulfilled, the Digvijayī sang his praises. Crying, "Victory, victory to Advaita!" he fell at Advaita's feet, and my lord retracted his four-armed form.

That Digvijayī became a devotee of my lord. He practiced dispassion—he was absolutely the best.

And that is the tale of my lord's defeat of the Digvijayī who revealed his name as Advaita. Advaita was revealed as nondifferent from Kṛṣṇa. He became a scholar and proclaimed the scripture(s) of devotion.

The Ācārya had another aim, as revealed by order of Svayaṃ Bhagavān in the scriptures. For,

> One should recognize the Master as me and never treat him disrespectfully nor take him to be a mortal; for the preceptor contains all the gods. (*Bhāgavata Purāṇa* 11. 17. 27)

Kṛṣṇa was revealed to be the scholar who saved the whole world with the Kṛṣṇa mantra. The illustrious Advaita Ācārya became the mantra-guru. Lord Nityānanda, the other "lord," is to be equally revered.

One who witnesses Mahāprabhu's compassion attains Rādhā-Kṛṣṇa, so pay attention!

He who does not consider the three lords one is just an infidel. The One is in all three; in the One is no differentiation among the three. This apportionment has occurred for His eternal pleasure.

Praise, Brother, praise Advaita Gosvāmī, from whom we got Nitāi and Lord Caitanya. He got the Vraja-*dhāma*, this is again Rādhā-Kṛṣṇa's domain. In particular he waits on Rādhā-Kṛṣṇa during their lovemaking.

May I attain the feet of the lord of Shantipur—my lord—in birth after birth. The kindness that my lord Advaita, Sītā, and their children have shown me has fulfilled my desires. I have committed my life to the feet of Rādhā-Kṛṣṇa. I've wandered through many lives and yet remain fallen. Fit for service in the groves of Vṛndāvana by your mercy, I am completely healed.

Haricaraṇa Dāsa whose hope is at the lotus feet of the lord of Shantipur recites the *Advaita Maṅgala*.

This is chapter 4, "The Revelation of the Name Advaita and the Defeat of the Digvijayī," in book 3—the *Kaiśora Līlā*—of the *Advaita Maṅgala*.

Book 4

Chapter 1

The Theology Described in the Conversation with Kṛṣṇadāsa

Victory to my lord Advaita, compassion itself, who brought in Mahāprabhu, the abundance of *rasa*. Affectionately I will praise my lord's sons, by whose mercy the *līlā* was revealed.

I proclaim and praise the feet of Kṛṣṇadāsa and the other devotees, unparalleled in *rasa*; I saw that very Kṛṣṇadāsa's notebook and heard the specifics from Śrīnātha Ācārya.

My lord's innate *līlā* is infinite; who has the power to describe it?

Listen a bit: I'm writing of his "youth" activities. The fourth book tells of those games. Everyone, listen to the verses of the fourth book. I bless Kṛṣṇadāsa who told it all.

He explained his actual true form, and named Haridāsa "Brahmā." He revealed the worship of Rādhā-Kṛṣṇa's bower, and more. I'll tell it all, thanks to his sons.

Everyone, pay attention, please listen to me! Brahmācārī Kṛṣṇadāsa worshiped so assiduously!

One day Kṛṣṇadāsa had been worshiping intensely. Pleased, my lord said, "Kṛṣṇadāsa, Kṛṣṇa has great mercy on you; whatever you ask, I'll grant you, I promise. Your worship has made the guru one with Kṛṣṇa. There's nothing more I can tell you."

Kṛṣṇadāsa fell down like a stick and joined his hands in prayer. "Dispel my doubts! Tell it all! I have seen your four-armed form many times. Say the name 'Vṛndāvana' and save my life! You blather on as a *sakhī* of Rādhikā. Everyone knows you as Īśvara. You are a natural devotee," said Kṛṣṇadāsa. "Please tell me about him."

My lord laughed and replied, "Listen, Kṛṣṇadāsa. Let's sit down in private and I'll tell it all. You know it all, but lately you've forgotten. I'll just remind you."

Sitting privately the pair discussed it all, from alpha to omega, delighting in their blessed memories.

"Had you not seen my four-armed form you would never be convinced, and that's why I revealed myself as Vasudeva's son. Some say (I am) Nārāyaṇa, lord of Vaikuṇṭha. Some say (I am) best known as Vāsudeva. Some say (I am) Mahaviṣṇu, lying in the Ocean of Milk. Some say (I am) Īśvara Sadāśiva. Kṛṣṇa takes the form of his every wish. Everything is possible for him; it's no surprise. He takes the form appropriate to the devotee. This is the lord's work: he reveals various forms.

"I'm telling you the truth! Listen carefully. Vāsudeva was born in Vasudeva's house. Kṛṣṇa, darling lord of Vraja, is Svayaṃ Bhagavān. The part and its container are one—that's his plan. Pūrṇatama, the most complete, is Kṛṣṇa who sports with Rādhikā. And Pūrṇatara the more complete is Vāsudeva who enacts the mood of friendship. So that Pūrṇatara—there's no difference. They became one and play out the Vraja *līlā* eternally. And so I tell you—listen carefully! As Pūrṇatama the most complete he sports with Rādhikā.

"When it's time for worship, that same Kṛṣṇa became Pūrṇatara, the more complete. As a *sakhī* he worships most intimately. He serves Rādhā and Kṛṣṇa most intimately as Rādhikā's youngest *sakhī*.

"Kṛṣṇa is the lord of my life, so I'm telling you that serving Rādhā and Kṛṣṇa is my treasure. The youngest girl has great affection for Rādhikā and is her eternal servant in the amorous *līlā*. In that regard, my *svarūpa*—my real form—is Rādhikā's *sakhī* Sampūrṇā Mañjarī. As Kṛṣṇa's male companion I take the name of Ujjvala. I am that Ujjvala, *rasa* personified, who assists the love play of Rādhā and Kṛṣṇa."

Kṛṣṇadāsa says "There are Vāsudeva, Rādhā, and her girlfriend. That's clear. But I have one remaining point of confusion: How can he possibly be in Vraja when he's someplace else at the same time?

In reply, my lord recited a verse, explaining the matter through the Vedas.

For (49. 2)—(text missing). And in another Purāṇa: (text missing)

"How is it possible for Kṛṣṇa to have Icchāśakti, the power of desire? He becomes a *sakhī* by mere desire and worships night and day. This philosophy I'm expounding is that Kṛṣṇa's handmaiden Rādhā is the treasure of Vraja. Kṛṣṇa accomplishes everything through his *svarūpa*, his true form. As Rādhikā's *sakhī* he behaves like a servant. Rādhikā's love defies description, and it drives Svayaṃ Bhagavān Kṛṣṇa. He has come here to experience Rādhikā's love, to awaken the mood of devotion. The reason I have come to earth is to taste the love of Rādhā and Kṛṣṇa. When I got here, I found it devoid of devotion, and so I have undertaken lengthy austerities. If, as Kṛṣṇa, I reveal the whole reason I've come, oh my! It's no small matter.

"And so I am performing austerities on the bank of the Gaṅgā so that I can bring in his parents, Nanda and Yaśodā. I will make Balarāma appear in Rohiṇī's womb, and finally I will bring Kṛṣṇa to the city of Nadīyā. I will make the couple Rādhā-Kṛṣṇa appear as a single individual. Listen carefully! *Sakhas*, *sakhīs*—the whole eternal retinue—will appear in one house after another. Bringing the devotional mood, nearly all the companions will appear in their true forms. All the committed devotees from other realms will appear, following those of Vraja. Any low, miserable, poor people will certainly attain Rādhā and Kṛṣṇa, and arrogant haughty devotionless people will surely find hell.

"According to all the scriptures, the devotion of his devotees is dear to Kṛṣṇa. Devotion arises to destroy the pain of worldly existence. I will preach the love of Rādhā and Kṛṣṇa and will continue my austerities for some time. I will rescue the world through the 'sacrifice'[13] of devotional singing. I will make Rādhā and Kṛṣṇa a single being, and savor them. Then will my name of Advaita—not two—be fulfilled. I will bring the playboy of Vraja right here to the earth.

"And when I've brought him I will attend him as his servant to accomplish my mission. I will be delighted to serve Rādhā and Kṛṣṇa in their eternal loveplay. In this Kali Yuga the mood of devotion is the promise, and so I will make him descend as a devotee. I've promised everywhere to make him appear. If I kept it secret, no one would know."

With that, my lord returned to his austerities, and Kṛṣṇadāsa bowed and returned to his worship. My lord was merciful to Kṛṣṇadāsa in telling this, and by Kṛṣṇadāsa's grace, I can reveal it. For the sake of the theology Kṛṣṇa's *svarūpa*, his true form, is unique, but that same Kṛṣṇa sports with three forms. Anyone who differentiates among those three forms will be called a heretic, and totally ruined.

Kṛṣṇadāsa recorded what he'd heard straight from my lord Advaita, and I know all his writing.

Haricaraṇa Dāsa, whose hopes are at the lotus feet of the lord of Shantipur, recites the *Advaita Maṅgala*.

This is chapter 1, "The Theology Described in the Conversation with Kṛṣṇadāsa," in book 4, *Yauvana-līlā*, in the *Advaita Maṅgala*.

Chapter 2

The Revelation of Haridāsa and the Conversation about the Lord's Māyā

I praise my lord Advaita, lord of the helpless. I praise his sons, famous throughout the world.
I praise holy Shantipur, site of my lord's activities, and I respectfully praise the devotees.

Sītā's lord's *līlā* is so vast that not even Brahmā and the other gods can fathom it.

I am a worthless wretch, so how can I know about it? I'm going to write what Acyutānanda wrote. Acyutānanda is the touchstone; his touch turns iron to gold. I don't have the power to touch that! My heart is hard and my mind sinful, but I'm writing at his command. He is an *aṃśa*—a part—of Kṛṣṇa, as everyone knows.

Everyone, listen to another amazing tale: how Haridāsa Ṭhākura came to earth.

[13] A slur on the old Vedic method of elaborate ritual sacrifice. Now *kīrtana* does the job.

Advaita would roar out while he was worshiping the goddess Gaṅgā, and the gods and sages in heaven heard that roar. No one knew why he was performing austerities, so Indra and the other gods decided to bring him to their heavenly realm.

The gods created and sent an *āpsarasa*, a heavenly nymph, who tried very hard to disturb his meditation. She appeared and danced in front of the tulasī plant but could not break my lord's concentration, though she tried for a very long time. Everyone burst out laughing when they saw my lord; they laughed and laughed.

The *āpsarasa* danced for seven straight nights. No one can resist that divine dance! No one can withstand its divine splendor. She stayed on his left,[14] dancing as is her nature. Seven nights passed, and still my lord continued his meditation. He knew what the gods were up to, and just smiled.

The gods smiled and said, their hands joined, "Command us! We come before you ready to obey."

He glanced up angrily as soon as he heard them, so the *āpsarasa* was able to carry him on the wind to the assembly of the gods.

The gods asked why he had come. He told the whole story with bent head. He knew that if he went before them politely, he could not fail. "How can I fulfill my purpose? Please listen, O Gods. When you saw my angry look, you brought me on the wind to your assembly. You revived me to make me watch your singing and dancing. No human can watch it and survive. Do your duty, O Gods!"

Then all the gods approached Brahmā and bowed to him, their hands joined in supplication. Brahmā said, "Why have you all come here at once?"

Indra, the destroyer of strongholds, replied on behalf of all the gods, "A radiant human being is performing severe austerities by the Gaṅgā on earth. He's reciting the Name as he worships, roaring again and again. That roar has pierced heaven, and reached the gods' abode. I am afraid, he's doing everything so carefully, and no one can disturb his practice. No one does such austerities in the Kali Age! He's going to be able to enslave the gods![15] That's why we've all come to you. Do something! This is a crisis!"

Brahmā said, "Listen, Gods, fear not! Let's all go and take his shelter. Take birth on earth as human beings and serve him lovingly. Start spreading the practice of the Name for Kali Yuga. Nārāyaṇa has come down from his heaven of Vaikuṇṭha. *Aṃśa/aṃśī*, the part and the whole, will all descend at the signal of at his roar. I have commanded: Go to earth! Even I will worship that Supreme Being, and I will myself take human birth."

With that he bid the gods farewell, and each one took birth on earth. Brahmā was born in a low-caste home. From childhood the only nourishment he would take was milk. His mother died in childbirth, and a neighbor lady took the boy in.

[14] Just as a bride sits to her groom's left at a wedding.

[15] Austerities confer power and may make their practitioner even stronger than the gods.

When he was five he came to Shantipur and went to my lord's—that ocean of mercy—place. He kept his distance, bowing again and again.

My lord said, "My Haridāsa, you have come! I recognize you as Brahmā Haridāsa. Your lotus lips will preach His Name. Praise Lord Kṛṣṇa! Take Kṛṣṇa's Name! Kṛṣṇa will quickly show you His mercy."

Then Haridāsa said, his hands joined in supplication, "I'm from a low-caste family. How can you say such things?"

My lord smiled and said, "Listen, Haridāsa! I'll tell you the reason. Listen and believe. Kṛṣṇa appeared in Vraja as a cowherd boy, and sang hymns by the river. No one who sees his unworldly *līlā* can understand it, and to confuse people, that child stole things. So Kṛṣṇa was everyone's child and everyone looked after the boy. He went into every single house, great or small, with his friends, and drank their milk. In the middle of one such exploit the pest that you were swore at him, you mean boy! For that offense you lost caste and were born in a low family. Now concentrate on worshiping Kṛṣṇa, and spread the practice of the Name in Kali Yuga."

Haridāsa replied, "I don't know anything at all. I will obey whatever order you give. Your roar cracked Brahmā's ribs. You have brought me here; now teach me. Be so kind as to bestow on me the Name. What other purpose can there be but the Name?"

Haridāsa sat listening under the tulasī dais as my lord explained the mantra systematically.

"Hare Kṛṣṇa Hare Kṛṣṇa Kṛṣṇa Kṛṣṇa Hare Hare
Hare Rāma Hare Rāma Rāma Rāma Hare Hare

These sixteen names, thirty-two syllables, constitute the great mantra. Rādhā and Kṛṣṇa and their companions, male and female, are the whole system.

"The syllable '*ha*' and the color yellow—the best of all the colors. The syllable '*ha*' burns a sin, committed ignorantly or knowingly, in an instant.

"The syllable '*re*' is the color red, chosen by Gopāla. The syllable '*re*' burns a sin committed by an elder in an instant.

"The syllable '*kṛ*' is the color of lampblack. The syllable '*kṛ*' instantly overpowers the god of love and his wife Rati and immobilizes them.

"The syllable '*ṣṇa*' in its different forms is widely praised. The second he pronounced the syllable '*ṣṇa*' Dhruva was saved from hell. The syllable '*ṣṇa*' instantly burns off even sin accumulated in a hundred lifetimes.

"And the syllable '*ra*' is the color white; the power of the *rasa* is indestructible in the world. It shines like the sun and the moon, and can burn through great darkness in an instant.

"And the syllable '*ma*' has the form of pure light. The syllable '*ma*' instantly burns sin committed by lying. May it reflect the sixteen names on the entire body of the glorious Rādhā-Kṛṣṇa.

"And here is the whole list of his female companions: Lalitā and Viśākhā and Citrā and Campakalatā; Raṅgadevī and Sudevī, Tuṅgavidyā, Indurekhikā, Śaśīrekhā and Vimalā, Pālikā, Anaṅgā Mañjarī, Śyāmalā, Madhumatī Devī and Dhanyā and Maṅgalā. Rādhikā is primary among them.

"And a separate list: Śrīdāmā and Sudāmā and Vasudāmā, and further, both Subala and Arjuna, Kiṅkinī and Stokakṛṣṇaka; Varutha and Aṃśumān, Vṛṣari and Vṛṣabha; Devaprastha and Uddhava, Mahābāhu and Mahābala.

"Listen to these: Kṛṣṇacandra has many companions. These thirty-two male and female companions constitute the Rādhā-Kṛṣṇa mantra. Hari's name is the great mantra, the essence of his esoteric doctrine. Recite this day and night; it is the supreme doctrine."

Then Haridāsa built a tulasī platform and carved out a cave beside the Gaṅgā. He sat in it and recited the name three hundred thousand times. In this way he became skilled in worship.

In Shantipur my lord performed his Vedic rituals according to tradition. That venerable man fed Haridāsa lovingly. So all the people started gossiping, "The venerable master is feeding a Muslim!" Four classes of people live in the town of Shantipur, and all the brahmins are above reproach.

Some say "the Ācārya is a powerful ascetic."[16] Some say "the Ācārya is the mighty Īśvara." Some say "the Ācārya has lived a very long time. What will befall us if we offend him! The scholar has gone crazy, he's always proud; if we speak ill of Haridāsa he goes crazy."

Then Haridāsa said to my lord, "This isn't fair! You're behaving improperly! People can't understand Īśvara's doings. I'll accept the blame so they don't fault you."

My lord smiled and said, "Listen, Haridāsa! They *will* eat and drink freely in your presence. Tomorrow at dawn you will perform the fire ceremony and reveal something of your own power. Unless they see your true nature, people won't understand. Foolish children do not understand righteousness and responsibility."

The next morning, no house in the whole town had any fire, and when they brought it in from the next town, it went out immediately. The ritual brahmins could not start their fires. Without food, their children and elders were starting to suffer. The entire day passed, and then it was twilight. All the children and the elderly humbly approached Advaita and threw themselves at his feet.

"Please forgive our offense at your house. We fools did not realize you are the lord of Vaikuṇṭha, and we all have suffered for our verbal abuse. Forgive this insult and restore our fires. Today we have learned our lesson. Now please give us back our lives!"

[16] Cf. IV.1.

My lord replied, "You people are ritual brahmins. Someone, recite the Vedas and the dharma literature. If you speak righteously you will always have fire. Take grass in your mouths as a sign of your humiliation and then light your fires."

One brahmin caught on quickly and immediately made everyone put grass in their mouths. Without food a virtuous brahmin perishes.

My lord said, "Listen! Perform the fire ceremony publicly. You spoke ill of Haridāsa out of ignorance. The consequence of that, you've seen for yourselves, for Haridāsa is actually Brahmā. Go to him, all of you, you'll get your proper fire."

When they arrived at Haridāsa's cave they all ritually circumambulated him and spoke very respectfully. "Please restore our lives today, give us our fire! Forgive our sin, we were all ignorant."

Haridāsa replied compassionately. "As soon as you give me the grass, I'll give you the fire."

They brought the grass and offered it to Haridāsa, and as the four-faced Brahmā he produced fire in all four directions.

"Victory, victory to Haridāsa!" everyone cried, and carried the fire home. From that day on, they all sang Haridāsa's praises.

Before they had seen his might, foolish folk had no respect for him. Thus he revealed himself publicly, as a promise. My lord enacted many other dramas with Haridāsa. No one could possibly write them all down.

I am a miserable creature and have written this; at my lord's order I watched and listened, and then wrote it down.

Who could describe my lord's endless dramas! They are proclaimed throughout the four directions. By whom could such deeds be proclaimed? Īśvara himself enacts his esoteric dramas.

Haricaraṇa Dāsa whose hope lies at the feet of the lord of Shantipur recites the *Advaita Maṅgala*.

This is chapter 2, called "The Revelation of Haridāsa and the Conversation about the Lord's Māyā" in book 4—the *Yauvana Līlā*—in the *Advaita Maṅgala*.

Chapter 3

The Description of Śyāmadāsa's Branch and the Disappearance

I praise the illustrious Advaita, lord of Sītā's life, who brought in Mahāprabhu, Govinda himself.

Praise the lady Sītā and Mother Śacī! Everyone praise her son, who is my salvation.

Praise Śyāmadāsa, his main confidant. His *kīrtana* delighted everyone around my lord.

Salutations at the feet of my lord's assembled disciples, by whose mercy I record the magnitude of his activities.

One day Advaita was dancing, engrossed in *kīrtana*, in Shantipur. He was Madana Mohana playing in Holy Vṛndāvana. Rādhikā took him into her warm embrace. Their love flowed well into the night. "Sing! Sing!" my lord commanded Śyāmadāsa.

Śyāmadāsa recognized that he had taken on the mood of Vāsudeva, the playboy of Vṛndāvana, with Rādhikā. Again and again my lord turned into his heart to sing. Late in the night, something amazing happened.

Śyāmadāsa paused in the *kīrtana* and lovingly fanned my lord. Shouting the names of Kṛṣṇa and Rādhā aloud, crying "Śyāma" quietly, my lord horripilated, quivering like a kadamba bud; his entire body ached. He kept falling in and out of consciousness, and began to cry out, "Alas! Rādhā! Gopāla!"

When Śyāmadāsa grabbed his hand to rouse him, Advaita thought he was seeing Rādhā and Kṛṣṇa dancing joyfully together. "When they finish dancing, I will dance, and the couple will be very pleased. The way Rādhā and Kṛṣṇa move, that charming stance with its three angles, pleases the eye and mind. It's delightful! Rādhikā put her flower-bud earring on Kṛṣṇa's ear to tell him more. As soon as he touched Rādhikā's lotus face Kṛṣṇa danced with great joy. Rādhā gave him a sidelong glance and laughed. 'Śyāma, Śyāma,' I said over and over. Smiling, then Rādhikā looked toward me. Touching Śyāma's feet I seated the pair. Then I worshiped the couple. Rādhā said, 'Sampūrṇā, you've kept Kṛṣṇa's name.' Chatting like this the pair went to a hut in the bower. I brought them betel nut and a blanket."

As he spoke, my lord's mood was innocent. People who saw this wondered at his affectionate nature. As he became aware of his surroundings he would babble. All his disciples worshiped at his feet.

Śyāmadāsa said, "My lord, what are you telling me—that you were worshiping in the bower in Vṛndāvana? For so long I've known the greatness of your mercy! Through this love I've realized the importance of your worship."

My lord said, "I had a crazy dream that I was worshiping Madana Gopāla in Vṛndāvana. He wouldn't let me stay in Vṛndāvana, but (told me to) preach his worship. By the time I revealed him, I had been worshiping on the banks of the Yamunā for a long time. He remained there, promising to reappear, and sent me back here."

As soon as he'd said that, my lord slipped into a state of *prema*, divine love, and he made us aware of everything.

When he first met the learned Śyāmadāsa he lovingly told him the whole story. The learned Śyāmadāsa was a very respectable brahmin from RāṚha. He recited scripture meticulously, but the devotional texts had no place in his heart. Wherever he roamed he would debate, knowing all the scriptures, but in devotion found his defeat. He knew the *gāyatrī* mantra, Mother of the Vedas, and performed austerities, and had been a very successful astrologer.

Then he went to Kāśī to the temple of Viśvanātha, the lord of the universe. Śiva noticed his zealousness and took pity on him, and told him everything that night in a dream:

"Why are you suffering like this here? Kṛṣṇa is nearby; go to him! You are reciting devotional texts like the *Bhāgavata Purāṇa* but you don't understand them. Look to your own kinsmen. You recite astrological texts; look at the horoscope and see: you will find Nārāyaṇa lord of Vaikuṇṭha in Shantipur. Go serve him, and by his grace your knowledge will flourish."

And then he woke up, and sitting there, he began to draw up the horoscope. Śiva's order was for him to go to Shantipur, and the horoscope confirmed that. Accordingly, he made his way to Shantipur, where he found the learned man deeply focused on his austerities. How long he kept up those austerities, without interruption! It defies description! He lovingly anointed the holy tulasī shrub with flowers from every village. He brought fragrant flowers and applied sandal paste, consecrated them to my lord, and sent them away in the current. The flowers floated upriver to arrive at my lord's feet, where he had been lovingly worshiping for many days.

But even then he did not break his concentration as he preached the meaning of the *Bhāgavata Purāṇa*. Finally, though, my lord interrupted his meditation to ask his particulars, and Śyāmadāsa fell at his feet.

My lord said, "Who are you and where are you from? Stay here and worship."

"Have pity on me and explain the *Bhāgavata Purāṇa*. Clearly you are Īśvara! I am your servant in birth after birth. Please be so kind as to teach me and correct my thinking."

My lord said, "What are you reciting? Tell me. You sound like some barnyard animal!"

Then by my lord's grace he recited the *Bhāgavata Purāṇa*; he'd lost his mind searching for devotion. He touched his feet and began. "Roaming here and there—I have come to you. Viśvanātha told me about your teachings. He told me how great they all are. Now please have mercy and grant me the *dīkṣā* mantra, by which one crosses the ocean of worldly existence."

He complied and bestowed the Kṛṣṇa mantra, and then explained it. "The four devotional attitudes are friendship, servitude, affection, and love," the learned man explained. "The deepest *līlā* of Vraja is the worship of Rādhā and Kṛṣṇa."

They sat in a quiet place and discussed this day and night. Then he explained his own *svarūpa*. His expertise in the devotional texts is tremendous; he never loses a debate. With Śyāmadāsa's initiation he performed austerities, and Śyāmadāsa served him with inner delight. At the same time Śyāmadāsa composed a poem in eight verses. He set its meter and began to recite.

(text missing)

Śyāmadāsa composed that poem—such ardent service as he praised my lord!

Many days passed in this manner, my lord's meditation interrupted only to discuss devotion. He stayed in Shantipur working on his *bhakti* commentary (to the *Bhāgavata Purāṇa*). Days and nights passed; no one had anticipated this. There was Govinda, Murāri the gentle; they performed the customary rituals. Puruṣottama Pandit's branch spread far and wide; Kāmadeva was the second one so steeped in *rasa*. These were both my lord's disciples in Purī-Nīlācala. They came and went on their own; no one knew. In keeping with the love of Rādhā and Kṛṣṇa they rescued people. Both, infused with Śakti, blessed people. Both worshiped with the attitude of friendship. My lord gave his blessing. Both were well-versed in *bhakti* scriptures. They conquered all creation with their devotion.

In Kali Yuga Mahāprabhu conquered the world through his two generals who were the Bird Garuḍa incarnate: Vāsudeva Datta and Śrī Yadunandana, his disciple Raghunātha Dāsa the great. Master Yadunandana was a great object of my lord's mercy; because of my lord's grace they saw all the scriptures.

And the description of the *svarūpa*:

(text missing)

I've already written about how Master Yadunandana described it. I wrote about how he got such devotion. I'll describe his *svarūpa* in another several verses.

Vāsudeva Datta was my lord's intimate. His life story is a wave of love. Thus he would converse with his disciples. Days and nights passed, and he didn't know the difference.

I've spoken a bit about his branch; Pañcānana-Śiva even with all five mouths could not say how far it reaches. I will list all his sons and disciples below. What we've said about Śyāmadāsa is well-known.

At the head of all these great men is Śyāmadāsa, and my lord revealed the scriptures to him. Śyāmadāsa served my lord a long time as an accomplished devotee.

Haricaraṇa Dāsa, whose hopes are at the lotus feet of the lord of Shantipur, recites the *Advaita Maṅgala*.

This is chapter 4, the description of Śyāmadāsa's branch and the disappearance, in book 4, the *Yauvana Līlā* of the *Advaita Maṅgala*.

Chapter 4

The Conversation with Śrīnātha and Description of Rūpa's and Sanātana's Mercy

I praise the glorious lord Advaita, the sole resort of the helpless. He rescued the souls of the Kali Yuga through *prema-bhakti*.

Praise his children, Sītā's complete mercy. I lovingly praise that devotee; he glows like the full moon.

In his youth my lord Advaita performed austerities. Sometimes he would discuss devotion, sometimes he would interpret it. Once he went to the south. Living in Shantipur he bathed and performed oblations in the Gaṅgā. Delighting in *rasa* with the devotees, he revealed the same *līlā* in his old age as in his youth.

I'll tell about his old age in book 5; as an old man and as a youth, his language was the same. I've laid it all out in these chapters. I said he married Sītā at an advanced age. I was old myself when she commanded me to marry. I'll tell you elsewhere about his life after marriage as an old man; I'm still writing about his younger years, prior to his marriage. Śyāmadāsa was very concerned that he marry.

Here I will describe the arrival of Śrīnātha Ācārya, who headed one of the large branches of my lord's followers. Earlier, when my lord had traveled to the South, he had met Śrīnātha and his great crowd of disciples. Śrīnātha was the most important scholar there, blessing the South with unequaled compassion.

One day my lord was sitting with the disciples, glowing like the moon of Shantipur, when Śrīnātha Ācārya appeared. My lord said, "All my efforts will now bear fruit."

Śrīnātha approached and bowed before him, and my lord took his hand and embraced him. He asked after his welfare, and Śrīnātha replied, "This is the *darśana* of Lord Kṛṣṇa's blessed feet."

My lord said, "The king of Gauḍa went to your country. His several sons have a part in your king's story." Śrīnātha told everyone to listen as he began to tell the story.

"Initially the king made great efforts, but the king of Gauḍa defeated him in battle. Once he'd subjugated the whole realm, he killed everyone in the king's capital city. The prince was killed in the great battle. His three sons fled to relatives in different places. Sanātana and Rūpa ended up at my house. (Their younger brother) Vallabha remained, king of the mountain. My lord's great rule was righteous and wise; the Deccan is our ancestral home. Now my lord had gone there by God's will. How can you treat him so rudely?"

My lord says, "A kingdom's territory is never fixed. If you've been graced by God, then leave that domain. No earthly king lives forever. Kingdoms like Māndhātā's are all gone. Tell the whole story of Sanātana and Rūpa: what they did and where they stayed."

Śrīnātha said, "I was their family priest. As boys they were very unusual. I taught both of them *alaṃkāra*, grammar, Vedānta, and *Bhāgavata Purāṇa*—many things! I gave them the Kṛṣṇa mantra at the bank of the Gaṅgā and carefully presented the devotional scriptures. Śrīvallābhā had brought his kinsmen here; they had been at court before they came here to my place. The king of Gauḍa had taken kindly to them and recruited the two brothers into his service. Soon both had become wise ministers, performing their duties. Look: they're ever young. They worked hard at their official duties. Both were like great renunciates. If you would show them compassion, they would cross the ocean of worldly existence and find salvation."

Hearing that, my lord replied to Śrīnātha, "There's a lot of work for these two servants of Kṛṣṇa to do. Haridāsa has preached the name-worship in the east. These two will spread devotion in the west."

Śrīnātha said, "O King! They were part of a large administration. Now that they've fallen from power they are dependent on us. What else will you do? Tell me truly. What work like this can we do?"

"Listen, Śrīnātha, you're one of Kṛṣṇa's people. By your mercy His grace will fall to them. I revealed Madana Gopāla in Vraja. I'll teach Sanātana to worship him and turn that task over to him. His younger brother is very intelligent. I can give him a lot of tasks for which he's skilled. He will reveal Śrī Govinda, and after that, many other things. There's never any distinction between those two eternal servants. I'm staying for ten days. Look how awareness of Kṛṣṇa is spreading! These two by their kindness will bless everyone for whom I will bring in Kṛṣṇa Caitanya. I will bring Śrī Rādhā and Kṛṣṇa to earth! Have no doubts! You will see this for yourselves very soon. He who is to be worshiped is always mine. I will accomplish my every obligation through him. I have come to taste unalloyed devotion; as a devotee I will know Rādhā-Kṛṣṇa's loving devotion. Through them I will do it all; look! How long! Have no doubts!

"Fix your mind firmly! When I went east to see Jagannātha, I met Mukunda. Mukundadeva Rājā was a leading scholar there, and treated me most hospitably. He came to meet me every day while I was in Purī. Listening to the deep meaning of the *Bhāgavata Purāṇa* I horripilated and rolled on the ground.

"Mukunda Deva asked me what Rādhā would have done, had she been the one abandoned in the *rāsa-līlā*. The eternal heroine, the eternal hero. He accepted her as *parastrī*—another's woman. If someone becomes Īśvara to make everyone his Śakti, that Śakti does not continue to participate in the human drama. I proceeded to expound on that, and as he heard (me speak), Deva Rāja was thrilled.

"Rādhā left the *rāsa* dance for a tryst in the bower. Were they not in private their love could not be realized. There the always timid Parastrī saw his majesty but did not realize this was Īśvara. 'The lord of my life will take me to a private place where we will make love. We'll stay there until our elders come.'

"With a *parastrī*, another's woman, love is ever new. It's not like that with *svakīya*, one's own woman. Revealing the attitude of another's man and another's woman as one's own eternal beloved, going to a secluded place to make love, that Kṛṣṇa, that Rādhā, marvelous, entire; their Vraja *līlā* is the essence of *mādhurya*, erotic sweetness. The essence of *mādhurya* is Rādhā's alone. The *mādhurya* Kṛṣṇa creates is very rare. Kṛṣṇa and countless cowherd maidens danced in the *rāsa līlā*, and not a one knew that Kṛṣṇa was with Rādhā.

"For that reason I say, 'Listen you scholars! The many *līlās* created through refuge in Yogamāyā: When Kṛṣṇa performs the *rāsa līlā*, the cowherd maidens don't know him. Yogamāyā does it all in various forms. The wisdom of the *parastrī* practice lies in the power of Yogamāyā. A husband has no desire for the woman who is near at hand.'

"For,

> Indeed, enchanted by Kṛṣṇa's magic the men of Vraja were not at all envious, thinking their wives were by their sides. (*Bhāgavata Purāṇa* 10.33.38)

"His every deed reveals Īśvara's power. He works through Yogamāyā, it has nothing to do with worldly power. The great *rāsa līlā* is Kṛṣṇa's greatest *mādhurya.* No one else knows; only the devotees know. The manifester became the manifestation and indulged in amorous activity. The manifester and the manifestation are actually a single form. The part and the whole have separate names, but the manifestation is unitary. All the Vedas proclaim that the manifestation is undivided.

(text missing)

"Kṛṣṇa's *mādhurya līlā* is the erotic play in Vraja, extended to his mother and father and his male and female companions. He dances through his eternal *līlā* in human form, for the human body is the container of *rasa*. His mother says, 'Kṛṣṇa is my son.' His friends say, 'Kṛṣṇa is my friend.' His girlfriends say, 'Kṛṣṇa is my beloved.' This *līlā* is the best of all, that's certain.

"Kṛṣṇa performs his Vraja *līlā*, ever new. Rādhā-Kṛṣṇa don't know this, nor do the cowherd maidens.[17] For this reason, everything is Yogamāyā. Of its own accord the three kinds of karma become those three. As Yogamāyā he experiences everything. Then as Paurṇamāsī he arranges their trysts.

"Rādhikā's girlfriend Kanakā Sundarī is described in the *purāṇas* as Ādyāśakti."

(missing citation from *Padma Purāṇa*)

"There is much evidence for this in the *purāṇas*. Yogamāyā enabled everything Kṛṣṇa did. In this way Kṛṣṇa's desires were fulfilled. Rādhā-Kṛṣṇa revealed all his *līlās*. I've said all this, having heard it from Mukunda. From time to time I asked questions of that great lake of *rasa*.

"Then I touched his feet and took my leave. I had very much enjoyed talking with him. He was a singular devotee of Kṛṣṇa's. His son Kumāra Deva was another. There will never be another scholar like Mukunda. Sanātana and Rūpa were his grandsons. These two will be your students in Vaiṣṇavism. Kindly preach to them."

"Master, rest assured that I will awaken their Śakti. Don't worry." Then Śrīnātha fell at his feet and bade him farewell.

"I've stayed in Shantipur living with my lord for a month, telling everyone many intimate tales."

[17] Cf. *Caitanya Caritāmṛta* 1.4.27.

Then Śrīnātha wrote and sent a letter to Gauḍa. The two brothers received the letter and proclaimed its contents: "Don't worry a bit. The two of you have a great reputation for kindness."

What I've said here is my lord's amazing tale. Whoever hears it reaches my lord's feet. My lord preaches the greatness of those devotees who know Rādhā-Kṛṣṇa's private *līlā*. He taught everyone their respective tasks to generate kindness and affection among the devotees.

Haricaraṇa Dāsa, whose hopes are at the lotus feet of the lord of Shantipur, recites the *Advaita Maṅgala*.

This ends chapter 4, called "The Conversation with Śrīnātha and the Description of Rūpa's and Sanātana's Mercy," in book 4, the *Yauvana Līlā*, in the *Advaita Maṅgala*.

Book 5

Chapter 1

The Lord's Marriage

Victory, victory to Lord Advaita, the only resort of the hopeless, who summoned
Mahāprabhu with his roar.
I praise the lady Sītā, my lord's Śakti. I praise her sons with devotion.

Over and over I praise the blessed feet of my guru. By his grace my *līlā* has bloomed.

Now I will write about my lord's activities in his old age, in what I have called book 5.

My lord's old age and his youth were one and the same. By his command I wrote this testimony as an old man. In book 5 I tell the great *līlā* of such great activities as his marriage to Sītā. He made Mahāprabhu appear—that's in book 5, and his delight with Nitāi and Caitanya.

Listen carefully to the tales in this fifth book. They will delight everyone; listen with joy.

Now I'm going to tell the story of my lord's marriage. Hear about the great magnificence of Sītā Devī!

There was a village in Saptagrāma called Nārāyaṇapura, surrounded on all four sides by an enormous marsh. Just as Lakṣmī appeared in the ocean of milk when the ocean was churned, so Sītā was born there.

The most respectable family in that village was that of Nṛsiṃha Bhāḍurī. His wife was completely devoted to him. They always gave generously to mendicants. Everyone respected their daughter Sītā Devī. From the day that embodiment of Lakṣmī appeared in Nṛsiṃha's house, he was blessed with Lakṣmī's wealth and the respect of all. Her *līlā* in Vraja was as Lalitā's older companion. This Lakṣmī of Vraja was known as Paurṇamāsī, and in the forest bower she was Kanakā Sundarī. I'll tell her whole story later. Now I'll tell you about her birth.

Very early on the fourth day of the bright fortnight in the month of Bhādra she touched the earth to be born. With loud music Nṛsiṃha bestowed wealth on the brahmins, and yet his own wealth remained undiminished. As soon as she reached the ground he took his daughter in his arms; the mother who had just delivered didn't know a thing.

The father who named her Sītā revealed her esoteric name of Kanakā Sundarī. The child grew more lovely with each passing day. Her younger sister was called Śrī. Both had been manifestations of Yogamāyā in the Vraja entourage. Lord Kṛṣṇa sent them for Advaita.

Their father was worried about their marriage. Meanwhile, Śyāmadāsa had told my lord that he should leave sons, through whom the earth will be rescued.

My lord replied, "Who will give his daughter to an old man like me? Well, Kṛṣṇa's desire must lurk behind your words! My lord and Īśvara's beloved exist at Īśvara's whim. If he feels like manifesting her, I will cherish her."

My lord said, "Śyāmadāsa, build me a big house. Kṛṣṇa's desire for devotees grows stronger."

Śyāmadāsa understood this roundabout way of speaking, and built a place for the women to live. He built another room to house the *Bhāgavata Purāṇa* and the *śālagrāma*.

Meanwhile, Nrisiṃha Bhāḍuri took a journey to the banks of the Gaṅgā. He reached the landing at Phuliyā worried to death. His wife had died, leaving him with two daughters, and he was doing everything he could think of to get them married. His two young daughters looked after their father. Sītā did all the cooking. Sītā's cooking was like divine nectar, and whoever ate it was pleased.

Since his health was good, Nṛsiṃha went here and there (looking for grooms), and took his two daughters along with him. One day everyone came to Shantipur for Bhāgavatī Pūjā, the festival of the Goddess. Bhāḍurī took his daughters and came, and approached the tulasī and bowed.

My lord was reciting his rosary, his topknot[18] bobbing in the breeze. He looked just like Kandarpa, the god of love. His body outshone gold and caught the gaze of Sītā Devī's deer eyes. Sītā's eyes were caught in my lord's eyes. When their eyes met, their pledge was sealed. Bhāḍurī recognized my lord's power and began a steady stream of praise. Bhāḍurī realized his daughter's inmost feelings and became flustered.

He recognized my lord as his son-in-law, and returned home with his daughters. Śyāmadāsa joined them. Bhāḍurī received Śyāmadāsa cordially and seated him, and he asked Bhāḍurī about marrying his daughter.

[18] Devout Vaiṣṇava men often kept their hair cropped very short, letting only a bit grow to form a sort of ponytail in the back. Kṛṣṇa then can use that topknot to pull his devotees to him at the time of death.

Bhāḍurī said, "I have found a bridegroom worthy of my daughter. I want to get her married; I can't keep her another night."[19]

Śyāmadāsa replied, "Your daughter is a goddess. Please consent to marry her to Īśvara."

Nṛsiṃha said, "This ascetic—he's an old man, and doesn't know our family traditions. We've always known his tremendous power, but if I give him my daughter, the family won't take it well. I will ask all my kinsmen, and then give you my answer. My lord, if they're willing to promise my daughter, I will give her."

Śyāmadāsa asked Sītā what we mean by "brahmin," and she replied that a brahmin is one whose word is true. "You know that everything is by Īśvara's will. If you ask your kinsmen, then you're allowing someone else's will to dictate what you do."

Heeding his daughter's words, Nṛsiṃha consented, saying, "I am your servant."

Śyāmadāsa came to tell my lord that the wedding would take place the day after next. All the villagers and the local king accepted the invitation. Some said, "We're going to see an ascetic get married." Some said, "He's Īśvara, let's be sure to go!" All his disciples were thrilled to come. The king brought food and gifts.

Music, dancing, and singing—the king assigned these responsibilities to his courtiers. That king was a disciple of Yadunandana, who had sent the king to the wedding. This king was a great devotee of my lord's and performed tremendous service without being asked. An inexperienced servant does only what is asked, but one who serves without being asked is best. I recognize the visible signs of inner joy and consider the diligent servant, best of all.

Yadunandana Ācārya was very close to my lord. That scholar took his disciples Hiraṇya and Govardhana, brothers of the king, and decreed that they had been able to do whatever he asked. They brought my lord in a new litter and performed one of Īśvara's *līlās* in the court.

On the bank of the Gaṅgā at the Phuliyā landing they convened the community, and Bhāḍurī gave his daughter in marriage. Whatever scripture prescribes by way of wedding rites, they did it all right there, then went home.

Sītā serves my lord carefully and attentively with her cooking, and cooks for the *śālagrāma*. My lord sat with his retainers and distributed the *prasāda*. The food Sītā cooked was like divine nectar. My lord said it was certainly worthy of Kṛṣṇa. Kṛṣṇa ate only food from Rādhikā's hands, and he wouldn't touch anyone else's cooking. Since Sītā Devī entered the house, he eats the *prasāda* from Sītā's own hands.

The lady Śrī was Sītā's younger sister, and their father gave her to the bridegroom, too, to serve them, so Sītā's lord also married Śrī. The two served at his feet together, recognizing Advaita as their husband.

Śrī took charge of the deity worship. Sītā would rise at dawn and bathe and ready the materials for her husband's worship. She would take the offerings to the

[19] Because of her age; keeping girls unmarried beyond their first menses was considered risky.

bank of the Gaṅgā herself, then go home and immediately start cooking. She placed food before the *śālagrāma* with great joy. When my lord saw what she had cooked, he spoke with great passion.

"Truly, your cooking is fit for Kṛṣṇa! Kṛṣṇa comes to eat out of your hands!"

Sītā said, "You are Kṛṣṇa, lord of my life. I am your servant; please take this *prasāda*."

My lord wanted everyone to meet his new bride so they could see how pious she was. People's minds are unfathomable; no one could say what they were thinking.

He asked his students to recite for their *prasāda*. He brought them all together and sat in the middle. Sītā in the circle, my lord feasted, his students surrounding him on that empty beach.

As she was serving all the food, her hair came undone. Two hands were serving the food, and with two more hands she modestly retied her hair. Everyone was amazed to see her four hands! But my lord gently reprimanded her, "Sītā, we're in the Kali Yuga."[20] Sītā concealed the two extra hands, but from that day on, all the devotees knew her as Īśvarī.

Previously the couple had disported in Gokula, and now everyone sees them in Shantipur. The lord of Goloka has appeared in Shantipur. My lord announced that he had come to earth to experience the devotional mood, which had not been his nature as Kṛṣṇa. "Now I will bring the darling of Vraja here: Rādhā and Kṛṣṇa, the two forces, together as one."

Commitment made, he returned to the waters of the Gaṅgā and resumed his austerities.

I have now told of Sītā's marriage. Everyone was pleased to hear this.

I am a wretched creature; what can I describe? I just write what my lord had me write.

Haricaraṇa Dāsa whose hopes are at the lotus feet of the lord of Shantipur recites the *Advaita Maṅgala*.

This was chapter 1, "The Lord's Marriage," in book 5, the *Vṛddha Līlā*, in the *Advaita Maṅgala*.

Chapter 2

Sītā's Initiation

Victory, victory to my lord's noble lord Kṛṣṇa-Caitanya! Victory, victory to the village of Navadvīpa where his treasure lies.

Victory, victory to the lotus feet of Sītā's lord. Victory, victory to Shantipur, that pure abode.

[20] His reprimand to his wife that the form of divinity she was exhibiting was inappropriate for the present times.

Victory, victory to the chief Vaiṣṇava, the guru. You have blessed me and made me describe (these events).

One day Sītā Devī, her hands joined in prayer, propitiated my lord to rescue the wicked.

"You have descended to earth to bless all creatures. What kind of justice is this, if I don't get that same compassion?"

My lord said, "You are Rādhikā's companion. As Paurṇamāsī we saw you as the guru of the community. You have authority over all Kṛṣṇa's activities. People look to you for rituals like initiation. The theme for worshiping Rādhā-Kṛṣṇa is *para-tattva*, the doctrine of 'another's.' I will tell you something of its importance."

He gave Sītā the eighteen-syllable mantra and introduced her to the dual form of Rādhā-Kṛṣṇa: Kṛṣṇa's cleverness is countered by Rādhā's erotic sweetness; Rādhā's mood is the guru that makes Kṛṣṇa a guru. Rādhā's lovely nature, her sidelong glances; Kṛṣṇa is eager to speak to her. Rādhā's smile when she sees him smitten; Kṛṣṇa is embarrassed and not in control. Kṛṣṇa is always overwhelmed by Rādhikā's love; Kṛṣṇa has no quality of which she is not the foundation. They live in Vṛndāvana acting out that love. That is what Kṛṣṇa does, and nothing else.

"You assist Rādhā-Kṛṣṇa in all they do by day and by night. I am the power of Kṛṣṇa's desire in that secluded place. I am called Sampūrṇā Mañjarī; Kṛṣṇa is my lord. I am Rādhikā's companion by my lord's command, and I attend them in their secluded amorous activities. When I wait on them no one else is present. When I ask her, Rūpa Mañjarī approaches. She serves their feet, dresses them, fans them, and offers them betel. Rādhikā's intimate friend is Kṛṣṇa's power of desire, his Icchāśakti, and Kṛṣṇa's intimate looks at Rādhikā with devotion. That very Rādhā-Kṛṣṇa I will now cause to appear. I will bring them to Navadvīpa and make them appear. I will worship them passionately. I've told the whole story; listen, you fortunate people!"

Sītā bowed and spoke, "Kṛṣṇa has many loves among the cowherd girls in Vraja. Candrāvalī is one of them; she's very proud. She's well-known in the town of Vraja, and has quite a reputation."

My lord interrupted, "Listen, I'll tell you Kṛṣṇa's side (of the story). Kṛṣṇa's desire is to maintain all dharma. Candrāvalī is also his lover. There are many cowherd girls, and all are eternally Kṛṣṇa's. Candrāvalī was one of the most beautiful among them, and had been his lover previously. Every *sakhī* played an important role in increasing the flavor of the *parakīyā līlā*. Kṛṣṇa's desire was intense, and all the gopīs, as desire personified, were just as strong. There were a great many of these gopīs, and among them Rādhā and Candrāvalī, the most important. When Kṛṣṇa smells Rādhikā's perfume, Candrāvalī tricks him and goes to him herself. Candrāvalī's affection is like a wound, but Rādhikā's tastes sweet. To make us know the full excellence of Rādhikā he made many impassioned *sakhīs* appear in

Vraja. The amorous activities of Vraja are the *parakīyā* practice. These eternal amorous activities are *parakīyā* love. As it says in the *Sanatkumāra*,

> *Parakīyā* practitioners are his favorite people; for they make love with their own beloved in secret. (*Padma Purāṇa*, Pātālakhaṇḍa 52. 6)

Kṛṣṇa's adolescence was fulfilled in Rādhikā's love; Kṛṣṇa didn't leave Vraja for a second.

For,

> I never leave Vṛndāvana to go anywhere! I always live right here with her. (*Padma Purāṇa*, Pātālakhaṇḍa 51. 78)

You know this whole story. You practice as Kandarpa Sundarī. Kṛṣṇa is very pleased with your service and gave you the name Kanakā Sundarī. That is you, that is I; I will explain the philosophy. Now we will worship Kṛṣṇa as his servants."

With that, my lord asked for Śrī's hands, and at her lord's request, Sītā attended the couple. He gave the lady Śrī initiation in the tradition. He knows her reputation as a very sharp woman. And so he bestowed upon both the tradition of initiation. Jaṅgalī and Nandinī are their two chief servants. These two people were the lady Sītā's disciples, and had been Vīrā and Vṛndā back in the forest of Vraja. Jaṅgalī was very intensely strict and Nandinī gentle and sweet. The lady Sītā had made them fully female, and accordingly both worshiped.

Jaṅgalī was Vīrā in Vṛndāvana. When she came to Vṛndāvana, she learned to worship Kṛṣṇa. He had so kindly infused them both with Śakti that their male bodies looked female.[21] They had been Paurṇamāsī's disciples Vīrā and Vṛndā, and now they are Īśvarī's eternal servants.

Everyone, hear about the magnificent Jaṅgalī. She learned the power of worship from Sītā.

In a deserted forest near the town of Gaur lived tigers, bears, and very evil people. No one went there alone, for if they did, they never came back. Jaṅgalī built a hut in that forest, living there and worshiping in solitude with mental focus, as a woman. She assembled all her own materials for worshiping Kṛṣṇa.

One day several hunters came to the forest. They saw a woman and approached that house but saw no one coming and going. Tigers and bears surrounded her, and she just sat there unperturbed. They saw someone in women's clothes churning milk at the house. Later, at the end, they saw her as a *vairāgī*. They fell like sticks with great devotion. They informed the king of this wonder they had seen.

[21] For the full story of Jaṅgalī and Nandinī, see the *Sītācarita*.

The local ruler listened to their whole story and then set out to go hunting. They got there around midday, all dying of thirst, and asked for water. She placed a pot of water before them, and they all quenched their thirst. The ruler asked the woman why she was there. Jaṅgalī replied, "I worship here."

A hunter said, "Your majesty, this is an important man who has become a woman, you know."

Then the king said, "You're a man. Why are you here in the forest dressed like a woman?"

Jaṅgalī said, "I really am a woman!" And so the king ordered a woman brought to inspect her.

The woman from the village undressed Jaṅgalī and saw that she was menstruating. The Badshah was amazed to hear that. Then she again revealed her male form. The Badshah fell at her feet with devotion. Gently, she bade him return to town, saying that she regarded the forest as her home, and intended to remain there.

The Badshah asked if she wanted anything from him. Jaṅgalī said, "I only want this: allow me to stay as Jaṅgalī." And so he commissioned a town to be built, naming it "Jaṅgalī Kothā."

Such was Jaṅgalī's great power. In her *sādhaka*-body she attained perfection, the blessing of *rasa*. The lady Sītā's disciples are beyond compare. Sītā's great devotee is Nandinī. I've described them both in brief. I've tried not to let this book get too long.

Haricaraṇa Dāsa, whose hopes are at the lotus feet of the lord of Shantipur, recites the *Advaita Maṅgala*.

This is chapter 2, "Sītā's Initiation," in book 5, a brief description of this branch, in the *Vṛddha Līlā* in the *Advaita Maṅgala*.

Chapter 3

The Story of Lord Nityānanda's Birth

Victory, victory to that master, Sītā's lord. Be kind, lord, Caitanya's guru.

Victory, victory to Sītā Gosvāmī, ocean of mercy. She looked at this wretch and showed me mercy.

Victory, victory to Sītā's lord in the holy site, Shantipur, who brought Caitanya and Nityānanda and through them, peace.

I praise my lord's many followers with devotion. I praise them all together, hundreds and hundreds of devotees.

By your mercy, gathered devotees, the lame can leap over mountains. Let's look at everyone connected to that mercy.

I am an ignorant child. Grant me the power to describe something of Caitanya's and Nityānanda's births. Nityānanda is the object of my lord's great respect.

Advaita and Caitanya are one and the same. Hear the stories of their births—miraculous occurrences! You'll get joy in listening—unparalleled joy!

In this particular appearance Rohiṇī and Vasudeva are Padmāvatī and HāṚāi Pandit. My lord Advaita first brought in Baladeva-Saṃkarṣaṇa as the next phase of his plan to experience Kṛṣṇa. He had been the elder brother, previously born from Devakī's womb, and now Nitāi was born from Rohiṇī's womb. Ananta-Saṃkarṣaṇa appeared at Advaita's will—he brought him to be born on earth.

In time Padmāvatī delivered, and he was born on the thirteenth of the auspicious month of Māgha. It was the most auspicious day, the thirteenth in the bright fortnight, when the lotus-eyed Baladeva arrived. The sounds of "Victory! Victory!" filled the earth. "Haladhara is born!Behold a miracle!"

He grew rapidly in strength, heroism, and prowess. He was always happy, never sad. His father the pandit delighted at the child's nature. He (gave him the proper haircut, and) left a tuft of hair at the back of his head. The pandit couldn't come up with a name for his son. He bathed in the Gaṅgā and made many offerings.

Everyone knew Advaita performed austerities. When they thought of Advaita, all the child's ills departed. HāṚāi Pandit came to Shantipur and told my lord about his son.

"He doesn't have a name, O all-auspicious lord! Would you take a look at him and give him a name? I'll bathe in the Gaṅgā and shave the child's head. We always follow the family's traditions; that's our way. If you like, I'll bring the boy to the riverbank. You can see him and give him a name."

My lord replied, "pandit, you are most fortunate! Bring your son, and I'll go and take a look, O Wise Man." So he brought the child and its mother to the bank of the Gaṅgā; he calmly brought him to Advaita. With hands joined in prayer, he presented the child to Advaita. Advaita took a look at the naked child, and said, "Don't worry about a thing. Your son is Īśvara, don't think of him as an ordinary infant."

My lord took a boat to the other side of the Gaṅgā, and when he showed him the boy, the pandit was overjoyed. Advaita smiled and placed his hand on the boy's head. The pandit said, "May my son live a long life!"

"Listen, Pandit, you are very fortunate. Your son is Ananta, so take good care of him. How can I give him a name; tell me, what jurisdiction do I have in this matter?" The pandit said, "His name is up to you."

My lord said, "Strength and heroism, unequaled joy, I proclaim his name to be Nityānanda—Eternal Joy. This is his name in every age, countless times. This humble scholar will make him a savior. In any case, raise him carefully." He tied a protective thread around his right upper arm.

The pandit took the child and returned home, and my lord Advaita returned to his austerities. As the days passed Nityānanda became more and more (radiant) like a second full moon. Infancy, childhood, adolescence, his parents' deaths, all occurred in due course. He took his close friend Uddhāraṇa Datta and systematically made a grand pilgrimage tour.

They had no particular agenda; at one point they found themselves at an *avadhauta* Śaivite hermitage. Another day when there were staying in a desolate area they encountered an enormous demon. This had been an area where brahmins performed sacrifices, but the demon had frightened them off and they'd run away. The demon told the two men his story, amazed to see their gentle eyes.

The demon shouted, "Listen, you two humans! Why have you come here to give up your lives? The whole town has up and left; did you see anyone there? I'll eat you two brothers this morning."

Then lord Nityānanda asked the demon to tell him what he planned to do.

Datta[22] said, "My lord, we're brushing up against danger here. Let's grab some weapons and kill him."

Nityānanda replied, "Where will we get weapons? We'll use Hari's name to chase the demon away."

At dawn the demon wanted to eat them, but he couldn't come before them, and held back.

Nityānanda said, "Arm yourself with Kṛṣṇa's name. The demon will end his life and become a repository of virtues."

The demon laughed derisively, saying, "Kṛṣṇa, Kṛṣṇa." And repeating Kṛṣṇa's name, he was finally converted, and asked them to tell him who they were so he could serve them properly.

Nitāi then showed him something amazing: he made his body immense, obliterating the entire kingdom.

The demon said, "Save me! I understand what you're doing." He fell at his feet and became a great devotee. He covered his head with his garment and sang their every praise. "Tell me what I can do. I'm a habitual murderer. I've destroyed a lot of brahmins' sacrifices, and have killed hundreds and hundreds of brahmins. Please forgive all these offenses of mine, and initiate me now with the name of the savior of the downfallen."

My lord said, "What you have to do is go to the bank of the Gaṅgā, and the contact with its waters will cleanse your sins."

The demon said, "I have no right to touch the Gaṅgā!" But my lord said, "Just go! It's joy unequaled. Go to Advaita Ācārya's place across the river and tell him this whole story. I'm continuing my pilgrimage journey for a while, and I promise we'll meet again after that. When you touch the Gaṅgā your life's purpose will be fulfilled. You'll have no trouble doing so."

The demon did everything Nityānanda asked. He came to Shantipur, Advaita's town, and found Advaita just finishing his practices. The demon abruptly threw himself into the water there. He took on a divine form and fell at my lord's feet, praising him.

[22] Some manuscripts read "the demon."

My lord said, "Who are you and where have you come from?" The demon told him his whole story and became a god and departed for Vaikuṇṭha in his eternal body.

I've just told something of the importance of the Gaṅgā, and a bit about Nityānanda's greatness.

Haricaraṇa Dāsa, whose hopes are at the lotus feet of the lord of Shantipur, recites the *Advaita Maṅgala*.

This was chapter 3, "The Story of Lord Nityānanda's Birth," in book 5, *Vṛddha Līlā*, in the *Advaita Maṅgala*.

Chapter 4

Mahāprabhu's Birth

Victory, victory to that great lord Kṛṣṇa Caitanya, my lord's lord, who blessed the world.
Caitanya says, "My noble-minded Advaita is my example." Advaita says, "My lord Caitanya is foremost."
I praise them both with my head at their feet. Praise the lord Nityānanda throughout the earth.
Victory, victory to Nityānanda, root of joy, Rohiṇī's son, in his next appearance in the sequence of manifestation.
Victory to that moon Advaita and to the Lady Sītā. Praise my lord's sons, and the Lady Śrī.

My guru-lord has been kind to me. As I wrote about Mahāprabhu's birth, he made him appear in my heart.

At the feet of the Vaiṣṇava Gosvāmīs I humbly beg them to forgive my offenses. This is my praise.

Kavi Karṇapūra has described Caitanya's activities, and you can learn all about them from him.

Advaita and Caitanya are unequaled in *rasa*. They've been described in many ways. I'm going to emphasize things that have not been described elsewhere.

In my attachment to my lord's son I bow and write a bit about Caitanya's birth. The village of Navadvīpa is situated in the middle of the continent, a site almost as full of virtue as Vṛndāvana. The half moon of the Yamunā River surrounds it, and the Gaṅgā, like the moon, flows there, too. The Gaṅgā and the Yamunā have the same source. One flows here (in Navadvīpa), and one flows there (in Vṛndāvana). Important brahmins came from every land and settled in Navadvīpa to perform austerities. The Gaṅgā, a stream of the Yamunā, flows through Navadvīpa, built centuries ago and now very large. Śiva Lord of Crops lives there in the form of a *liṅgam*, and brahmins, kṣatriyas, and vaiśyas all worship him.

Kṛṣṇa the cowherd god is in charge in Vṛndāvana, and his *aṃśa* is in Navadvīpa. Mathurā, Vṛndāvana, and the Yamunā are most worshipful, as are the realms of Navadvīpa and Shantipur. Mathurā is eternally proclaimed Īśvara's place. The brief ritual of Kṛṣṇa's birth is in Gokula. Gokula is about six miles from Mathurā. Navadvīpa is twice that far from Shantipur. Navadvīpa and Shantipur are in the middle of the earth. There are no places like it anywhere. This Navadvīpa is Mahāprabhu's birthplace. Listen carefully—it's all divine nectar.

Advaita performed many miracles in public view. He performed austerities and brought in the whole guru lineage, bringing about the appearances of Nanda and Yaśodā as Śacī and Jagannātha, and his own birth in Sylhet, with his wife and sons. They had six sons, who died one after the other. Out of grief for their sons they came solemnly to live by the Gaṅgā. They came to Navadvīpa and settled at the Gaṅgā. Advaita paid great respect to Jagannātha Miśra. And so in time they had a son, and his father named him Viśvarūpa.

As a teenager Viśvarūpa became a renunciate; such was his nature. He left his parents, and Śacī Miśra was beside herself with grief. She wept day and night for her son, so much that the neighbors had to restrain her.

People said that the master in Shantipur was a very good man and told her to go see him, as he was very well-respected, an ascetic and very eloquent. No one knows how much longer he'll be there. Jagannātha and Śacī came to Shantipur, where Advaita was performing austerities on the bank of the Gaṅgā. They circumambulated the tulasī bush and bowed to my lord with joined hands and thought, "Let's stand a little way down the beach so we don't disturb him."

My lord turned around and saw Śacī and Jagannātha, and smiled and said, "Son, it's fine. Why have the two of you come here? Tell me."

They approached and prostrated themselves. Jagannātha joined his hands in prayer and began to speak. "We've been living in Navadvīpa on the Gaṅgā for some time. Deeply bereaved over our sons we've come to you. First, our sons departed this life, and now the last one has become a renunciate, and our grief is for him. Please tell us—you are Lord Nārāyaṇa—how we can dispel this sorrow and grief."

My lord said, "Sorrow and grieve no more! Know that all this has been by Kṛṣṇa's will. I tell you, you will have a wondrous son. Stay here for seven days, promise me."

The couple forgot everything and stayed as he asked. Advaita went back into the water with a roar. For seven days he performed austerities, roaring, and earth and water shook. No one understood what he was worshiping for. His roar split the earth and reached all the way to Vṛndāvana. He attracted Rādhā and Kṛṣṇa with his roar.

Two tulasī buds came floating upstream on the tide, and Advaita picked up one in each hand. He had Śacī eat the larger bud, and he fed the smaller one to Sītā herself. Then Śacī and Jagannātha took their leave, and he sent them home with much ceremony.

From that day forth Kṛṣṇa appeared in Śacī's house, and they were honored; a treasure had come into their home. Jagannātha told Śacī he'd had a dream in which a brilliant radiance had entered his heart. "That same radiance settled in your heart. I realize that the Master's promise has been fulfilled."

Śacī's pregnancy progressed, and the master soon said, "You will have a son this month."

When the full moon in the bright part of the month of Phālguna came, just after twilight, during an eclipse, he was born, and everyone rejoiced. It felt like the banks of the Gaṅgā were ringing with the sound of Kṛṣṇa's name. The words "Hari, Hari" filled the earth. The moon-Caitanya was born!

Though he was in Shantipur my lord became aware of this, and told Sītā of Caitanya's birth. On the pretext of the eclipse he bestowed gifts on the brahmin community. Overwhelmed with joy, he sang the holy name. And in Navadvīpa, that Indra Jagannātha Miśra generously gave the brahmins many gifts to celebrate his son's birth. When morning came he sent people far and wide with the news, and he sent a brahmin to Shantipur.

When they saw their son the parents quivered with joy. The land of Gauḍa became as beautiful as Vraja. A son was born! Their joy was tremendous. But they were disheartened when he wouldn't nurse. Miśra went to see the master in Shantipur and told him what was going on.

"Lord, you went to all the trouble of giving us a son. Why won't he drink any milk?"

My lord said, "Don't worry, I'm coming back with you," and he set off with his disciples.

There was a large, tall neem tree next to the door. Śacī was sitting under it, rocking the baby. When she saw my lord, she fell at his feet, begging him to restore her son.

My lord sent the crowd away and approached her. He smiled at the child and asked, "Why are you doing this?"

Mahāprabhu replied, "You have not initiated my mother. Kindly give her the Kṛṣṇa mantra. Give her the sixteen-syllable (mantra of the) names of Hari. Then I will drink her milk. Give my mother initiation and save her!"

My lord told Śacī to listen. "Your son will drink your milk; I've seen what the problem is. Go bathe, and when you return, I'll give you the mantra. You and your son will be just fine."

Śacī bathed in the Gaṅgā and returned quickly, and then he bestowed the mantra on her.

"Always recite this thirty-two-syllable, sixteen-name mantra of Hari's name. Do not tell anyone this Kṛṣṇa mantra. You will accomplish every purpose through this mantra. Love Kṛṣṇa affectionately day and night; know that this son of yours is actually Kṛṣṇa. If he cries out hungry for milk, offer him your breast, with Hari's name."

Śacī placed her hand on her son's head and recited the mantra, and my lord placed the infant on Śacī's lap. Then the little boy nursed greedily. Cries of victory filled the earth.

"Raise this baby with the name 'Nimāi.' Later, he will acquire many other names."

She paid homage to my lord with devotion. "In life after life I am your servant."

My lord returned to Shantipur, delighted, and told Sītā all the details.

And so Mahāprabhu began to grow. In time, he would perform many *līlā*s.

All this was the dance of my lord Advaita Ācārya. He descended as a devotee in Caitanya's market. This *līlā* unfolded by Advaita's mercy. Caitanya cannot be merciful without Advaita's mercy. He blessed his mother by being born, and everyone knows he did much more. The Ācārya's mercy precedes any mercy that Mahāprabhu demonstrates.

Anyone who honors the master earns my heartfelt respect. Mahāprabhu Caitanya's words are critical.

Haricaraṇa Dāsa, whose hope is at the lotus feet of the lord of Shantipur, recites the *Advaita Maṅgala*.

This was chapter 4, "Mahāprabhu's Birth," in book 5, *Vṛddha Līlā*, in the *Advaita Maṅgala*.

Chapter 5

Kāmadeva's Good Fortune and the Advent

I praise my lord Advaita himself. Second, the one known as the lord Caitanya.
Praise the lady Sītā and her sons, at whose request you have this book.
Praise Pandit Puruṣottama, the wise man who made Advaita and Caitanya one.
The pandit was the object of both men's mercy. Listen, everyone, to what he said.

Previously they were born as one, and now one came after the other, independent.

For, (text missing)

First Kṛṣṇa himself was Advaita's true form, and then became two separate forms.

For, as Jadunandana says, (text missing)

Making Rādhikā and Kṛṣṇa one, my lord made them appear as Kṛṣṇa Caitanya. His body internally dark and outwardly fair, he appeared in Jagannātha's house. As "*pūrṇa*"[23] my lord was his servant and his pride, and his primary role was as the model devotee. Advaita's habit was roaring out, "Say it! Caitanya is my lord! Go and worship him!"

[23] At least one manuscript reads "*pūrṇatara*, "fuller."

Caitanya said, "I will show mercy, Brother, to whoever worships me, if he worships Advaita."

Listen carefully to this theological point: the person who worships Advaita, gets Caitanya. The person who does not believe goes to hell when he dies. Nityānanda is Caitanya's elder brother Balarāma. The form Advaita has revealed is Caitanya Gosvāmī. The One is in all three; the three are in the One. There is no division or distinction. The person who differentiates among them does not get Kṛṣṇa.

Kāmadeva Pandit composed a poem in eight verses on my lord. It pleased Mahāprabhu, who showed him kindness.

As, (text missing)

When Mahāprabhu had heard the poem he decreed that this Kāmadeva who had spoken, was his.

"This Kāmadeva is an *aṃśa* of Kṛṣṇa who was destroyed by the great god Śiva's curse. Everyone should know him now as Advaita's left hand. Worship him to conquer the senses. Listen, Kāmadeva, to what I'm saying. You made Kṛṣṇa tend the cows in the forest. Now keep your *līlā* secret, worship Advaita's feet attentively."

Mahāprabhu smiled and embraced him, and when he released him, showered him with mercy. Kāmadeva came and reported this to Advaita. Delighted, my lord embraced him.

One day in the autumn Sītā's lord was sitting on the bank of the Gaṅgā with his golden mane. Kāmadeva was on his left, Puruṣottama on his right, and all his disciples were lined up behind. My lord contemplated the Vṛndāvana activities: "The Yamunā where Kṛṣṇa plays is most fortunate. Rādhā and Kṛṣṇa play together in her waters. Kṛṣṇa kept telling Rādhikā to look."

Advaita said, "Kāmadeva, look at this Kṛṣṇa of yours! Kṛṣṇa is putting pressure on my *sakhī*!"

With that he took Kāmadeva's hand and stepped into the water. He took Rādhikā's part and defeated Kṛṣṇa. Advaita took all the devotees into the water to play. He cried out, "Rādhikā won!" and laughed and laughed.

The lady Sītā heard all the noise and came down to the river herself with Śrī. They watched my lord playing in the water, from a distance. My lord said, "Now Kṛṣṇa's delighted. You've come to Kṛṣṇa's aid. You and I defeated Kṛṣṇa before."

The two ladies went back home, laughing, and my lord got out of the water, commenting that his wife had gone home laughing, but the disciples were confused, and no one understood what he meant. Kāmadeva asked my lord to dispel his confusion. "Why were we playing in the water?"

My lord said, "Kāmadeva, Puruṣottama, listen! I am Rādhikā's *sakhī*, her intermediary. Like me, Kṛṣṇa was defeated by his *sakhī*. Who can resist a tussle with Kṛṣṇa? Acting as the *sakhī* I defeated him, but Sītā came to the bank to take

Kṛṣṇa's side. Kṛṣṇa had allowed someone else to win. When Sītā heard that, she just laughed. I told you Sītā is Kanakā Sundarī. She is a younger *sakhī* than Lalitā and the others. She's on the side of whomever Kṛṣṇa defeats. I am on Rādhikā's side. This is how the eternal Vraja *līlā* goes. That Kṛṣṇa, that Rādhā, are the lovers of Vraja. That *sakhī* serves the couple. Kṛṣṇa is eager to serve Rādhikā. At that time, I am the best of all the *sakhīs*. Remember all this. Keep it safe and don't tell anyone."

With that, my lord sat in the midst of his students, the full moon shining on him. They heard from my lord what he had seen, and committed it to writing.

1. Hands joined over head, I've told about Sītā's lord; my lord, gaze with mercy. Your *līlā* is such—how can I talk about it? Promise this time.
2. Returning in human form in birth after birth to let us touch your feet; you've taught everyone about Rādhā-Kṛṣṇa's activities in Vraja. Please show us the same mercy this time.
3. Your sweet words soothe my mind; you are innately merciful. I am a miserable wretch with neither devotion nor accomplishments; I come thinking of your feet.
4. You—Kṛṣṇa, the moon of Gokula; you're walking the earth as all three, Advaita, Caitanya, and Nityānanda. The three of you are in the One, the One is in all three, in your respective *līlās*: this is Rādhikā's highest mood.
5. You took on Rādhikā's mood and appeared as Gaurāṅga to act out the Vraja *līlā* before us. He is to be worshiped constantly; you've instructed young and old; I am proud to be your servant.
6. You accept whoever recognizes you, and you do your Hari *līlā* with him. Only Nityānanda knows your theology; who else can explain this game?
7. You descended to earth, you constantly roar the sound "HUM!" and you made Rādhā-Kṛṣṇa appear. This is all your *līlā*. You gave the Kṛṣṇa mantra to the world. I'm a wretch in constant danger.
8. You taught your holy *līlā* to gods and brahmins. Kṛṣṇa Caitanya calls you guru. I am just a miserable soul, how can I realize this? Only through his mercy.
9. Lord Kṛṣṇa took the form of Caitanya. Nityānanda is his *svarūpa*. You are foremost of our community. You made them all come down to earth, there's no confusion. Now please bless me, a sinner.
10. If you can save me then I will know you are great, for I am a chronic sinner. Sītā's Lord, please have mercy, show your compassion, and save Haricaraṇa Dāsa!

This was my lord's *līlā* in Shantipur: he enacted many games with supreme delight. Not even Brahmā knows the extent of my lord's *līlā*. I'm just a miserable wretch; how can I possibly describe it? Whatever I write is because of his mercy. I hold his order in the lotus of my heart.

Haridāsa and Kṛṣṇadāsa taught complex things. I, Haricaraṇa Dāsa—my lord, please have mercy. I've described just one day's *līlā*. I'm going to write a bit about his *līlā* day after day.

Haricaraṇa Dāsa, whose hope is at the lotus feet of the lord of Shantipur, recites the *Advaita Maṅgala*.

This was chapter 5, "Kāmadeva's Good Fortune and the Advent," in book 5, *Vṛddha Līlā*, in the *Advaita Maṅgala*.

Chapter 6

The Appearances of My Lord's Sons

Praise the lord of Shantipur, no different from Caitanya! By bringing in Caitanya he blessed the world.
Praise the lady Sītā, as Rādhā, his life's companion. Praise her sons, full of love.
I praise the village of Shantipur diligently, for there my lord's *līlā* continues, day and night.

The Gaṅgā flows through Shantipur for about eight miles; on both sides, branches from the rows of vandana trees float on the stream. Coconut trees on either side interspersed with rows of paths, we move among the aśvattha trees. Under a khāju tree is some nice shade, as if that wonderful tree were inlaid with gems. The brahmins' houses all surround my lord's. That skilled Vedic scholar is a great renunciate. In the summertime, beside the Gaṅgā, at twilight, they all come sit on the bank. Vedic recitation, the din and bustle of scriptures and grammar: gods, sages, and *gandharvas* all would go for his *darśana*. No one knows who might come to him in human guise, then bow to my lord and go back home.

What can I say about the splendor of Shantipur, where Kṛṣṇa appeared, whose lord is Kṛṣṇa!

Now I'll tell about my lord's children. He had a son like Pradyumna. Acyutānanda was born as an *aṃśa* of Mahāprabhu Caitanya, after (Advaita) had fed (his mother) the smaller tulasī bud. My lord's eldest son was the best of them all; Sītā's son known as her eldest was the best. Sītā's child was a charming blossom. He charmed the hearts of Rādhā and Kṛṣṇa with his worship.

My lord's branch of the school was like my lord; the world knew him as no different from Caitanya. One day Sītā set aside and covered some milk for Caitanya. Acyuta and Caitanya were bathing in the Gaṅgā, playing in the water as children do. When they were late returning, my lord went to the riverbank. Caitanya was embarrassed, and Acyuta headed home.

"You played in the water for so long your food has dried out. Śacī is terribly worried! Stay at my place; that'll make her happy. Come eat!" He gestured him to come.

Laughing, he came with my lord. "I'll eat, then move on."

Meanwhile, Acyutānanda reached home before them and was happy to see the container of milk. He drank the whole pitcher. His mother got angry and slapped him, leaving a large imprint from her hand.

Mahāprabhu sat down by himself for the meal. He called Acyuta and everyone to eat, but when they all sat down, Mahāprabhu had the mark of the slap on his body.

Sītā asked how he'd gotten that mark. "I think Śacī's sending it! Every time Śacī hears that you're out playing, she hits herself hard enough to leave a mark."

Mahāprabhu replied, "Tell me who you just hit. Just look at the mark of your hand. Is this the way for a mother to train (her child)? When Acyutānanda drank that milk, you hit him. You were amazed. Acyutānanda and I share the same body. Never think that we are separate."

Then my lord Advaita said to Sītā, "You didn't understand what I said."

From that day on everyone noticed Acyuta's tremendous power. Kṛṣṇa Caitanya had manifested as Acyutānanda, who frequented Vraja as one of the intimate companions. No one should have any doubt about this. The Vraja retinue came along with Caitanya.

Whichever devotees came from various other holy sites, Mahāprabhu included them in the Vraja entourage. As Mahāprabhu said in the *Caitanya Candrodaya Nāṭaka*:

> "This is my desire: that I will go to Vṛndāvana as a *rasa*-full form, and there I will make one of you hand over a son whose devotion to Vṛndāvana is like your own—then we'll all meet there and float on the surging ocean of love. This ineffable action is the only thing I have not accomplished, and I want to complete it as soon as possible."

And also:

> "Among the devotees some will favor the attitude of service, some friendship; of these, moreover, some will be devoted to Rādhā-Mādhava, some to the lord of Dvarakā, still others to Rāma, Nṛsiṃha, and other *avatāras*; whatever, I will bring all these people to my feet and bind them with the dust of divine love, and grant them the attitude of deep love for Vṛndāvana."[24]

My entourages in other holy sites became devotees in Vraja. The Vraja retinue always comprises the eternal *līlā*.

My lord's second son, Balarāma, was most worthy of the name of Aniruddha[25] in form and temperament. This child of Sītā's was peerless. According to my lord,

[24] *Śrīśrīcaitanyacandrodayam (carita-nāṭakam)*, Kavi Karṇapūra, Bangla translation by Manindranath Guha, 2nd ed. (Calcutta, self-published, 1378), 380–81, Scene 10, verses 72–73.

[25] The fourth evolute; Kavi Karṇapūra equates Vakreśvara Pandit with Aniruddha.

he was the best of all. My lord made him well-versed in scripture. He preached devotion to and worship of Rādhā and Kṛṣṇa. One day my lord said, "Listen, Balarāma. Kṛṣṇa really likes the sound of the flute."

Balarāma said, "How sweet is the sound of Kṛṣṇa's flute! It charmed not only the cowherd women, but the women of the three worlds, as well. Whoever hears his flute becomes oblivious to the world. They all become devoted and cannot remain in the world. It destroyed all the gopīs' composure and made them wander around confused. Kṛṣṇa made his flute the weapon to attract the minds of the cowherd women and weaken them. People couldn't go into the forest out of fear of shame. They would glance toward the path and start crying. This *līlā* of Kṛṣṇa's is inconceivable and unparalleled. My lord said, 'Who can fathom the extent of Kṛṣṇa's *līlā*?'"

That Balarāma is a stream of love of Rādhā and Kṛṣṇa, who is unequaled with the name 'Venu Mañjarī.'

My lord's third son is Śrī Gopāla, Sītā's son, and very strong. Mahāprabhu had great mercy on him. Gopāla said that Mahāprabhu had called him to Gokula. The other two sons were Jagadīśa and Rūpa. These five holy ones were Sītā's sons.

The lady Śrī's son was called Kṛṣṇa Miśra. His devotion was tremendous; he was like the navel center of Vraja.

The lady Sītā's sons were devoted to my lord. My lord entrusted them with the painting of Madana Gopāla. When he rediscovered Gopāla in Vṛndāvana, the painting was as important as the *Bhāgavata Purāṇa*. At the end of his life my lord brought his *Bhāgavata Purāṇa* and called both Balarāma and Kṛṣṇa Miśra. He bestowed his *Bhāgavata Purāṇa* to Balarāma, and entrusted the painting of Madana Gopāla to Kṛṣṇa Miśra.

My lord's six sons are the most important of his branch, and all the disciples, like Jagadīśa, Murāri, Vijaya Kṛṣṇa, Kamalākānta, Mādhava Pandit, and Śrīkānta, are all-virtuous.

Kamalākānta demonstrated great power. Kamalākānta Gosvāmī said that my lord had called him. He had been a celibate student (*brahmacārī*), a householder, an ascetic. He was a great object of my lord's mercy and had much praise for him.

Īśāna Dāsa,[26] my lord's disciple, was intense in his service. He had the sole responsibility year-round for the household's water. He would bring Gaṅgā water in a pitcher on his head, and that is the water Sītā would use for cooking. He served wholeheartedly with body and mind by bringing water for my lord.

One day Sītā happened to notice some maggots on his head, from carrying the water. "Īśāna, you're suffering so much, but you still bring us water. Shouldn't you say something to my lord? You'll die from all these maggots." Īśāna merely worried that he would feel badly about the maggots.

[26] Acyutacaraṇa Caudhurī Tattvanidhi will later use this character as the putative author of his own *Advaita Prakāśa*.

Sītā Gosvāmī took his hand and stopped him, and beseeched him at my lord's feet, "My lord asked you to do many things. Now do what Sītā asks of you: Īśāna, get married! If you have children you can rescue the world."

Laughing, Īśāna said, "I'm an old man! Who will give his daughter to me now!"

Sītā said, "If it's God's will, you'll get a bride. As I've said, get married!"

And so he got a bride and married her, and that was a great blessing.

What I've written, my lord's son told me. There's a little about his branch in it. The three lords' branches are all my lord's branches, so I didn't describe them separately.

My lord's sons enlightened my heart. Their influence is apparent in what I write. My famous lord's sons are well known. My lord's sons enlightened my heart. I am proud to be his disciple, for as a disciple I will never be born again. I don't know how to worship, I am absolutely without devotion. If he grants me mercy I'll be sanctified. I am greedy, deluded, lustful, angry, and drunk; these things fill my heart. If Sītā's lord can forgive so many faults then he can save this sinner. I beseech you, lord, with grass between my teeth (like a lowly animal), please let me die in Vṛndāvana when I call your name. If I am such a chronic sinner, then your servant is proud. If you show me even an ounce of mercy, please grant me service at the feet of Rādhā and Kṛṣṇa. Whatever you do to me, I have no fear; your lotus feet remain always in my heart.

Haricaraṇa Dāsa whose hope is at the lotus feet of the lord of Shantipur recites the *Advaita Maṅgala*. My lord, promise Haricaraṇa Dāsa that the sorrows of material existence will cease.

This was chapter 6, "The Appearance of My Lord's Sons," in book 5, *Vṛddha Līlā*, in the *Advaita Maṅgala*.

Chapter 7

Caitanya's Mercy to Advaita

Victory, victory to Mahāprabhu, to Advaita, and to Nityānanda! I praise the feet of the three lords, my sole delight.

Victory, victory to my lord's sons, all praiseworthy. Victory, victory to the peerless devotees of these three lords.

Victory, victory to those who dwell in Navadvīpa and Shantipur! Victory to the Gaṅgā and the Yamunā, dwelling together there.

Now I will tell of my lord's remarkable activities, the joy he had with Caitanya.

From his very birth Mahāprabhu revered my lord as his guru. But in public, he said no such thing to my lord. In private, if my lord called Caitanya "my lord," Mahāprabhu would rebuff him, saying that Advaita was the elder. Mahāprabhu came and fell at my lord's feet, crying "Kṛṣṇa! Kṛṣṇa." My lord lifted him, then fled.

"I did the work of bringing you here, and the first thing you do is destroy my dharma. Therefore you need to think about becoming a *sannyāsī*-renunciate; it has been proclaimed that in the Kali Yuga the *avatāra* will be a *sannyāsī*."

Mahāprabhu considered this command. Keśava Bhāratī came and initiated him as a *sannyāsī* on the spot, and then Caitanya wandered around RāṚha for a while. Later when he returned to Shantipur, Advaita bowed deeply to him.

Mahāprabhu said, "Kṛṣṇa! Kṛṣṇa!" and embraced him. "Don't mock me like this!"

My lord replied, "You are a *sannyāsī* and Nārāyaṇa himself. In the past I praised you and now I still serve your feet."

Mahāprabhu said, "You are the guru of a *sannyāsī*! Why do you mock me! People will berate me—you are my mother's guru! You're Mādhavendra's disciple, so I am his disciple. You are the guru for all the rituals, a Vedic reciter, and yet you fall at the feet of a child, calling *him* a renunciate? You are full of splendor, like the full Brahmā. Don't make me your equal!"

Then my lord said, "Śrī Kṛṣṇa Caitanya! I brought you here and you've blessed the world. If I'm going to be your guru, with authority over others, then tell me, why did I bring you?"

Mahāprabhu said, "You know the whole story. You and I are one, there is no difference between us. But to maintain propriety in the eyes of the world, you, as the elder, must treat me like a child."

My lord said, "Don't ever say such things! I don't know why you became a renunciate."

As much as Mahāprabhu tried to stop him, my lord kept coming and falling at his feet. Mahāprabhu got upset and refused to stay. He told the disciples that he was leaving.

"My lord the Ācārya is my elder. He's not listening to what I'm saying, and is behaving like a servant."

Sadly, Mahāprabhu was actually afraid. He was absolutely speechless. Then my lord promised that he would set aside all his devotion and let him punish him. He placed his hand over his heart and said, "I am Caitanya's servant. He'll make me believe by humiliating me."

And then my lord danced energetically. The devotees filled the courtyard, and they floated in divine love. Śyāmadāsa sang *kīrtana* like a nightingale. Mahāprabhu, that crest-jewel of renunciates, danced. The two rode wave after wave of emotion and clung to each other so tightly you couldn't tell where one's body ended and the other's began. No one knows what those two talked about. Everyone knows Nityānanda, who remained in divine love. They were overwhelmed in divine love like this for some time. Though they were out of their minds they spoke like ordinary men.

Mahāprabhu stayed for many days, then told the group that he was leaving because Advaita was worshiping him. And with that, Mahāprabhu set out. The master reached a decision: "In my *Bhāgavata Purāṇa* commentary, I obscured devotion. I'll preach that commentary to the world. Then because he reveres me, he'll punish me, and I'll be able to abandon my pride."

And accordingly, Advaita preached his full Vedānta commentary. He propounded monism and discussion of Brahmā and raised the issue of the formless god. One disciple, named Śaṅkara, learned this doctrine; he didn't understand what my lord was doing, and a few others were also confused.

Mahāprabhu's devotees all saw this as perversion. They said nothing to his face, but out of his sight were very sad. A few went to Mahāprabhu and told him that the master was preaching monism. "He's an old man, an expert in scripture. Aside from this commentary, we've never seen his like. It doesn't acknowledge Īśvara, it doesn't acknowledge the *avatāra*! With this commentary the scholar has gotten lost in worldly illusion. O great lord! If you don't stop him, his thinking will spread throughout the world."

Mahāprabhu listened time and again, increasingly disturbed. He sent Gaurīdāsa Pandit to investigate. Immediately Gaurīdāsa headed to Shantipur to see what was going on.

Asked why he had come, Gaurīdāsa fell at Advaita's feet and explained that Mahāprabhu had sent him."He's very upset about you. Come with me to see him."

My lord said, "Why should I go to him? He's a *brahmacārī* living a holy life, and I'm outside that realm. He's a renunciate; what use does he have for the world? I made him come to earth, I decide what his duty is."

The pandit said, "He is Kṛṣṇa, everyone is his servant. And you, as Kṛṣṇa, made him appear."

Then Advaita revealed his four-armed form to Gaurīdāsa. Dumbstruck, Gaurīdāsa returned to Caitanya and related their whole conversation, concluding with his running away when my lord showed his four-armed form.

My lord said, "Īśvara is all majesty. I know that he is the ultimate authority for everything always. Whatever job he's sent you to do, why has he insulted me by sending you? In whatever form you've praised and brought him, when he's revealed his majesty you can't restrict him. I will not eat until you bring him here. I'll beat him and teach him a lesson."[27]

Gaurīdāsa returned to Shantipur to the master's place, and relayed his master's order.

My lord said, "Is he greater than I? Take a good look at what I'm showing you." He revealed Kṛṣṇa's four-armed form many times. "Now look—the six-armed form!" Then my lord Advaita became six-armed. The pandit was awestruck and could not speak.

"Mahāprabhu has quit eating because of you. How can you stay here? Tell me, O Great Blessed One!"

[27] This story can also be found in 2.10 of the *Caitanyabhāgavata*.

Then with a loud shout of "HUM" he reiterated to Gaurīdāsa, "Bring him here! Then he'll take me and tie me up. You do as he's asked and then I'll go."

The pandit said, "My lord, I don't understand your *līlā*, or why you're talking like this, or why you're playing games."

"I'll go there and make him bind me," my lord said, and took his disciples with him. He preached such a hostile commentary Caitanya brought everyone. Advaita stood before Mahāprabhu with bound hands.

Mahāprabhu, his head bent, began to speak. "You brought me here by such deception. You are the lord Īśvara, I know the whole story. You have produced a monistic scriptural commentary. If you do such a pointless thing, and I find out about it, then I'm going to come."

My lord said, "The reason I brought you is that you show your mercy to the entire group but not to me. That's why I wrote that countercommentary. Now I see you'll do what's right and stop me. If you beat me it will be a great blessing, and I'll then be Caitanya's best servant."

When he said, "Caitanya's servant," my lord danced. Mahāprabhu pulled him up and embraced him. They were both senseless with divine love. Eventually they grew calm and sat down.

My lord said, "You renounce anyone who propagates monism; now that's why." At my lord's request he abandoned them all. Śaṅkara didn't leave; he remained and persevered.

My lord said, "Śaṅkara, bring me the manuscript. Throw it in the water; give up that practice."

Śaṅkara said, "Let's debate the matter. If I lose the debate, I'll throw the manuscript in the water."

My lord said, "Śaṅkara has become a mongrel. Should I forsake him? I'm trying to decide. If I forsake him, he'll be known as Varṇaśaṅkara the mongrel. I'll have nothing further to do with him, nor will anyone else in town."

Then Śaṅkara grabbed the manuscript and ran. Śaṅkara sprinkled water on it in consecration and placed it reverently. Śaṅkara became widely known for having left my lord. No one would associate with someone who had rejected his guru, that's certain.

Mahāprabhu said, "Brothers, listen everyone! No one who has forsaken Advaita can associate with me. Anyone Advaita praises is my man. Without Advaita's mercy it's hard to find me. There is no devotion in *advaita*, monism, for those who worship me. I show no mercy, he's sunk in hell. Mark my words, I speak the truth. I was brought to earth because of *advaita*, monism, I know. The man who recognizes no difference between me and Advaita, receives Kṛṣṇa's mercy." And so Mahāprabhu returned to Shantipur with Advaita and all the devotees.

There was no end to the joy in the village of Shantipur. All the devotees eventually came there. At my lord's instigation, a great celebration ensued. Sītā Devī cooked with particular joy.

One for whom the feet of Caitanya, Nityānanda, and Advaita are the sole focus understands these *līlās*. May the three lords have mercy on me. The disease of worldly existence is cured; we all see this. The devotees of the three lords are most compassionate. I'm a miserable wretch; all of you, please bless me. My blessed guru Advaita is an ocean of mercy. Once again he has shown mercy to a vile man.

As you well know, the ladies Sītā and Śrī have Kṛṣṇa's mercy. When they see a vile man, they are merciful to him. May the name of the savior of the downfallen be proclaimed!

I sincerely hope to be assigned to the service of Rādhikā's lotus feet. I hope I will reach your feet. I'm a fallen cātaka bird. But if you say you don't know the cātaka's nature, then carefully teach this ignorant one.

Haricaraṇa Dāsa whose hope is at the lotus feet of the lord of Shantipur, recites the *Advaita Maṅgala*.

This was chapter 7, "Caitanya's Mercy to Advaita," in book 5, *Vṛddha Līlā*, of the *Advaita Maṅgala*.

Chapter 8

The Display of Sītā's Majesty and the Feast at Advaita's House

Victory to my lord Advaita, lord of Sītā's life, who brought Mahāprabhu and his brother Nityānanda.

Victory, victory to Sītā Gosvāmī, Rādhikā's *svarūpa*, in the form of the senior *sakhī* Kanakā Sundarī.

Victory, victory to my lord's sons and all the devotees, through whose mercy the *līlā* spread.

Listen carefully to the Shantipur adventures. My heart cannot contain the joy of the three lords.

One, Mahāprabhu, was intoxicated, and the other two stayed up all night in Shantipur for great *kīrtana*. Their disciples and servants all came and delighted in the great celebration.

During the day the great celebration was Sītā Devī's cooking, like divine nectar; everyone loved it. The contents of Sītā's pantry never ran out. Each day she spent twice as much as the day before, and the pantry lacked nothing. Sītā planned the meals and prepared them, and the lady Śrī collected all the ingredients. They served the *śālagrāma* every four hours and then took the food and placed it before Mahāprabhu.

Nityānanda sat to my lord's right and the devotees sat all around them, singing Kṛṣṇa's virtues. Sītā and my lord both served the food. The lady Śrī came and helped. My lord gave everyone whatever they asked for.

Mahāprabhu said, "I especially like the *sukta*,[28] bitter vegetables. Please give me a larger helping."

Nityānanda said, "I love sweets! Please give me some rice pudding!"

They happily enjoyed their second helpings. I can't describe how happy the master was. Those who witnessed the splendor of the feast said the food at Advaita's house was all great. The devotees had all heard about the banquets in that previous era in Gokula at Yaśodā's house. They had the same sort of feast every day. Every day their joy expanded, it never diminished.

One day Mahāprabhu unexpectedly invited the whole village, to demonstrate Sītā's greatness. My lord told Govinda to take his drum and announce Mahāprabhu's invitation throughout the village. Govinda did so, and in four hours they were enjoying their food.

They prepared heaps and heaps of food, in two houses. There was so much food it was piled in every corner.

Mahāprabhu served the *śālagrāma*, and he and Nityānanda started to look at the food.

"Dear devotees, we've invited you all here as a group to see this *prasāda* that's been cooked for Kṛṣṇa."

Four hours later, there wasn't much food left. Hundreds of people all saw the food. The aroma of the *prasāda* drove them crazy. They began to dance, crying, "Kṛṣṇa's *prasāda*!" Such food Sītā Devī fed Kṛṣṇa! That's why cooking for Kṛṣṇa is no burden.

Advaita and Nityānanda sat on either side of Mahāprabhu, and the devotees surrounding them floated in the taste of divine love. "Look, look master! Today she's made a stupendous heap of rice!" He began to dance all around the house. Mahāprabhu danced for a long time in divine love. Advaita embraced him like a flower in his heart. Then my lord told him how much time had passed. Mahāprabhu said, "This very day we will honor Sītā.

Don't worry, Sītā, that your hands will ever be empty." Mahāprabhu looked, and praised her pantry. "You'll make known that this pantry of Advaita's is inexhaustible. As long as Sītā's name is fulfilled, your guests will be, too." With that Mahāprabhu sat down to feast, with the two lords, one on each side. The devotees sat in a circle around them, sitting as was proper. And all the various villagers sat in their own proper rows. Brahmin, kṣatriya, kāyastha, and vaidya sat next to my lord according to their respective positions.

Sītā served all these people, and Īśāna and Śyāmadāsa served everyone else. Laughing and bowing to the three lords, Sītā Devī served them, like a star. She served seconds even before their leaf-plates were empty; she kept going back and refilling the food.

[28] A Bengali favorite to this day!

Mahāprabhu had given his dear devotees a clue to his intentions, so they all asked at the same time for their favorite thing.

Mahāprabhu said, "Please give me some of the *sukta*." Nityānanda said, "Please give me some rice pudding."

My lord said, "Give me the banana flower dish." The devotees all wanted their favorite things.

Then Sītā Devī realized what was on my lord's mind, and there was a Sītā in front of each person present! She served each person what he'd asked for, with undivided attention. The master and Nityānanda looked at Caitanya. "You've made Sītā do just what you did in the *rāsa līlā*!"

Then all the devotees indicated by their body language that no one can explain this to a nondevotee. Mahāprabhu told the assembly not to be so surprised; "You should know she's practically the same as Rādhikā! No one had ever seen Rādhikā's majesty. Now see Rādhikā's majesty and meditate on it."

The *nityasiddha* associates are like Mukunda: whatever he wants, making it happen is foremost in their minds.

As it says in the *Sanatkumāra*,

> Hari's servants, companions, parents, and lovers, O best of sages, are all eternal and possessed of the same qualities he is. (*Padma Purāṇa*, Pātālakhaṇḍa 52. 3)

His lovers have all the same powers Kṛṣṇa does. I believe this, and know he is the Ultimate. By my lord's desire he revealed it all. In the blink of an eye, it all returned.

Mahāprabhu said, "Master, just as you attracted Kṛṣṇa, so is Sītā specifically Rādhā's *svarūpa*."

My lord said, "I know your pretense.... You are both Rādhā and Kṛṣṇa in a single body! Anyone else is only your *aṃśa*. What you are is the crown of our whole assembly." Laughing conspiratorially he said, "No one else understands. Ocean of Mercy, you promised the assembly they'd understand."

My lord fed everyone he'd invited and sent them off. Sītā said, "There's as much food as you want. By your mercy, there's no shortage of anything."

Then all the devotees asked for whatever they wanted and laughed. They laughed, and all praised her cooking. Mahāprabhu said, "How can I praise her? If I had a thousand mouths, then how I'd praise her! Everyone says that whoever eats what Sītā has cooked, is a very lucky man."

He asked for some food and ate it. He rinsed his mouth and enjoyed some betel nut.

The assembled devotees were amazed. Mahāprabhu said, "Master, all this is your doing. By your mercy you will make Kṛṣṇa promise; you captured the heads of the assembly one by one." Then the devotees fell at my lord's feet. The master, my lord, showed much mercy.

Each of the three lords had so many devotees! At Mahāprabhu's command, they fell at the feet of the two lords. The two lords wrapped their arms around each other at Mahāprabhu's feet. Mahāprabhu said, "Now these are the devotees! I owe my very life to the mercy of these two lords! There is no deliverance except at their feet."

Then the three went off by themselves and decided to act out the *Dāna Līlā*, the story of the toll. He made them appear here with the same pride they felt in their earlier *svarūpa*.

Haricaraṇa Dāsa, whose hope is at the lotus feet of the lord of Shantipur, recites the *Advaita Maṅgala*.

This was chapter 8, "Seeing Sītā's Majesty and the Feast at Advaita's House," in book 5, *Vṛddha Līlā*, in the *Advaita Maṅgala*.

Chapter 9

The Dāna Līlā

Praise the glorious lord Advaita, lord of Sītā's life, renowned for bringing Mahāprabhu to earth.
Praise Mother Sītā, my lord's helpmate, renowned in Vraja as Kanakā Sundarī.
I praise Acyutānanda, Balarāma, Kṛṣṇa Miśra with devotion and a thousand obeisances.
I praise my lord's intimates Gopāla and Jagadīśa; praise the feet of the assembly, who are outstanding.
Praise the feet of all three lords and the thousands and thousands of devotees; I am a miserable wretch.
I carefully praise the lovely banks of the Kālindī-Yamunā, Kṛṣṇa's holy site Vṛndāvana.
I enthusiastically praise the feet of the three lords with the desire to serve the lady Rādhikā's lotus feet.
I praise her companions, all those girlfriends; praise the girlfriends devoted to service—my king.

All together, be merciful to this miserable wretch. Now I'll write something about the three lords' *dāna līlā*.

One day the three lords were in Shantipur, and thinking about the *dāna līlā* they had previously revealed. The three lords showed the glory of Shantipur. Mahāprabhu called it the knowledge of the city of Gokula. Lord Advaita was Lord Kṛṣṇa's *svarūpa*; Mahāprabhu was Rādhikā.

Nityānanda bragged a lot to Advaita. Śrīvāsa and the others were the *sakhī*s and the old woman who was the lovers' go-between. Kamalākānta and a lot of others were the *sakha*s: Gaurīdāsa, Narahari, Subala, and Madhumaṅgala.

All these male companions assisted Kṛṣṇa; they took the cows to graze in the pastures.

Her girlfriends helped Rādhikā get dressed and put on her jewelry. The maid-servants took the things and helped her dress. Lalitā and Viśākhā were the most important, and all the *sakhī*s surrounded her in the forest. They were always together. People were amazed to see them, and all sorrow vanished.

The splendor of Shantipur defies description. The great effulgence that is the Yamunā is also in the Gaṅgā. An old man had brought his boat to the bank of the Gaṅgā and was worshiping it with sandal and vermillion. There's a kadamba tree there on the bank, at the foot of which is an altar. On the altar are containers of vermillion and sandal, and he had decorated it with garlands. Kṛṣṇa took all his male friends there, to the sounds of horns and flutes.

All the cows moved toward the forest on the riverbank, and Kṛṣṇa and all the *sakha*s were under the kadamba tree. They played stick games for a while, and in the distance they could see Rādhikā's group. They dropped the games and ran to the kadamba tree. The old lady was at the front of Rādhikā's group. Rai came with her *sakhī*s, all dressed up, sparkling like lightning against a dark cloud.

Muralī leans against the tree in his three-angled pose, surrounded by his *sakha*s, and indolently plays his flute. And then Rādhikā's entourage arrives, with the old lady, as all the shining *sakha*s were watching for them.

"Where are you people from? Why are you here? Tell us; we need to find out what's in your baskets."

The old lady said, "We cowherd women are dressed up to go to Mathurā. We have yògurt, milk, cheese, and milk solids."

Subala said, "Why have you come to this landing? The king has just put a new tax on this landing. There are a lot of young women with you, and there will be tax on each one. Śyāma is in charge of this landing, and we are all subject to his command. We can let you go if you settle up. Otherwise we take your goods and eat them."

The old lady collapsed, laughing and sputtering.

Then Muralī Kṛṣṇa appeared, stick in hand, and said to Rādhikā and the *sakhī*s, "Listen to me, ladies. Pay the tax and get in the boat. The tax on all of you is substantial. I'll collect that large tax and then ferry you across."

Lalitā stepped forward smiling and said, "Tell us, Nanda's son, what tax you want to collect. We always come this way to sell our goods, and no one's ever told us any such thing before. You've exceeded all authority to become the superintendent of the landing. You have to treat everyone the same. Little by little you'll catch everyone with this strictness. We've packed our wares carefully in our baskets. You're a prince and yet you behave this badly! Quit stalling and let us cross!"

Kṛṣṇa spoke haughtily to Rādhikā, "Hey Pretty Girl! I made you face me. Listen, Cowherd Maid: the landing tax is simple. Every single person who goes pays one silver coin. The tax on two baskets is one coin. If you want it doubled, listen, you *sakhī*s. Since you are young women, you have lovely nice large hips, and your breasts are very heavy, O Cowherd Maidens. Each young woman must give two rupees. Large-hipped women pay double the tax. Your high breasts are very heavy; that'll cost a lot. But if you show us your faces, the price will not increase. My little boat is very old, and there are waves on the Yamunā. I can take you across the Gaṅgā one at a time. Don't take so long! Pay the tax! Otherwise, you deer-eyed ladies, you'll be stuck and won't go at all. And all that jewelry is very heavy; you know, the boat will sink. Look, look how large is this necklace! I'll pretend to break it; that'll get her attention. Then I'll surreptitiously put it in Rādhā's hand." The old woman steps forward and scolds.

1. The old woman's fire touched the hand of the wicked toll collector. Why has he come here? What a problem! This toll collector is very bad! We are weak women, and he's playing all sorts of tricks, laughing and saying sweet words.
2. The fire rages: when did they set up a tollbooth on this path? If we had decided to stay home and sell the milk, what business would we have in Mathurā? The milk is turning sour, the yogurt is at risk of spoiling, we can't afford this delay.
3. You've thrown us into the hands of this terrible toll collector; he asks a huge tax for our high breasts, and when he saw our broad hips and expert sidelong eyes, he doubled the tax.
4. He wants those long eyes, his restless eyes speak; we can only imagine what's on his mind. If he's a tax collector he should keep his distance; there's never been such a tax collector. When he came we pulled up the ends of our garments to hide.
5. He wants to get money from each of us—he wants ten cents, and double that for the baskets. He's behaving so badly, his friends are dying of laughter. We're scared to hear that.
6. We see a broken-down boat at the landing; we look toward the red mountain; we can't all cross at once. He'll take us across one by one. They all decided. His friends are dying of laughter.
7. Listen, Old Woman. I'm not going to cross. They've damned me to the hands of your toll collector. As soon as you brought him, I knew you were capable of this. This is my heart's desire.
8. The old lady laughed and said, "What are you afraid of? I am right here with you. This son of Nanda has just become the tax collector of his own accord to see you.
9. I'll hold him off in front, and your companions will follow and pick up our baskets. I'll follow with a stick in my hand. Don't worry about a thing.
10. The goods are in no danger. He's asking for a tax; he's in charge. If you want to go back, then don't pay the toll, and we'll see what happens."
11. Lalitā heard that and replied, laughing, "The old lady's right!" Haricaraṇa Dāsa says, "The old lady has guessed what Kānāi is up to."

When he'd heard what the old lady said, Nanda's son smiled and saluted her with great respect. "There will be great danger in what the old woman's suggested. The goods will be stolen and you'll lose your clothes. Old Woman, take the *sakhī*s and go. I'll take you across one at a time. These young ladies, these deer-eyed ladies; don't talk about their broad hips and their breasts. All these heavy women will sink the boat. Take them and go. I forbid the tax. I'll be their guard; don't worry about a thing."

Hearing that, Rādhikā and her *sakhī*s turned around and headed for home, and didn't cross the river. But then Kṛṣṇa and his *sakha*s surrounded them. They grabbed whatever goods they saw. They got into the boat with the goods and forced the young women to get in. In knee-deep water the boat began to sink. They stole the yogurt, the milk—all their wares.

Then they started playing in the water, the boys and girls together. The three lords were as one; divine love surged up. They lost consciousnesss and fell in the water. The devotees pulled the three lords out of the water and brought them to the bank in their arms. Śrīnivāsa, Narahari and Śyāmadāsa, Murāri, Mukunda, and the vaidya Kṛṣṇadāsa, all sang the *kīrtana* of the tax of Gokula. They moved from toll to divine love unrestrained.

Before long the three began to return to normal awareness, embracing, unable to speak. "Let's go, brother, let's go to my Vṛndāvana," all three cried as one.

All the devotees were very upset to hear what my lord said. They wanted to take him to the others. When the three saw their disciples' anxiety, they regained consciousness and Advaita roared out a loud "HUM!" Mahāprabhu danced with Nityānanda. Saying, "Hari, Hari!" Advaita placed his hand on his head. There was a lot of very strenuous dancing. When they saw that effort, all the servants fell at their feet.

They stopped dancing and went home, and it took a lot of nursing to dispel their fatigue.

This writing describes my lord's activities in Shantipur. His longing for Mathurā was overwhelming.

I've carefully written only a tiny fraction of my lord's activities, at the request of his son. Now I'll recap everything from the beginning, step by step. Listeners will derive great joy from what I've written. Everything in the book is significant.

In book 1 are praise of the gurus and a list of Kṛṣṇa's activities.

In book 2 are five chapters beginning with Vijaya Purī's holy advent.

In book 3 are the conversation with Vijaya Purī and my lord's taste for the meaning of the *Bhāgavata Purāṇa*. Overwhelmed with divine love, Purī, Durvāsa himself, was a classmate of Mādhavendra.

In book 4, Vijaya Purī spoke of my lord's birth. He who roamed Shantipur blessed the king's son. I wrote four parts for the first chapter, where I told of the conversation with Vijaya Purī.

In book 5 I described the king's conversion. The king in Sylhet became a Vaiṣṇava. This king had been a staunch opponent of Vaiṣṇavism but became a *vairāgī* renunciate after getting my lord's mercy. He attained perfection in Vṛndāvana. What can I say about his wonderful luck!

Book 6 is about my lord's move to Shantipur. He left Sylhet then. He began to study scriptures first. My lord has a tremendous reputation for his uninterrupted scriptural recitation.

These two chapters constitute book 2. Everyone is familiar with the stages of his adolescent life.

In two books I wrote six chapters. Now, everyone, hear the book of his *kaiśori līlā*.

Chapter 5 was my lord's trip to Vṛndāvana, and his parents' death. He conducted all the proper Vedic rituals, then proceeded to Vṛndāvana. Chapter 8 was the appearance of Madana Gopāla. He was in a bower near Sūrya Ghāṭa. Then there was the command to find Madana Gopāla. Gopāla had promised to appear. Previously he'd been Madana Mohana. My lord preached about him. At Gopāla's order my lord came to Shantipur and there performed arduous austerities. Chapter 9 is the conversation with Mādhavendra, known for having bestowed initiation on my lord. Lord Mādhavendra remained in Shantipur. Gopāla, full of *rasa*, appeared at Govardhana. Both appeared through each other, and the joy, the divine love, of both overflowed. Chapter 10 is the victory over the Digvijayī, who gave Advaita that name. By my lord's grace the Digvijayī was pivotal. He ordered my lord to reveal his true form. When he saw the four-armed form he sang his many praises. That man was an object of my lord's mercy.

These four chapters are the *kaiśora līlā*. That's book 3 of my lord's. There are a total of ten chapters in these three books.

Now I'm writing about book 4. Chapter 11 covers Kṛṣṇadāsa Brahmācārī, who called his (Advaita's) *svarūpa* the Shantipur-*vihārī*, the playboy of Shantipur. Kṛṣṇadāsa was the great object of my lord's mercy. Everyone knows all about his doctrine. He served my lord throughout his life, was his companion in Vṛndāvana, and came to Shantipur.

Chapter 12: getting a divine vision. He went before Brahmā, hesitantly. The *āpsarasas* could not captivate my lord. At Brahmā's order the gods came and worshiped him. Brahmā came and took birth as Haridāsa. My lord proclaimed Haridāsa's majesty.

Chapter 13 described my lord's internal state in which he was taught *kuñja-sevā*, serving the divine couple in the bower. Serving the divine couple in a secluded place, he taught the meaning of divine love.

I recited Śyāmadāsa's earlier book; he was a singular object of my lord's mercy. Śyāmadāsa delighted everyone with his *kīrtana*. And there are so many more branches (to Advaita's tree).

Chapter 14 is the conversation with Śrīnātha; my lord's blessing on both Rūpa and Sanātana. The work my lord would do in anticipation of Mahāprabhu through the two of them, I've described step by step.

These four chapters are the *jauvana līlā*; they constitute book 4. These four books contain fourteen chapters. I'll go through it step-by-step, so pay attention.

Chapter 15: my lord's marriage—the wonderful tale of the wedding with Sītā. Their father brought her younger sister, the lady Śrī, and gave them both to my lord. Sitting with their guru, his disciples were blessed, and Sītā's hair came undone as she was serving the food. She was serving the food with two hands, holding the platter, and with two more hands she tied back her hair. She revealed her four-armed form in public, amazing everyone.

Chapter 16: Sītā Devī's initiation. My lord told her all the theology and had her learn it. He explained his own *svarūpa* and Sītā's *svarūpa*. The lady Sītā's children were excellent.

Chapter 17: the birth of Nityānanda. He taught the esoteric truth that Nityānanda was Baladeva. Nityānanda showed mercy to the demon and revealed the importance of the Gaṅgā in the assembly. He made him take my lord's Gaṅgā water after his rituals, and the demon abandoned his body and attained liberation.

Chapter 18: I write about Mahāprabhu's birth. The entire universe trembled when Advaita roared "HUM!" Yelling "HUM!" he brought in the darling of Vraja, Rādhā and Kṛṣṇa, the two became one, Śacī's darling. He worshiped him himself to show how it should be done and, at Mahāprabhu's order, gave Śacī initiation.

Chapter 19: my lord's water-*līlā*. He proclaimed Sītā as Rādhikā's elder *sakhī*. My lord was a younger *sakhī* in Rādhikā's entourage. In the eternal *līlā*, they both took on the mood of the female companions. Kāmadeva had the good fortune to be an object of Mahāprabhu's mercy. He composed an eight-line poem describing my lord's theology.

Chapter 20: the appearance of my lord's sons. Mahāprabhu showed Sītā a great point. Sītā had set aside some milk for Mahāprabhu. She was surprised when Acyutānanda drank that milk. Sītā slapped Acyuta, and the mark of that slap appeared on Mahāprabhu's body. He demonstrated to her that the bodies of the two boys were one. The *Paugaṇḍa Līlā* he revealed to the community in Shantipur.

Chapter 21: Advaita's posturing. Caitanya punished him. Mahāprabhu beat him and was embarrassed. He revealed Advaita's majesty to Gaurīdāsa. That Advaita is my very life. Know that this is indeed Mahāprabhu's order.

Chapter 22: the feast at Advaita's house. Mahāprabhu's revelation of Sītā's majesty. One time Sītā had manifested a lot. She served the community as Mahāprabhu had desired. Mahāprabhu said that Advaita's pantry was never empty. The three lords enjoyed the feast a great deal.

Chapter 23: *Dāna Līlā* in Shantipur. The three lords as One, tremendous fun. They appeared before the community in their previous forms. People praised this Shantipur *līlā*.

I wrote my lord's book 5 in nine chapters. I've written all twenty-three chapters.

Lord Caitanya, Nityānanda, Advaita, Sītā, the gurus, the Vaiṣṇavas, the *Bhāgavata Purāṇa*, and the *Bhagavad Gītā*.

Haricaraṇa Dāsa, whose hope is at the lotus feet of the lord of Shantipur, recites the *Advaita Maṅgala*.

Chapter 23, the *Dāna Līlā*, in book 5, Old Age, in the *Advaita Maṅgala*, is finished.

Lauḍīya Kṛṣṇadāsa's *Bālya-Līlā-Sūtra*

Chapter 1

The Family History

1. I praise the glorious Madana Gopāla, who satisfies Rādhā's desire, who engenders devotion, whose picture Viśākhā displayed with devotion.
2. My lord's perfect mantra drew him to descend from Purandara into Śacī's womb at Navadvīpa and to emancipation while still alive.
3. I praise the glorious Gauḍa Gopāla Hari, that ocean of love, whose greatness is so nicely described in the *Ananta Saṃhitā*.
4. I praise my guru Kamalākṣa, by which lord, with his nectar of great mercy, I have been liberated from the bondage of transmigration and the inevitable hazard of kingly pride.
5. And O best of lords, O Vaiṣṇavas, I praise you; please grant my heart's desire.
6. I composed this *Bālya-Līlā-Sūtra* with my feeble brain to propagate the type of devotion to Kṛṣṇa (advocated by) that moon, Advaita.
7. Brahmā the four-faced speaker of the Vedas was born from Nārāyaṇa; Aṅgiras, foremost chief of sages, was born from him, and from him the guru of the gods, Bṛhaspati.
8. The serene sage Bharadvāja was born from him; kind, well-versed in scripture, he was a master because he taught the sacred texts; a wise man, founder of the greatest clan.
9. The guru named Droṇa, well-versed in scripture, who trained the Kurus and Pāṇḍavas in archery and related sciences, was born from that great sage; Drauṇi Aśvatthāma, who knew battle, was born from the sage Droṇa.
10. The very wise man known as Harṣa, best of brahmins, knower of sacrificial ritual, was born into this clan. He came right here to Gauḍa. I will recite his lineage as best I can.

11. The high-born King Ādīśūra of old was of the noble lineage of the kings of Gauḍa. Strong and virtuous, he observed the timeless brahminical rituals and was pure-minded.
12. Seeing that there were no brahmins in the country capable of performing sacrifice, he recruited five brahmins from various clans in Kānyakubja.
13. He commissioned those brahmins to perform the sacrifice he wanted, and thanking them with gifts of wealth and clothing, sent them (back) to Kānyakubja.
14. But when they went back to their own country, people no longer respected them, so these brahmins returned to Gauḍa and set up residence in RāṚhā, with the king's permission, on land the king bestowed.
15. The so-called seven hundred brahmins (already) living in RāṚhā who had fallen into evil ways had daughters as beautiful as Lakṣmī. The five newcomers married them and settled happily into family life.
16. After their virtuous sons were born, some of those wives died, and then the maternal grandparents used the orphans' inheritance to take care of them.
17. Among those five brahmins brought to Ādīśūra's domain had been one brahmin named Harṣa, born in Bharadvāja's lineage.
18. In time his firstborn son, called Gautama, came to Gauḍa from Kānyakubja and told the pious king he was destitute.
19. "My father was your sacrificing priest; today his own community claims he committed the sin of arrogance. O King, how can I live there."
20. When he heard that, the wise King Ādīśūra welcomed him with great honor and gave him a very lovely, choice village in Vārendra.
21. Gautama, knower of many scriptures, accepted the village from the generous king and with his permission, took up residence there along with his wife, children, and servants.
22. Guṇākarācārya, called the Sky-dweller, the best of the yogis, was the son of that great Vedic scholar Gautama.
23. Ṛṣi Guṇākara had a son called Nārāyaṇa, known as "Pañcatapas" of the five fires. He was an ascetic devoted to performing austerities.
24. His son was a brahmin called Viṣṇu Miśra who best knew the scriptures, an ascetic who knew dharma fully; he was most celebrated for his Vedic interpretations.
25. After him came Kākutstha who was virtuous, handsome, and wise. Prajāpatyagnihotra, a very good sacrificer, was his son.
26. The son of that Vedic scholar was a master called Mātaṅga. (His son) was called Jikṣmaṇa Ācārya; he was well-versed in scripture.
27. His son was called Bhāskara, blessed with the title of "Ornament of Masters Learned in Vedānta." He attained the highest rank among all the councilors at the court of King Vallālasena.

28. After he got the title "Vārendra" from the king at the time of the Vārendra-RāṚhā division (of the brahmin community), he died and attained heaven (and) the lotus feet of his Lord.
29. His brother Parāśara, who knew the Vedas and other great scriptures, got the title "RāṚhi" from the king and wandered through RāṚhā to spread the Veda in that land.
30. In time Vallāla instituted the social rankings based on different qualities among the brahmins of RāṚhā and Vārendra, respectively.
31. Indeed, here are the qualities of a *kulīna*: scholarship, austerity, discipline, liberality, tranquillity, steadfastness, visiting many pilgrimage places, good conduct, devotion.
32. Here are the qualities of a *sacchrotriya*: scholarship, steadfastness, disçipline, great tranquillity, good conduct, strong devotion, visiting pilgrimage places, pure generosity.
33. One is called a *vipra* because of being in the brahmin class; one is said to be a twice-born (merely) because of *saṃskāras*, and a knower of the meanings of scriptures, wise and disciplined would be a *kaṣṭātmaka-śrotriya*, a *śrotriya* through his own effort.
34. From Bhāskara, that best of brahmins, was born the serene Āru Ojhā, widely respected and praised by his own people.
35. The brahmin Āru Ojhā was adorned with the eightfold virtues, knowledge, et cetera; a Ṛg Vedin, he knew the essence of sacrifice and rose like the moon over the mountain of his lineage. He attained the position at court called *siddha-śrotriya* through King Vallāla, because of the impartial pure mind of his divine guru.
36. Āru, best among Vedic scholars, was adorned with the title of Ojhā; and because he lived in the village of Naduli he became known as the Naduli-villager.
37. Yadu Paṇḍit was the son of the brahmin Āru Ojhā; he knew many scriptures, Vedas, et cetera, and was compassionate, calm-minded, and great.
38. Yadu's son (was) called Śrīpati Datta, a virtuous brahmin who was versed in *smṛti* and *śāstra*. He meditated on these scriptures and wrote a book, the *Smṛtisāra*.
39. The magnanimous king of Lauḍa, Sūrya Siṃha, a brahmin king in the most meritorious land of Śrīhaṭṭa, heard of that goodness manifest as Śrīpati Datta,
40. (and) very graciously brought him from the village of Naduli to his capital, the little village called Navagrāma, and settled him there.
41. That brahmin Śrīpati Datta settled in the region called Lauḍa, which was full of great riches, and the good Sūrya Siṃha very reverently appointed him his adviser.

42. With his advice, the kingdom became very rich and well-ruled. The king most gladly entrusted the responsibilities of his kingdom to that learned one.
43. The wise brahmin Kulapati was born from Śrīpati Datta. Kulapati the brahmin had a righteous son called Vibhākara.
44. His son was called Prabhākara, a great scholar, conversant with Ṛg Veda and a speaker of truth, born into Bharadvāja's clan.
45. He had three sons, Vidyādhara, Śakatari, and Nṛsiṃha.
46. Nṛsiṃha, friend of the distressed, generous, famous, humble, self-controlled, benevolent, took a vow and left that region and took up residence in Gauḍa.
47. He learned the fourteen *śāstras* of the barbarian and the Jaina scriptures from Jaṭādhara, crest-jewel of scholars, who held that title with respect to all authorities.
48. King Gaṇeśa, specialist in many scriptures, was completely captivated by the splendor of the perfume of the reputation of the great-minded Nṛsiṃha, as its loveliness burst forth.
49. That refuge of good brahmins who know the Vedas, like an eagle on the mountain of good bloodlines, is the suppressor of the wicked, protector of sages, generous, virtuous, the peak of devotion to Hari.
50. King Gaṇeśa brought Nṛsiṃha and his ambassadors to his capital, Dinājapura, where there were many courtiers. Nṛsiṃha mastered politics and then became his skilled minister.
51. Then, aided by Nṛsiṃha's cleverness, the great noble King Gaṇeṣa overthrew the barbarian sons of the foreigners who controlled Gauḍa, and he became sovereign in Gauḍa.
52. In 1229 Śaka (c. 1307 CE) Gaṇeśa brilliantly defeated the Muslims, and Gauḍa came under single rule.
53. In time Nṛsiṃha's virtuous wife Kamalā, who was like Lakṣmī, gave birth to one daughter and one son.
54. That beautiful, slender, sweet-voiced, and intelligent daughter called Kulojjvalā was the flame of the family.
55. Her (Kamalā's) son was actually Kubera, the god of wealth, and was known in this world as Kubera. He appeared to reveal Sadāśiva, the essence of Vāsudeva.
56. In time the dear son of the semidivine Nṛsiṃha, the brahmin Kubera, who read many scriptures and was very clever, came to be known as Tarkapañcānana.

This is the first chapter in the *Bālya-Līlā-Sūtra* composed by the noble Lauḍīya Kṛṣṇadāsa, entitled "The Family History."

Chapter 2

The Family History

1. Nṛsiṃha, his heart set on living in a place of pilgrimage, took his wife, son, and daughter to the village of Shantipur.
2. It was full of many kinds of people, and embellished by its markets, et cetera; it was like Tapoloka, the eternal penance-world, on the bank of the Gaṅgā, because of (all) the sacrifices (being performed there).
3. That brahmin, scion of the lineage of teachers, lived there for a long time. People called him Naduli because he was originally from the village of Naduli.
4. One day Nṛsiṃha began to consider the best possible groom for his daughter: a *kulīna*, the best among pious men.
5. Just then a great brahmin scholar approached on his way to bathe in the Bhāgīrathī River.
6. As soon as Nṛsiṃha saw him, he was happy to offer him a seat and bid him welcome.
7. "Where have you come from, O Lord? Tell (me) what is your purpose, Sir? Now that I've seen you today, the night has become a beautiful dawn."
8. Rejoicing to hear those sweet words, the scholar smiled and replied to the wise Nṛsiṃha:
9. "The land of Bhārata is glowing with the moonbeams of your fame. I am a Kula sage and I've come to you from Madhyagrāma."
10. Nrsiṃha joyfully saluted the brahmin and quickly replied, "Please tell me, Sir, what you have determined: to which *kulīna* groom should I give my daughter?"
11. The family priest made his decision there and replied sweetly:
12. "In Madhyagrāma there is an outstanding *kulīna* named Madhusūdana, in Maitreya's family, who stands out from the others.
13. Suṣeṇa, (one of the five Kānyakubja brahmins) who had come to Gauḍa, had two sons, Kratu and Maitreya. Maitreya had a son named Sthirācārya.
14. Mahānidhi was his son, and his son was Bṛhaspati. His sons were Sola and Kupa, well-versed in all the scriptures.
15. Kupa went to Madhyagrāma. His son was called Nṛsiṃha. Suki was born from Nṛsiṃha; Madhusūdana is his son.
16. If you offer your daughter to that groom, her good reputation with the *siddaśrotriya* community would be ensured.
17. This speech is the truth. Go to Madhyagrāma as you wish, but you will accomplish your goal at great cost and trouble."
18. Then the brahmin accepted the money Nṛsiṃha had offered, conferred his blessing on the teacher, and went home.

19. That brahmin's speech sounded like a voice from heaven to Nrsiṃha, whose sole concern was his family's position. He set off for Madhyagrāma with many jewels.
20. Nṛsiṃha took a *śālagrāma* stone, a cow, (and) his daughter Kulojjvalā, stepped into the boat, and began the journey.
21. And in just a few days the boat reached the river dock near Madhumaitra's house.
22. The good-hearted Madhumaitra had just finished his evening prayers and was about to go home when he saw the boat. He said:
23. "Where has this boat come from, and who is that standing in it? Speak quickly, Boatman, I need to get home."
24. The wise, magnanimous Nṛsiṃha announced his name and address and said:
25. "By what name is Your Honor called; where is your house? Please tell me quickly, O brahmin; I am eager to hear."
26. Maitreya Madhusūdana gave his name and residence quite politely.
27. Nrsiṃha heard his words and thought, "This is the one!" Filled with great joy, he raced toward him.
28. His mind at peace, the brahmin took Maitreya's hand and respectfully brought that lord among brahmins into the boat.
29. The wise Nṛsiṃha, resolute and suppliant, said to Madhusūdana, who was sitting on the seat he'd offered:
30. "O Brahmin, please grant my wish by marrying this daughter of mine, Kulojjvalā."
31. Immediately upon hearing these words, Maitreya, surprised, said, "*Kulīnas* marry *kulīnas*, not *śrotriyas*.
32. Long ago someone foretold that I would marry without the consent of my children.
33. If I transgress the ancient rules in my marriage, there's no doubt that the destruction of the *kulīna* lineage will follow."
34. The calm, magnanimous Nṛsiṃha listened to the intended groom's refusal and again spoke.
35. "I am indeed a *siddha-śrotriya* Naduli-villager, a high-principled *Ṛg Veda* scholar of Bharadvāja Muṇi's clan.
36. The *siddha-śrotriya* line is considered equivalent to (that of) the *kulīnas*, and so according to scripture, you may consider this marriage blameless.
37. And if you don't take my daughter, you will be to blame for killing a cow, a brahmin, and Viṣṇu's wife."
38. Thus addressed, that Maitreya, terrified that he might accrue sin, agreed to marry the girl.
39. Thus Madhusūdana, the lion of the *kulīnas*, married her according to the custom of the *kulīnas* by touching a water-filled clay pot, and with darbha grass in their hands, they were purified.

40. He uttered the mantras for engagement and marriage, speaking words suitably auspicious, and joyfully released the (water from the) marriage pot into the pure waters at the landing.
41. When Madhu's son heard about the wedding, he was very upset (and) said angrily, "I will not allow my father, defiled by this vile deed, to enter this house today."
42. He and his brothers concocted an astonishing plan and barred the front door of their house with sharpened bamboo poles.
43. Meanwhile, the marriage finalized, the wise Nṛsiṃha returned home to Naduli.
44. But the cheerful Madhu could not go home peacefully after he had contracted the marriage. Angry to find the door of his house barred, he blurted out:
45. "Learning of my legitimate marriage (contracted) today with that pure brahmin named Nrsiṃha, my own evil sons, intent on mischief and consumed by anger, have barred themselves in the house.
46. I am certainly not at fault by having contracted a marriage with the great Nrsiṃha, who is a *siddhaśrotriya*."
47. When they heard their father's proclamation, those sons of Maitreya said, "Even though you are a *kulīna* who recites the Gāyatrī mantra, you have fallen from your own dharma.
48. Society cannot accept you who are a fallen evildoer. Think about all this, then do as you see fit."
49. Ānai and Madhu's other sons and their followers deliberated about their father's transgression, and then after consultation with the ministers and their own people, banished their father from the community.
50. The great-souled brahmin Madhusūdana of the Maitra lineage sought the help of a *kulīna* named Dhoyī Bāgchi.
51. Through the efforts of Dhoyī, crest-jewel of the *kulīna*s and a Vedic priest, Maitreya regained his good name and caste.
52. Except for Arjunai and Ānai, Madhu's sons who had (previously) censured their father ran to beg his forgiveness.
53. Arjunai and Ānai remained estranged from their father. Dhoyī called them impostors because of their deceitful minds.
54. Those two sons of Madhu were banished from the community as rogues, villains, and cowards, and the others returned home.
55. Then Madhu, along with the righteous brahmins including the *kulīna*s, went to Nṛsiṃha's place and married Kulojjvalā.
56. The drums sounded. Nṛsiṃha joyfully gave property, gold, et cetera, to his daughter and to Maitreya.
57. Nṛsiṃha pleased Maitreya's friends and relatives with fine cloth and other goods and food of excellent quality.
58. All of those disagreeable *kulīna*s who did not go to the wedding, who had been expelled from the community, came to be known as *kāpa*.

59. In honor of his daughter Kulojjvalā's marriage to a *kulīna*, Nṛsiṃha delivered a column of praise to the heavens.
60. That brahmin called Nīlamegha, best among *sacchrotriya* Vedic scholars, generous, famous, disciplined, serene, great-souled, born into the family of Mayura Bhaṭṭa,
61. wanted to give his own blessed daughter Lābhā, who was filled with a multitude of virtues, to Nrsiṃha's dear son, the wise Kubera.
62. So at an auspicious moment Nīlamegha gave his daughter Lābhā to Kubera with due ceremony, and rejoiced.
63. Then Nṛsiṃha left his body on the bank of the Bhāgīrathī at Shantipur and went to heaven.
64. Kubera, who was very wealthy, offered various items to his father in places like Gayā and in his house, as was customary.
65. And then wise Kubera, well-versed in the great scriptures, calm, traveled from Shantipur to Lauḍa; he was constantly honored by the king of that country.
66. The king of that realm, who was very well-versed in scripture, employed as his councillor that epitome of nobility Tarkapañcānana, conversant with many scriptures on politics, et cetera.

This is the second chapter in the *Bālya-Līlā-Sūtra*, composed by Lauḍīya Kṛṣṇadāsa, called "The Family History."

Chapter 3

The Birth of Lord Advaita

1. Lābhā, Kubera's wife, a very virtuous woman, gave birth to six sons and a daughter, one each year.
2. Her six sons, Lakṣmīkānta, Śrīkānta, Hariharānanda, Kuśala, Sadāśiva, and Kīrtticandra, died.
3. Her daughter also died. Lābhā was beside herself with grief for her children,
4. and cried day and night with her suffering Finally she said to her husband, "Dear, I cannot stay here."
5. With those words the brahmin Kubera and his wife left the comfort of their home in Lauḍa for Shantipur on the banks of the Gaṅgā to worship Hari.
6. One day while the noble Kubera, beloved of ascetics, was meditating on the feet of Viṣṇu, a clear vision appeared before his very eyes.
7. The radiant river goddess Gaṅgā Devī spoke to the transfixed brahmin: "My lord will be born as your son, as a portion of himself."
8. Then she who rose from the water at Viṣṇu's feet, Gaṅgā Devī, disappeared. Kubera went home and told Lābhā what had happened.

9. And after some little time had passed in Shantipur, Lābhā, whose womb was a jewel, became pregnant.
10. When the wise Kubera discovered that his wife was pregnant, he fed brahmins, et cetera, to get Lord Nārāyaṇa (as his son).
11. And meanwhile Mahāviṣṇu, noticing the decline of righteousness in Kali Yuga, decided to come to earth.
12. "That teacher with his intense devotion is a noble man who seeks me, and with his wife has been performing austerities. I (shall) be born on earth as their son."
13. Thus Mahāviṣṇu, with his infinite potency, together with Gopeśvara and Ādiśiva, decided to take up life in the world (and) entered the ocean of milk of Lābhā's belly to take away the suffering of the world through love.
14. At this point, the teacher Kubera, at the order of King Divyasiṃha, brought his wife back to Lauḍa.
15. When he saw them, Divyasiṃha, the king of that country, bowed and saluted and asked delightedly after their welfare.
16. The great-minded Kubera replied to the king, "My wife has conceived again back there."
17. At that very moment an aged brahmin soothsayer arrived and happily told Kubera:
18. "O learned one, an exalted being has entered this woman's womb. Her son will be long-lived and versed in all the scriptures,
19. and a giver of great compassion; and he will unquestionably appear in your devout and sanctified house to establish righteousness."
20. And the brahmin soothsayer vanished. Kubera was bewildered and searched everywhere for him, to no avail.
21. One night Lābhā saw Viṣṇu and Śiva in a dream, as one most splendid spirit in her own lotus heart.
22. They were singing "Hare Kṛṣṇa" and dancing joyfully. Sinners go straight to heaven the moment they hear those names.
23. This situation frightened the god of death, Yama Dharmarāja, who hastened to throw himself down humbly before Viṣṇu and praise him.
24. When Lābhā awoke she told her husband that dream, and Kubera was pleased.
25. On the auspicious seventh day in the bright fortnight of the most auspicious month of Māgha in 1356 Śaka (c. 1434 CE) the glorious Advaita, out of compassion (for the world), took birth in Lauḍa.
26. A fragrant breeze blew; the gods in their happiness rained down flowers. The gods and demigods came and praised him and recited the Vedas.
27. "You alone are the cause for hope for the world, you create the world and you destroy it. We do not know exactly who you are, but we take refuge in that eternal form.

28. You alone are life itself, compassionate, O Viṣṇu-Śiva, and you have appeared to present pure devotion, and above all, you reveal the ocean of divine love which is the eternal energy that is Kṛṣṇa.
29. We gods and sages, along with our retinues, will appear here on this good earth just to serve Kṛṣṇa and eternally worship you. This is our proclamation."
30. They praised Mahāviṣṇu and bowed to his lotus feet, and then the delighted gods and sages returned to heaven.
31. When the great wise son of Nṛsiṃha had bathed and completed his sunrise prayers and worship of the divine mothers, he greeted his new son,
32. and after finishing the proper birth rituals he gave the priests money (and) gave the singers and musicians money, clothing, et cetera.
33. He gave heavenly goods and as much wealth as they wanted to the blind, deaf, and hunchbacks, and to those who were sick and miserable.
34. He honored the women with rivers of betel and money. He put on a great festival for the wise inhabitants of the village of Lauḍa.
35. The midwife got money and clothing and quickly cut the placenta. She bathed the newborn with water and all kinds of herbs.
36. The midwife worshiped the crying child in his mother's lap. Lābhā offered her breast to her divine son.
37. The sight of her son's lotus face made Lābhā happier than humanly possible. When she saw the auspicious mark of the virtuous on her son's body, she knew he was the best of men.
38. On the eleventh day, with tremendous joy Kubera gave his beautiful son with the lovely eyes the name Kamalākṣa, as the astrologer had instructed.

This is the third chapter, called "The Birth of Lord Advaita," in the *Bālya-Līlā-Sūtra* composed by Lauḍīya Kṛṣṇadāsa.

Chapter 4

The Appearance of the Paṇā Tīrtha

1. And so on the right day under an auspicious constellation, Kubera worshiped the ancestors properly and performed the baby's first-food rite, with sacred words (uttered) by brahmins who knew the Vedas.
2. King Divyasiṃha himself had been invited and arrived with his wife, his ministers, and his attendants, delighted to see the divine child.
3. And the noble Kubera, overcome with joy, provided delicious food to everyone at his son's festival and many jewels to the brahmins, his priests.
4. All the people, rejoicing, set out loudly to bless his house. The generous queen gave the son of Kubera Pañcānana an elephant pearl.

5. As Kamalākṣa grew in joy, he behaved exactly like an ordinary child.
6. Within a few days, even though he was only a child, he would eat no food or water except what had (first) been offered to Viṣṇu, to provide an example.
7. He spoke sweet words, summing up all the scriptures: "Whatever food and water are not offered to Viṣṇu are excrement and urine. If one eats and drinks all this, only penance can erase that sin."
8. Kubera worshiped Hari with the brahmins and had his son's education begun at an auspicious time.
9. One day Lābhā, (that) virtuous woman whose sole purpose was righteousness, had placed a young tulasī leaf in the chapel to use later in her worship of Gopāla, and went about her household chores.
10. Meanwhile, little Kamalākṣa entered the chapel and exuberantly began to worship Gopāla with fragrant flowers, et cetera.
11. The lovely Lābhā heard the bell ringing and went to see what the boy was doing, and said to her little son:
12. "Son, since you have not been initiated you cannot worship the image of Gopāla."
13. The lord of the universe, smiling, replied sweetly to reassure his mother.
14. "Mother, there are no restrictions as to who may worship Kṛṣṇa, nor are there any restrictions regarding initiation.
15. Initiation and such rituals are for those who do not inherently find supreme joy in worshiping Kṛṣṇa.
16. Devotion itself is the *cit-śakti*, the mental power of the Lord, the bestower of his love. This, and never anything else, pleases the Lord.
17. Devotion is the best form of worship; Hari accepts it unfailingly. When it comes to devotion, only purity of heart matters, not time and place.
18. If a non-Hindu (Muslim) ventures onto the path of devotion even by chance, then he automatically becomes better than a brahmin.
19. If a brahmin endowed with the 200 virtues be devoid of devotion, he is considered the lowest ignorant barbarian; so say the divine sages."
20. When she had heard these remarkable words from the lotus of her son, Lābhā was amazed; further, she was captivated by his supernatural power.
21. From here on I shall tell of the birth of Lord Paṇā Tīrtha, just by hearing of whom the world becomes pure.
22. One night Lābhā, her son at her breast, dreamed of two shining boys, one like a silver mountain, one darkish and beautiful, covered with jewels, as playing resplendently in a lovely courtyard.
23. And those two merged and entered the body of Kamalākṣa. Lābhā woke up, got out of bed and told her son:
24. "O Mahāviṣṇu, Creator of the Universe, give (us) the nectar of your lotus feet. All the pilgrimage sites rest upon your lotus foot."
25. He said, "Why do you say this, Mother, to your son? I will bring the pilgrimage places here today; this is my solemn promise."

26. Thus by the power of the pull of the command of Mahāviṣṇu, Creator of the Universe, all the pilgrimage sites appeared on the mountain at Lauḍa.
27. Kamalākṣa addressed Gaṅgā and the other pilgrimage sites with delight: "You will always abide on this mountain in the thirteenth day of the dark fortnight in the month of Caitra.
28. One who bathes with devotion here at Paṇā Tīrtha can earn the collective devotion of all the *tīrthas*."
29. Lābhā heard him welcome Gaṅgā and all the pilgrimage sites, and delighted, approached her son.
30. As Lābhā stood to bathe on the mountainside, a lovely waterfall poured over her head with much shouting of Hari's name (and) blowing of conches.
31. The lord addressed words like nectar to his own mother. "Look at this unpolluted dark water of the Yamunā.
32. But look, the cool water of the Gaṅgā is white. This water, each a different color, is the source of the respective *tīrtha*s.
33. Mother, this is salt water from the ocean, the king of *tīrtha*s. Taste it, (then) you will realize that I'm telling the truth.
34. Blessed are those people who see this great miracle and wretched are those who will not, even in a hundred lifetimes.
35. Those people who bathe here on the thirteenth day of the dark fortnight in the month of Caitra will in effect be bathing in the waters of all the *tīrthas*."
36. Just then a deer, shot by a hunter's arrow, plunged into the flowing water of that Panā Tīrtha, and died and took on a divine body.
37. Lābhā was thoroughly amazed to see that marvelous great miracle of the Paṇā Tīrtha—the deer's heavenly transmutation.
38. Charmed, that virtuous woman drank water from all the *tīrtha*s and, praising her son, picked him up and took him home.
39. "On the thirteenth day of the dark fortnight of the month of Caitra, Paṇā Tīrtha, which consists of all the *tīrtha*s, always purifies the whole world; there is no doubt about it.
40. Thus whatever pure-minded person bathes with devotion in the king of *tīrtha*s called Paṇā on the date of Vāruṇī attains salvation at the feet of Viṣṇu.
41. When the thirteenth day of the dark fortnight of Caitra falls in the constellation of Śatabhiṣā on a Saturday it is called 'Mahavāruṇī.' The person who bathes in it then is freed of all sins; he goes to my world.
42. If Vāruṇī falls on a Saturday on an auspicious date it is called ' Mahāmahā'; that Vāruṇī is very rare. Whoever bathes in the Paṇā Tīrtha at that time is liberated from the bonds of existence, (and) indeed attains me," the lord said.

This is the fourth chapter, called "The Appearance of the Paṇā Tīrtha," in the *Bālya-Līlā-Sūtra* composed by Lauḍīya Kṛṣṇaḍāsa.

Chapter 5

The Manifestation of Superhuman Powers

1. At the proper time the king of Lauḍa sent his son to the guru's house, (where) he spent his time studying the Kalāpaka grammar and the lexica with the (other) students.
2. Kubera's son was also in the house with the students. That subtle-minded one had mastered all of that grammar with the lexica and literary criticism in just three years.
3. And one evening the king's son went from his guru's house to a Devī temple with his teacher's son and bowed to her respectfully. The teacher's son did not bow to Caṇḍikā.
4. The prince, overcome with anger, harshly rebuked his guru's son: "Bow to Kālī or I will beat you for this insult."
5. Kamalākṣa, the husband of that goddess, bellowed out a loud "HUM," and the prince collapsed on the ground, unconscious.
6. When they saw their prince lying on the ground, his trembling servants went to the king, wailing and stammering.
7. "The pandit's son stunned the prince with his 'HUM' sounds. He's collapsed on the threshold of the temple of the blessed goddess Kālī."
8. That disturbing news upset the king, who was in the Kātyāyaṇī temple with a wise courtier, and he raced off.
9. Seeing his dear son lying dead, he fell to the ground like a mountain shattered by a thunderbolt, wailing with distress; his ministers lamented to each other.
10. Master Kubera, best of scholars, suppressed his own grief to comfort the bereaved king:
11. "O King, don't grieve; I will bring my son here and find out what he has done, my lord."
12. Immediately, with the king's permission, Kubera took a lamp in his hand. Distressed in his thatched hut in the forest, he kept saying "O Son" over and over. He wandered all over the country, and the great brahmin saw him emerging from an anthill, as the sage Vālmīki had appeared from an anthill.
13. He lifted his son onto his lap and firmly but calmly demanded, "Tell me the truth, son, what happened to the prince? "
14. Kamalākṣa demurred and told his father Kubera, "The prince became furious and said some bad things. He has only fainted."
15. They continued talking on their way back to the unconscious prince in the temple of the goddess.
16. Divyasiṃha saw them coming, and with trembling heart he rose quickly, bowing. The king spoke to the son of the best of sages with the words, "Tell me, has my poor son been embraced by the fire of Brahmā because of a guru's

anger? How can anyone civilized take offense when a wise man speaks the truth?"

17. When Kamalākṣa heard this he was ashamed and told the king, "The fire of raging anger has not killed him; he is (only) unconscious.
18. Sprinkle holy Gaṅgā water (lit., water from Viṣṇu's feet) all over his body, and he will regain consciousness and we'll all be very happy."
19. As soon as he had heard that good news, the king joyfully gave the boy the foot-water from a *śālagrāma* brought by a brahmin. (Then) seizing Kamalākṣa's lotus feet and fixing his thoughts on the lord, Divyasiṃha praised the lord, Kubera's son Kamalākṣa, with devotion.
20. "You are truly a form of Śiva, the teacher of Brahmā for the world. God has placed this brahmin's footprint in my heart.
21. Sir, you are of a brahmin family, brahmin-like, a delighter of brahmins. Nowhere in the world does a lion give birth to a jackal.
22. Have mercy, my lord, with me; restore (my) son to life like I am alive. May the River Gaṅgā be your eternal glory."
23. Thus the beneficent Kamalākṣa instructed him to sprinkle the nectar of immortality, the holy Gaṅgā water, over the prince's entire body.
24. The prince regained consciousness instantly and got up. He grasped Kamalākṣa's feet and bowed again and again.
25. The waters of a sacred river purify when one drinks them and bathes in them and sees them; (but) the mere thought of the water from Hari's feet truly (purifies) the three worlds.
26. Then he thought, "They should know who I really am." The true lord of yoga made his magic manifest to them.
27. Everyone was overcome with joy when the prince got up. They returned to their homes with the names of Hari on their lips.
28. The king returned to his own city with his ministers, convinced that some powerful medicine had restored his son's life.
29. He put Tarkapañcānana's son on his (Kubera's) lap and caressed him and went quickly home, amazed by the child's deed.
30. Kubera told his wife the whole story. Full of love for her son, she marveled.
31. Thus Kubera, ornament of the brahmin lineage, absolutely devoted to righteousness, looked at this apparent child, bright golden like a sage, his son. Seeing that the time was right, he quickly invited the scripture-knowing brahmins and the sacrificial priests (and) his relatives (and) gave him (Kamalākṣa) the sacred threads as ordained by scripture.
32. After his initiation Kamalākṣa studied the six Vedāṅgas from his father. Even though he was only a child, because of his intelligence he memorized the Vedas with their six *aṅgas*.
33. Before long they saw that he was thoroughly conversant in all the scriptures, and everybody said, "He is maintaining the Vedas in the world."

This is the fifth chapter, called "The Manifestation of Superhuman Powers," in the *Bālya-Līlā-Sūtra* composed by Lauḍīya Kṛṣṇadāsa.

Chapter 6

The Goddess Kālī Vanishes

1. Then on the auspicious evening of the new moon in the month of Kārtika (Dīvālī) the king went to Caṇḍī's most holy temple to worship. He praised the goddess, bowed with devotion, and presented her with many kinds of offerings to please her. Then he entered the assembly of his wise and dear ministers to hear the concert of instrumental and vocal music.
2. Kamalākṣa arrived with all his friends and sat down without bowing to Kālī.
3. Infuriated, the king said, "Why do you not bow to the stone image which everyone should worship, the goddess who tames the fear of death, the female form of Brahmā? Tell me why; did some scripture-knowing guru teach you this, or is it your own idea, brahmin boy?"
4. The god of gods, his moonlike face smiling, kept the true reason to himself and humbly replied to the good king: "Mahātma, listen to me: Of course I know that gods, demons, and men should always praise Śarvāṇī.
5. This goddess, Viṣṇu's magic personified, keeps people from worshiping Hari. She gives people puny bodies of her own creation and keeps them roaming continuously in this miserable world where they have already been crushed so many times. Therefore Māyā is something of an enemy to embodied souls, and so I do not bow to her.
6. But if Kālī is a form of Brahmā and pervades the worlds and beyond, alas, O Refuge of Men! She is not confined to that stone image in the corner, and if you think that's the case, you are blind to worship her. Look at scripture, O King: the *Gītā* proclaims this."
7. Completely stunned, the poet drank in his son's lovely words. Kubera, ever mindful of scripture, wisely replied to his son:
8. "Indeed all the gods worship and serve the goddess Māyā, the female form of Brahmā, source of all virtues, attested in all the scriptures, with austerity, sacrifice, prayer, and meditation. As the cause of creation, preservation, and destruction, she grants liberation and sustains all life. Son, you know what is right; join your hands in devotion and bow to Kālī this minute.
9. Son, scripture consistently acclaims Viṣṇu's beautiful Śakti. Even Lord Rāma fashioned a pure clay image of Viṣṇu's Śakti and worshiped it, and brought about the destruction of the demons and so brought joy to gods and men. Sītā got her lord; the young milkmaids in Vraja, Kṛṣṇa."
10. In response to his father's true words the great-souled one politely said: "My head is fixed on the feet of Lord Janārddana and cannot be removed."

11. His father wisely replied, "Māyā is no more separate from Viṣṇu than heat from fire. Therefore, son, bow with devotion to this eternal and universally auspicious power of God."
12. The lord smiled and answered his father sweetly, "I am telling the truth, Father. Listen carefully!
13. Just as a cātaka bird would not drink water from a river, tank, or well; just as a cākora would by its nature drink only moonbeams and ingest nothing else,
14. So naturally this very cākora who guides my senses does not feed on the honey of the lotus feet of the Mother without the nectar of the lotus feet of Sacchidānanda, the lord who is truth, consciousness, and bliss."
15. That supremely wise man was about to say more when Kamalākṣa continued, respectfully, his head bowed.
16. "The resplendent primal goddess is described by the bowed heads of flocks of gods—Viṣṇu, Śiva, et cetera, and by god, man, and sage as wearing a garland of skulls. She certainly cannot be captured through the courtesy, praise, and prostrations of a living being. For one who drinks divine nectar, there is no desire for anything but the moon."
17. When he had heard his son's words like nectar of utter humility, the wise Kubera, realizing that he was acting like a devotee of Kātyāyaṇī, was pleased, and that great-souled one answered his dear son,
18. "She who is compassionate to all, who looks upon the three types (best, mediocre, and worst) as equal, bestows heavenly joy even on the lowly. She is the mother of Gaṇeśa as surely as the River Gaṅgā flowed down from heaven."
19. When he had heard his father's words, he who appeared to be a child (said): "Then I am bowing to Bhavānī." Śiva's wife, with trembling heart, quickly turned her face away to avoid her husband's bow.
20. The daughter of the mountain, destroyer of the fear of existence, worshiped by gods and men, said to Pāśupati:
21. "I appeared in Lauḍa to see you in your full form, my lord. Now I'm leaving the palace immediately."
22. He who had descended to earth as a devotee addressed that supreme goddess, "You are (my) soul, my power, you know my every thought.
23. O Mahāmāyā in the form of devotion, you will resort to human form in Gauḍa and become my helpmate.
24. Kṛṣṇa himself will appear with a fair form in Navadvīpa, bestowing the loving devotion that is Hari's name on embodied souls.
25. I will settle in Shantipur, Devī, and promise to bring Hari as Parabrahmā Himself, that the world might be saved through Him."
26. Thus addressed the blazing Mahāmāyā burst open the stone image with her splendid power and fled, making the ten directions shine,
27. and simultaneously this human form of Śiva disappeared. The courtiers were astonished when Kamalākṣa vanished before their very eyes.

28. And when everyone saw that lovely dark and moonlit stone image stand in that pavilion with eyes averted and suddenly burst open, they were sore amazed.

This is the sixth chapter, called "The Goddess Kālī Vanishes," in the *Bālya-Līlā-Sūtra* composed by Lauḍīya Kṛṣṇadāsa.

Chapter 7

The Meeting with Advaita

1. Kubera, discovering his son had disappeared, set out from home, grief-stricken, bursting into tears again and again.
2. When he saw his virtuous wife Lābhā approaching him, Kubera, out of his mind with grief, wailing, told her everything that had happened.
3. The moment Lābhā heard from Kubera of her son's departure, she fell to the ground unconscious, crying, "Alas!" Her eyes, filled with the tears which are a woman's treasures, went blind. Kubera saw his wife unconscious, and he fainted, too.
4. And both Kubera and Lābhā, stunned, beat their breasts and wailed in their tremendous grief, staining their faces with their tears.
5. Kubera could not eat, and fell asleep in Hari's temple. Lord Viṣṇu appeared and spoke these profound words with deep compassion: "Give up this longing for your son. He is not your son, he is Śiva, and he will cause Hari to appear and make Hari's name manifest.
6. In reward for your virtue, Śaṅkara, worshiped by (all) the gods beginning with Brahmā, became the one you cherish as your son. When he entered the room, Bhavānī's image split open in response to his bow, and then he went to Shantipur.
7. You are Kubera the wealth-giver. The compassionate Lord Śiva was born to Lābhā and you because of your past merit.
8. Neither of you will return to the phenomenal world, nor to hell; (rather) you (will attain) a perfected form."
9. In his dream Kubera the wise and eloquent spoke with Lord Viṣṇu, recapitulating his son's greatness with a glad heart and tears in his eyes. He bowed to the Lord Gopāla who grants devotion and saves his devotees from this violent existence. Comforted, his heart anointed with love for Kṛṣṇa, he then recounted his dream to Lābhā.
10. When she heard her husband's happy words, Lābhā's eyes (filled with) tears of joy, and her hair stood on end. She said, "O Lord of my life, I pray that the message of this dream of yours is not false.
11. If my son is Śiva, the essence of Kṛṣṇa who is devoted to his followers, then when I die I will go to hell because of my sins.

12. Once our son stole some sesame candy and ate it, and I got angry and beat him with a stick.
13. Another time our son begged for a banana, and when he did not get the banana he rolled around on the ground, crying loudly over and over.
14. Lord Śiva is to be worshiped, but thinking only of my own family's welfare, I bound him. He did various deeds to please me, (his) mother, with a glad heart, like any other child.
15. Perhaps my son Śiva, the best of men, is living happily in heaven, but this separation from my son is like a fire in which the log of my heart burns eternally.
16. Alas, alas, when will the light of my son's moonlike face fall upon me to put out the heat of this fire in my heart and give (me) peace?"
17. When he had heard Lābhā's words, wise Kubera, hoping to console her, said:
18. "Do not fear, O devoted mother, Harihara is always compassionate. He gives peace, protects his devotees, is self-reliant, and squelches the wicked. Since you carried him in your belly you will attain the ultimate success of liberation at death. O lovely-minded one, you will reach your desired lord."
19. Lābhā, the mother of Śiva, listened and then replied to her husband: "Sir, Fate has not granted us the happiness of having a son. My Lord knows this. Śiva became our son and disappeared from us. Let's leave this householder life behind and take up the path of yoga, which destroys sorrow."
20. The couple resolved to do so, controlled their passions, and experienced the joys of yoga with the support of knowledge.
21. Meanwhile, in Shantipur, Kamalākṣa became aware that his parents, in Navagrāma, had taken up yoga.
22. Then Lord Mahāviṣṇu, who had taken on human form by his own will, sent a servant who could run quickly to them.
23. His messenger raced to Navagrāma and delivered the lord's kind letter to Kubera, while he himself went to Lauḍa.
24. Kubera, reading that letter which his son's lotus hand had written, told Lābhā, her heart full of the fire of separation from her good son, these cheerful words to extinguish the pain of her longing: "My dear, your son is in a comfortable house on the bank of the Gaṅgā."
25. Lābhā and Kubera immediately set out for their house in Shantipur and with great joy found the lotus of their son's lovely face. Their faces streaming with tears of joy, they embraced their son, bathing his head with their glistening tears.
26. The great lord Maheśa immediately took the dust of the sacred feet of his mother and father and made something like a *tilaka* on his forehead and praised them to instruct the world. "You two are yourselves gods who have appeared solely to please me. Let my mind praise your two feet; I pray for nothing else."

27. Thus addressed, Kubera spoke to his son: "Cut that out! You need to study *dharma-śāstra*. A very wise man predicted that you will live for one hundred years. At first study scripture to the best of your ability.
28. In the town of Pūrṇavatī lives the peaceful-minded Śānta, a Vedic philosopher, the best of brahmins. He has all the qualities of Kṛṣṇa's tutor Sāndīpani.
29. Make up your mind and go to him immediately. What you need to do, young man, is to study scripture with him."

This is the seventh chapter, called "The Meeting with Advaita," in the *Bālya-Līlā-Sūtra* composed by Lauḍīya Kṛṣṇadāsa.

Chapter 8

Kubera's Ascent to Heaven

1. And so in accord with his father's words, Kamalākṣa went straight to Pūrṇavatī and bowed to the brahmin Śānta.
2. Śānta, the lofty-minded master of the Vedas, asked Kamalākṣa, "What is your name, son, where do you live? Tell me why you have come here."
3. The brahmin Kamalākṣa told the guru his particulars (and) proceeded with his study of the six great schools of philosophy.
4. The brahmin Śānta and many of his students would go to an oblong lotus pond to carefully collect lotuses for their worship of Śiva and Viṣṇu.
5. The brahmin scholar Śānta noticed a particular lotus in the middle of the pond and said to the students, "Who can bring (me) that lovely lotus?" The students said, "We cannot."
6. But Lord Kamalākṣa walked right into the middle of the lake full of lotuses and picked that especially lovely one for his guru and returned to the shore.
7. When the dharma-knowing guru saw this miraculous deed, he knew Kamalākṣa was a god, but all the others thought him an impostor.
8. Then the guru asked Śiva in private, "Tell me, son, what god are you?" The son of the sage Kubera replied, "I am not a god; I am a portion of Śiva."
9. Then that serene guru realized that Śiva stood before him, and requested: "O Śiva, (take) great pity on me! (you are) the chief of the gods who lead us off (to liberation)."
10. The wise brahmin Kamalākṣa concealed his true form and said to the well-restrained guru, "O Guru! How can you praise me, born as a human, as the nondual one (Śiva)? Tell me now."
11. The brahmin Śānta replied, "You have taken a lovely human form to play as a mortal.
12. Indeed you are the guru of the world. You made me (your) guru and you are studying the holy scripture of the Vedas. Now that I have become the guru

of my Lord, a living master, I shall attain liberation, which is difficult to attain."

13. When he had said this to the lord, the brahmin sage Śānta praised him as enjoined by holy scripture as he taught, and then both master and student each performed their respective sacred duties according to the *Ṛg Veda*.
14. Thus after the brahmin Kamalākṣa had studied the Vedas and other scriptures to his satisfaction, he asked his guru, master of Vedānta, (for permission) to go home, as was proper.
15. The learned Śānta thus addressed these stammering words to Kamalākṣa:
16. "My wife and child and I are sunk in the ocean of bliss of your devotion. Therefore just as a poor person cannot leave his property, my mind does not want to abandon you, who give pleasure to heart, eye, and ear."
17. The incarnation of Mahāviṣṇu responded to his affectionate guru's misery.
18. "This is the proper duty of the wise toward a child who is deaf and blind, as the natural wetness of water proves. Now please be so kind as to grant me permission to attend to my dear parents, by which service a living being attains the highest immortality, O Sage."
19. Śānta, surrounded by wise men, replied to that lord, "Your devotion to your parents is like Rāma's.
20. O Child, I am very pleased with you and (so) name you Vedapañcānana, Five-Faced Śiva of the Vedas, because of your guru-like knowledge of scriptures."
21. When he had heard the sweet words which had come forth from the blue lotus face of his guru, Lord Śiva was somewhat embarrassed but delighted in his knowledge.
22. Then with great respect Kamalākṣa ritually circumambulated his guru three times and bowed to him with incessant devotion, and returned to Shantipur.
23. When Lābhā's Kubera, the brahmin, saw his son returned, he jumped up and kissed his head (smelled his head).
24. The great lord respectfully bowed to the lotus feet of his parents with his hands in the gesture of *añjali* and praised them, as was proper.
25. "Satisfying you two gods pleases the Lord Nārāyaṇa himself. The embodiment of compassion will grant the eternal joy of liberation while still alive.
26. Just as Sacchidānanda sent a portion of himself to live here, similarly you two godly parents bathe your son in the *rasa* of parental affection.
27. I cannot repay you (even) through many lifetimes, even with the fragrant flowers of true devotion. Your efforts make even the light of the sun look dull.
28. O Mother and Father, now I serve your lotus feet eternally. This is my ultimate duty and through it comes your salvation."
29. When those two heard their son's speech the hair all over their bodies stood on end and they wept tears of love. "O Son, you are truly the answer to our prayers.

30. Well, Son, as our son you should both take care of yourself and strive for immortality, just as when the ocean becomes a cloud its own waters bestow (both) jewels and prosperity (rain).
31. After we are gone, O Child, you will remain here in human form to make the offerings to the ancestors and perform service for brahmins at the Viṣṇupada Temple in Gayā and deliver us from this bottomless pit."
32. Then their son Kamalākṣa, tears in his eyes, his body thrilling with joy, bowed at the lotus feet of his parents. For the year (remaining in) their lifetime Śiva dwelt in supreme peace, fixed on the worship of his parents' feet, overflowing with love.
33. When those two had reached the age of ninety, they again contemplated their divine son Keśava-Hara. They received a beautiful jeweled chariot that was turned toward Upendra (Viṣṇu) while saying Hari-Hara, climbed into it and ascended to the abode of Viṣṇu.
34. Then when Lord Gopeśvara's parents had given up their human form, he performed the ritually ordained rites for them. From then on, on auspicious days that virtuous one gave money and various types of clothing and excellent food to the brahmins and to the blind and the deaf.
35. I bow to that god who was given the name Kamalākṣa by the divine voice of the scholar called Śyāmadāsa at the time of his (naming) ceremony. He alone is known by the name of Advaita. I praise that god known as Kamalākṣa.
36. With the permission of my guru, my lord Advaita, I, an insignificant fool desirous of good, have praised the ancestors of his lineage. You wise men (please) forgive my many errors.
37. I who am extremely old and ignorant have described some of the childhood exploits of that moon Advaita who points out the truth.
38. Kṛṣṇadāsa composed this *Bālya-Līlā-Sūtra* in the month of Vaiśākha in the year 1409 Śaka (1487 CE).
39. The venerable divine master Śyāmadāsa, best of brahmins—this book was completed because of his help from the beginning.
40. O Vaiṣṇavas, please be so kind as to forgive me who is ignorant (and who makes) a million bows to your lotus feet.
41. I, ignorant, wrote this *sūtra* just as I saw and heard from good men. I beg that the good people will correct it.

This is the eighth chapter, called "Kubera's Ascent to Heaven," in the *Bālya-Līlā-Sūtra* composed by Lauḍīya Kṛṣṇadāsa.

Om! salutations to Śrī Gaura Gopāla!
Om! salutations to (my) guru Śrī Advaitacandra!
Om! salutations and salutations to the Vaiṣṇavas!

Īśāna Nāgara's *Advaita Prakāśa*

Chapter 1

The Advent

Invocation

I praise the glorious guru Advaita, that very Advaita who is himself no different from Hari, who is Parambrahmā the Supreme Lord who made Hari descend to earth. I worship the source of every power, Sacchidānanda the eternal, blissful, omniscient god, the ocean of love known as Kṛṣṇa Caitanya, who was dark within, fair without. I praise the glorious Nityānanda Rāma, the compassionate light of love; and Gadādhara; (and) Śrīvāsa, the servant of Rādhā's lord.[1]

> Victory, victory to Lord Caitanya. Victory to Sītā's lord.
> Victory to Nityānanda Rāma, and their followers.

"Kali Yuga is full of wickedness," Pañcānana the Five-Faced Śiva observed, and thought to himself, "How can I rescue living beings (from the depths of *saṃsāra*)?" He discussed this at some length with Yogamāyā, concluding, "No one but Hari can rescue living beings." Sadāśiva, that great yogi whose mind is in perpetual bliss, sat down at the shore of the primeval ocean in the appropriate yoga posture to begin his meditation. He meditated for seven hundred years.

The creator Mahāviṣṇu was pleased by this fierce austerity, and granted Sadāśiva a vision of himself. Words are inadequate to describe the many ways in which Pañcānana praised Mahāviṣṇu-Nārāyaṇa when he beheld him with his own (many) eyes.

[1] This is a reordering of the *pañca-tattva* prayer the Gauḍīyas use to celebrate Caitanya and his four closest associates. The usual ordering is Caitanya, Nityānanda, Advaita, Gadādhara, and Śrīvāsa, but Īśāna places Advaita's name first to show us which he thinks is the most important in the list.

Mahāviṣṇu said, "No one else is like you! You and I share a single soul, only our bodies are separate," and when he embraced Pañcānana, their two bodies merged. Who can fathom his intention? Most astonishing! Listen carefully, people: the two of them merged to form one pure radiant golden body. The lord roared out "Kṛṣṇa, Kṛṣṇa!" (in response), and then a divine voice rang forth from heaven." "Listen, Mahāviṣṇu, you take this form and descend to earth through Lābhā's womb, and I will follow you down to Nadīyā. You will find me in the house of Śacī and Jagannātha. Balarāma and all the other devotees will likewise be born to rescue living beings."

When he heard that, Mahāviṣṇu, who had not detached himself from Śiva, descended to Shantipur, and entered the womb of Lābhā Devī, a devout woman, chaste and virtuous, the wife of Tarka Pañcānana Kubera Ācārya.

In a prior age Kubera, the god of wealth, had been extremely devoted to Śiva, and prayed and performed austerities over a long period that Śiva might be born as his son. Pleased with the austerities, Śiva acquiesced, and thus Kubera was born on earth with the name Kubera ācārya. Everyone respected him for his virtue and knowledge. I do not have the power to describe the many qualities of that highly-praised son of Nṛsiṃha. That Narasiṃha, a lion among men, was known as Naḍiyāla; he was born into the lineage of Āru Ojha, a *siddha ācārya*. The three worlds proclaimed the fame of that Narasiṃha who was an excellent scholar, very learned in all the scriptures. With his wise counsel Rājā Gaṇeśa overthrew the foreign ruler in Gauḍa and became king. Some called him a heretic because of his marriage, and he settled in the province of Lauḍa. Kubera Ācārya became the pride of his lineage. He held the position of court councillor in the capital.

He got married and produced one son after another, but they died, and he became dejected. Sometime later he and Lābhā moved to Shantipur, a lovely town on the bank of the Gaṅgā. In time Kubera Tarka Pañcānana realized that Lābhā was again pregnant, so he worshipped Nārāyaṇa in a host of ways, and fed brahmins, the poor, and the blind to their satisfaction.

Just then King Divyasiṃha summoned Kubera and his wife back to their homeland in Navagrāma. The villagers welcomed Kubera and his wife as soon as they arrived in Navagrāma. The king and his chief minister were reunited after a long separation. The king greeted him and joyfully inquired about his welfare. "Tell me, tell me, Tarka Pañcānana; why have you been away so long? I delight in your company. My throne means nothing with you gone."

The scholar replied, "O King, you are a veritable treasure trove of mercy, and you have exhibited endless compassion toward this poor brahmin. The bank of the Gaṅgā is a holy, lovely place, and living there was like living in heaven. I had no thought of leaving there, but have returned at your command. By the grace of God, (my wife) has again become pregnant, and (we hope that) by His (grace) this (time it) will come to fruition."

The king said, "She conceived in a holy place, which will prove auspicious, I am certain. Forget your past sorrows and call on God; by His mercy you'll have an exceptional son." The two had discussed the matter at some length, when an astrologer appeared and said, "Listen, Great Scholar. There is no doubt that you will have a godlike son. He will live long and be an accomplished interpreter of sacred texts. It is clear that he will inculcate a pure dharma." And with that pronouncement, the astrologer vanished. The king could not find him anywhere. The courtiers were amazed and told each other, "This person must be a divine being descended from the heavens."

The astrologer's words encouraged the scholar Kubera, and he went home and related the whole story to Lābhā. Lābhā replied, "God's majesty is boundless. By His kindness, the weight of our sorrow will be lifted. Holy men say a person who worships Viṣṇu with devotion is blessed in every way."

Kubera knew she spoke the truth and said, "My dear, this is true, it is the testimony of the Vedas. Devout worship of Viṣṇu, whereby one gains all powers and which cuts the bonds of illusion, constitutes worship of all the gods."

Assuming an attitude of devotion, Kubera honored Nārāyaṇa with great ceremony and with offerings of various substances. To brahmins he fed food consecrated to Viṣṇu, and to the blind, the sick, and the poor he distributed clothing.

But there is an even more amazing story. Late one night Lābhā had a dream in which she saw the image of Hari-Hara in the lotus of her own heart, streaming radiance in all directions. Oblivious to his surroundings, he was dancing and weeping with arms upraised, singing the praises of Hari in a very sweet voice. He roared, "Hare Kṛṣṇa." Yama, the son of the Sun and the god of death, came when he heard that and beheld that sweet form: just as Hara conjoined with his wife Gaurī (to form Ardhanarīśvara), Hari-Hara had assumed a single body. Who could ever describe such a form, as beautiful as countless suns? He cried out, "Hare Kṛṣṇa," his hair standing on end, with tears flowing from his eyes as steadily as the Gaṅgā herself. His body overflowed with pure love, and that love surged outward in waves through his dancing.

When Tapānandana the son of the Sun witnessed this unearthly burst of emotion, he prostrated himself completely. He praised Hari-Hara in more ways than words can tell; then with palms pressed together (in supplication) he continued, with sweet words: "Listen, Lord, dark is this Kali Age! Your descending into it would be a wondrous thing. The wicked will be saved at the mere sight of you, but that would undermine my dominion and authority. Therefore, Lord, please remain unmanifested. Have mercy on your servant, please remove this threatening possibility."

When he heard this, the lord spoke gently to Yama with a smile, "Calm down, King of Dharma, you are mistaken. Just think about the dreadful suffering of the wicked, and know that the wise and the good suffer, too, with the pain of others. For instance, who holds the power to destroy the bonds of karma of a person who relishes his own activities? A person mesmerized by the magic of the world does not know what is good for him. Those lowly people imagine their senses exist for their own benefit. But just as an invalid suffers further from eating badly cooked food, so too one stuck in the trap of karma becomes further enmeshed in *saṃsāra*. Living beings who succumb to their own desires, especially in the Kali Age, are buffeted about in a conflagration of dreadful suffering. I am deeply distraught to behold the unbearable misery of living beings, and so I make this promise: I will teach the great mantra to destroy the bonds of karma and to create that devotion which is the pure love of Kṛṣṇa. I will infuse people with the power of that wisdom-bestowing name of Hari; I will rescue the wicked. For this reason I am taking birth; the wise will say that the Kali Age is blessed.

"I have one more very solemn promise, and that is that I will cause Svayaṃ Bhagavān, God Himself, to appear. Mahāprabhu the great lord will descend with his friends and associates, and the land will be completely flooded with pure love. Your dominion and authority will not be destroyed. Vile atheists will not be rescued."

When he heard this, Yama Rājā went home. Lābhā Devī awoke from her dream and sat up. She told her husband about her strange dream, and wonder grew in his heart, and he marveled.

When Lābhā Devī's pregnancy finished its tenth month, on the seventh day of the lunar month of Māgha, the lord appeared. On that auspicious day the voice of Hari washed over Lābhā; throngs of lovely women cried out their approval. Deep joy grew in the hearts of the wise, though they did not understand the source of this joy.

Kubera summoned the astrologer, who selected the name "Kamalākṣa" for his son.

Look at the miracle that was the lord at the age of five! He would eat nothing but food which had been offered to Kṛṣṇa. At the proper time his father put chalk in the child's hand, and within a month, my lord had learned to read and write.

Īśāna Nāgara, whose hopes are at the feet of Lords Gaurāṅga and Advaita, narrates the *Advaita Prakāśa*.

Chapter 2

Childhood

Victory, victory to Lord Caitanya, victory to Sītā's lord,
Victory to Nityānanda Rāma, and their followers.

The blessed land of Lauḍa is the causal ocean out of which the glorious Advaita's childhood activities arose. Listen to something amazing. One day Lābhā took her son to her breast and went to sleep, and late at night she had the most marvellous dream: the son at her breast was Śiva himself, and he was the unknowable lord Mahāviṣṇu, with four arms, conch, lotus, discus and mace, and white complexion. He was as beautiful as the glowing autumn moon; the sight of it would drive away the all three—spiritual, material, and supernatural—afflictions of mortal existence and make peace seem possible.

The virtuous Lābhā saw this ethereal beauty and prostrated herself completely, then joined her palms in supplication and exalted him in many ways.

My lord said, "Why are you praising me?"

Lābhā said, "Give me the water (from washing) your feet."

My lord said, "One's parents are the guru."

Lābhā continued, "You are Sadāśiva, the guru of the whole world. You have many souls and manifest eternally in every heart. You are the cause of creation; how can you have a mother? (And) you are Mahāviṣṇu Himself, the father of the universe, at whose reddened feet lie countless holy sites. Anyone who drinks the nectar of your feet attains liberation, so, my Lord, please give me that saving water."

My lord said, "Do not say this sort of thing again. If I bring you all the holy *tīrthas*, say that you will bathe and drink there, and establish righteousness."

This is the sort of strange dream she had, and she (immediately) awoke and sat up, contemplating Nārāyaṇa, and said, "What an amazing dream I had last night. According to popular wisdom, a dream at dawn is the one that comes true."

My lord got up and said, "Mother, what are you trying to say?"

Lābhā said, "I had a dream."

My lord said, "Tell me, Mother, what did you dream?"

Lābhā said, "Why do you need to hear the story?"

My lord said, "You must tell me the dream, or I will not dance or sing *kīrtana* for Kṛṣṇa."

Lābhā said, "Child, you are just a foolish boy. What would be the point of telling you the story?" But she described her strange dream from beginning to end, weeping as she spoke.

My lord said, "Mother, I promise you this. I will bring all the holy places here and install them for you."

Lābhā Ṭhākurānī trembled and said, "Then, child, I know my dream is true."

My lord said, "Tonight all the holy places will come here. Tomorrow, bathe in them, and all your desires will be fulfilled."

Lābhā said, "Who could believe this prediction?"

My lord insisted, "This story is true, it is true." That night my lord meditated and drew all the holy sites by the power of his concentration. The *tīrthas* came at the lord's summons just like iron filings at the pull of a magnet. The glorious Yamunā and Gaṅgā themselves, and the other holy places paid their respects to my lord, and all were fulfilled. He welcomed the holy sites with great respect and then bowed at the lotus feet of the glorious Yamunā. The holy sites asked, "Lord, why have you called us?"

The lord said, "Please come live on this mountain."

But the holy sites objected, "If we live here, many holy places will lose their efficacy."

My lord said, "My word must not be in vain, so you will all gather here on one day every year."

The holy sites replied, "Lord, you decide which day we should appear on this mountain."

The lord said, "Promise me that you will all come on the auspicious thirteenth day of the dark fortnight of Madhu (Caitra)."[2]

The *tīrtha*s responded, "That we promise you, and we shall never fail to keep our promise to you."

And ever since, the name of this site has been Paṇā Tīrtha, the place where promises are kept, because one's desires are fulfilled by bathing here.

My lord requested, "All you *tīrtha*s, go to the top of the mountain, and stay there as a waterfall." The holy places complied with his request and proceeded to the mountaintop, where they flowed naturally and unrestrained.

In the morning, Advaita Ācārya reported to his mother, "All the *tīrtha*s have appeared at the top of the mountain."

Lābhā said, "How can I believe this?"

My lord said, "It is truly a miracle, you must see it," and he took his mother. When they reached the mountain, he blew a conch and rang a bell. As soon as he called out "Hari" in a loud voice, the waters of the holy sites began to trickle down.

My lord said, "Look, Mother, the water is trickling steadily, and if you blow a conch or the like, its flow will increase. Just look at the dark ambrosial waters of the glorious Yamunā! Your body would look like it was covered by a cloud in there. Look opposite, the Gaṅgā puts crystal itself to shame. Immerse yourself in its sacred immortal waters. Again, look at the red, yellow, and other sacred waters. They are falling, babbling, around your head."

Lābhā witnessed these marvels and paid her respects and finished her ablutions with devotion. From that time on this place has been known as Paṇā Tīrtha, and a bath at the right time of Vāruṇī brings great reward.

Then Lord Kubera reveled in Kamalākṣa's (brilliance) and arranged to have him study with the king's son. My lord, who could remember everything he heard, studied grammar and could memorize verses with their meanings and commentaries with one reading. In three years he had mastered the texts, and everyone felt Kamalākṣa had attained divine knowledge.

Listen to an astonishing tale of those days, a tale of Divyasiṃha's son and Kamalākṣa. The boys went to show their devotion to the goddess, a stone image of Kālī, in the temple. The prince noticed that my lord was simply standing and gazing at the beauty of the Kālī image, and said, "Bow, Ācārya."

[2] The month in the Bengali calendar that corresponds to the period from mid-March to mid-April.

My lord did not hear him and simply stood there. This angered the prince, and he scolded him. My lord in turn became furious and bellowed a roar. The king's son fell into a dead faint. All the courtiers cried out in dismay and ran quickly to report to King Divyasiṃha. As soon as the king heard this terrible news, he and his ministers rushed to his son. Meanwhile, Kamalākṣa had run away and hidden behind a large anthill, as he always did (when in trouble).

The king saw his son dead and wailed in misery. Kubera ran to find Kamalākṣa, and after searching high and low, he finally found him and brought the boy to the temple of the goddess.

The king demanded, "Kamalākṣa, you are a king among brahmins. Why have you done this terrible deed?"

Embarrassed, my lord said, "He is not dead, he is still alive; he is just unconscious," and he sprinkled some of the water that had been used to bathe Lord Nārāyaṇa's feet over the king's son, and the prince revived. (Even) Brahmā and Śiva do not understand the supernatural powers of the water used for bathing Lord Hari's feet. The mere thought of the water used to bathe Viṣṇu's feet confers the same result as bathing in or seeing a holy place.

The king, delighted to see his son was alive, pleased the poor and the brahmins with rich gifts. Everyone observed, "This is auspicious, very good," (but) Kubera remained troubled.

Then on an auspicious day the scholar Kubera Tarka Pañcānana had his young son's initiation ceremony performed and gave the boy the sacred thread. My lord's glorious countenance was most wonderful. Thereafter Lord Advaita studied the literary lexicons; he mastered rhetoric, astrology, et cetera.

Listen to another day's strange occurrences. On Divālī a tremendous celebration was under way. Everyone in the country, noble or otherwise, had come to the temple of the goddess, where according to custom various dance dramas were to be performed. My lord entered the assembly and sat down.

The king inquired, "Kamalākṣa, what kind of behavior is this? You did not bow to Kālī; what are you thinking?"

My lord said, "Paraṃbrahmā, Svayaṃ Bhagavān, is my goal, no one else. Whoever thinks otherwise deludes himself; for the wise he is the sole object of worship."

Tarka Pañcānana heard his son's wise words, and even though he was on the king's side, he began to ponder the matter. "O Kamalākṣa, you have not gotten to the bottom of this. According to the Vedas, the one Brahmā has many forms, and antagonism toward the gods and goddesses is very wicked. So worship these gods, and everything else will follow. In the Treta Age, Rāmacandra, who was actually Nārāyaṇa, worshiped the Goddess so that he would be able to rescue Sītā. All seekers of knowledge who worship the most merciful Mother of the Universe attain liberation, so bow to Mother Kālī. Do not make trouble; she will fulfill all your desires."

My lord replied, "Listen, Father, do not be angry. If you do not focus on a single goal, you will have serious problems. If you water a tree at its root, the branches and leaves will also be nourished. Similarly, should you worship Nārāyaṇa, the root of all the gods and goddesses, no further worship is necessary. Viṣṇu's creation is the external form of the Goddess, and living beings, dazzled by her magic, forget this fact. (Further), offering animal sacrifices is not the proper way to serve the Goddess. If she is the mother of the world and all it contains, then the world is her son; is killing one's children scripturally enjoined?"

Kubera said, "What is the point of irrational debate? Slandering the Goddess yields inauspicious results. Just as the king deliberates and punishes criminals, and rewards the just, according to the law, so the Goddess grants liberation to her aspirants and drowns ordinary souls in the ocean of illusion. Killing animals for sacrifice is not violence, for they are liberated and go to heaven and thus are glorified."

My lord said, "If it is true that the means to success is easy, why is it so hard to save one's parents?" The debate between father and son continued in this manner, to the amazement of everyone assembled there.

One's father is to be regarded as the great guru, so out of respect for his father, my lord quit speaking. Then he said, "Father, please forgive my disrespect. I will bow to the Goddess now," and to the Goddess he bowed.

And at that very moment something amazing occurred: the Goddess withdrew and the image cracked, astonishing everyone present. This happened because as soon as the soul of the image came into contact with her husband, the two merged. This marvelous sight stupefied the king and his ministers, and Kubera Ācārya. Then Kamalākṣa, who had assumed the form of Hari-Hara, vanished, reciting Gauralīlā, the exploits of the Golden One. At the age of twelve he went to Shantipur and began to study the scriptures of the six philosophical systems.

Īśāna Nāgara, whose hopes are at the feet of Lord Gaurāṅga and Lord Advaita, narrates the *Advaita Prakāśa*.

Chapter 3

Education

Victory, victory to Lord Caitanya, victory to Sītā's lord,
Victory to Nityānanda Rāma, and their followers.

One day Advaita Ācārya wrote a letter to his parents back in the blessed land of Lauḍa. Kubera missed his son terribly, and his eyes were always full of tears from seeking him in vain. He kept saying, "O Gopāla, what have you done?" Then by Kṛṣṇa's mercy he would recover somewhat and go home sadly.

Lābhā missed her son so much she wailed constantly and could not sit still at all. Her eyes flowed continuously with tears, and she babbled incoherently like a madwoman. She was completely oblivious to her surroundings and at times lay as still as a corpse.

Her husband Kubera comforted her as best he could, with such statements as, "Bhagavān is very generous to those for whom he is the goal; he displays no partiality." "The most important thought is devotion to the lotus feet of Hari." "One who thinks this illusory body is the Self, is a miserable creature. Worldly pleasures conceal a wealth of suffering, for contact with pleasures is like (contact with) a snake, so full of deadly poison. But worship of the glorious Hari is a mine of eternal bliss in the midst of misery; it is like an herb which has the power to bestow bliss."

After she had heard many such words of wisdom, Lābhā Ṭhākurānī became somewhat calmer. But in her sorrow she spent the night in the temple room, and Kubera went to bed without eating.

At dawn Gopāla called to him in a dream. "Greetings! Your son has gone to the bank of the Gaṅgā. Kamalākṣa is not a (ordinary) man, he is the divine embodiment of the model devotee. His disciples will soon follow him into this world."

Kubera described his dream to Lābhā and happily took those words about my lord's future to heart.

One day Lābhā and her husband rejoiced to receive a letter from Kamalākṣa. Kubera said, "Why should we stay here any longer? We should go to the bank of the Gaṅgā, where we will attain liberation."

Lābhā said, "I was thinking the same thing. We should live out our lives there." So the couple climbed into a boat and set out, and happily arrived at holy Shantipur.

When he saw his mother and father, my lord ran to his parents. He bowed at their feet with devotion, and they embraced him and kissed his head and blessed him. Lābhā said, "O child, without you, I am as dead as a fish without water."

Kubera said, "Child, what have you learned?"

"The six philosophical systems, from beginning to end."

Kubera said, "Now learn the four Vedas. You should certainly learn about the *Brahmā Sūtras* also."

"I would like to go to Pūrṇavaṭī to study at the house of the brahmin Śānta Vedāntabāgīśa."

His father agreed, "Your education is not yet complete. It takes great effort to blend knowledge with common sense. Go there immediately, and write (to let us know) that you are well. Study freely, you have our blessing."

So my lord bowed at his parents' feet, took his books, and left, thinking of Lord Hari. He soon arrived in the village of Pūrṇābaṭī and bowed before the calm brahmin Śānta. The brahmin was amazed to see my lord's beauty, and blessed him and asked him to introduce himself. That best of brahmins discussed scriptures with him. He admired the boy and was very pleased, and said, "Study what you want, child." My lord studied the Vedas assiduously under him. In this human drama my lord could remember everything he heard, and mastered the Vedas in two years.

Listen to something very strange. One day Śānta took his students to bathe in a big marsh with a lot of weeds near the Gaṅgā, whose waters were extremely deep. One lotus shone in the middle of it, its lovely fragrance filling all directions, and black snakes were playing there. Who could possibly pick that lotus? Vedāntabāgīśa smiled and said to his students, "Who can pick this lotus?"

The students said, "No one can get it."

My lord said, "Were you to ask me, I would not be afraid."

Śānta said, "There are thorns and snakes here, so do not boast that you can accomplish this difficult task."

At this, my lord smiled slightly. He leapt from lotus to lotus, and picked that shining flower, and offered it with devotion to his guru. Everyone who saw this miracle said it must be magic.

The brahmin thought, "I am blessed by this master." Privately, Śānta, king of brahmins, asked my lord, "My boy, how did you manage this miraculous accomplishment, by the power of God, or did you do it by magic? Or are you some god come to earth? Tell me the truth for, I am your guru."

My lord said, "These three worlds are part of Hari. A person with a pure heart who has gone to take refuge at Hari's feet can do anything."[3] Then Śānta Vedāntabāgīśa, jewel among brahmins, heard the final secret dogma from my lord's mouth. A normal living being cannot understand the explanation, but Īśvara spoke through my lord, I guess.

One day Kamalākṣa said to his teacher, "Please, with your permission, I would like to go home."

Śānta said, "Your name is (now) Śiva-Veda-Pañcānana, Five-faced Śiva who knows the Vedas. I give you leave to go, albeit reluctantly, but if you must go, I have this one earnest request: that I be able to see you just by thinking of you."

My lord then prostrated himself fully before his teacher. The master held him and began to weep, and the other students wept, and the master's wife wept. My lord consoled each one with sweet words. "Don't grieve about me. We'll see each other again and again, and I won't forget your affection," my lord said, and then vanished. Everyone ran here and there but could not find him.

My lord returned to his father and mother and bowed, praising them a great deal, and showing deep devotion. Both were greatly delighted to see their son, and kissed him on the head and gave him many blessings.

Nāgara Īśāna, whose hopes are at the feet of Lord Caitanya and Lord Advaita, narrates the *Advaita Prakāśa*.

[3] The text says "attains the eight powers," a reference to the eight yogic powers described in Patāñjali's *Yogasūtras*. The general cultural understanding is that assiduous practice of austerities automatically results in one's obtaining magical powers. These are *aṇimā* (the power to become tiny), *laghimā* (the power to become very light), *prāpti* (the power of obtaining everything), *prakāmyam* (the power of irresistible will), *mahimā* (the power to become very large), *īśitvam* (the power of supremacy over everything), *vaśitvam* (the power of great radiance), and *kāmāvasāyitvā* (the power of suppressing desire).

Chapter 4

Pilgrimage Tour

Victory, victory to Lord Caitanya, victory to Sītā's lord,
Victory to Nityānanda Rāma, and their followers.

Kamalākṣa devoted himself to serving his parents and set about the task of meeting their every need. This continued for one year, with both parents very pleased with their son's help.

One day Kubera said to Kamalākṣa, "You have served your mother and father enough. A person who serves his parents with devotion will live a long life, and his fortune and fame will increase. Now, son, listen to something very mysterious. I am more than ninety years old, and your mother is the same age. Very soon a flower chariot will come for us from heaven. When we have left this world, perform our funeral rites at the Viṣṇupada Temple."

No sooner had he said this, when the gods' flying chariot arrived. Only the eyes of the enlightened could see it; it was beyond the perception of ordinary physical eyes. They both climbed into it and flew away to heavenly Vaikuṇṭha. Kamalākṣa roared out "Hari!"

Lord Advaita grieved and completed all the proper rituals in accordance with custom. Then, remembering his father's words, he went to the holy city of Gayā, sacred to Viṣṇu. He offered rice balls at Viṣṇu's lotus feet and spent many days there praying for his ancestors. Then Advaita thought, "Now I shall go to Nābhigayā,[4] if Lord Viṣṇu is willing."

So he set out for Purī, and on the way visited Gopīnātha[5] at Remunā. When he saw how sweet was that glorious image, he was filled with love. He laughed and cried and danced, roaring the whole time. Much later Advaita regained his senses and bowed before Gopīnātha, praising him. Then he proceeded to Nābhigayā and offered rice balls to his ancestors, and when he considered his obligation complete, he set out for Purī, where Jagannātha, Balarāma, and Subhadrā play.

He prostrated himself completely before the images, offering praise, and as he did so, the Jagannātha image took on Kṛṣṇa's form. As Advaita watched, his love overflowed, and crying, "Alas, Lord of my life!" he fainted. Shortly thereafter Advaita regained consciousness and roared out, "I have found the treasure of Kṛṣṇa!" He jumped up and down and danced; words fail (to describe the sight). Sometimes he would laugh, sometimes he would weep aloud. Day and night passed with Advaita lost in ecstasy, and at dawn he regained his senses. Then Advaita bathed and played at that king of holy sites and was delighted when he

[4] Advaita is punning with this name for the city of Purī and the city of Gayā.

[5] Temple images have individual names, and people speak of visiting them in the same way one might describe a visit to a beloved relative.

received the consecrated food. Advaita wandered from temple to temple in that holy domain, full of devotion. He spent many days in this way, then he set off for the holy site of Setubandha.

On the way he wandered through many other holy places. He bathed in the Godavari River. As he traveled he become more enrapt in love with every step. Words cannot tell how many holy places Advaita visited. He saw Śivakāñcī and Viṣṇukāñcī, he went to bathe in the sin-destroying Kaveri River, and wandered through such places as Madurai, the southern Mathurā.

Then Advaita reached the great holy site of Setubandha, in which blessed place he experienced bliss bathing. He saw the Śiva (*liṅgam*) at Rāmeśvara and bowed, and worshiped him devoutly with many kinds of praise. Rāma was his lord, he was Rāma's servant. As soon as he said this, he experienced the great joy of love. With arms raised, Advaita danced, sometimes laughing, sometimes crying, sometimes unconscious. Sometimes he said, "Where are you, Rāma, my life's treasure?" and noisily slapped his cheeks and clapped his hands. For a long time Advaita was filled with divine love and spent the night reading the *Rāmāyāṇa*.

Eventually Advaita had wandered through many holy places and finally arrived at Madhva Ācārya's place. Many wise men belong to Madhva Ācārya's school and live there, enjoying the taste of devotion. He has lovingly written devotional commentaries on the *Śāṇḍilya Sūtra* and the *Nārada Sūtra*. Hearing these (commentaries) kindled Advaita's love. "Goddess of devotion, have mercy!" he cried aloud, and did a strange dance with his arms raised, weeping and running here and there. A wave of the ocean of love was gradually growing. My lord fainted and fell to the ground.

When the great teacher Mādhavendra Purī saw that, he said, "This is a prime exponent of the path of devotion. This kind of pure devotional love does not exist in an ordinary soul but can only thrive in a consciousness-filled vessel. He has drunk the wine of pure love; he has inner bliss, and no external awareness. I see the marks of greatness on his body and can tell that he has been born to save the world."

Those wise and good men were delighted (to hear this) and surrounded Advaita and cried out, "Hari, Hari!" Absorbing the great medicine of the name of Hari through his ears, my lord roared out, "Grant me devotion!" The wise and good men began to float on a flood of love. Advaita revealed many different moods in his enjoyment of love, and after some time he calmed down and bowed to Mādhavendra, the wishing tree of devotion.

Mādhavendra embraced him lovingly, and said, "What is your name? Tell us where you are from. You are eternally perfected, a storehouse of pure love. All of us are very fortunate to have seen you."

Advaita said, "My name is Kamalākṣa Ācārya, and my home is the village of Shantipur, on the bank of the Bhagirathi. You are a supremely dispassionate master of the devotional scriptures. Teach me the doctrine of devotion. Make me your servant."

Mādhavendra was overjoyed to hear this and encouraged Advaita to stay there. Mādhavendra recited the *Bhāgavata Purāṇa* with Madhva Ācārya's commentary to Advaita, and preached. Advaita memorized it all as soon as he heard it, and the wise men saw this and marveled.

One day Advaita said to Mādhavendra, "This is Kali Yuga; living beings are not heeding dharma. Wherever I go I see wicked behavior, and you never once hear the names Hare Kṛṣṇa. I cannot figure out how living beings can be saved. Tell me the right way to help living beings."

Mādhavendra replied, "Kamalākṣa, you are a storehouse of compassion. You are always thinking about the benefit of others. Such a thought would not spring forth from an ordinary creature; what has manifested here is divine power. Now, there is no easy way to rescue living beings unless Parabrahmā Himself appears. Svayaṃ Bhagavān will appear soon to establish dharma in this Kali Age. The *Ānanta Saṃhitā* is the best witness to this. His coming to India is (foretold) in the *Bhāgavata Purāṇa*."

Advaita said, "Where is the *Ānanta Saṃhitā*? I have a deep desire to see it."

When he heard that, Mādhavendra Purī showed him the *Ānanta Saṃhitā*, and Advaita was overjoyed to read it. Advaita said, "Nanda's son is full of the six majesties. He will incarnate in a fair body in Navadvīpa. He will rescue the world with the love of the name of Hari, and then he will surely fulfill the desire of this miserable creature."

As soon as Advaita spoke, his love caught fire. He chanted the name "Gaura" for three hours. "Gaura is the lord of my life. I, a transgressor against Vedic dharma, will go where I can find him." Advaita sang this verse and danced, and many of the holy men sang and danced with him. Gradually a wave of the Gaṅgā of love swelled up. Many people cried, "Oh Gaurāṅga!" Saying, "I will find that fair Gaurāṅga," Advaita ran here and there, from time to time fainting and rolling in the dust. After some time Advaita contained that divine love. He read the book *Ānanta Saṃhitā* and kept it.

One day Advaita rose at dawn, bowed to Mādhavendra Purī, and left quickly. On the road, he visited many hundreds of *tīrthas*. Advaita spent several days in the Dandaka Forest. He saw many more holy places, including Nasika, and then proceeded to holy Dvaraka. He bowed before Vāsudeva, Lakṣmī, and the other deities, and enrapt in love, recited many kinds of praise. Then he went to Prabhasa, Pushkara, and still more holy sites and eventually came to Kurukṣetra. Then Advaita went to Haridvara. He bathed in the Gaṅgā and circumambulated the pilgrimage site. From there he went to the ultimate holy place, the hermitage of Lord Badrika, and saw Naranārāyaṇa Vyāsa. Enrapt in love, he danced for some time; my lord paid his respects there and left.

After several days he came to the sacred Gomukhi Rock. Then he went to the domain of the glorious Gaṇḍakī Śālagrāma. Advaita bathed and rested there, ceaselessly reciting the name "Hari Nārāyaṇa." He saw a stone disc with especially auspicious marks and devotedly took it with him when he left.

Next my lord Advaita came to Mithilā. When he saw Sītā's birthplace, he rolled in the dust. Enrapt in love, he danced and sang *kīrtana*. Just then—listen to something wonderful! Advaita heard someone singing a very sweet, very beautiful song of Kṛṣṇa's virtues, and followed the sound. He saw a great brahmin sitting under a banyan tree, singing the nectar of Kṛṣṇa's virtues like an angel. Astonished, he listened to the brahmin's description of Kṛṣṇa's beauty. Engrossed in love, Advaita embraced him—my lord revealed his mercy through an embrace—bestowing on him the gift of love and arousing his divine power. Advaita's touch filled the brahmin with love, just like iron turns to gold upon contact with the touchstone, and he bowed to Advaita's divine wisdom.

Thinking of Viṣṇu, Advaita asked him, "Brahmin, please tell me your name. Who composed this very sweet song? I have never heard anything as sweet as this composition, with your wonderful vocal introduction. This sort of sweet music is my favorite; it has intoxicated me and drawn me here."

The brahmin said, "My name is Vidyāpati, and I earn my rice in the king's service. I lost my mind and composed this song. You are a holy man who has grasped the spirit; there is so much love in you. What person bears the power to attract you? You have recited your own virtues as the means to rescue me."

My lord said, "This song-nectar you have composed could attract Kṛṣṇa (himself), let alone a humble wretch. I am fortunate; Kṛṣṇa has shown me his kindness: He let me meet the poet Vidyāpati," and embraced him.

Advaita went to holy Ayodhyā, thinking of the glorious Hari. When my lord got there, he saw the glorious Rāma's birthplace and bowed, so thrilled he got goosebumps. He contemplated Rāma's marvelous activities and wept, engrossed in love.

A wave of the ocean of the nectar of love began to swell up. "Slay Rāvana!" he roared. He followed Rāma's activities, absorbed in ecstasy. After some time, when Advaita's mind had recovered, he bathed in the Sarayu Gaṅgā. After he had seen the sites of Rāma's activities, he again set off.

Advaita proceeded to the holy city of Vārāṇāsī and bathed in the Gaṅgā at Maṇikarṇikā Landing. When he saw the Adikeśava image he prostrated himself completely. Engrossed in divine love, he glorified him in many ways.

Then Advaita saw Vindu Mādhava and danced and sang *kīrtana*, filled with love. His delight in the divine love kept increasing. He bowed again and again, and praised him. With hands joined in prayer, he said, "Listen, Lord Mādhava Hari. I am rendered completely speechless by your kindness. Your divine image is a tree that fulfills the wishes of the devotees. Grant this inert soul eternal liberation. Brahmā and Śiva cannot comprehend your majesty, so how can someone as base as I describe it?"

Then he went to Viśveśvara, engrossed in ecstasy. Advaita performed his worship as an example, in order to instruct people. "Grant me devotion," he babbled, and glorified him. With raised arms he danced and sang *kīrtana*. He bowed, and proceeded to the Annapūrṇā temple. When he saw Annapūrṇā, he glorified her highly. My lord paid her his respects and moved on.

He saw many sites sacred to Śiva and others. He preached the supremacy of devotion to *yogis* and various types of renunciates and other holy men. At night the glorious Vijaya Purī, the ultimate *Bhāgavata Purāṇa* scholar, met with Advaita. The two of them enjoyed the bliss of love in discussing tales of Kṛṣṇa. Sometimes laughing, sometimes weeping, calling "Govinda," sometimes whirling around, sometimes unconscious, sometimes lost in ecstasy, the two embraced. In this way the blessed night turned into dawn, and when they had to part, their sorrow had no end.

Then Advaita traveled until he came to Prayāga. He had his head shaved, and bathed in the confluence of the three rivers. He offered rice balls to his ancestors with devotion and performed all the rituals according to the injunctions.

When he saw Veni Mādhava he praised him and bowed. When he saw Bhīma's mace, he praised it repeatedly. As soon as he reached the eternally perfect site of Svayaṃ Bhagavān's eternal activities, he drowned in love. Crying, "O Kṛṣṇa," he let out a roar. A flood of love swelled up and flooded Mathurā, and children, old people, and youths drowned in it.

Engrossed in ecstasy, he saw the glorious Yamunā. Praising her, he bowed repeatedly; words are inadequate. An earlier devotee of Hari by the name of Dhruva had worshiped Kṛṣṇa in this very spot, known as Dhruva's Landing. Offering rice balls here yields the same results as one hundred (pilgrimages to) Gayā. Advaita bathed in the Yamunā and devoutly offered rice to his ancestors in that spot.

Then he saw the glorious image of Kṛṣṇa, and he was drowned in the essence of pure love. Advaita circumambulated all the sites of Kṛṣṇa's activities, and there was no limit to the bliss he felt.

Advaita proceeded to the holy town of Vraja, and as soon as he touched its sacred soil he was captivated by love. Even though Mathurā and other places are sacred soil, there is more love in Vraja because of the inspiration of the *gopīs*.

After some time, Advaita regained consciousness. "Where is the lord of my life?" he said, weeping. He ran here and there, lost in great ecstasy. He rolled in the dust, proclaiming, "This is sacred dust." He roared loudly, always calling Kṛṣṇa, sometimes laughing, sometimes jumping up and down and dancing. Afflicted alternately with sweating, trembling, stupefaction, et cetera, Advaita went to Mt. Govardhana, and the moment he saw it, a wave of love swelled up. Advaita raised his arms and began to dance. He saw the various sites of Rādhā's and Kṛṣṇa's eternal activities and fell asleep under a banyan tree.

As he slept, he had a dream late at night. The glorious Nandanandana came and revealed Himself to him, with the beauty of a young cloud, this world-enchanter with a peacock's feather in his hair, the flirt with the flute at his mouth, dressed in yellow with gold anklets on his feet, his creamy body full of the nectar of divine love. Advaita felt great joy when he saw this magnificent form, and raised his arms and danced a great dance.

Kṛṣṇacandra Himself said, "You are part of me. A wave of love will radiate out from you. You are Gopeśvara Śiva, most compassionate, who has appeared for the sake of living beings. Restore the lost holy sites and preach devotion, and rescue living beings with the name of Kṛṣṇa.

"There is a bejewled image of me called Madana Mohana in a bower, which Kubjā used to worship. Its body is covered with a little earth at the shrine of the twelve Ādityas on the bank of the Yamunā. Finally, it was hidden, out of fear of foreigners. Bring the people of the village out and reveal its worship for the good of the world."

With that, Kṛṣṇacandra disappeared. Advaita awoke, filled with pure love. Then he set off, singing the name of Hari aloud with his arms raised, and dancing. Advaita entered the village, and when people saw this holy man, they all came to him. Advaita said, "All of you go quickly to the shrine of the twelve Ādityas on the bank of the Yamunā. Whether young or old, come with me. We are going to raise a lovely image of Kṛṣṇa bent to play his flute."

The villagers were excited to hear that, and ran to bring back axes and shovels. They dug up the image with a great deal of effort. The image enchanted them with its most wondrous form. Then they lashed together a small hut under a banyan tree and consecrated it and installed the deity, and Advaita enlisted a virtuous Vaiṣṇava brahmin to serve the image.

He circumambulated Vṛndāvana and left. Listen to something marvelous that happened then. Some mischievous youths had realized the significance of the image and thought they would destroy it, to strike a blow at Hindu pride. While these Muslims were in one place plotting, Advaita took some weapons to the banyan tree. Madana Mohana became afraid of the Muslims and hid Himself under some flowers, and turned himself into Gopāla. The Muslims entered the holy temple and went away frustrated when they did not find the holy image.

When the brahmin came to worship the image in the morning, he could not see it and returned home wailing. A child told the brahmin that the Muslims had vandalized the temple and thought, "Those Muslims have taken the image. God has been cruel to me." He was too upset to eat.

That evening, Advaita came to that temple and heard the story and wept profusely to see the empty temple. Advaita said, "Kṛṣṇa Himself was merciful and came. He must have hidden again because of this offense." Advaita was so upset he could not even drink water. At night he fell asleep under a tree.

Madana Mohana Himself appeared in a dream and, smiling, told my lord these sweet words: "Get up, Advaita, I turned into Gopāla out of fear of the Muslims and hid in the flowers. Brahmā and the others cannot show themselves like this. I shine forth only because of the devotion in your eyes. I appeared previously in a perfected form, and when all the people saw, they received endless delight."

After this dream, Advaita went straight to the temple and saw Gopāla shining out from under the flowers. The image was completely filled with the sweet nectar of divine love. He wept with pure love and had no external awareness. He was sometimes stupefied, sometimes trembling, sometimes his hair standing on end, sometimes dancing and crying "Hari," sometimes fainting. After some time Advaita came out of his trance and worshiped the lord Gopāla with fruit and water. Advaita took the consecrated food and meditated on Kṛṣṇa's incomparable mercy. At dawn, he got up and went for his morning bath and met that same brahmin on the bank of the Yamunā. Advaita said, "Brahmin, go quickly to the temple and wake up the image and worship it immediately. Perform the worship using the name 'Madana Gopāla.' You do not need to hear the whole story."

The brahmin said, "But the holy image is not in the temple."

Advaita said, "Kṛṣṇa cannot abandon His devotee."

The brahmin, thinking this was wondrous, went and unlocked the door and saw the image. Overwhelmed with love, the brahmin sang many praises and worshiped the image using the name Madana Gopāla. Since then, that holy image of Madana Mohana has been known as Madana Gopāla.

Another night in a dream, Madana Gopāla spoke very sweetly to my lord, "O Advaita Ācārya, listen to a story. A brahmin from Mathurā who has been harrassed by mischievous Muslims will come here. You must give me to him."

Advaita said, "Listen, Madana Gopāla. You are my life's treasure, the strength of my soul. How can I live without you? I would die, like a fish without water."

Madana Gopāla smiled and said, "May your obedience to me endure for a long time. Without you, my activities would not prosper. Wherever you are, there also is my eternal essence. But give up this image of me. Please fulfill the desire of my devotee.

Remember the painting that was originally made by the lady Viśākhā? The image in that painting is no different from me. When Rādhikā saw it, she became infatuated. This eternally perfect object is in the Forest of Nikuñja. Go there, and you will certainly find it easily. Take that painting and return to your own country. Worship this picture and rescue living beings."

Advaita was overwhelmed with love by this dream. With raised arms he danced, crying, "Shout 'Hari!'" Three hours later he recovered, and just then the brahmin from Mathurā arrived. When he saw Advaita, he put a blade of grass between his teeth (like an animal, to indicate submission).[6] He bowed, and spoke with joined hands. "Omniscient man, you are a divine embodiment who has rescued the image worshiped by Kubjā. Madana Gopāla commanded me in a dream, 'Take it to Mathurā and install it, quickly.' So my lord, I have come to you. Please be so kind as to turn over the image to me."

[6] Cleverly, *The Last Kashmiri Rose*, 113: "if a man comes . . . with a tuft of grass in his mouth to indicate that he is subservient like the animals . . ." he may not be refused.

When he heard that, Advaita handed over the image. Upset by this separation, he wept as he walked away and found himself in the holy Forest of Nikuñja. When he found the painting, he drowned in the ocean of love and lovingly took the eternally perfect painting home to Shantipur.

Īśāna Nāgara, whose hopes are at the feet of Lord Caitanya and Lord Nityānanda, narrates the *Advaita Prakāśa*.

Chapter 5

Mādhavendra Purī and Madana Gopāla

Victory, victory to Lord Caitanya, victory to Sītā's lord,
Victory to Nityānanda Rāma, and their followers.

One day Mādhavendra Purī rose over Shantipur like a moon of devotion, with the sound of Kṛṣṇa on his lips and the ecstasy of divine love in his body. He was an actual manifestation of the wish-fulfilling tree of Vraja. Mādhavendra had supreme dispassion and needed nothing else; nonetheless, he came to Advaita's place, out of affection. As soon as he saw Mādhavendra, my lord Advaita was overwhelmed with love. He respectfully covered his head with his garment and fell before him like a stick. Mādhavendra embraced him and inquired after his health.

Advaita said, "Madana Gopāla has been kind."

Mādhavendra said, "Serving Kṛṣṇa brings unworldly power and eternal divine protection." Then when Mādhavendra saw Viśākhā's painting, he was overwhelmed with love, alternately laughing, weeping, and dancing. Who can understand the truth about that great lord Mādhavendra Purī!

After some time Mādhavendra came to his senses and explained the easy way to reach Kṛṣṇa. He said, "Child, you are full of pure love. Commission a painting of Rādhikā. The sight of Rādhā and Kṛṣṇa incites the mood of the *gopīs*, so worshiping the divine couple is the best (worship) of all. And I tell you something else; listen carefully. Get married and dedicate your life to Kṛṣṇa. By Kṛṣṇa's grace you will have many sons. They will all rescue living beings through the name of Kṛṣṇa."

Advaita said, "There are blessings in the worship of a holy image, (but) if I do it incorrectly, everyone in my lineage will go to the lowest level of Hell."

Mādhavendra said, "Kṛṣṇa, that ocean of compassion, depends on you. You will accrue no sin for fourteen generations."

Love enveloped my lord's mind because of his guru's request, and he installed the blessed Rādhikā's painting. One who sees these two perfect images easily attains the treasure of the love of Rādhā-Kṛṣṇa. Then Mādhavendra consecrated the blessed Rādhikā and Lord Madana Gopāla with great delight. He offered various types of sweets and foods, rinsed their mouths, and offered camphor and betel. All who saw the extraordinary double image prostrated fully and sang many praises. Everyone was drawn by the divine sweet smell of the food offerings and ate Kṛṣṇa's leftovers with devotion.

Then Advaita lovingly brought people to Mādhavendra Purī to learn the Kṛṣṇa mantra, the best (mantra). After several days Mādhavendra begged leave (to go), and Advaita protested vehemently. Mādhavendra said, "I want to go to Purī. Gopāla has asked me to get him some sandal paste."

Advaita said, "Why has Gopāla asked for sandal paste? I would like to hear about this."

Mādhavendra said, "Lord Gopāla, the independent lord, kindly appeared to miserable me in a dream and told me, 'Mādhavendra, my body is burning up. Go to Purī and bring me some Malayan sandal paste. If you smear that perfume on my body, I will feel cool.' No one can ignore Gopāla's stern command, so I have come here to you in the peaceful town of Shantipur, drawn by your noble desire for that sun which is devotion to Kṛṣṇa, (on my way) to get the sandal paste."

Advaita became overwhelmed with love and roared. "Kṛṣṇacandra is most merciful, the source of the great power of affection for his worshipers, whose good qualities are ever increasing. No one can determine when he will appear to a devotee," Advaita said, and fainted.

Mādhavendra revived him and begged leave (to go). Advaita prostrated himself completely before Mādhavendra. Mādhavendra embraced him and blessed him and then set out, full of great love.

He went to Remunā, where Gopīnātha had appeared, and saw the Gopīnātha image. He raised his arms and danced. After a while Mādhavendra returned to his senses and then prostrated completely before Gopīnātha. He sat before the enchanter of the world reciting the Name. Just then he saw a brahmin approaching. "Hey, O best of brahmins! Tell me what noble person produced this holy image."

The brahmin said, "Listen, Holy Man. I will tell you what my elders told me. In Treta Age, the Absolute God, Rāma, disguised as a yogi, went to live in the forest with Sītā in accord with his father's vow. One day a female yak wandered through the forest with her calves. When Rāmacandra saw them, he smiled a bit, and Sītā asked why he was smiling. Rāma replied, 'You do not need to know.'

"Sītā said, 'Tell me, Lord, I am at your feet. Devotee-calves are God's eternally dependent devotees. He eternally gives His devotees the gift of love.'

"The glorious Sītā was his pure delight, a crest-jewel of devotion. Out of love for her, the jewel of the Raghu clan said, 'Listen Jānakī, in the future, at the end of the Dvāpara Age, I will appear in Vraja in a dark form, where I will tend cows with the cowherd boys and girls; my name will be Gopāla.'

"That lady Jānakī said, 'What will you look like? Please show me.'

"Then Bhagavān Himself, lord of the universe, created a lovely divine image of himself with a divine jewel. Sītā was amazed when she saw that image of Kṛṣṇa and said, 'No one has ever seen such a lovely form! This well of every sweetness will attract the hearts of the universe; its otherworldly form is as lovely as a new cloud.'

"Then the pious Sītā worshiped that very image with great devotion, with various fruits and flowers. Everyone knows it as Gopīnātha, and anyone who sees it attains pure devotion to Kṛṣṇa.

"I have told this old story in brief. The wishes of those who hear it are fulfilled."

Then Mādhavendra Purī worshiped Gopīnātha, engrossed in love. "Gopīnātha, have mercy," he said repeatedly. Everyone marveled to see his love. Then he saw the *ārati* devotional ceremony and set out.

Mādhavendra sat down to rest beneath a tree and recited the name of Hari. Six hours later, at nightfall, the priest came with a pot of sweetened milk in his hand.

"Where is Mādhavendra?" he called repeatedly.

Mādhavendra said, "That miserable creature is here."

The priest said, "The ocean of your good fortune has overflowed. Gopīnātha has stolen some milk pudding for you.[7] Gopīnātha commanded me in a dream, 'Take him some milk pudding, and I will come with you.'"

With that, the priest offered Mādhavendra the milk pudding, paid his respects, and went home.

"Kṛṣṇa has shown me amazing inconceivable mercy," Mādhavendra lovingly said, and fell into a trance. He shed many tears, and then his mind became calm, and he received the offered pudding with devotion. As he took the consecrated food, love again welled up. He raised his arms and danced. My countless bows at the feet of that Mādhavendra Purī, through whose devotion Gopīnātha got the name Kṣīracora, the milk pudding thief.

Then Mādhavendra proceeded to Nīlācala. When he saw Jagannātha, he danced most happily. Falling like a stick he sang many praises, and engrossed in love, he burst into song.

Mādhavendra rested there for several days and then took the best sandal paste and set off. He appeared again at Remunā and bowed to Gopīnātha, reciting praises. At night, Lord Gopāla spoke to him in a dream. "Listen, listen, O King of Renunciates, do not hesitate; smear the aromatic substance on Gopīnātha, because the stuff will break my fever."

When he'd had this dream, Mādhavendra was overwhelmed with love and said, "What an amazing command Lord Gopāla has given. God's will is incomprehensible; who can understand its constancy? His wish is my command." Then he offered all the sandal paste to Gopīnātha.

Mādhavendra rested there for a few days.

[7] The young Kṛṣṇa's most popular antics include his stealing dairy products from the women of Vraja. This petty theft is viewed as endearing rather than criminal.

Thereafter Mādhavendra, for the sake of love, would go back and forth frequently between Nīlācala and Remunā, always drawn by divine love. In the end, he attained final emancipation at the feet of Gopīnātha.

Mādhavendra's virtues and activities are like an ocean. Lord Advaita described them to me. I, miserable creature, cannot touch a drop of them but have written down just a few points at my lord's request.

Nāgara Īśāna, whose hopes are at the feet of Lord Caitanya and Lord Advaita, narrates the *Advaita Prakāśa*.

Chapter 6

The Digvijayī Names Advaita Ācārya

Victory, victory to Lord Caitanya; victory to Sītā's lord,
Victory to Nityānanda Rāma, and their followers.

Now listen while I describe the amazing story of how my lord came to be known as "Advaita Ācārya." A brahmin who had conquered many lands with his erudition appeared in Shantipur. He had heard of my lord Vedapañcānana and was very eager to meet him. My lord was sitting near his tulasī tree reciting the Lord Gopāla mantra when that master of debate approached and composed a poem describing the greatness of tulasī:

"Pushkara, Prabhasa, Kurukshetra, and the other holy sites;
Holy Yamunā, Gaṅgā, and all the other holy places;
Brahmā, Viṣṇu, Śiva, and all the other gods
Always dwell on a leaf of Tulasī.
Tulasī Devī seen tramples all sins.
Queen Tulasī touched purifies all bodies.
Tulasī Devī adored destroys all ills.
Tulasī bathed is Kṛṣṇa's *śakti*, the destroyer of time.
Tulasī Devī sown is an offering for Kṛṣṇa's body.
Tulasī offered to Kṛṣṇa bestows liberation in this lifetime.

I pay my respects with these verses on Holy Tulasī. Viṣṇu eats no food without (a leaf of) Tulasī."

The brahmin in this way continued to expostulate on the greatness of tulasī, quoting from various scriptures. Then he began to speak of the greatness of the Gaṅgā, and my lord opened his eyes. The master of debate said, "The Gaṅgā's majesty is unparallelled. Since she was born at the feet of Viṣṇu, her name is Viṣṇupādī. Śiva's matted locks are her eternal playground. Brahmā worships her with many gifts. She rescued Indra and the other gods; as Mandākinī she is a jeweled necklace at the throat of the world. Through his meditation, the sage Jāhnu learned the essential truth of the Gaṅgā. Pretending to rinse his mouth, he drank the Gaṅgā. Later, he decided to help living beings and let the Gaṅgā flow out between his knees. The Gaṅgā was like a devotee of Viṣṇu on earth in liquid form. She consolidated her power to save embodied souls. The blessed Mother Jāhnavī-Gaṅgā is a vessel of the virtue of compassion; bathing in it immediately destroys the three kinds of suffering. If a person drinks one drop of the Gaṅgā he will definitely go to heaven at his life's end. Therefore my hundreds of salutations to the feet of the Gaṅgā. I have come to debate with you."

When he heard this, Kamalākṣa Veda Pañcānana smiled slightly and spoke sweetly, "O Crest Jewel of Poets, you who have understood much! The top of the tree of your fame touches heaven. You have told me about the divine greatness of Holy Tulasī and the Gaṅgā, and my heart is spinning with the taste of love. But you are wrong about the essential truth of the Gaṅgā. You say it is like a devotee of Viṣṇu, (but) it is liquid Brahmā. Svayaṃ Bhagavān, to rescue living beings, melted and took the name of Gaṅgā. It says in the Purāṇas that one day Nārāyaṇa turned to liquid because of Five-Faced Śiva's song. The Gaṅgā with its musical/divine waves is actually liquid Brahmā, at the mere recollection of whose name a living being will have no more births. Bhagavān's inseparable *śakti* wears the form of the Gaṅgā. Death-conquering Śiva bore the Gaṅgā on his head. Without the Gaṅgā no task is successful, and one who worships Brahmā attains the fruit of his own desires. The wisdom of the Gaṅgā has been attributed to all waters; scriptures say: 'That water is Nārāyaṇa Himself.' If an old person drinks Gaṅgā water and dies a year later, the soul goes to Vaikuṇṭha. If one offers a tulasī leaf to the Gaṅgā intending it for Kṛṣṇa, Lord Kṛṣṇa becomes that person's servant."

Śyāmadāsa heard my lord's reasoning and thought, "My reputation as a master of debate has been ruined. Be that as it may, I will ask about Lord Brahmā. How do scriptures establish him as having form?" he thought, and said, "Listen, Veda-Pañcānana. The Vedas say that Brahmā is all-pervading. This thing is beyond the senses, without qualities, formless; there is no alteration in the uncreated Supreme Brahmā. So how do you imagine him as having form? By 'having form' I mean 'perceptible by the senses.'"

My lord said, "Parabrahmā is not formless. He has an unmanifest form full of *saccidānanda*, eternal bliss, and omniscience. He is all-powerful, absolutely complete; he is the cause of all causes of creation, et cetera. He has a special body, a special mind; he has special eyes, special qualities. He has no correlation to ordinary qualities. The scriptures say he is without qualities. He is beyond the senses, there is no doubt. He can never be known through the physical senses. Just as a fruit has form but its flavor does not, so Brahmā's physical beauty has no form. Kṛṣṇa is the supernatural Brahmā, Kṛṣṇa is Svayaṃ Bhagavān. His abode is in the eternal Vṛndāvana. With his young adolescent form, the eternal nectar of every devotional sentiment, his ecstatic state is influenced by his intrinsic energy. Kṛṣṇa's worshipers are supernatural beings. This sort of beauty can only be seen with the eyes of devotion. Hari is supremely merciful; his devotees are his life. He bestows the gift of pure devotion on His devotees. Finding Kṛṣṇa on the path of dry knowledge is very difficult; finding Kṛṣṇa on the path of devotion is extremely easy."

My lord propounded many similar concepts. When the master of debate heard them, he was amazed. Previously this Śyāmadāsa had himself gone to Vārānāsī and had worshiped Śiva because he desired knowledge. Śiva was pleased by his several days in austerity, and late at night he smiled and said to Śyāmadāsa, "O Brahmin, the tree of your austerities has borne fruit. Sarasvatī has taken up residence on your tongue. You are the real victor among the learned, excluding me. You will be known throughout the land of Bharata as a master of debate."

The brahmin traveled throughout the land, by Śiva's blessing, and finally came to Shantipur. Now when he realized that he had been defeated by my lord's brilliant reasoning, he thought he had lost Śiva's blessing.

Just then, a divine voice spoke from the sky. "O brahmin, listen, quit thinking like this. This Master Kamalākṣa is actually Hari-Hara, and that is why he is known as Lord Advaita."

When the master of debate heard this strange divine voice, he looked up but could not see anything. The brahmin thought, "He really is Hari-Hara Himself. Debating with him was a terrible sin," and said, with inner devotion, "O Glorious Lord Advaita, have mercy on me!"

The glorious Advaitacandra had abundant mercy and revealed his true form; it was most wonderful. When he saw (that), Śyāmadāsa trembled with love. Weeping, laughing, dancing, he sang Hare Kṛṣṇa.

Lord Advaita smiled when he saw how saintly the brahmin was and said, "You are blessed; you have gotten such good fortune because you ceaselessly sing the name of Hari, which is embued with endless power. Today I am a lucky man, every moment is lucky; hearing the name of Hari has satisfied my heart and soul."

As soon as he had spoken, my lord was overwhelmed with love. He said, "Call out 'Lord Kṛṣṇa Caitanya,' call out 'Nityānanda.'" After some time he regained his external awareness. My lord Advaita understood his own emotional state. My lord and his divine duty are matters not of this world. Not of this world is his knowledge, not of this world the power of his fame.

The crest-jewel of poets saw and heard all this, and diligently took mantra initiation from my lord. When he received the Kṛṣṇa mantra, he was overwhelmed with love. He fell like a stick at my lord's feet, praising him. "O Lord, by your great mercy I have been effortlessly freed from the bonds of karma." Then the brahmin learned how to worship Kṛṣṇa. When he read the *Bhāgavata Purāṇa* he drowned in love. My lord said, "Your name is Bhāgavata Ācarya," and Śyāmadāsa replied, "Your order is to be obeyed." A few days later the brahmin bowed at my lord's feet and with his permission left for his own country.

One day the glorious Advaita, the devotee-incarnation, thought to himself, "How will living beings be saved? As yet Svayaṃ Bhagavān has not appeared. How will I impart loving devotion to living beings?" My lord continued to think like this for some time.

Meanwhile, King Divyasiṃha arrived from Lauḍa. This was that same king who had earlier, under my lord's influence, left his mistaken ways and become a Vaiṣṇava. Lord Advaita stood up as soon as he saw him. The king said, "Lord, consider me your servant," and fell like a stick at Advaita's feet. He humbly praised my lord, and Advaita revealed his doctrines to him.

My lord said, "Get up, get up, you are Kṛṣṇa's servant." From then on, the king's name was Kṛṣṇadāsa. Kṛṣṇadāsa studied the devotional scriptures for ten years, saying, "Kṛṣṇa is lord of all," and his faith became firm. He abandoned the Śakti mantra and took up the Viṣṇu mantra. My lord said, "Today you have become Viṣṇu's son."

Kṛṣṇadāsa said, "You are an ocean of compassion. You have rescued this misguided person; this is most wonderful. Now send me into seclusion. I will always be completely satisfied by reciting Kṛṣṇa's name," he said, and went to the bank of the Surādhāni River, where he lashed together a small hut and lived for a long time. He made his very lovely home in a garden amid many flowers, so from that time on the name of the village has been Phullabaṭi. He was a favorite of my lord's because of his devotion. He composed my lord's *Bālya-Līlā-Sūtra* in Sanskrit, and at the end of his life Kṛṣṇadāsa went to Holy Vraja. He attained salvation gazing at Kṛṣṇa with the eyes of devotion.

Nāgara Īśāna, whose hopes are at the feet of Lord Caitanya and Lord Advaita, narrates the *Advaita Prakāśa*.

Chapter 7

The Tale of Brahmā Haridāsa

Victory, victory Caitanya, victory to Sītā's lord,
Victory to Nityānanda-Rāma, and their followers.

Now hear the tale of Brahmā Haridāsa. I'll describe it rather briefly.

Kṛṣṇa, Svayaṃ Bhagavān, had taken on human form in holy Vṛndāvana and was the pride of the cowherd boys. One day while he was tending the cows, Nanda's Gopāla ate some fruit that someone else had bitten into. The four-faced god Brahmā saw him do that and thought, "This cannot be the creator of the universe. I see what he is doing in human form; if this is the lord, why this wrongdoing?" He thought about this in his meditation, and with his divine vision he saw Kṛṣṇacandra himself sparkling in the fields of Vraja. Again he saw Kṛṣṇa eat someone's food leavings and thought, "This is not Kṛṣṇa, it must be someone else."

Brahmā had been enchanted by Kṛṣṇa's magic, and under its spell, he kidnapped the calves and the cowherds.

The primordial Nārāyaṇa learned what Brahmā had done and created an amazing, tremendously astonishing scene. Kṛṣṇa distributed his own power among many bodies, and the calves and cowherds appeared to be just as they had been originally. The yogi carried out his unperceived activities just like before. Gradually a year in human terms passed. Meanwhile, Brahmā happened to see the marvel of Kṛṣṇa engaged in tending the cows, just like before. Brahmā thought, "How could he have retrieved all the calves and boys? They are still where I hid them." Then Brahmā looked with his divine vision and saw that Kṛṣṇa himself had assumed the forms of the calves and cowherd boys.

"I am stupid not to have recognized Kṛṣṇa! I stole the calves and everything, and I am drowning in wickedness. I will praise him and make him forgive this offense," Brahmā thought, and the Creator approached Hari Himself. In order to teach the Creator spiritual truth, Kṛṣṇa created an otherworldly city with his magic. He sat on his throne and meditated, and countless Brahmās and Viṣṇus and Śivas appeared, along with countless attendants of Mahāviṣṇu. They all came and took refuge at Kṛṣṇa's feet.

Brahmā presented himself at the first gate, which was guarded by an eight-faced Brahmā. When he saw the four-faced one, the eight-faced one smiled and said, "Who are you? Where do you want to go? Tell me."

The four-faced one said, "My name is Brahmā. I want to see the cowherd-Kṛṣṇa." The eight-faced one laughed out loud and said, "I had never heard of a four-faced Brahmā, but Nārāyaṇa's creation is infinite! I am an insignificant Brahmā; today I have been enlightened!"

Now the four-faced one thought to himself, "There is an eight-faced Brahmā? Who knew that?" Then Brahmā spoke with a dry mouth to the sixteen-armed one, "Please let me see Kṛṣṇa."

The eight-faced one said, "I am an insignificant Brahmā, but the great engineer of the universe is beyond many more doors. You are entreating (me) to open the door, but no one has the power to do so without Kṛṣṇa's command. (But) there is no prohibition against brahmins entering Kṛṣṇa's inner chambers. You stay here; I will go and get his permission."

While they were talking, the infinite lord Ananta arrived, constantly praising Kṛṣṇa's greatness. When Brahmā saw his unworldly beauty, he bowed before him and took the dust of his feet. Lord Ananta said, "Who are you?"

The Creator said, "I am the four-faced Brahmā. I have come to see Lord Kṛṣṇa. Please take me, I depend on your mercy."

The lord said, "First tell me who can count the number of four-faced Brahmās?"

Brahmā thought, "How amazing! Brahmā certainly is infinite, yet I am insignificant compared to the magnitude of Kṛṣṇa's essence. Now by what sign will I be saved..." As he thought, Brahmā lost consciousness. Brahmā regained consciousness by dint of Kṛṣṇa's mercy. He said, "Sanatkumāra and the others are my sons."

Lord Ananta said, "I know which one you are. I saw you in Goloka as a very pure yogi."

The four-faced one thought, "I am most fortunate. By what scores of merit have I gotten such sons? Those wise ones have descended from me just like the moon rises from the ocean. By the incomprehensible power granted a servant of Kṛṣṇa, I am now freed from a shame worse than death."

Then the four-faced one joined his two palms in supplication and said, "Kṛṣṇa is so hard to see! Please let me see his moonlike face."

Lord Ananta said, "Without an order from His illustrious mouth, who has the power? I will go to Kṛṣṇa," and he approached the glorious Govinda and told him, "Sanatkumāra's father is at the gate."

Govinda said, "Bring him here. That very one is the Creator of this tiny universe."

Lord Ananta thought, "Blessed is the father of a servant of Kṛṣṇa. Brahmā has been honored because of his *sādhu*-sons." Then Lord Ananta quickly returned to Brahmā at the second gate. The gatekeeper there was the sixteen-faced Brahmā. When he saw him, the four-faced one said, "Who is this person?"

Saṃkarṣaṇa-Ananta said, "He is a Brahmā, the great Lord Kṛṣṇa's gatekeeper Viśvakarma, the engineer of the universe. There are hundreds more gates like this, and successively more-faced Brahmās are assigned to each gate. There is no end to the creation of the primeval lord Nārāyaṇa. He has so many assistants more important than I."

Talking and listening, he passed through many gates, and finally presented himself at the court of Govinda, the Supreme Being. Assembled there he saw countless Brahmās and Śivas; so many Gaṇeśas, Viṣṇus, Mahāviṣṇus; divine sages, celestial musicians, how many hundreds of sixteen-faced ones, hundreds of millions of Indras and Anantas. Tens of millions of moons and suns—but who was counting! The embodied Vedas were singing praises. Kṛṣṇa's unworldly splendor is so wondrous; it outshines millions and millions of suns. That young cloud-colored lotus shaped like the sun; nothing compares with Kṛṣṇa's splendid black color! Millions and millions of great emeralds, mountains of gems together cannot match Kṛṣṇa's splendor. Rādhā, his great delight, sat at Kṛṣṇa's left. Her unworldly splendor lights up the three worlds, with her hundreds of millions of golden lotuses more splendid than the moon. The splendor of Rādhā's radiant body intoxicates Kṛṣṇa's mind. The luster from Rādhā's body would outshine many hundreds of mountains of new orpiment. Lalitā and the other female companions encircle the couple and serve them as they taste love.

When he saw them all, the four-faced one trembled. But he could not see Rādhā and Kṛṣṇa, only their divine radiance. Praising Lord Ananta, Brahmā said, "Where is Lord Govinda? Let me see him."

Ananta said, "The crime of stealing the calves is no trifling matter, and consequently you have been denied the sight of Kṛṣṇa."

When he heard this, Brahmā confessed his crime, and with tears on his face, he sang Kṛṣṇa's many praises. Lord Mādhava, beloved by His devotees, is an ocean of compassion. When he heard Brahmā's profuse praises, he was satisfied. Then he revealed his own eternal form to Brahmā and said, "You have committed the crime of stealing cows, so you will be (born) a Muslim in the Kali Age, but when you see the glorious Kṛṣṇa Caitanya, you will be acquitted."

Brahmā was amazed when he saw Kṛṣṇa's form. When he heard His decree, Brahmā drowned in the ocean of the bliss of divine love. He bowed fully, hundreds of times, before Rādhā and Śyāma, then took his leave of Kṛṣṇa and went home. He watched the arrival of the Kali Age from his lotus seat, and descended to earth.

Brahmā appeared in the village of Budana in the year 1450. Some say Prahlāda had incarnated in Haridāsa, but my lord Advaita Ācārya says the two—Brahmā and Prahlāda—have come together in one body. He is known as just an ordinary Muslim with no clue that he appeared primarily to rescue embodied souls. Though raised as a Muslim, Brahmā drank only milk.[8] Day by day he waxed like the moon. Brahmā Haridāsa could remember his previous earthly births, and because of his prior inclinations he always chanted the name of Hari.

At the age of five the child left home and roamed from place to place and eventually came to Shantipur. He appeared before Lord Advaita as a mass of splendor with arms reaching to his knees. Lord Advaita, a mine of all knowledge, immediately recognized Haridāsa as Brahmā in human form. Since Haridāsa was playing a human part in this earthly drama, Advaita said to him, "What is your caste? Why have you come?"

Brahmā Haridāsa replied, "I am a vile Muslim. I have come to see you."

My lord said, "Stay here and rest. Study the scriptures, and your heart's desires will be fulfilled."

Haridāsa said, "By good fortune I have reached the ocean of compassion. I will cool my heart and soul in its waves." Thus Haridāsa diligently studied grammar, literature, et cetera, with Advaita and eventually became proficient in philosophy, et cetera, and after that he studied the *Bhāgavata Purāṇa* and developed pure devotion. The meanings of its verses formed a jeweled necklace for his throat. No one can match the greatness of Haridāsa, who memorized everything he heard.

One day Haridāsa was sitting in an isolated place. He paid his devoted respects and told my lord, "I realize that you are actually an incarnation of Īśvara. Who but you is the savior of the lowly?"

The glorious Advaitacandra heard his humble words and said, "Listen, child, to the voice of the pure scriptures. Whether one is young or old, he knows no

[8] That is, he would not eat solid food because in a Muslim household food would not have been offered to Kṛṣṇa.

security, but one whose conduct is virtuous is considered most excellent. If the eight types of devotion arise in a Muslim, his low birth becomes irrelevant and he is considered to be a brahmin. Anyone who worships Kṛṣṇa is most excellent, and any who turn away from Kṛṣṇa are most vile. One cannot reach Kṛṣṇa's feet except through the mood of the *gopīs*; in that attitude one finds the priceless jewel of divine love."

Haridāsa said, "Not even countless lifetimes of merit can inculcate the incomprehensible mood of the *gopīs* in a person. Lord, please reveal the easy means by which one can transcend illusion and reach Kṛṣṇa."

Advaita Ācārya said, "Nothing is beyond your perception, yet you have accepted me as master. Chant the name of Hari for the purpose of establishing righteousness. Rescue living beings by spreading the mantra of the Name. Just as Bhagavān's power is infinite and divine, so the power of Brahmā's Name is eternally perfect. Merely suggesting the Name dispels the three afflictions (spiritual, material, and supernatural). Pronouncing the name breaks the bonds of illusion. The touchstone of the Name is Kṛṣṇa, Svayaṃ Bhagavān. In the entire universe there is no Truth like the Name. Deep faith in the Name kindles divine love, and its ceaseless repetition confers the treasure of divine love. If the wishing tree of divine love is vigorous, it bears the fruit of Svayaṃ Bhagavān.

"Kṛṣṇa said the Name is even more powerful than the one who bears the Name. Repeating the Name erases all crimes. Therefore, taking Kṛṣṇa's Name is the best course of action, and if one has any inclination at all toward the Name, all desires are fulfilled. But without the counsel of the illustrious Vaiṣṇava gurus, there is no salvation in Kṛṣṇa, even after millions of ages, for the illustrious Vaiṣṇava teachings constitute the essence of all religions. Among Vaiṣṇavas, the ascetics are the best. The marks of complete renunciation in the ascetic stage are that the twice-born should wear the Vaiṣṇava garb, et cetera. This sort of dispassion dawns, if one is lucky, and then devotion to Kṛṣṇa arises. Such a person will spontaneously decide to wear these pure marks and will surely reach the feet of Rādhā-Kṛṣṇa."

And with that, Advaita Ācārya shaved Haridāsa's head, et cetera, and put *tilaka* marks and a tulasī necklace on him. He awakened the divine power within him, tied the loincloth around his waist, and gave him the name of Hari. In a cave by the Gaṅgā he got the touchstone of the Name, and that crest-jewel of Vaiṣṇavas went mad with divine love. When he regained consciousness he prostrated his body full-length.

Advaita Ācārya said, "May you reach Kṛṣṇa," and blessed him, saying, "Your name is now Brahmā Haridāsa."

Haridāsa said, "I am your slave." He donned simple garments and made a daily practice of reciting the Name three hundred thousand times, and then preaching. His otherworldly activities amazed people.

One day—listen to an amazing story—Brahmā Haridāsa was chanting the Name when an accomplished logician came and said, "I think this boy is crazy."

The great scholar Kṛṣṇadāsa explained, "He is drunk on the divine love of the Name, and has no trace of sorrow. The goddess Sarasvatī resides on his tongue, ceaselessly unfolding the name of Hari, and all the scriptures dwell in his heart. By his guru's command, his name is Brahmā Haridāsa."

Just then Haridāsa completed (reciting) his Names. The logician arrogantly asked him, "Brahmā's body is both with form and formless. Which is the true causeless cause? Why did that Supreme Brahmā create this world and moreover, why (such) a diverse world? Why do living beings experience a succession of joys and sorrows? This is Īśvara's dominion; why does wickedness pervade it?"

When he heard this, Haridāsa spoke humbly and politely. "This insignificant creature wants to say something. Kṛṣṇadāsa Pandit, please remain calm. Please listen, My Lord Cakravartī. Saccidānanda Brahmā is the infinite Īśvara, proclaimed in scripture to be eternally perfect. The loveliness of his body is all-pervasive and formless, like the splendor of the one sun which pervades the universe. Scholars do not understand Parabrahmā's eternal form, and they consider the loveliness of his body to be Brahmā, but one can only know his eternally perfect form through pure devotion; it is not revealed otherwise. All the scriptures say that creation is as eternal as the omnipotent Brahmā, and in this Kali Age it is both manifest and unmanifest. It is eternal by Īśvara's decree, and so creation collapses at the end with the Great Dissolution. I am just describing a few points about this. As soon as Lord Caitanya,[9] the foremost cause of all causes, is mentioned, illusion turns to wisdom and one tastes eternal bliss. The sovereign lord produces many types of Creation, the Vedas testify, and creates the material world as a duty, by his own desire. For this very reason Brahmā is fixed in the Vedas as immutable. Living beings are covered with illusion according to their own karma and wander through many births, experiencing joy and sorrow. In this Parabrahmā there is no inconsistency. Think about this and you will see it is true; and do not become angry."

When the brahmin had heard all this philosophy, he was amazed. The glorious Advaita, whose form was (radiant) like ten million suns, arrived, and when that best of brahmins saw Advaita Ācārya's form, a mass of splendor, he bowed to him, his palms joined in supplication.

My lord said, "Why are you behaving so humbly, sir?"

The brahmin said, "Lord, I understand who you are."

Advaita said, "I am just a powerless wretch."

The brahmin said, "You are the evil-destroying lord of the universe." Compassion arose in Advaita Ācārya, that ocean of the nectar of compassion, and he awakened the brahmin's divine power and gave him the Kṛṣṇa mantra. Lord Yadunandana prostrated himself completely.

Advaita Ācārya said, "May you obtain the treasure of love of Kṛṣṇa."

[9] Who has not yet been born!

Yadunandana Ācārya came to lead one branch of Advaita Ācārya's followers, and he is everywhere described as Tarkacūḍāmaṇi, crest-jewel of debate. As proficient as a celestial musician in music, by my lord's grace he found the essence of the truth about devotion.

Brahmā Haridāsa has power not of this world. By repeating the name of Hari three hundred thousand times every day he found pure loving devotion. He repeated it mentally, under his breath and out loud. Then he took consecrated food and tasted the essence of Kṛṣṇa from my lord's mouth. Whoever constantly remembers Haridāsa's good conduct will surely have the pearl of worshiping Kṛṣṇa. Brahmā Haridāsa Ṭhākura is a storehouse of compassion. My millions of salutations at his feet.

Īśāna Nāgara, whose hopes are at the feet of Lord Caitanya and Lord Advaita, narrates the *Advaita Prakāśa*.

Chapter 8

Marriage

Victory, victory to Lord Caitanya, victory to Sītā's lord,
Victory to Nityānanda Rāma, and their followers.

One day when Lord Advaita took his followers to the Gaṅgā to perform their usual bathing and other rituals, Nṛsiṃha Bhāḍurī and his two daughters rowed up to the same dock. In that boat was Sītā, beautiful and virtuous, and beside herself with joy, entirely smitten by the beauty she saw in Advaita. "No ordinary man can look this attractive. His entire magnificent golden body shines brighter than the River Jambu, from the lotus-like hands at the ends of arms which reach his knees,[10] to the graceful lotus buds of his fingers. As soon as I saw his lovely face, sweet as a beautiful lotus, the lotus of my heart blossomed. I surrender my life to this great man; if I do not get him, I will die!" she said, and like the cākora bird, turned her eyes to the moonlight of Advaita's glorious face and drank in his radiance.

The lovely Śrī, the sister of the virtuous Sītā, like her sister as beautiful as Lakṣmī, thrilled to see my lord's charm. She said, "Sister, look at that magnificent man on the bank of the Gaṅgā! He looks like ten million golden full moons descended to earth all at once. The fragrance of his body is so ethereal, it would put to shame ten million lotuses. One look at that lovely radiant face soothes me to my core. A woman who has such a man for her husband is blessed and is fortunate to have been born a woman."

Then Nṛsiṃha Bhāḍurī, jewel among brahmins, caught sight of my lord Advaita and felt blessed. He greeted my lord very courteously, as was proper.

[10] An indication of spiritual power.

Advaita Ācārya in return said, "Praise God," and sweetly asked the brahmin his particulars.

Bhāḍurī humbly and respectfully replied, "I live in the village of Nārāyaṇapur. My name is Nṛsiṃha Bhāḍurī. I have heard about your spiritual qualities, and so have come to see your true form. I have been wanting to see you for a long time, and today, by great good fortune, my desire has been fulfilled."

My lord said, "I am just a miserable creature; what power do I have? Please, make yourself at home in my house."

Nṛsiṃha said, "You are Sadāśiva incarnate! No one can ignore your command," and he and his two daughters happily proceeded to Advaita's house. My lord received them with proper hospitality and blessed Bhāḍurī with a vision of his four-armed form. Bhāḍurī thought, "Today my life is fulfilled! Today the results of ten million good deeds have borne fruit for me! I have seen something with my own eyes, that until now I had only heard about. This is a sign that this man is a suitable groom for my daughters. Just as two essences fuse to form one body, so love has dawned in the hearts of this couple. If only Hari will grant me this grace, my heart's desire will have been perfectly fulfilled."

Then Advaitacandra in his omniscient glory used his divine powers to make himself look like an emperor. Advaita's house was transformed into a palace like Indra's city, adorned with various flowers whose heavenly scent cast a spell over blessed Shantipur. Lord Advaita sat on a jeweled throne, his lovely form as beautiful as many moons, more sparkling than the gold of the Jambu River. On his head he wore a jeweled crown, on his wrists, bracelets, earrings glistened in his ears, and on his lovely feet, anklets. His garments were of white silk, and his body had been anointed with the best sandal and musk. White flowers decorated his neck and chest. Male and female servants fell at his feet surrounding him, and courtiers were seated close to their lord. Yadunandana Ācārya was the chamberlain, Pandit Kṛṣṇadāsa was the scribe, and Brahmā Haridāsa sat at the feet of the ministers. Śyāmadāsa Ācārya was the matrimonial go-between, by whom this marriage was arranged.

The sight of this assembly amazed Nṛsiṃha. Just then Śrīvāsa Pandit arrived. The incarnation of Nārada, this member of Gaura's inner circle had the power, by Kṛṣṇa's grace, to know what other people were thinking. A bestower of pure devotion to brahmins, always engrossed in Kṛṣṇa, his appearance in Navadvīpa was an extraordinary mercy. The only word out of his mouth was "Hari." As soon as my lord saw him, he stood up to welcome him. Śrīvāsa and Advaita greeted each other, and when they sat down, Śrīvāsa proclaimed, "Listen, everyone. This Lord Advaita is no different from Hari: he has appeared on earth to rescue living beings. How can I, a miserable wretch, comprehend his majesty? The lotus-born Brahmā Himself knows (only) a little of his greatness.

"(And) this is the exalted Nṛsiṃha Bhāḍurī, sprung from the union of the ocean of milk and the Himalayas. A wise speaker of truth, he is foremost among the virtuous, learned in dharma treatises, venerated among the *kulīnas*, the highest of brahmins. His daughter Sītā is that very Yogamāyā, Kṛṣṇa's Magic personified, born in Vraja in Kṛṣṇa's play as Paurṇamāsī. People do not realize that Sītā was not born from a womb; Nṛsiṃha got her as a reward for many good deeds. Let me tell you the story of Sītā's birth; just thinking about it destroys all evil.

"Nṛsiṃha Bhāḍurī, a *kulīna* brahmin always concerned about the welfare of others, lived in Nārāyaṇapur. He worshiped Nārāyaṇa daily with tulasī blossoms he picked himself. A great many lotus flowers had come into bloom in a lake near the village, and their lovely fragrance wafted into town. Nṛsiṃha caught their scent with great delight and thought, 'Whoever worships Nārāyaṇa with a lotus flower goes to Vaikuṇṭha at the end of his life.'

"Thus virtuous Nṛsiṃha went to the marsh and picked a quantity of lotus blossoms. While he was picking, a hundred-petaled lotus caught his eye. In the center of that lotus was sitting a dazzlingly beautiful girl the size of his thumb, clearly a member of the eternal inner circle of Rādhā-Mādhava. He thought, 'This must be the goddess Lakṣmī, since her physical beauty is more radiant than the sun's. Lakṣmī's lotuses adorn her glorious body, and her nails are like moons. I have never seen such incomparable beauty. I will take this jewel of a girl and her lotus home.'

"Then he picked that great lotus and carried it straight home. Meanwhile, by God's will, that very day Nṛsiṃha's wife had given birth to a beautiful daughter named Śrī. Nṛsiṃha's wife's name was Narasiṃhī. She was chaste and virtuous, a real Lakṣmī-Menakā. Bhāḍurī stealthily entered the childbirth room and ecstatically showed his wife the girl in the middle of the lotus. She was amazed to see the extraordinary girl and spoke sweetly to Nṛsiṃha: 'O Lord, the beauty of this thumb-sized girl is as dazzling as the sun. I think Mahāmāyā has come to us magically as this girl; her living with us would be Mahāmāyā's kindess.' And the couple discussed the matter for some time.

"This divine child grew quickly. Word of their twin daughters spread, and many village women came to see them and said, 'These two girls are like Lakṣmī.' People assumed that Sītā was older and Śrī younger."

Who can describe the activities of Śrī and Sītā at all? At the age of five they went to the bank of the Gaṅgā and studied with various types of renunciates. This is the gist of that story.

"One day a shining renunciate came to visit Nṛsiṃha Bhāḍurī," Śrīvāsa continued, "and many people came to see him. Sītā and Śrī, too, came for his blessing. Everyone bowed with devotion before that best of yogis. But when he saw Sītā and Śrī, although they had concealed their yogic powers, he became agitated. He praised them both and bowed in complete submission.

"Sītā asked, 'Why are you, a very powerful, splendid yogi, praising the two of us?'

"The yogi said, 'Mothers, you are as beautiful as the Supreme Lakṣmī. Please tell me how I can attain liberation. What will please Viṣṇu? Reveal the truth and drive out my wickedness, and news of your greatness will spread all over the world.'

"Sītā, the embodiment of kindness, smiled and said, 'Liberation is the servant of the goddess of devotion; devotion is the mistress of all. A person can attain the five types of liberation but still not have reached the feet of the eternal Hari. The liberated person naturally takes pride in being liberated but is sent into the world again and again because his understanding is inadequate. None can rival the spiritual greatness of the goddess of devotion; whomever she graces is not born again. Devotion earns a sincere worshiper the bliss of divine love. He attains Kṛṣṇa's feet, before which the bliss of Brahmā is nothing.'

"Then Śrī smiled and said, 'Listen, O best of yogis. That liberation by which one merges into Viṣṇu is most terrible. If honey is available wouldn't you rather taste honey with the bliss of the divine love of a follower of Kṛṣṇa who relies on Kṛṣṇa?'

"Thus the two girls expounded the tenets of devotion, and when he had listened to their explanations, that renunciate became a pure Vaiṣṇava.

"Now hear what happened to Sītā on another day, when the two girls went to the bank of the Gaṅgā. Many people had gathered for a celebration with nonstop singing and chanting of the Name, on the other side of the Gaṅgā. Bhāḍurī had planned to take his two daughters, but when they reached the riverbank a fierce wind came up, and the waves on the Gaṅgā frightened them. That great brahmin left his two daughters with a servant and crossed the Gaṅgā in a huge boat. But Sītā and Śrī crossed the river themselves, using their divine powers. Nṛsiṃha marveled to see what his daughters had done, and ran to embrace them. Some wicked barbarians had watched Śrī and Sītā walk across the river, and arrogantly set out to cross the Gaṅgā the same way, but they fell into the deep water and had to struggle to keep from drowning. Everyone who saw that laughed out loud."

Sītā and Śrī performed so many similar miracles in their childhood, I cannot begin to describe them. Lord Advaita described the greatness of a follower of Kṛṣṇa: "Nothing is impossible for Kṛṣṇa's servants, male and female, who have inconceivable powers. They acquire yogic powers instantly, and one by one those powers of his followers purify the world."

The brahmin Śrīvāsa humbly told the lord, "You are Kṛṣṇa incarnated as his devotee; you are the philosopher's stone, the catalyst to instill devotion in us all. You have appeared as a mine of the principles of devotion to Kṛṣṇa. You alone know (what it is to be a) follower of the Lord. You alone are Īśvara, Gopeśvara the omniscient. This Sītā Devī is your Yogamāyā. Sītā and Śrī have a single soul housed in separate bodies. Marry these two girls (and) your storehouse will be inexhaustible. They will be useful in serving Lord Kṛṣṇa's Vaiṣṇavas, and allow your lineage to rescue living beings." The lord agreed to the marriage immediately, and accordingly, Bhāḍurī gave his two daughters.

Advaita Ācārya gave a feast for Rādhā and Madana Gopāla on the occasion of his marriage, with various sorts of food and sweets. He distributed this consecrated food to men and women, and they all ate it and went home happily.

He considered Sītā Ṭhākurānī and Śrī Ṭhākurānī as one soul in his love for them. Their faithfulness in serving the Lord and waiting on their husband increased day by day.

One day Mādhavendra Purī came to Mother Sītā in a dream and spoke with sweet words, "Listen, Sītā Devī, my name is Mādhavendra. Lord Advaita took initiation from me. I will give you the same Kṛṣṇa-attracting king of mantras, the eternally perfected Kṛṣṇa mantra, that I gave him. Kṛṣṇa will not eat food cooked by a noninitiate; it would be a great offense if you knowingly fed him without that mantra."

Sītā said, "I am most fortunate to meet you. Please purify my body and soul with mantra initiation."

Then Mādhavendra initiated Sītā with the Kṛṣṇa mantra and vanished immediately thereafter. Sītā woke up and told the whole story to her husband. "How wonderful! Mādhavendra Purī gave me the mantra in a dream!"

Advaita responded, "By this good fortune, your karmic bonds have been broken." Her lord bestowed the mantra again on his wife Sītā, in accord with scriptures, at the auspicious moment.

I have revealed just a glimpse of this deep truth which Mother by her kindness revealed.

Īśāna Nāgara, whose hopes are at the feet of Lord Caitanya and Lord Advaita, narrates the *Advaita Prakāśa*.

Chapter 9

The Trials of Haridāsa

Victory, victory to Lord Caitanya; victory to Sītā's lord,
Victory to Nityānanda Rāma, and their followers.

One day Brahmā Haridāsa humbly expressed his heart's desire to my lord Advaita Ācārya. "O Lord, with your permission, I would like to go off by myself to taste unceasingly the nectar of Hari's Name."

My lord said, "My heart bursts at (the thought of) separation from you, (but) I cannot forbid it, for that would create an obstacle to your worship."

Haridāsa fell at my lord's feet, and Advaita Ācārya, overcome with divine love, pressed him close. Haridāsa said, "I am a vile untouchable. Why have you committed the offense of touching me?"

My lord said, "I recognize neither high birth nor low birth. Anyone who worships Kṛṣṇa belongs to the Vaiṣṇava caste and is said to be highest of all. 'High' and 'low' are determined by one's actions (alone). You are the best of the Lord's pure followers, and devotion takes root in the soul of everyone you touch."

Haridāsa said, "My lord, your most unblemished kindness makes everything possible, (even) for an ordinary person." With his lord's permission, he departed for the village of Phuliya, his mind ever on Hari.

When the brahmins living in that town saw Haridāsa, their hearts melted. One very scholarly brahmin named Rāmadāsa was well-versed in the treatises on dharma and always behaved accordingly. When he saw Haridāsa, devotion welled up in him. He began to speak humbly in sweet language: "O Wise Man, your coming here sanctifies my house. I had no idea how much merit our village had accrued. Please be so kind as to make your home here."

Brahmā Haridāsa said, "O Best of Brahmins! In the words of the Vedas, a brahmin alone is the body of Viṣṇu, but I am lowborn, not worthy of your touch. It is I who have been very blessed by you."

Rāmadāsa said, "Sādhu, why are you behaving so humbly? Caste is not important for those who follow the lord. Just as iron turns to gold when it comes into contact with the philosopher's stone, everyone involved in the worship of God belongs to the highest caste. What is human praise but praise for one's dharma? One is considered high or low according to his own deeds. The devotee of the lord who has renounced worldly affairs is the best of all creatures, entitled to liberation."

Haridāsa said, "You are eternally wise and good. You show an ascetic's form to all creatures. Whoever worships God through practices based on intellectual knowledge gets liberation according to the strength of his learning, but a cleverer seeker does not long for liberation. A living being does not obtain eternal liberation through practices based on intellectual scholarship."

The brahmin said, "By what, other than intellectual knowledge, can one attain the complete essence of Parabrahmā?"

Haridāsa said, "The method of devotion is the best because it allows one to attain the eternal Brahmā, the Lord of All. Hari gives his servants a *siddha-deha*, a meditation-body, so that they can use the practice of devotion to reach an understanding of their servitude. The eternal Brahmin is really Svayaṃ Bhagavān, composed of truth, awareness, and bliss, full of every power. One who ceaselessly repeats Hari's Name, the motivating factor of pure devotion, attains the realm of divine love. Gradually, as one's love deepens, one (first) attains the mood of the *gopīs* and then attains Rādhā-Kṛṣṇa in the erotic mood."

This news caused the brahmin's hair to stand on end. He said, "Have mercy on me, purify me!"

When he heard this, Haridāsa was filled with divine love and transmitted that power to the brahmin and gave him (the mantra of) Hari's Name. The brahmin's eyes cascaded (with tears) as he bowed to Haridāsa and praised him. Eventually the brahmin and the (other) holy men became Vaiṣṇavas, and the heavenly creeper of devotion covered the fields of their hearts. With the help of the brahmin, Brahmā Haridāsa built a small hut and lived there happily, always tasting the nectar of Hari's Name, and many of the villagers became his disciples.

One day the thought occurred to Haridāsa that it might not be good to stay in one place for any length of time because one can fall into illusion through association and conversation. And in time a person becomes blind to his worldly attachments. It is not necessary to maintain an ascetic's lifestyle, but still, renouncing human company is best, he thought, (and) he left home late at night, singing Hari's Name, and went to Venapola. There, deep in a great forest, he sang *kīrtana*, and the village people came and worshiped him. Devotion to this mere mortal arose in everyone who by Kṛṣṇa's mercy had the great good fortune to see him, so when the villagers saw Brahmā Haridāsa's splendid form, one by one they became his disciples. The village disciples lovingly built him a hut right there in Venapola Forest, so he stayed there and worshiped Tulasī. In one month he recited the Name ten million times. He would beg a handful of rice at the homes of the Vaiṣṇava brahmins every day, and out of kindness instruct people in moral principles.

One day a wanton woman came to Haridāsa, all dressed up as beautifully as a celestial nymph. She sat in the doorway of his hut and gestured her intent. Haridāsa innocently asked her, "Why have you come here this evening?"

The woman said, "I fell in love with you when I saw how young and beautiful you are. Quit chanting the Name and let's have some fun!"

Haridāsa replied with a smile, "Leave here immediately! Anyone not wearing tulasī around the neck, without *tilaka* marks on the forehead, and without Kṛṣṇa's name on her tongue is vile and wicked. The point is that they have turned away from Kṛṣṇa, and no intelligent person can ever look (at them). On the other hand, Kṛṣṇa will fulfill every desire of those who come with good intention." And Haridāsa began to chant the Name, and the wanton woman left.

The next day there was a tulasī necklace around her neck and she had made a *tilaka* on her forehead with sandal paste. She had written the name of Hari on her body and dressed like a Vaiṣṇava, and then came to Haridāsa's place in the evening. The fallen woman bowed and sat in the doorway of the hut, and ostentatiously chanted "Hari, Hari" aloud.

Association with holy men has great spiritual power, and anyone dressed as a virtuous person, even under false pretenses, attains liberation while alive. It is as if one gets the whole tree along with the fragrance of the sandal paste. So when he heard the ceaseless Name of Hari from the mouth of the sinful woman, the crest-jewel of Vaiṣṇavas was awestricken by the bliss of divine love. She told Haridāsa what kind of woman she was, and said, "My lord, I have come in the hope that you will have mercy on me."

Haridāsa replied, "It is good that you have come. Say 'Hari, Hari' just once, sincerely," and he began chanting the Name. While he was singing to her, the woman's mind drifted away as if floating on a wave of his goodness. She realized her promiscuity was the enjoyment of wickedness. She joined her palms in supplication and bowed to Haridāsa and said, "You, great sage, are the magnet which has attracted me. You, my lord, the guru, are full of compassion, a wish-fulfilling tree. Be so kind as to give me the fruit of liberation."

The crest-jewel of holy men was overcome with the feeling of divine love by the wanton woman's change of heart. He had her head shaved as a penance, and he infused her with divine power and whispered the name of Hari in her ear. As soon as she got the (mantra of the) Name of Hari, the sprout of divine love took root. Haridāsa named her Kṛṣṇadāsī and said, "Stay here and recite Hari's Name. Because of Kṛṣṇa's mercy, your heart's desires will be fulfilled. Brahmā's Name has the same power as Parabrahmā, so one can reach Kṛṣṇa through His Name; liberation occurs at the whisper of His Name."

After he said this, Haridāsa moved on to another place, and Kṛṣṇadāsī continued to repeat the name of Kṛṣṇa night and day. By the incomprehensible power of the mercy of such a wonderful holy man, even a poisonous tree bears the fruit of spiritual nectar.

Now hear about Haridāsa's unprecedented accomplishments—he converted many Muslims to Vaiṣṇavism! When the Vaiṣṇavas who lived in Phuliya saw Haridāsa, they drowned in divine bliss. They always chanted the Name together; this became a sharp knife in the hearts of the wicked.

The Muslim ruler had learned of Haridāsa's religious beliefs and very angrily said to his servants, "There is a Muslim named Haridāsa in Phuliya who is behaving like a Hindu. If he suffers for this and people ridicule him, Islam too will eventually suffer. Arrest him and bring him here, and punish him."

And so his wicked servants set off to arrest him. They seized Haridāsa and tormented him, and brought him into the court at the end of a rope. The Muslim ruler asked Haridāsa, "Why are you, a man of noble birth, acting like a Hindu? Surely any person who abandons his own religion and practices yoga will go to hell at death. If you have any desire in your heart to find heaven, say your prayers in the Muslim way and recant this heresy."

Haridāsa responded very seriously, "I tell you, the best scripture is the most rational one. One should obey a logical scripture which prescribes what is best for all castes. The Muslim scripture is somewhat irrational. Look at what it says. The cow is (our) mother and father, so harming the cow is irrational, and eating its flesh is the same as eating the flesh of one's father. Those wrongdoers whose scripture advocates killing cows, get more births; as a result of their own religion they wander through many births.

Parabrahmā comprises all natures, his form is without beginning, complete with the six splendors, his body composed of pure truth. Reading a scripture in which He is said to be formless and indifferent strengthens the spell of illusion. In actuality there is no difference between God and a living being, just as fire exists equally in every light. Thus just as fire is the underlying property, so Hari, Lord of

All, is the Creator of all. If a living being worships Hari, his illusion disappears, so I have taken shelter at Hari's feet because of that desire."

When they heard this logical testimony from the ascetic, everyone assumed he must be a Sufi saint. Then the ascetic revealed his full glory, and the Muslims were afraid. The Muslim ruler submitted completely (and) said, "O Holy Man, have mercy on me, a miserable wretch. I am a wicked fool not to have recognized you; please forgive my offense. I bow ten million times at your feet. Now rescue this contemptible person through your own virtues."

Compassion arose in Haridāsa's heart. He blessed them, saying, "May you be devoted to Kṛṣṇa." He raised his arms and said, "Chant 'Hari, Hari.' You will cut the bonds of karma and cross (to the other shore) on the boat of devotion."

Devotion arose in the hearts of everyone present, and they all began to dance and cry "Hari, Hari," and thus Haridāsa converted the Muslims. From there he went to Kulia city.

The greatness of Brahmā Haridāsa has no equal. Not even the gods can understand, let alone a wretch like me. Raghunātha Dāsa Gosvāmī, in whose good company I got the seed of devotion, had faith in Caitanya. How amazing that the man through whose mercy a snake became liberated should cause the salvation of the Muslims.

Let me tell you now a little about the salvation of that snake. The Vaiṣṇava great souls who heard it were thrilled.

Haridāsa was sitting in a cave reciting the Name of Hari. Everyone in the village heard him and came to investigate. When they saw the holy man's delight in divine love and the Name, they began to chant the Name along with him. Meanwhile, a very long black snake, a divine jewel shining like the sun in its head, positioned itself in front of Haridāsa and coiled up to listen to the Name of Hari. Everyone trembled in fear when they saw this, and said, "O best of holy men, today we will all die!"

But fearless Haridāsa wrapped that snake around his neck and infused it with its own divine power and gave it the (mantra of the) Name of Hari. He clapped his hands and sang the Name of Hari, and the snake began to dance and sway with divine love, his eyes flowing ceaselessly with tears, and he lowered his head again and again to the feet of the Vaiṣṇava. He took the dust of the feet of the Vaiṣṇava and thought of God as the Name of Hari. Right before their eyes, the snake got an eternal body and went to divine Vṛndāvana in a four-armed form. All the people who saw this incomprehensible greatness became Vaiṣṇavas attached to (chanting) the Name of Hari.

After several days Haridāsa became anxious and went to Shantipur at dawn. When my lord Advaita saw his beloved Haridāsa, he called him to him with great affection. Brahmā Haridāsa fell at my lord's glorious feet and spoke humbly. My lord embraced him and spoke sweetly, "You have cast off your base birth, and I consider you very dear." The two dear friends were sunk in divine love in their conversation. Crying "Hari," they raised their arms and began to dance, and so their great celebration expanded daily.

The *kulīna* brahmins said to each other, "If Advaita Ācārya does not give up associating with Haridāsa, we will shun him." The master did not pay them any mind, and these wicked people did shun my lord. My lord said, "Good, good, the bad company has gone. The Blessed Lord has shown me his kindness."

Listen to a wonderful story. One day...There was a rich *kulīna* brahmin in Shantipur. More than a hundred brahmins very gladly came to his house at his invitation for an auspicious function. Everyone was greeted and took their seats. Just then a renunciate arrived, his body as splendid as the sun, its loveliness throwing light in all four directions. He sat down under a tree and did not say a word. Everyone came and bowed to him; the blind, the mute, et cetera, all came, and everyone smeared the dust of his lotus feet all over their bodies. The touch of the dust of that holy man's feet dispelled disease. Everyone began to dance with great joy. All afflictions were cured: the blind could see, the lame could walk, the mute could speak. The *kulīna* brahmins, the proud scholars, and the wicked people saw this wonder, and they all came and bowed at his feet, praising him in many ways with great humility, and many took great pains to serve the holy man. But he said, "I eat nothing but food consecrated to Viṣṇu. Viṣṇu's consecrated food is most sacred, and substances unfit to offer Viṣṇu are (no more than) excrement and urine. The gods, ancestors, holy men, et cetera, take nothing except what is fit to offer Viṣṇu. If one ignores these words of the eternal scriptures, he will definitely fall into a dreadful Hell."

The host said, "Nārāyaṇa is at my house," and offered Him consecrated food. The holy man said "amen" and accepted it. Then that best of holy men was seated among the brahmins, where he looked like the moon surrounded by the stars. The host attentively served the holy man before he served the brahmins.

Just when the brahmins had finished eating, my lord Advaita Ācārya arrived. The glorious omnipresent Advaita, guru of the universe, was the wish-fulfilling tree of pure devotees. He saw Brahmā Haridāsa seated among the brahmins and smiled indulgently and spoke sweetly. "Dear Haridāsa, what a scene you have created! You have made so many brahmins lose caste!"

Haridāsa said, "My lord, I had no intention of doing so! The brahmins insisted on seating (me here)." He hurriedly rinsed his mouth and bowed to my lord with many praises. This surprised the brahmins, who told Advaita, "He is actually an incarnation of Viṣṇu! This very Haridāsa, whose company we wanted to make you give up as wicked, has spiritual virtue. A devotee of Hari has a pure body, and moreover, one who recognizes caste is a great evildoer. We have offended the glorious Advaita, who has blessed us and instructed us through his own devotion."

Then the brahmins joined their palms in supplication and approached Advaita Ācārya with great humility. My lord kindly displayed his true form: Mahāviṣṇu and Sadāśiva, the two in a single body. The sight of it flooded the brahmins in bliss, leaving them weeping and trembling like the leaves of a kadamba tree, their hair standing on end. They said, "Lord, we take refuge at your feet. Forgive our offense and place your feet on our heads." They prostrated themselves completely and praised him, and everyone drank the water used to wash the lord's feet.

My lord said "Brahmins, do not fear. The power of Hari's Name is incomprehensible. Repeat this *mantra* of the Name, and all your desires will be fulfilled effortlessly."

After he had spoken, Lord Advaita returned to his own house, and by great good fortune those brahmins became Vaiṣṇavas. The feet of the glorious Vaiṣṇavas have infinite greatness. I am a miserable creature who cannot understand an iota of this. If by God's kindness a barbarian finds devotion to Kṛṣṇa, he becomes a brahmin; this is sung in the Vedas. Just as bell metal becomes gold on contact with any mercury, so purity of soul comes about through contact with devotion. Those brahmins had detestable characters, but under Vaiṣṇava influence, they were purified.

My lord, in order to teach the superiority of Vaiṣṇavism to the ignorant, kept the brahmins waiting and served Haridāsa a great feast. Haridāsa said to my lord with palms joined in supplication, "Why are you feeding me without having fed the brahmins?"

My lord said, "The glorious Vaiṣṇavas have spiritual strength, so if I feed you, the result is (the same as) feeding ten million brahmins."

Haridāsa said, "You are the Vaiṣṇava Master. Your commands are fixed in the form of the dharma treatises." When he heard the title "Vaiṣṇava Master," that best of lords was overwhelmed by divine love and roared out loud. His joy with Haridāsa grew; they always delighted in chanting the Name of Hari.

One day Haridāsa said to my lord, "The wicked barbarians are destroying our eternal religion. They are breaking our gods and images into pieces and completely disrupting the implements for our worship of the gods. They are forcibly throwing the *Bhāgavata Purāṇa* and our other scriptures in the fire and burning them, and taking away the brahmins' conches, bells, and drums, and they are slapping the brahmins because of the seals and *tilaka*s on their bodies. These wicked people are defecating in the temples and pouring dogs' urine at the base of our sacred tulasī (plants). If we sit for worship they spit on us, and they flog the holy men and call them crazy. They are degrading religion entirely and destroying it with hundreds of such acts of vandalism. I know Kṛṣṇa's solemn promise in the scriptures, "Whenever there is a decline of righteousness and an excess of unrighteousness, Kṛṣṇa appears." This is such a time, so why has Kṛṣṇacandra not been born here? My lord, how will dharma be preserved? I think about this constantly, and my mind is very anxious."

Advaita Ācārya said, "This is the way people behave in the Kali Age. The only remedy is for Kṛṣṇa to appear." Suddenly he became furious and said, "The firm promise I made must certainly be carried out. I will spread the Name to reveal

Kṛṣṇa; I will effortlessly save the whole world," he said, (and) roared loudly. Haridāsa danced, overcome with divine love. Even though Advaitacandra knows all Truth, still he made a promise in accord with worldly law.

Nāgara Īśāna, whose hopes are at the feet of Lord Caitanya and Lord Advaita, narrates the *Advaita Prakāśa*.

Chapter 10

The Advent of Viśvambhara

Victory, victory to Lord Gaurāṅga, victory to Sītā's lord,
Victory to Nityānanda Rāma, and their followers.

One day as Lord Advaita was bathing in the Gaṅgā he suddenly cried out, "Hari, Hari," and wondered, "When will that golden-bodied Gaurāṅga appear and bring me peace?" Then he offered tulasī leaves and flowers and Gaṅgā water to Kṛṣṇa, with great faith. The master's roar attracted Kṛṣṇa's attention, and he drew one of the offered flowers upstream. Advaita, realizing this was Kṛṣṇa's doing, followed the flower upstream. Haridāsa ran after him, meditating on Hari's Name, and the flower floated all the way to Nadīyā.

My lord said, "O, dear Haridāsa, listen. Kṛṣṇacandra will appear in this village. The divine prediction in the *Ānanta Saṃhitā* is today revealed as truth."

Just then Jagannātha Miśra's wife Śacī Ṭhākurānī, who looked like Kṛṣṇa's mother Yaśodā, came to the Gaṅgā to bathe. She was pregnant, and that flower adhered to her body. Śacī thought, "What an inauspicious thing has occurred today, as these cast-off flowers have come and stuck to my body." Śacī quickly finished bathing and stepped onto the bank. My lord, engrossed in divine love, recognized her as the mother of Kṛṣṇa, and when he saw that she was pregnant, he thought, "Kṛṣṇacandra may have already entered this womb." As a test, he prostrated himself before her womb, but since this was an ordinary pregnancy, Śacī immediately miscarried. Distraught at the loss of her child, Śacī went straight home. When Miśra saw his wife's condition, he said, "Why are you so upset today?"

Śacī said, "Where did that old brahmin come from? He prostrated before me and made me miscarry."

Jagannātha said, "I did not notice anyone. Truly Īśvara is the cause of everything. Let your grief go; meditate on Nārāyaṇa through whom all obstacles are removed."

Lord Advaita Ācārya decided to found a school there in Navadvīpa in preparation for Gaurāṅga. The many good scholars in Nadīyā counted my lord as their chief and went to him.

The scholar Śrīvāsa Ṭhākura, the embodiment of Nārada, enjoyed endless joy with my lord. During the day the lord taught the students both the *Bhagavad Gītā* and the *Bhāgavata Purāṇa*, along with Veda and other scriptures as the students desired. At night he met with Haridāsa and loudly sang the name of the Lord. When Viṣṇudāsa Ācārya saw my glorious lord Advaita's spiritual work, he took mantra initiation from him. He studied the *Bhāgavata Purāṇa* with my lord, and the sound of the recitation attracted many Vaiṣṇavas. Nandini and others like Vāsudeva Datta took mantra initiation from the lord and became successful. Advaita discussed Kṛṣṇa with many students. Sometimes they were so intoxicated with divine love, they babbled deliriously.

Jagannātha Miśra's wife Śacī suffered successive miscarriages as the result of Advaita's bows. Finally, in her eighth pregnancy, a very despondent Śacī spoke tearfully to Jagannātha Miśra, "We have been completely undone by Advaita's bows. How will we continue the lineage? You must do something."

That calm, refined man who exemplified the best of brahmins now became anxious himself and approached the lord Advaita, bowing and offering various praises. The lord blessed Miśra and asked him to sit down, and asked why he had come.

That scion of the Miśra lineage joined his palms in supplication and said politely, "I take refuge at your feet. If I have committed some offense, please forgive it, but please, my lord, the future of my lineage is up to a luckless fellow like me, so please grant me this boon."

Advaita sent him home, promising to take care of the problem.

Miśra took his leave and went home to give Śacī the lord's heartening message. The next day, my lord finished his morning ablutions and went straight to Jagannātha Miśra's house. Miśra fell at his feet and gave him a place to sit and water to wash his feet, and welcomed him cordially.

Śacī Devī entered the room and also bowed. The lord said, "Child, may you bear a son." Hearing that, Miśra, king of brahmins, said, with great joy, "Please make your words come true."

My lord said, "I will give you a mantra in a dream. You must both repeat that mantra faithfully, then all your bad luck will certainly be broken. You will have a divine son who will be an outstanding scholar."

After they heard this decree, the couple went to the river and bathed. My lord Advaitacandra worshiped Nārāyaṇa in accord with scriptural injunction and then initiated them both with the great four-syllable Gaurāṅga-Gopāla mantra. They were both overwhelmed with emotion when they received the mantra, bowing to the lord and praising him humbly. My lord granted them their boon and said, "May your minds remain on Kṛṣṇa." He fed them, and they went home.

Within a few days Śacī conceived a son they named Viśvarūpa, who was full of virtues. He was dispassionate from birth, and people marveled at him. My lord said, "This is Kṛṣṇa's first evolute Mahāsaṃkarṣaṇa," and told her, "(Even) Brahmā cannot understand his greatness. He will be a great scholar and preach righteousness."

Now I will tell about the advent of Mahāprabhu Caitanya, by the mere thought of whom a person is greatly blessed. Every day when Lord Advaitacandra had finished worshiping Kṛṣṇa, he would roar, "Come, Gaurahari!" Advaita's great Kṛṣṇa-attracting mantra of a roar disturbed Kṛṣṇa's heart tremendously. Kṛṣṇa honored his previous kind promise and descended into the town of Nadīyā. The scholar could tell from the glow emanating from Śacī's body that the moon that was Gaura was rising over the ocean of milk which was her womb.

One day my lord was sitting in a cave by the Gaṅgā, worshiping Kṛṣṇa with tulasī, sandal, and flowers. He had placed a mental image of Kṛṣṇa in the Gaṅgā and then made three flower offerings to the river, and they floated away. Kṛṣṇa's will pulled the flower offerings upstream, and as they had before, the flowers adhered to Śacī Devī's body. Śacī became very upset and wondered who had sent the flowers this time. Then she quickly pushed a tulasī blossom away and climbed onto the bank, pleading, "Rāma, Nārāyaṇa, Hari."

Divine love arose in the lord when he saw that. Lord Advaita loudly roared out "Gaurahari," then circumambulated Mother Śacī and prostrated himself.

Śacī said, "Stop, stop, Ācārya Ṭhākura! My sins must be immense! Your bowing has already destroyed so many of my pregnancies! Tell me, lord, why have you bowed again to my child?" and she fell at his feet.

The lord blessed Śacī and told her, "Fear not, Mother, for truly you carry a child the equal of Kṛṣṇa."

When she heard this, Śacī went home joyfully. My lord, overcome with divine love, roared "Hari." But after ten months of pregnancy, Lord Kṛṣṇacandra had still not been born. By the time twelve months had elapsed, Jagannātha Miśra and the others were very frightened. Śacī's father, Nīlāmbara Cakravartī, the embodiment of Gārga of the astrological treatises, cast a horoscope and told the assembly, "A great being is present in this womb. He will be born after thirteen months of pregnancy, when all the auspicious signs converge. His birth will be very beneficial for living beings."

Everyone sank into bliss when they heard that. Just as Nṛsiṃha sprang from a crystal pillar, so Lord Caitanya came forth from Śacī's womb. "In Svayaṃ Bhagavān, who is the eternal, blissful, and omniscient god, the ocean of love, there is no possibility for deception. Anywhere he resides is Vṛndāvana. He takes human birth to rescue living beings. His mother, father, and all his relatives are divine; their residences, et cetera, are divine; they are all inherently full of bliss, but unbearable sorrow is a natural part of human existence. They will all appear, drawn in by Kṛṣṇa's manifestation."

Nanda's dear son remembered his three wishes. He took on Rādhā's mood and fair beauty and descended to Nadīyā, where he spread pure love and blessed the world. On the full moon in Phālguna[11] in 1486, on the day in Leo when Rahu came

[11] Corresponds to mid-February to mid-March.

and eclipsed the moon, with Leo rising, with all auspicious conjunctions, the earth shivered in delight with love of Kṛṣṇa. In the evening, as people were chanting the divine Name of Hari, Lord Kṛṣṇa appeared as Gaurāṅga. The world was already covered in bliss for Kṛṣṇa's swing festival,[12] but the great bliss at this eclipse was over and above that. Some, being very virtuous, performed charitable acts and meditated; some danced and some sang "Hari, Hari!"

At Mahāprabhu's appearance, Lord Nityānanda, in RāṚha, roared like a thundercloud with divine love. Lord Gaurāṅga's body glowed like the golden moon, and this golden moonlight lit up the childbirth room. He had arms that reached to his knees, and lotus eyes; I am not capable of describing a fraction of that beauty.

Śacī was charmed when she saw his ethereal beauty. Jagannātha recognized him as Viṣṇu and began to praise him, until Gauracandra cast his magic, and then they both saw him as merely their son. Living beings delighted at Kṛṣṇa's appearance, and his followers drowned in divine love. When Lord Advaita learned of Kṛṣṇa-Caitanya's appearance, he let out a roar, considering himself blessed. Haridāsa and the others chanted the Name. Some danced with joy, some fainted.

From the moment Lord Gaurāṅga was born, he kept his eyes closed like a great yogi and would not drink any milk. Śacī Devī wept at his refusal, and Jagannātha Miśra and the others became very concerned.

At that point my lord Advaita arrived to see the lord. Miśra fell at his feet, and the lord asked him why he was upset.

Miśra said, "Best of lords, you know everything. I have been shown the treasure of a son, and now he is being taken away again."

The lord said, "Best of the Miśras, do not grieve. Rest assured that your child will truly be well," and the lord entered the childbirth room. Śacī seized the lord's feet and began to cry, but Advaita said, "Mother, do not cry. Step aside, your son will be fine."

At her guru's order, Mother Śacī stepped aside, and the lord approached Mahāprabhu. Advaita saw his body, overflowing with divine love. The fair lord Govinda laughed and stood up, and when the master saw that Kṛṣṇa Himself had taken birth in that form, he drowned in pure divine love. Advaita remained entranced for quite some time, then prostrated himself and prayed with cupped hands: "O God, today I am fifty-two years old. I, your servant, came to earth for your sake. The world is filled with sin, terror, and darkness, and similarly has been pervaded with fear. Now at the sight of you my fear is dispelled. I left home and have been wandering from place to place seeking you, but because of the ignorant wickedness from my past, I could not find you. After so long, my heart's desire is fulfilled. The moon of Gokula has risen over Navadvīpa."

Gaura said, "I am eternally dependent on and under the control of my manifest and unmanifest followers."

[12] A spring festival for which images of Rādhā and Kṛṣṇa are decorated and placed on swings.

Lord Advaita said, "Since you have come to earth, tell me why you will not drink your mother's milk."

Mahāprabhu said, "Listen, Pañcānana. Drunk on dispassion, you have forgotten the law. First bestow the mantra, give the Name of Hari, because the ears are purified by the pure Name. If one puts the great mantra into an impure ear, the initiation is incomplete; you certainly know this. Since my mother was initiated without being told Hari's Name, I will not drink her milk."

Mahāprabhu recited the eternally perfect sixteen Names:

> "Hare Kṛṣṇa Hare Kṛṣṇa Kṛṣṇa Kṛṣṇa Hare Hare
> Hare Rāma Hare Rāma Rāma Rāma Hare Hare."

Even though the master had been aware of these sixteen Names, when he heard them from Gaura's mouth, he became drunk with divine love. Then the lord felt blessed and picked Gaura up and gently laid him down at the base of a nim tree and said, "Hari, Hari!" That tree was liberated by the touch of Gaura's foot.

My lord spoke to Śacī and initiated her with Hari's Name, and again reminded her of the mantra he had given her earlier. Then the lord placed Gaura in Śacī's lap, and Mahāprabhu drank the nectar of his mother's milk. Mother Śacī drowned in bliss, and Miśra and all the others delightedly roared "Hari."

The brahmins and their wives blessed them, and Sītānātha announced that his name should be Nimāi, and roared out "Hari." Everyone said, "This old man is Śiva."

The lord said, "This is wrong; why are you praising me? This baby got well because of the qualities of the nim tree. Who can tell the virtues of the nim tree, in whose shade a person's every ailment is removed; at whose fragrance witches and demonesses flee; at whose foot Lord Kṛṣṇa was born."

Advaita took his followers and spent the night singing the Lord's name. As soon as the followers of God saw this drama, their desires were realized; it was a great blessing. Through Kṛṣṇa's mercy they saw the play of his birth, which cannot be seen even with the merit accrued in ten million births.

Eternally perfected Paurṇamāsī, Yogamāyā herself, is Advaita's wife Sītā Devī, the embodiment of devotion. She saw the eclipse on the day of Kṛṣṇa's Swing Festival and thought of Kṛṣṇa's activities with deep dispassion. In her mind's eye she saw Kṛṣṇa in Navadvīpa, where he had manifested his own body covered with Rādhā's beauty. Sītā drowned in divine love at this extraordinary sight and filled herself with divine power and quickly came to Navadvīpa. When she saw Lord Gaurāṅga, she felt her life's purpose had been fulfilled.

She blessed Gaura (as was traditional) with rice straw. Many people heard about Lord Caitanya's appearance in the town of Nadīyā and came to see him. They saw the marks of a great man on Gaura's body and felt that this was the holy lord. Śacī's son is like a magnet who attracts followers like iron from all directions. Everyone enthusiastically sang the Lord's name, from time to time using Gaura's name.

The brahmin Nīlāmbara who was as adept in astrology as Gārga gave him the name "Viśvambhara." When he saw Jagannātha's son's golden body, he affectionately named him "Lord Gaura Gaurāṅga." Śacī Devī sometimes called her child "Goracanda," sometimes "Gaura," out of pure affection.

Everyone, listen to something even more amazing. Śacī's son enacted a drama not of this world. In his baby guise, when he would cry, he would smile if he heard the name of Hari. When so many of the men and women of Nadīyā saw that, they wept, and when they had composed themselves, they cried "Hari, Hari." He would pretend to cry so they would chant the Name of Hari for him. Kṛṣṇa's followers understood Gaura's true identity.

All the women saw Gaura's excellent nature. They joyfully called him "Gaurahari." Kṛṣṇa's pure followers were drunk on the bliss of divine love and gave Mahāprabhu the name "Lord Gaura Govinda."

At the proper time, Miśra performed Gaura's first solid food ritual and fed everyone food consecrated to Viṣṇu. Gaurāṅga's childhood activities are an ocean of nectar. I, a miserable creature, cannot touch a drop of them.

When Gaura was five years old, Miśra put chalk in his hand at the proper moment. Lord Gaurāṅga, best in the world of those who could remember everything they heard, learned the alphabet in a short time, and then Miśra carefully sent Gaura to study with the scholar Gaṅgādāsa. Gaura mastered grammar in two years, which amazed the scholars. In time, Bhāratī gave him the sacred thread, and Miśra gave him the Viṣṇu mantra, in accordance with scripture. How can I, a miserable creature, understand Gaura's unparallelled drama? I merely write what I heard from my lord's mouth.

Īśāna Nāgara, whose hopes are at the feet of Lord Caitanya and Lord Advaita, narrates the *Advaita Prakāśa*.

Chapter 11

Advaita's Sons, Part I

> Victory, victory to Lord Caitanya, victory to Sītā's lord,
> Victory to Nityānanda Rāma, and their followers.

I will briefly describe the members of the community who constitute the main branches of that wish-fulfilling tree, Lord Advaita.

Mother Sītā became pregnant at an auspicious time, and the hearts of all Kṛṣṇa's followers swelled with joy to hear that news. Sītā Devī's son was born in the year 1492 on the most glorious of auspicious days, the full moon in the month of

Vaiśākha.[13] The baby's extraordinary beauty charmed everyone, and they said, "I have never seen such beauty before. I think some god must have descended here."

The astrologer came and cast the horoscope and proclaimed, "One of the *gopīs* of Holy Vraja has taken birth. She has become male so she can instruct people. He will be dispassionate from early childhood, know for certain."

This news overwhelmed the devotees with divine love, and they began chanting the Lord's name all together. Some danced, some wept in the spirit of divine love, and Advaita roared out like thunder, "Cry 'Hari!'" Gaurāṅga realized a beloved disciple had appeared.

Then in due time my lord summoned the priest for his son's naming ritual. The priest came and cast the horoscope and said, "This son of the master is not an ordinary (boy). His heart and soul are in Kṛṣṇa, his joy is in Kṛṣṇa, so I will name him Acyutānanda, the Bliss of the Imperishable Lord."

When they heard the name, the devotees cried "Hari"; all the lovely ladies ululated with joy. Acyuta loved Kṛṣṇa like a cowherd girl of Vraja, so the sages called him "Lord Acyuta Sakhī."

Sometime later the lord recognized the auspicious moment and performed Acyuta's first food rite, with great pomp. He set a feast before Madana Gopāla and held a great festival to put food in his son's mouth. The brahmins, Vaiṣṇavas, et cetera, ate consecrated food, received clothing, and blessed the child.

At the proper time, when Acyuta was five years old, his father put chalk in his hand. On the very day Acyuta began his studies, my mother came to Shantipur and took refuge at Lord Advaita's feet; I was five years old.

My lord kindly initiated my mother with the Kṛṣṇa mantra and purified me and gave me (the mantra of) Hari's Name. When they got me, Sītā Devī treated me affectionately and raised me like her own son. My mother was obedient to her guru. I remember a little about this. My lord said, "Īśāna's mother is a virtuous woman. She will live in Vaikuṇṭha when she dies."

So listen to another remarkable story, about Mother Sītā's second son. On the thirteenth day of the dark fortnight in the month of Madhu[14] in 1496, late at night, Sītā Devī gave birth to a remarkable prince. His spiritual beauty was like that of a divine incarnation. At the same time—hear about an act of God! The glorious Śrī Ṭhākurānī had a son who died as soon as he was born. Mother Śrī wept when she saw that, and Mother Sītā, crying, told Advaita, "I cannot bear it! My sister's suffering is my suffering, too. She finally had a son, and God has been unkind, and taken him away. With your permission, I would like to offer this son of mine to my sister."

My lord said, "Good, this idea of yours is good. This is the best plan to console Śrī."

[13] Mid-April to mid-May.

[14] The last month of the Bengali calendar, also called Caitra, from mid-March to mid-April.

Then Sītā said, "Wipe away your tears. Sister, do not cry, do not cry, calm your mind. I am offering you this son of mine, and we will let it be known that he is your son," she said, (and) put the child in Śrī's lap. Letting go of her grief, Mother Śrī put her son to her breast.

Others do not know all this secret information. (Only) my mother and three other people know. Padmanābha Cakravartī was a special favorite of Advaita's, so by my lord's mercy he knows the whole truth.

Then at dawn the Vaiṣṇavas and brahmins came and, with very soft words, cast the horoscope and spoke. "This second son of Advaitacandra has manifested to preserve devotion to Kṛṣṇa. Kārtikeya, that very general of the gods whose function is protecting the gods, is now Advaita's son."

When they heard that, the devotees became drunk on divine bliss and all began to dance and chant "Hari, Hari." Then at the proper time my lord brought a priest, who was delighted to perform the naming ritual. The astrologer-priest read the horoscope and told everyone that the boy would be a great scholar. "He will be attached to serving Kṛṣṇa and the Vaiṣṇavas, and indifferent to the world. Thus I name him Kṛṣṇadāsa, Servant of Kṛṣṇa."

Kṛṣṇa's followers were delighted, and they spent the day blissfully chanting the name of Hari.

In time the lord recognized the proper moment and held Kṛṣṇadāsa's first-food ritual. He placed a feast before Lord Madana Gopāla and gave his son his first solid food from the consecrated offering. He fed the brahmins and the Vaiṣṇavas with devotion, and gave the blind and the poor much food. He greeted everyone with gifts of clothing and blessed them, and they left.

Then, at the proper time, the glorious Advaita had Kṛṣṇadāsa begin his studies.

Everyone, listen to one more remarkable tale, of how the lord's third son appeared. In the month of Kārttika[15] in 1500 on the twelfth day of the bright fortnight, Sītā gave birth to a son. The boy was born with his eyes closed like a corpse. My lord shouted "Gaurahari" and roared like a mighty lion. As the name of Gaurahari entered the infant's ears, his eyes released tears in divine love. Everyone roared "Hari" in the bliss of divine love, and the wives of the lineage ululated.

Just then the brahmin astrologer arrived and calculated the boy's horoscope. "This, Lord Advaita's third son, is Lord Gaṇeśa himself. He has come to destroy obstacles on earth, and people will find the treasure of devotion when they see him."

When the devotees heard that, their joy grew, and they spent the day chanting the name of Hari.

Then my lord summoned the priest and had him perform his son's naming ritual. The brahmin said, "He will be a servant of Kṛṣṇa, so I'll name him Gopāladāsa, servant of Gopāla."

[15] Mid-October to mid-November.

Now hear about Gopāla's otherworldly nature, the mere thought of which confers devotion to Kṛṣṇa. When Kṛṣṇa's followers would chant the name of the Lord, Gopāla would stop drinking milk and listen. Tears would fall from his eyes, and he would laugh, and he would roll his eyes like a drunkard. When the chanting would stop, that mood would leave him, and he would cry aloud and finally would drink his mother's milk. This was always Kṛṣṇadāsa's nature; it was apparent to the wise, but the ignorant were unaware of it.

I have told just a bit of the stories of the births of these three sons of Advaita Ācārya, for the benefit of living beings.

Nāgara Īśāna, whose hopes are at the feet of Lord Caitanya and Lord Advaita, narrates the *Advaita Prakāśa*.

Chapter 12

Gaurāṅga: The Early Years

Victory, victory to Lord Caitanya, victory to Sītā's lord,
Victory to Nityānanda Rāma, and their followers.

One day when Lord Advaita Veda-Pañcānana was instructing his students in the Vedas and philosophy, Gaurāṅga and Gadādhara arrived to study. My lord was overcome with emotion when he saw them. "Come in, come in," he said, and laughed heartily. Gaura and Gadādhara understood the significance of that and bowed to the master, as an example to others.

The master embraced them both, and the three sat together. Advaita softly asked Gauracandra, "Where have you come from, Nimāi? Tell me in detail. It has been a long time. Have you been studying all this time? Tell me the story."

"Listen, Guru Pañcānana. We have come to your house from Nadīyā. I am not interested in studying any other scripture; I have come here to hear the meaning of the Vedas," Mahāprabhu said, (and) smiled slightly.

Gadādhara understood and began to speak: "Listen, Veda Pañcānana, and I will tell you all about Gaura's studies. First, he mastered grammar in two years under the scholar Gaṅgādāsa. Next he studied literature and rhetoric for two years, and then he went to the revered Viṣṇu Miśra and studied astrology for two years. From there he went to Pandit Sudarśana and studied the six philosophical systems with him for two years, and now he has come to you to study the Vedas."

When he heard this, the master's joy grew boundless. He said, "He clearly has the power to remember whatever he hears."

When he heard that praise, Mahāprabhu bowed his head. Just then a student asked him a question. "Tell me, Nimāi, how do we know that God exists?"

Gaura said, "We infer it from our perception of the phenomenal world."

The student said, "The world is established by nature."

Gaura said, "How can something temporal be eternal?"

The student said, "Atoms are eternal."

Gaura said, "Inanimate objects never have any creative power. There is so much more; five other things do have creative power. The sages say that Īśvara, the source of consciousness and bliss, is One. No effect can occur without that Creator, the one in whom all power most certainly exists, as its cause." In this way they debated a great deal, but no one was taking notes.

Just then Advaita's five-year-old child Kṛṣṇadāsa saw them there. He laughed softly and settled the discussion. "O student, first acquire the eyes of devotion, and then you will see the image of God before you. He has placed the truth before you and you cannot recognize it, and I am very sad to see your ignorance."

My lord said, "This is good!" (and) let out a roar. He embraced Kṛṣṇadāsa and danced for a long time. Then Mahāprabhu picked up Kṛṣṇadāsa and joyfully called his name, "Kṛṣṇa Miśra."

Gaura studied the Vedas with the utmost care, and the master taught him most attentively.

Listen to something even more excellent. One day Sītā, Mother of the World, devoted to Gaura, had set aside a few of Gaurāṅga's favorite kind of bananas to feed him. No one was home when she went to bathe in the Gaṅgā. Meanwhile, Kṛṣṇa Miśra came home looking for something to eat and found the ripe bananas. The child, firmly devoted to Kṛṣṇa, debated with himself: "Mother wants to feed Gaura these bananas, so it would be wrong for me to eat them." Again he thought, "I will offer them (to Gaurāṅga), and then I can eat them. If they are consecrated to Gaurāṅga, there is no problem."

First he pronounced *Om* and the great mantra, and he made the offering, saying, "*Om*, Salutations to Gaura." The child touched the bananas to his head, acknowledging them as consecrated food, and ate them gleefully.

Mother Sītā came home after her bath and thought about offering the bananas to Gaura. She could not find the bananas where she had put them. Disappointed, she thought that her sons must have eaten them. First she called Acyutānanda and asked him if he had eaten the bananas she had been saving for Gaura.

Acyuta said, "Mother, you are omniscient; you know everything I do and my inner thoughts. In my childish impertinence I once drank some milk intended for Gaura, but I learned my lesson from your scolding."

How can a miserable creature like me describe the greatness of Acyuta, who is inseparably united with Lord Kṛṣṇa Caitanya? In his attachment to Gaura, Acyuta drank some milk intended for Gaura, and his mother slapped him for it. The bruise from that slap appeared on Gaura's body, to the amazement of all who saw it. Bhagavān's eternally perfect followers and their devotion: these two things have inconceivable power. Consciousness-filled devotion and consciousness-filled followers are inseparably united with Kṛṣṇa; this is written in scripture.

Then Sītā spoke to Kṛṣṇadāsa Miśra and asked him if he had eaten the bananas intended for Gaura. Kṛṣṇa Miśra said, "Mother, what is wrong? I offered them to Gaura before I ate them."

When she heard that, Mother Sītā smiled indulgently and ran after the child with a stick in her hand. Kṛṣṇa Miśra ran, frightened, to Advaita. Advaita saw Sītā right behind him and said, "Do not hit him in front of me; I want to hear his story."

Sītā stopped when she heard her husband's plea. The lord asked, "What has Kṛṣṇa Miśra done wrong?"

In a soft voice, Kṛṣṇa Miśra replied, "Mother was saving some bananas to feed Gaura. I offered them to Gaura before I ate them, (so) I know I did nothing wrong."

My lord said, "Did you offer them with a mantra?"

The child said, "Yes: *Om salutations to Gaura*."

My lord said, "You should have said 'to Kṛṣṇa' instead of 'to Gaura.'"

The child said, "Kṛṣṇa's name is incorporated in Gaura's name."[16]

The lord acknowledged him as a master because of his words, and overcome with divine love, he kissed the child's face. Sītā was amazed to hear her son's discourse and thought, "My son is indeed blessed." Then she called everyone to eat.

Gaura said, "I have already eaten."

My lord said, "How could you have eaten?"

Gaura said, "I ate some bananas in my sleep," he said, (and) he let out a belch. Everyone could smell bananas and was amazed.

The lord Advaita thought, "Kṛṣṇa is dependent on His followers. He certainly enjoyed the bananas Kṛṣṇa Miśra gave him. I am most fortunate to have such a son through whose exploits the world will be purified." My lord's heart melted with love as he thought, and his eyes remained constantly full of tears.

When Sītā heard the story she became filled with love. She thought, "No one is more blessed than my son. I, from whose womb a pure follower of Kṛṣṇa was born, am most fortunate to be a producer of excellent children."

Then one day a brahmin's son came and bowed at my lord's feet. Lord Advaita said, "Whose son are you? Why have you come here? Tell me."

The brahmin's son said, "I am your servant's son. My name is Lokanātha Cakravarttī, the son of Padmanābha Cakravarttī, of Jessore, an object of your mercy."

My lord recognized him when he spoke, and embraced him. Lokanātha said, "You are so merciful."

The lord said, "Why have you come so far alone?"

[16] The child is expressing an important view that sets the Bengali Vaiṣṇavas apart from their colleagues who relocated to Vraja. For those who remained in their movement's homeland, Caitanya is no different from Kṛṣṇa, and so worship of one is worship of the other. The Vraja community, on the other hand, places no importance on worship of Caitanya.

Lokanātha replied, "I have come to study with you."

My lord said, "Good; stay here. Study whatever appeals to you."

Lokanātha said, "My father has agreed that I should study the *Bhāgavata Purāṇa*, the nectar of Kṛṣṇa's activities."

Lord Advaita said, "Your father is full of devotion. He is always drunk from drinking the essence of the *Bhāgavata (Purāṇa)*."

So Lokanātha studied the *Bhāgavata Purāṇa*, with commentaries, with the revered scholar Gadādhara. The two of them recited while Gauracandra listened. He memorized the meanings of the verses and found great bliss.

One day Sītānātha was thinking about the proper time to perform Gopāla's first solid food ritual. Listen to an extraordinary event from that day. Various substances were placed before the child, according to scriptural injunction, but he would not touch any of them. Instead Gopāladāsa touched Lord Gaurāṅga's lotus feet. My lord became drunk with divine love when he saw this and said, "This child will be a pinnacle of righteousness. A brahmin's feet are the same as the feet of Viṣṇu. All the holy places are present in the feet of a brahmin." My lord similarly explained many things, and in this way Gaurāṅga's true nature was revealed. Their followers' bliss grew when they heard this, and all began to chant the name of the Lord. Lord Advaita danced, and Haridāsa danced; Acyutānanda danced, and Kṛṣṇadāsa. Mahāprabhu smiled when he saw Kṛṣṇa Miśra's dancing, and his followers tried to make Gaura dance.

In this way their bliss increased day by day, and every day their followers held a great festival. After one year had passed, Gaura had mastered the Vedas and the *Bhāgavata Purāṇa*. Realizing that, the master summoned the scholarly community and told them of Gaura's spiritual qualities and Gadādhara's incomprehensible greatness; not even Brahmā can delineate his virtues. He had extraordinary mastery of the *Bhāgavata Purāṇa*. My lord said that Gadādhara was Kṛṣṇa's greatest intimate. The virtues of Lord Gaurāṅga's associates are most wonderful. Lokanātha had expertise in the *Bhāgavata Purāṇa*, and tears of divine love would always fall when he heard the explanations of the verses. Everyone said, "Kṛṣṇa has shown His mercy to Lokanātha."

One day Lokanātha said to the master, "Tell me, my lord, how to find Kṛṣṇa."

The lord said, "Adopt the Kṛṣṇa mantra; it attracts Kṛṣṇa quickly."

Lokanātha was delighted to hear that, and my lord initiated him with the mantra in the Gaṅgā. The glorious Vaiṣṇavas' king of mantras has incomprehensible power. As soon as he repeated it, he attained pure loving devotion. Then Lokanātha clutched Lord Advaita's feet, overcome with divine love, and wept and humbly sang many praises. My lord said, "Do not cry, calm down. You will soon find Rādhā-Kṛṣṇa," and took Lokanātha's hand and presented him to Mahāprabhu.

Advaita Ācārya said, "O Nimāi, listen carefully. Teach Lokanātha how to realize Truth," and saying that, he offered his dear student to Gaura. Lord Gaurāṅga accepted Lokanātha.

Then one day Gaura said to the Master, "With your permission, I want to go home."

The lord said, "If I give you leave to go, my heart will burst. My separation from you will be both manifest and unmanifest," and sank into an ocean of divine love. Then he restrained that love and told everyone, "This Nimāi has become such an expert in all the scriptures that I have given him the title Vidyāsāgara, Ocean of Knowledge."

When everyone heard that, they yelled, "Victory, victory!" The students said, "O Ocean of Knowledge, give us sweets and betel nut."

Mahāprabhu gave them all treats as was proper, and then he set out for home.

What more can I say about Lord Gaurāṅga's departure? My lord and his family shed many tears.

Meanwhile, back in Navadvīpa, Mother Śacī missed Gaura and was wandering here and there like a cow without its calf. Then when Gauracandra came home, Śacī's empty life was filled. Gaurāṅga bowed at his mother's feet, and Śacī grabbed his neck and wept unceasingly. Gauracandra said, "Mother, do not cry, do not cry. I am hungry; go cook for me, quickly."

Śacī immediately went to cook, and Gaura went to bathe in the Gaṅgā with his followers. They worshiped Viṣṇu and offered food, and then Gaurāṅga and his followers ate happily. In the afternoon, Mahāprabhu wandered around town defeating great scholars in debate. Everyone said, "Nimāi is the crest-jewel among scholars. We have never heard such an ocean of knowledge."

Gradually the sun of the fame of Gaura's knowledge rose. He got married right in Navadvīpa. The royal sage Vallabhācārya, who looked like Bhīṣma, honored in his lineage for his character, regarded as noble among the brahmins, had a daughter, Lakṣmī, who was just like Rādhā, virtuous, full of all the good qualities, and very beautiful. My lord called her Rukmiṇī. The handsome lord Gaura married her.

Then Gaura founded a Sanskrit school and taught students, who studied whatever scripture they were interested in. Advaita's son Acyutānanda came. He was as erudite as Bṛhaspati the guru of the gods, very skilled in scripture. Mahāprabhu's joy was unbounded at getting him, and he taught him grammar and rhetoric.

One day Acyuta said to Gauracandra, "How is it that the comparison between the moon and a face is good? I can see there are a lot of spots on the moon and its faint silver color is only secondary."

When he heard that, Nimāi, the Ocean of Knowledge, was in bliss, and praising Acyutānanda affectionately, said to him, "The comparison with the face is in respect to joy. Nothing can be compared in every respect."

When Acyuta heard this, he said, "Now I understand. This has sparked another question of mine. Madana Gopāla Kṛṣṇa is Svayaṃ Bhagavān. Whom can I compare Him to? I can not find a simile for Him. Give me a simile and dispel my doubts."

Śacī's son listened to the boy and was deeply amazed, and said, "Listen, dearest. The eternal blissful omniscient god is full of all powers. Other things are compared to him. Since he is the object of comparison, there is no simile for Him. Similarly, ambrosia is the object of comparison for other juices, and many things are compared to ambrosia."

Acyuta said, "You know everything! The intensity of the flavor that is the ambrosia of the Name of Hari is from that ambrosia."

Lord Gaurāṅga said, "How do you know this?" Acyuta said, "The thing is manifest by its power. One who has drunk the ambrosia of the name from the divine cup is considered to have reached the ultimate goal, according to the scriptures."

Mahāprabhu melted with an invisible love when he heard that. He kissed Acyuta's head and took him onto his lap.

Lord Caitanya's activities with his followers are most mysterious. I do not have the power to describe even a bit of them.

Nāgara Īśāna, whose hopes are at the feet of Lord Caitanya and Lord Advaita, narrates the *Advaita Prakāśa*.

Chapter 13

Gaurāṅga's Youth and Marriages

Victory, victory to Lord Caitanya, victory to Sītā's lord,
Victory to Nityānanda Rāma, and their followers.

Now listen while I tell a wonderful story. The omniscient Īśvara Purī, whom my lord called the embodiment of *mādhurya*, the erotic sentiment, and whose sight could cause divine love and devotion to arise in anyone, came to Navadvīpa. He had been to my lord Advaita's house before. Īśvara Purī was the ultimate Vaiṣṇava, unattached and dispassionate, so when Sītā's husband saw the great, splendid renunciate, he said, "Praise Lord Nārāyaṇa" and fell at his feet. When Īśvara saw Advaita, he was convinced that this scholar would be the cause of Kṛṣṇa's manifestation. [Then one day that brahmin's son came and bowed at Advaita's feet.][17]

The revered Īśvara Purī was a disciple of Lord Mādhavendra Purī, and when my lord Advaita met him, a stream of divine love flowed from him. The stream surged up into a wave as the two discussed Kṛṣṇa, and they gradually sank into the ocean of the nectar of divine love, sometimes weeping, sometimes laughing, sometimes fainting, always roaring deeply like lions.

After some time, they regained normal consciousness. Sītānātha gave Īśvara alms. Then Īśvara wandered around Navadvīpa and, at an auspicious moment,

[17] Found only in the manuscript, not in any published versions of the text.

found Lord Gaurāṅga, whose lovely body was as beautiful as countless suns. He became ecstatic and thought, "This man is truly Svayaṃ Bhagavān, come to live in Navadvīpa in this fair body."

When Viśvambhara saw the effulgent Īśvara, he thought, "This man is a great disciple of God, the best among renunciates." Gaura came forward and bowed to him, and Īśvara blessed him, saying, "All your heart's desires will be fulfilled." They got acquainted and discussed scripture, floating in bliss. Then Gaura enthusiastically gave alms and other things to Īśvara. Īśvara stayed there for some time, then realizing he was too early for Gaura's revelation (of himself as Rādhā-Kṛṣṇa), he left on pilgrimage.

One day Lord Gaurāṅga told his mother, "Mother, I am going to take my students and go to the east. I will come straight back, so do not be sad and do not worry about any danger to me; stay home and worship Kṛṣṇa. If you keep yourself wrapped in the bliss of divine love, you will not miss me." And he bowed at Śacī's feet, and his anguished mother blessed him.

Then Gauracandra set out for the east. He went to Padmanābha's house at dawn. Mahāprabhu's companion Lokanātha Cakravartī called out to his father Padmanābha, "Please come to the front (of our procession)." The very pious Padmanābha Cakravartī, who was a special favorite of the glorious Advaita's, realized by my lord's mercy that Kṛṣṇa had manifested in Navadvīpa in this fair form. This realization threw him into an ecstatic trance.

When he regained his composure the brahmin covered his head with his garment respectfully. He recognized Gaurāṅga easily as soon as he saw him and fell at his feet, but Gaura, crying "Viṣṇu, Viṣṇu," went in the other direction.

Padmanābha said, "Gaura, don't tease me. Your deep philosophy is embodied in your disciples. You are Kṛṣṇa Himself, full of every devotional sentiment. You have taken birth to rescue living beings." And Padmanābha offered Gaura the deity's seat.

Keeping his mind on Viṣṇu, Gaura seated himself there. Padmanābha received him warmly, as was proper, and Mahāprabhu stayed for several days. Word circulated that the scholar Nimāi had come. Scholars came, and hundreds and hundreds of wealthy people: children, old people, youths, and many women. There was a great din and tumult to see Gaura. Gaura contemplated the situation and then climbed to the roof of the house. Gaura's radiant, lovely golden form, with arms reaching his knees, was a well of the ambrosia of *rasa*. His bright eyes, his full-blown lotus face, Acyuta's neck encircled by his left arm; everyone bathed in the nectar of the Gaṅgā which was his unprecedented beauty. Some were lucky enough to drink it and became intoxicated. Some shed many tears and were overwhelmed with divine love. Some raised their arms and danced with joy. At night when the learned people assembled, it looked like jewels were shining their light in all directions. Gaura brought his students to the gathering, and everyone rose respectfully when they saw him. Gaura sat in the midst of the assembly like the moon, and the ascetics sat around him like stars.

Among them was one wise brahmin, a crest-jewel of logic, very skilled in scripture, a jewel in the crown of the scholarly community. He asked a question from the treatises on logic, and Lord Gaurāṅga refuted it as soon as he heard it. That brahmin posed question after question, and Mahāprabhu easily refuted them (all). The brahmin's propositions flew away as he could not support them, so the scholars considered him defeated. Everyone said, "Nimāi the Ocean of Knowledge has proclaimed his divine philosophy to us, and proven it very well."

One day a great brahmin, a devotee of Viṣṇu, told my lord, with hands joined in supplication, "I see that this is the Kali Age; the world is covered with wickedness. Tell me how living beings will be rescued."

Mahāprabhu replied, "The Name of Hari is the key. Living beings will be rescued by hearing it and taking it up; they have no other recourse. All sin is dissolved in the Name, and one finds pure devotion."

When he heard that, the great brahmin felt the joy of divine love. He cried "Hari" and danced and wept, entranced. (Even) atheists were happy to see that, and laughed and became interested in Kṛṣṇa and the Vaiṣṇavas. Padmanābha Cakravartī, in whose house Lord Caitanya had this triumph, felt very blessed.

Eventually Gaura reached the bank of the Padmāvatī River. When he saw the Padma, Gaura said, with inner joy, "This Padmāvatī is Lakṣmī's second body. In this place, wickedness will be destroyed." Gaura stayed in a lovely place on the bank of that merit-conferring Padmāvatī and enjoyed himself. Gaurāṅga's lovely fragrance pervaded everywhere. Holy men began to tell each other, "A mighty scholar has come from Navadvīpa, a place on the eastern shore of the Gaṅgā where wise men live. Nimāi, called the Ocean of Knowlege, is the same scholar who composed the commentary called 'The Ocean of Knowledge.'"

When they got word, many scholars came there and were purified by the teachings and the sight of Gaurāṅga. Teachers came, bringing various items, and were delighted to talk with Gaura. Many scriptural experts and students came to study; prominent people studied a bit with him.

Meanwhile, in Navadvīpa Lakṣmī Devī died from the bite of the snake of separation from Gaurāṅga.

A few days later Śacī's son decided to go home. At that moment a very righteous brahmin came to Mahāprabhu about a dream (he had had) and prostrated himself fully at Gaura's lotus feet. Gaura interpreted the dream, privately, and said, "Keep this to yourself, and set out for Kāśī. In time, you will be with me in person. Your heart's desires will certainly be fulfilled." His name was Tapana Miśra; his heart was simple. He went to Kāśī at Mahāprabhu's request.

In this way Viśvambhara accomplished his purpose in east Bengal and went home with a lot of money, but when Lord Gaurāṅga arrived in Navadvīpa and learned of Lakṣmī's death, he grieved. When he saw Mother Śacī he became very distraught, and she tried to comfort him in various ways. Then Gaura's devotees and his close friends arranged his (second) marriage. The royal scholar Sanātana Miśra, a great brahmin whom Advaita Ācārya called "the incarnation of Śatrujita," had a daughter, Viṣṇupriyā, a crest-jewel among virtuous women. She was full of every good quality, a mine of the nectar of beauty, so my lord called her Lakṣmī, his true delight. Lord Gauracandra married her, and then there was a great celebration at Śacī's house, for Śacī was thrilled to have found a bride for her son.

My lord Acyuta told me this true story. I have just recounted a few points.

Īśāna Nāgara, whose hopes are at the feet of Lord Caitanya and Lord Advaita, narrates the *Advaita Prakāśa*.

Chapter 14

Gaurāṅga's Conversion and the Advent of Nityānanda

Victory, victory to Lord Caitanya, victory to Sītā's lord,
Victory to Nityānanda Rāma, and their followers.

Some time later Śacī's son went to Gayā to conduct his father's funeral rites. He offered food with devotion at the Viṣṇupada Temple and had an interview with Lord Īśvara Purī. Nimāi prostrated himself as soon as he saw that great renunciate, who embraced Gauracandra with deference. Īśvara spoke and Viśvambhara listened, and they discussed Kṛṣṇa all night. They imbibed the ambrosia of stories of Hari, and both became intoxicated and danced and wept like drunkards, absorbed in divine love. The next day Mahāprabhu recognized the right moment and took mantra initiation from Īśvara. Kṛṣṇa is present in that ten-syllable mantra, so Kṛṣṇa appeared in person before his eyes. When Śacī's son saw how extraordinarily beautiful he was, he became drunk on pure divine love and wept. He bowed and said repeatedly, "You have shown great mercy in saving this miserable creature."

Īśvara said, "You are God-realized, (so) don't belittle yourself. You have descended to instruct living beings in this world. You are the self-reliant lord, the source of cognition and bliss; who has not gotten lost in the dance of your creation? You saw your invisible reflection in the mirror of the mantra and were amazed, just as a child sees its reflection and plays (with it). Similarly, I see my own reflection in your blossoming love. You have clothed your body with Rādhā's physical beauty and are tasting your own sweetness through Rādhā's emotions."

When he heard this, Mahāprabhu meditated on Viṣṇu and said, "How can you call me 'guru'; I am unfit. Everywhere you look is Kṛṣṇa's form, the source of cognition and bliss; you have no awareness except through your otherworldly eyes of devotion."

Īśvara, absorbed in divine love, did not hear him, for he was laughing and dancing, with arms raised. When he saw the people gathering, he subdued his divine love and embraced Gaura tightly, and felt fulfilled.

Then the fair Viśvambhara went to Kumārahaṭa, Īśvara's very sacred birthplace. Gaura praised Kumārahaṭa a great deal, then bowed and asked leave to go.

Eventually Mahāprabhu returned to Navadvīpa and met his dear friends and devotees. When they saw Gaura, his friends smiled and said, "Why do we see new clothes on your body, Nimāi? You have put *tilaka* marks on in twelve places, and have written the name of Hari all over your body. You have put a tulasī necklace around your throat, and why have you put on the marks of conch and discus?"

Gaura replied, "Do not laugh at me! You know the importance of wearing *tilaka*, et cetera. It says in scripture that the evening worship and other pious acts of someone who does not wear *tilaka* and tulasī necklace are useless. So, I consider it the proper attire; the great sages say this proper attire has endless power. Wearing proper attire causes the mind to be purified. The worship (taught by) a succession of masters is most honorable. A living being who puts on proper attire finds liberation while alive. In the proper dress, Pūtanā found the path to heaven.

When they heard that, everyone realized that Gaura had had a change of heart, and the crocodile-hearts of the devotees drowned in bliss. Gaura's beloved Pandit Gadādhara asked him, "Tell (us) the good news from Gayā."

Mahāprabhu said, "Blessed Gayā, the pilgrimage place of His holy lotus foot, is the king of holy places. Hari, the friend of the helpless, storehouse of compassion, rescues living beings through the mark of his foot. Whoever envisions the foot of the lord of Gayā planted on his head finds that foot, which is even difficult for the gods to reach, at death. Whoever offers rice balls to that foot(print) of Hari obtains deliverance for his ancestors. Hari is merciful in many places and in many forms; a fortunate and very faithful soul can awaken Him."

Divine love built as he spoke. People had not expected it, and wept. Gaura roared out with the sound "Kṛṣṇa, Kṛṣṇa." When they saw Mahāprabhu's divine love, the disciples proclaimed, "God has been revealed," and wept, and all began chanting the name of God. The divine love and bliss increased progressively with the chanting. Gaura and Gadādhara both danced a long time. Śrīvāsa and the others said, "We have won now; that great divine love has dawned in Lord Gaurāṅga."

Many students heard that Nimāi Pandit had returned from Gayā and came to study with him. Some studied grammar, some philosophy, but with every text, Gaura described Kṛṣṇa. The students said, "O Ocean of Knowledge, what are you saying?"

Mahāprabhu said, "Have no doubt here. It says in the four Vedas that Kṛṣṇa is the Vedas personified. No other meaning occurs to me."

When Acyuta heard this, the spirit of renunciation awakened in him, and he joined Gaurāṅga in singing Kṛṣṇa's virtues. And those students who were most fortunate found dispassion through Acyuta's teachings. When the disciples saw

Mahāprabhu's delight in divine love, they told my lord Advaita the whole story. Even though the master already realized Gaura's essential nature, he became intoxicated with divine love when he heard about his conversion. Overcome with emotion, Sītā's lord told the devotees, "Listen, listen, let me tell you something mysterious. I have the daily habit of reading the *Gītā*, and the more I read, the more I understand. One day I was confused about one verse. I had contemplated it for a long time and still could not resolve my confusion. I could not eat, and stayed in bed, and in a dream, someone smiled and told me, 'Get up Master, why aren't you eating? This is definitely what that verse means.'

"When I heard that, I was amazed. I saw the fair Viśvambhara before my eyes, and as I was looking at him, he disappeared, and I understood Nimāi to be the Supreme. Just as the sight of smoke implies fire, so Īśvara's proof is in his supernatural qualities. Kṛṣṇa is Svayaṃ Bhagavān, a great ocean of love. How can a wave of that (ocean) remain hidden? The lord's activities are a reflection of the truth; he teaches people righteousness through his own example."

As soon as he said this, my lord was overwhelmed with emotion and proclaimed, "I will inundate every nation with this flood of divine love." He startled people with a deep roar, and boundless bliss arose in the minds of the disciples.

The holy men understood that Kṛṣṇa had descended and blessed the world with the gift of pure love. Then everyone chanted the name of God in the bliss of divine love, and laughed, wept, danced, and roared like thunderclouds.

Now hear about the birth of my lord Nityānanda, a story which makes love dawn in living beings. Nityānanda-Rāma appeared in northern Bengal, in a blessed village named Ekacaka. Vāsudeva's incarnation HāṚāi Pandit had a son Nityānanda who was always happy. My lord called Mother Padmāvatī, his crest-jewel of a virtuous wife, Rohiṇī, herself. Rāma was born on the thirteenth day of the bright fortnight in the month of Māgha[18] in the year 1473. That same Nityānanda had been Balarāma in Vraja, and descended to confer the bliss of divine love. My lord Nityānanda left home with the renunciates and wandered to many pilgrimage places and finally came to holy Vraja, where he stayed for some time. He found the bliss of divine love in his heart through Gaura's revelation, so he set out for blessed Navadvīpa and presented himself at the house of Nandana Ācārya. When Viśvambhara learned of Nityānanda's arrival, he secretly told the devotees, "A great man has come here, like a wishing-tree of the truth, to offer up the fruits of his devotion. Let's go, everyone, let's go to him. When you see him, you will realize the extent of his divine power."

When they heard this, the disciples became eager, and they all joyfully went with Mahāprabhu. They arrived at Nandana Ācārya's house, and when they saw Nityānanda, everyone was astonished by his supernatural beauty and his colossal body; his brilliance like ten million suns; his serious nature. The *tilaka* mark on his

[18] Mid-January to mid-February.

forehead shone like the light of the moon. A necklace of tulasī-wood adorned his neck. His smiling lotus face was extremely beautiful. That crest-jewel of renunciates was a mine of the virtue of compassion. When Viśvambhara saw the ever-perfect Baladeva, he and his associates bowed at his feet. The light of the sun-Gaura fell on the moon-Nityānanda, and the nectar of pure divine love steadily permeated the moonlight. When Nityānanda saw the marks of Svayaṃ Bhagavān on Gaura, he was stunned by the realization that this was Kṛṣṇa. When Gaura saw that Nityānanda was stunned, he created a way to show Nityānanda. He had his disciples recite the verses from the *Bhāgavata Purāṇa*, and when Nityānanda heard them, he fainted from divine love. When he regained consciousness Nityānanda was weeping, sometimes dancing, sometimes laughing, like a drunkard." Will I ever find Kṛṣṇa?" he said, letting out a roar. "Will he ever appear before my constantly tearful eyes?" Nityānanda's bliss in divine love was a cloud in a rainfall. The eyes of a devotee weep streams like the Gaṅgā. With that, a wave welled up on the ocean of love which was Gaura, and the crocodile-minds of the omniscient floated on it. After some time, everyone recovered, and Gaurāṅga humbly said to Nityānanda, "You have revealed the compassion which is the cloud of devotion, and have cleansed us with its rain. You roar like ten million mighty lions. You will inundate the world with the love you feel in your heart!"

Nityānanda smiled to hear that and spoke softly, "You have revealed a path of great importance to this base person. You are a great ocean of love, the source of the clouds, and your mercy is a second cause for the sun's attraction." In this way, he delighted in pure devotion, and Gaurahari revealed his mysterious true nature. Then Śacī's son took Nityānanda and the devotees and chanted the name of God daily.

One day Lord Advaita was thinking, "Kṛṣṇa has come to Navadvīpa to spread devotion. I will teach that intellectual scholarship is greater than devotion. How will Svayaṃ Bhagavān behave?" The great master was lost in this deep emotion. Cleverly interpreting the *Yogavaśiṣṭha*, my lord told his students that intellectual scholarship is greater than devotion. "Nothing is greater than scholarship, this is certain."

His students became distressed and thought to themselves, "Why has this contradictory idea arisen? The same lord who said 'Devotion is the empress; know for certain that intellectual knowledge is the slave of her slave. One will not find liberation through scholarship bereft of devotion, it is like a hailstorm, which only causes problems.' That same lord has (now) said, "What is the use of devotion? Scriptures say liberation comes through the realization, 'I am Brāhman.'"

Then the omniscient Viśvambhara, who was in Navadvīpa, realized immediately what was on the master's mind. He took Nityānanda with him and raced to Shantipur.

The master found out that Mahāprabhu was on his way and decided to make his scriptural interpretation sweeter. When Lord Caitanya and Nityānanda appeared before the glorious Advaita Ācārya, he was refuting devotion like the ocean of milk disgorging poison. Gaura-Bhagavān was amazed to hear this. He became furious and trembled with rage. In a loud voice he said, "Nāḍha, what is this idea of yours? You have cast aside the philosopher's stone and are venerating glass. People say 'The master is advocating devotion,' but now I see that you have been an obstacle to devotion. I will destroy you and establish devotion. Who in the three worlds can refute this?" Mahāprabhu said, (and) possessed by his lion-man form Lord Nṛsiṃha, he knocked the old man down off his seat. When the magnanimous Lord Advaita saw Gaura, he had a great desire to preserve devotion, and fainted from divine love.

The students wailed when they saw this, and the glorious omniscient Sītā wept with love. After a while my lord regained consciousness, and then Viśvambhara began to speak to him. "Hey Nāḍha, if this was your intention, then why did you make me appear? In the Vedas, it says that embodied souls are part of Brāhman, just as milk and yogurt occur in succession. Embodied souls offend Kṛṣṇa with the monistic idea 'I am that.' They attain a brief liberation and again return to earth."

When he heard this, the divine embodiment in the form of a devotee asked for eyes of devotion so that he could see the manifestation of Kṛṣṇa as (his own) devotee, two-armed, holding a flute, a peacock feather on his head, his whole body clothed with Rādhā's loveliness. Even though Advaita knew everything about Kṛṣṇa, when he saw this perfect form, he fainted from divine love.

When he regained consciousness, he said, "I was mistaken. Now, with your permission, I will spread devotion," he said, (and) carefully brought out two books and placed them before Gaura and Nityānanda. My lord had composed commentaries on both the *Yogavaśiṣtha* and the *Bhagavad Gītā*. When my lord respectfully showed Gaura those most wonderful commentaries on devotional behavior, Gaurāṅga read the two commentaries and melted with pure love and called out, "You churned out these two commentaries which you have written from a supernatural ocean of devotion."

My ten million bows at the feet of that divine embodiment in the form of a devotee who is like Kṛṣṇa Himself.

With raised arms the lord Nityānanda said, "The composer of this commentary deserves the praises of the whole world."

Lord Advaita heard that (and) said, "Everything is possible. It is Kṛṣṇa's nature to increase the status of his worshipers. By Kṛṣṇa's mercy, the eternal Sarasvatī lives in the heart of the devotee. When she stirs, the principle of devotion is revealed. Kṛṣṇa is most compassionate, the rescuer of the downfallen; he has taken birth to rescue living beings."

Then he wept, overcome with emotion, while Gaura and Nityānanda danced with divine love. "Hari!" Haridāsa roared deeply, and Acyuta and the others were stupefied with pure divine love.

Then Mahāprabhu and the two lords, overcome with great ecstasy, called loudly, "Come, come, everyone; who still fears? I will give everyone a panacea for the disease of illusion. If someone drinks a drop of that panacea, he will easily find the steady bliss of divine love."

Pure love arose in the disciples when they heard (that). They began to chant the name of Hari in unison. Mahāprabhu is the incomprehensible wishing tree of divine love, and the two lords Advaita and Nityānanda are his two main branches. The three contain a single essence; only their bodies are different, just as there are some differences among Rāma, Nṛsiṃha, and the other *avatāras* of Viṣṇu. One is the form of a devotee, one is the nature of a devotee, one is the embodiment of a devotee; three wells of divine love. The roars of these three are the texts of the three Vedas. They spread the Name of Hari throughout the whole world.

After a while they stopped chanting the Name and planned how they would spread righteousness. Meanwhile, Sītā, devoted to Gaura, was in the kitchen and covered her face with her garment[19] and wept joyfully as she prepared the many eggplants, spinach, and cakes and drinks, rice pudding cooked with ghee like ambrosia while this miserable creature supplied the water. Mother showed me such undying affection. Then she placed the feast before Madana Gopāla and placed a tulasī bud on top of the food. She gave them three places to sit and set out the feast. Nimāi sat in the middle, Nitāi on the right, Advaita sat on the left, behaving humbly. Sītā served them like Annapūrṇā; she waited on the three brahmins in various ways. Śrī asked for their leftovers for Īśāna Dāsa. After the meal, Mahāprabhu planned to take the two lords and go to Navadvīpa. The three together spread the Name of Hari; how many hundreds of great evildoers were saved! The rescue of Jagāi, Madhāi, and the Kazi[20] made such a strange drama, people marveled. I do not have the power to describe this drama, so I have just given a general overview.

Īśāna Nāgara, whose hopes are at the feet of Lord Caitanya and Lord Advaita, narrates the *Advaita Prakāśa*.

Chapter 15

Advaita's Sons, Part II, and Gaurāṅga's Renunciation

Victory, victory to Lord Caitanya, victory to Sītā's lord,
Victory to Nityānanda Rāma, and their followers.

Now hear about the other important branches of my lord Advaita's lineage; I interrupted the recitation earlier, before I had finished writing it.

[19] To avoid smelling, and so enjoying, the food before it is offered to Kṛṣṇa.

[20] These stories appear in Caitanya's own hagiographies.

Sītā's fourth son was born in the month of Pauṣa[21] in 1504. Some people said Indra had come and taken birth; some said the moon itself had appeared. The astrologer-priest came at the proper time to calculate the boy's horoscope and proclaimed, "This baby is an embodiment of Kubera, so Lakṣmī will be most merciful toward him. He will be as wise as Bṛhaspati, guru of the gods. He will be a scholar, and very handsome. He will consider sophistry, etc. to be true religion, but in the end he will remove that misconception from (the minds of) the holy men."

When they heard this, the Vaiṣṇavas cried "Hari" and the women ululated with joy. The brahmin said, "This boy will be strong, so I will name him 'Balarāma.'"

Then when Balarāma was seven months old, Sītānātha decided to hold his first-food ceremony. He convened a great gathering and offered Kṛṣṇa a feast, then fed the blind and the poor, brahmins and Vaiṣṇavas. He offered clothing and pleased everyone, and they all blessed him and went home.

Then in the month of Jaiṣṭha[22] in 1508, Sītā's twin sons were born. They held the naming ceremony for the two babies at the proper time and named the boys Svarūpa and Jagadīśa. The astrologer said, "These two will be intelligent; they will be like kings in worldly wisdom. They will love each other like Rāma and Sītā's sons Lava and Kuśa, and their voices will be as beautiful as angels'."

Then at the proper time Advaita Ācārya offered consecrated food and joyfully held the first-food ceremony for these two. He very happily fed the brahmins and the Vaiṣṇavas, and when they received the offerings of clothing they all blessed him.

One day after my lord had finished his morning worship and was loudly calling the Name of Hari with the devotees, a Vaiṣṇava arrived to report the news from Nadīyā and announced, "Nimāi has left home. He went to the town of Kantaka and had his head shaved, and Keśava Bhāratī made him a renunciate and gave him the name 'Kṛṣṇa Caitanya.' Mother Śacī is beside herself with grief and finds no relief anywhere. She fainted and fell down, and cries aloud with the heart-rending lament 'Ha, Nimāi.' She keeps running here and there like a drunk woman, and keeps going to the bank of the Gaṅgā to throw herself in. And I cannot begin to tell about Mother Viṣṇupriyā; she is drowning the world with the flood of her ceaseless tears."

My lord was stunned to hear this and could not stop weeping for three hours. Sītā too wept aloud when she learned the news, and Advaita's followers also drowned in the ocean of their grief. For the next three hours Advaita laughed aloud—who can possibly understand any of that?—and he remained lost in love for Gaura until dawn. Then he spoke with his closest followers, saying, "One can eventually reach the far shore of an ocean, but one can never reach the end of the ocean of Kṛṣṇa's compassion. Kṛṣṇa displayed his various activities to set living beings free; he fulfills

[21] Mid-December to mid-January.

[22] Mid-May to mid-June.

their desires so humbly. Indeed all the scriptures say Kṛṣṇa is eternally dependent on His devotees. He has revealed Himself fully in this drama."

As he spoke, he became overwhelmed with divine love. He continued, "Now I understand your whole act. Just as an actor plays many parts to entertain an audience, so you have adopted the role of a renunciate to instruct people."

Then Lord Advaitacandra regained his senses and began to chant the name of God in a loud voice. At that moment Ācāryaratna Mahāśaya appeared at Sītānātha's house. My lord was very excited to see him. "Tell me quickly, tell me the news from Nadīyā."

Lord Ācāryaratna said, "Listen, Gosvāmī. Nimāi has renounced the world and is on his way here." A chill ran down my lord's spine, and he said, "Where is he staying?" Ācāryaratna said, "He has been fasting for four days on the eastern bank of the Gaṅgā, lost in divine love. Take a boat and bring him back."

My lord sobbed sadly when he heard this and immediately took a boat across the Gaṅgā. When Gaura, enrapt with divine love, saw Advaita, he said, "How amazing, Master, you have come to Vṛndāvana!"

When my lord heard that, he said, "It says in all the scriptures that wherever you are is Holy Vraja," (and) took Caitanya and Nityānanda back across the Gaṅgā to Shantipur.

I cannot describe Mother Sītā's wailing when she saw Gaurāṅga dressed as a renunciate. Then Mother cooked a lot of food. She very lovingly prepared the type of cakes which Gaura loved, and many dishes full of divine nectar, and cooked substances with fragrant ghee. She put tulasī buds on the food and joyfully set the feast before Kṛṣṇa. Then she called Gaura and Nityānanda and lovingly seated them in places of honor. The master eagerly seated them both for the feast and stood to serve them himself. Gaura saw that, and smiled, and said to Sītānātha, "A sacrifice cannot possibly succeed without Śiva."

Smiling, my lord said, "You are the primeval Śiva.[23] By your mercy, all living beings reach Śiva."

Mahāprabhu said, "Stop all this nonsense. Without you, I can eat nothing."

When Nityānanda heard that, (he) laughed out loud and said, "O Compassionate Gaura, listen to one thing. Do not honor this gluttonous dwarf.[24] Even if he ate with four hands his belly would not be filled. He is always devouring the sacrifice, like a fire. He cannot make any claim to great learning."

Lord Advaita smiled at that and replied affectionately, "You take many forms and eat in different places. Even though you are one, you eat with countless mouths.[25] Who could possibly fill your belly?"

[23] The Bengali word *śiva* denotes both the name of the god and a condition of general welfare. In this conversation Caitanya and Advaita are punning to acknowledge each other's divinity.

[24] A reference to Viṣṇu's appearance as *Vāmanāvatāra*, the dwarf.

[25] Nityānanda is often associated with Ananta, the many-headed cosmic serpent.

In this way the two both revealed their essential natures. Gaura, seated between them, slowly began to laugh and said, "To compare these two, we should compare what they eat."

When he heard that, my lord said, very devotedly, "You are the immeasurable one who contains the measure of the endless universe. I see no point in further instruments of comparison."

This is the way Mahāprabhu and the two lords revealed their true natures: by hints and insinuations. After the meal the three lords rested and then shouted out, "Associating with the wise confers great power." With arms raised, they proclaimed, "Listen, everyone. Associating with the wise confers inconceivable virtues. Such people consider themselves lower than the grass, but they can endure longer than a tree; they have no desire to attain honor, (yet) are always undertaking vows and honoring others, and they constantly chant the name of Hari. These are the signs of the truly wise. Everyone, take refuge at the feet of the wise, for in them you will find the true eternal treasure worth seeking. One who can understand the essence of the *Ananta Śāstra* rides his chariot on the path of the wise, for the wise have distilled the essence from all scriptures to reveal the one true and attainable path. Whoever walks that path has vision, and whoever turns away from it is like a blind man. Just as string and things can pass through a hole and only a diamond can cut glass, even ignorant people who ride along the path proclaimed by the wise will be delivered from earthly life. This is why the ancient seers said, 'The heart does not become pure except in the company of the wise, for the wise are by nature equally kind to all beings; their mere association bestows their nature on other creatures. Crocodiles look like worms, because they have similar shapes, but they really are not worms; similarly, unless a person associates with the wise, he can make no discernment regarding (the true form of) worship. If a person is a great evildoer, a criminal, and then develops the proper conduct and devotion to Kṛṣṇa, he becomes as wise and holy as Dhruva. Just as iron turns to gold upon contact with the touchstone, so a soul is eternally liberated by association with the wise.'"

In hundreds of similar ways they described true religion, and as they listened, the Vaiṣṇavas drowned in bliss.

Back in Navadvīpa, Mahāprabhu's mother had heard from people that Gaura had come to Shantipur, so she joyfully came to Shantipur along with Gaura's Nadīyā followers. When Lord Caitanya saw his mother, he fell at her feet. Śacī began to weep as soon as she saw her son's face, and said, "Nimāi, seeing you dressed like this breaks my heart as if an arrow had pierced it." Gradually the mother's grief grew, a wave in the ocean, and all living beings began to float on its current.

Mahāprabhu explained the great yoga to his mother, and when she had heard, all her grief disappeared. Then Śacī cooked fragrant rice and prepared various of Gaura's favorite dishes with clarified butter. She offered him nectar, rice pudding, and other sweets and joyfully fed her son and his companions.

Who can describe the joy which transpired for so many days in Sītānātha's house?

During the day Mahāprabhu gave sermons on the Name, and at night he chanted the name of God with his followers. Gaura's associates were drunk on the bliss of divine love, and Shantipur was bathed in tears of divine love.

One day Lord Gaurāṅga very sweetly begged everyone's leave (to go). When they heard, the poison of grief surged up in all the disciples, and they were all tossed about in that conflagration. What more can I say about Śacī's burning grief, which was as if a fire had come and burned her to ashes. Mother cried "Alas!" and said to Gauracandra, "You've emprisoned me in the snare of grief; where will you take me? Why don't you go to Nadīyā? There's nothing wrong with staying here to worship Hari."

Mahāprabhu said, "Mother, do not say this. It is against the rules for a renunciate to stay in his own land." Śacī had requested this of her son, in her boundless ignorance, because she was a mine of affection for her son. His mother said, "Vṛndāvana is a distant land. Stay in Purī, then I will be able to get messages from you."

Lord Gaurāṅga heeded his mother's request and set out. His dear followers fell at his feet, wondering, "Will we find him, or not? If we could see him just once, we would be satisfied forever."

Lord Caitanya melted with compassion and said, "None of you must grieve for my sake. I cannot exist for a moment without you, not just this time, but in birth after birth. We will rejoice together in two more lifetimes as we have in this birth, with great festivals. I am just the body, and you are my five vital airs. I am not going to leave everyone and go anywhere with an empty body, but I have to travel to pilgrimage sites in different places to preserve the renunciate dharma. Always sing the Lord's name together, spread dharma, and serve the wise. You can certainly attain this bliss of divine love. No one should be depressed because of me."

In this way Gaura consoled all his disciples. Overwhelmed with love, he set out for Purī. Nityānanda and Mukuṇḍa, Dāmodara Pandit and Jagadānanda went with him. On the way, Lord Caitanya by his mercy rescued many fallen wicked evildoers. As they traveled his four companions sang the Name aloud, while that lion Gaura, engrossed in love, roared.

Eventually they came to Holy Remuṇā, and when they saw Gopīnātha everyone became very joyful. Gaurāṅga danced, besotted with divine love, sometimes weeping, sometimes running aimlessly, while Nityānanda's flood of divine love surged up, attracting every soul, and drowned them.

Then they saw Sākṣīgopāla, and reached Purī. When Gauracandra saw Jagannātha he became ecstatic, sometimes weeping, sometimes laughing, like a drunkard.

Then, overcome with divine love, Gaura fainted and did not regain consciousness for a long time. Sarvabhauma Bhaṭṭācārya, wise as Bṛhaspati, crest-jewel of scholars, recognized the divine ecstasy there in Gaura's body and said, "This person may be a god-realized being," and took Gaurāṅga to his own house. Nityānanda and the others came with them. They all surrounded Gaura and sang the Lord's name until Gaura got up and danced, crying "Hari!" Then Sarvabhauma brought consecrated food and graciously fed Caitanya and his companions.

Several days later Sarvabhauma was granted a vision of Gaura's divinity and felt the joy of devotion. Sarvabhauma had been a dry scholar before, but by virtue of the touchstone of Gaura he became the best of devotees.

From there Gaura wandered through the southern holy sites, where he met Rāmānanda Rāya. Rāya, whom my lord called "Kṛṣṇa's assistant," was an excellent scholar of the devotional scriptures, so when Rāmānanda spoke, Lord Caitanya listened. The intoxication of a devotee's mind produces a mood not of this world.

Then Gaura returned to Purī, and he sank in pure love as soon as he saw Jagannātha. He showed his mercy to King Pratāparudra, floating in devotion. He revealed his majesty to fulfill the desires of his devotees and took on a six-armed form. Gaura's mercy knows no limit. His disciples became filled with divine love when they saw this image. Some by good luck drank from that very Gaṅgā, nectar of beauty; some could not drink there, and wailed. Svayaṃ Bhagavān has a form which is the nectar of compassion, and his compassion is revealed through pure devotion.

Then, on the occasion of Jagannātha's chariot festival, my lord Advaita and a large number of his disciples went to Purī to see Gaurāṅga. Kṛṣṇa Miśra wanted to go with him, but Advaita said, "The route is very difficult, and there is no point in your going."

Kṛṣṇa Miśra said, "The only reality in this false world is refuge at Lord Gaurāṅga's feet." Even though Kṛṣṇa Miśra had eternal dispassion, his greatest dispassion was to meditate on Gaurāṅga.

Realizing that, Mother Sītā said to her son, "You are too young to go to Purī. Listen to your mother, Kṛṣṇa Miśra, you should stay home and worship Kṛṣṇa. Your elder brother Acyuta has princely dispassion. You should think of serving Kṛṣṇa and the ancestors (like he does). Take mantra initiation with your wife Vijayā, for one attains all one's desires by serving Kṛṣṇa, there is no doubt."

She took them both to the bank of the Gaṅgā and initiated them both with her mantra. The couple received that eternally perfect mantra, and bowed and praised their mother's feet in the bliss of divine love.

So Lord Advaita went to Purī. Gaura was very delighted to meet his own companions, and they wandered through the town chanting the name of God. They put the master in front (of their procession) to honor him, and the rest of the devotees proceeded with Gaura in the middle, and Nityānanda in the rear. This was an extraordinary dance; people were awed, and everyone's mind floated on the sweetness of the singing. Some laughed and some wept in the mood of divine love, and some roared "Hare Kṛṣṇa" like thunderclouds. The chanting of Hari's name continued for a long time, and then Mahāprabhu took the devotees and went to bathe. Advaita and Nityānanda enjoyed themselves even more, playing water games with their pure disciples. Engrossed in divine love, Gaura knocked Advaita down. My lord floated in the water, and engrossed in such ecstasy, Gaura climbed on his chest. My lord held Mahāprabhu and floated in dispassion. There is no end to the power he revealed. This sight filled their disciples with the bliss of divine love, for Gaura on Advaita's chest looked like Mahāviṣṇu lying on his Ananta-bed. The two had an unprecedented revelation of their human drama; all the devotees cried "Hari, Hari."

In this way Gaura enacted the drama of lying on Śeṣa. At Advaita Ācārya's invitation, Kṛṣṇa Caitanya took his associates and and fed them. Lost in love, Sītānātha praised him.

I have never seen such a strange drama, and those who saw it with their own eyes were very fortunate. I, however, was purified by drinking the ambrosia of this drama as it flowed from the lord Nityānanda's lotus mouth. The activities of Caitanya and Advaita are countless, and I have just written about a very few of them in these verses.

Īśāna Nāgara whose hopes are at the feet of Lord Caitanya and Lord Nityānanda narrates the *Advaita Prakāśa*.

Chapter 16

Gaurāṅga's Pilgrimage to Vṛndāvana

Victory, victory to Lord Caitanya, victory to Sītā's lord,
Victory to Nityānanda Rāma, and their followers.

One day Lord Kṛṣṇa Caitanya told his followers privately that he was going to Vṛndāvana. His followers reminded him that it was the rainy season, a time when travel to Holy Vraja would be unwise.

"The advice of Vaiṣṇava holy men is (like that of the) great Vedas; ignoring it brings about the destruction of all things good," Gaura said, and heeding his devotees' words, he returned home with his associates. He stopped at Advaita's house in Shantipur, where my lord was beside himself to see him. That frail man roared, and jumped up and down like a stick, and danced." Today I am so fortunate," he kept saying.

Gaura ran straight to Sītā without a word, tears flowing like the Gaṅgā from his eyes and down over his whole body. Acyuta, Kṛṣṇa Miśra, and Gopāla Dāsa were the most devoted of Sītā's most splendid sons. Their father delighted in their good deeds, and all three were completely devoted to Gaura. When they saw Gaurāṅga they bathed in the nectar of his divine love and outdid the celestial musicians with their singing of the Name. They roared, ever drunk on divine love. Gaura and

Nityānanda stretched out their arms and danced, and all the devotees sang the lord's name. I was lucky enough to have been employed in Advaita's household (at the time), so I bathed in the Gaṅgā-nectar of that lovely sight myself. Mother Sītā offered them nectar and cooked, and served the three lords and the devotees. Words cannot describe how joyous it was, and most fortunate were those who received that consecrated food.

Śacī Mother was delighted to get word of Lord Gaurāṅga's arrival, and she came to Shantipur. Gaura fell at his mother's feet, and Śacī Devī drew him to her breast affectionately. The feeling that arose in the lotus-hearts of the disciples was like that of Yaśodā at Kurukṣetra, with Kṛṣṇa at her breast. How could anyone observing such a scene remain calm? All hearts were pulled into the water of the ocean of divine love. Then Śacī cooked various of Lord Gaurāṅga's favorite dishes, like greens, gourd sweets, and rice pudding and sweet cakes. There is no comparison with the ambrosia she offered the assembly. Lord Kṛṣṇa Caitanya seated them for the feast, with Nitāi on his right and the virtuous lord Advaita on his left.

Mahāprabhu said, "The very best dish is the spinach."

Nityānanda said, "I would like some more." My lord laughed and said to Nityānanda, "Your love for the downcast is (as boundless as) the Gaṅgā."

Nityānanda said, "You are always looking up; you only see what is above you; how can you look down?"[26] Then the three lords laughed aloud. I was lucky enough to be able to understand a bit of that.

Mother served them more attentively each day, and every day a great celebration took place at my lord Advaita's house.

After several days, the glorious great lord Caitanya announced his departure for Vraja and left quickly. On the way he passed through the village of Rāmakeli, where he met Rūpa and Sanātana, repositories of all knowledge. They had been royal ministers, wise as Bṛhaspati, guru of the gods. Mahāprabhu showed them both great kindness, and they abandoned worldly pleasures and became free of envy.

Lord Caitanya announced his plan to go to Vṛndāvana. Rūpa and Sanātana quietly protested, saying, "Listen, Mahāprabhu, Ocean of Compassion: You should never go with so many people."

Again heeding the advice of his disciples, Lord Gaurāṅga now headed south and spent several days in Shantipur (on the way). The bliss of divine love swelled up at Gaura's arrival, and my lord held a great *sankīrtana* festival. Gaura saw Śacī Mother there and got her permission to go to Vraja, and continued south.

On the way, he met Raghunātha Dāsa, at whose hymns the holy men marveled. I lack the ability to describe anything about him whose dispassion Mahāprabhu praised, whose interest in worldly matters had been destroyed effortlessly by the fragrance drifting from the wishing tree of Gauracandra.

[26] A reference to Advaita's short stature, and correlation again with the dwarf *avatāra*.

On the day Lord Caitanya reached Purī, he melted in the *rasa* of love when he saw Jagannātha in the temple. At the sight of Gaura his disciples went mad with bliss and held a great festival of chanting the name of God. After several days that glorious Gaura-Viśvambhara decided to go to Vṛndāvana, and so late one night, he set out secretly for Holy Vraja, lost in ecstasy. Even though he avoided the main roads and traveled by side roads, when he set out on the road to Jharikhand loudly singing Hari's name, people marveled. When the animals saw Gaura their violent instincts were driven away as Mahāprabhu called out, "Hey, wild animals! The root of all bondage is sliced away when one says 'Kṛṣṇa.'" Since any command from Svayaṃ Bhagavān is unfailingly irresistible, the animals lovingly chanted 'Kṛṣṇa' and wept. A great festival ensued in the dense forest, and all the birds and beasts were liberated by saying the Name.

How can I tell of the greatness of Lord Caitanya's compassion? By Hari's Name, even inanimate objects became liberated. Lord Kṛṣṇa Caitanya's drama is a great ocean whose beginning or end not even Brahmā could find. I am the vilest of creatures; I do not know anything. This base creature, whose mind is in bliss, is just recounting the gist of it. The ignorant do not have the least faith in it, but be aware that it is certainly within range of the wise. It is very difficult to speak of the drama of Svayaṃ Bhagavān, but because a devotee is lucky enough to have divine powers, he can see it with his own eyes.

Mahāprabhu went on his way, spreading the Name, and on the road he infused many people with divine power and converted them to Vaiṣṇavism.

After several days Gaura came to the holy city of Kāśī and bathed at the Maṇikarṇikā Landing. Tapana Miśra was overjoyed to find Gaurāṅga there and bowed before him. He humbly invited him to his own house, and Gauracandra spent several days there.

Then Gaura saw the Vindu Mādhava image. He raised his arms and danced charmingly, and then restrained that love and prostrated himself and sang many sorts of endless praises.

When Gaura saw the Viśveśa image, his love overflowed. The only words from his mouth were "Chant Hari-Hara, chant Hari-Hara." He bowed to Śiva and recited divine praises, and recited the Vedas like four-faced Brahmā. Gaura had a supernatural form and supernatural love, and when everyone saw, they said, "This is the emperor of worshipers."

Then Lord Caitanya saw the Annapūrṇā image. Intoxicated with divine love, he called out "Paurṇamāśī!" Sometimes laughing, sometimes weeping, sometimes fainting, or sometimes roaring, he danced and roamed around. The residents of Kāśī saw this and found it wonderful, and some insisted he must be a divine embodiment.

Then Tapana Miśra took Mahāprabhu home and fed him, serving him and his friends consecrated food. Candraśekhara met Gaura there.

Then Lord Gaurāṅga saw the image of Ādikeśava and fainted from pure love. In this way a great festival took place in Holy Kāśī.

Gaurahari went from there to Prayāga. When he saw the confluence of the three rivers he was overwhelmed with love; all he could say was "Kālindī [Yamunā] Daughter! I've been lucky enough to catch sight of the Yamunā." He flew into the water, crying "Oh! Oh!" and remained submerged in the Yamunā all day. Mercifully he floated up to the surface in the evening, and some fishermen pulled him into their boat. Gaura sat in the boat singing the name of Hari, charming everyone with his very sweet voice. Most delighted, Gaura came to the bank.

When Śacī's son saw Mādhava at *ārati* time, he wept with love. Raising his arms, he roared repeatedly, "Grant me devotion, grant me devotion." He did a strange dance beyond human comprehension. Animate and inanimate beings wept at the wonder of Gaurāṅga's divine love.

Gaura eventually restrained himself, and then the sight of Bhīma's mace again kindled his delight.

He traveled from Prayāga to Vṛndāvana, rescuing living beings along the way with the treasure of divine love. In time Gaura arrived in the Mathurā area, where he forgot himself, lost in the mood of the *gopīs*. "Where is Kānu? Where is Kānu? Where will I find him? My heart is burning in the fire of separation; I must cool it." While he was singing this verse he began to stammer until he could say only "where, where," and began to weep. Gaura continued in this manner for three hours until finally he was whirling around, and people became quite concerned. After some time, overcome by the emotion of his own drama, Gaura roamed here and there looking for (the demon) Kāṃṣa, roaring like a lion and flailing his arms. He leapt up; who could imagine what he was thinking? In this way he displayed many emotions, until an entire day and a night had passed.

The next day Śacī's son went to the Dhruva landing, where he contemplated the story of Dhruva and wept. When he saw a group of people he controlled his emotions. He bathed, and gazed upon the holy image.

Then Mahāprabhu proceeded to Holy Vṛndāvana. As soon as he reached Vraja, he fainted from divine love. When he finally regained consciousness, Lord Gaurāṅga could speak only haltingly, "This, this." Even fully conscious, he kept rolling in the dust, calling out in great ecstasy, "Where is my beloved? Where is Kānu? Where is Kānu?" He searched for Kṛṣṇa day and night, his eyes constantly flowing with tears. He wandered from grove to grove, constantly sobbing. For three hours he kept laughing aloud, always roaring like a lion; who could comprehend it? Mahāprabhu's great ecstasy was beyond the comprehension of the gods, so what mortal can describe such emotion?

Gaura roamed the streets of Vraja, always crying "Chant Kṛṣṇa, chant Kṛṣṇa." At Lord Kṛṣṇa Caitanya's command the animate and inanimate made the sound "Kṛṣṇa, Kṛṣṇa" endlessly. Just then some cows and calves caught the scent of Kṛṣṇa and surrounded Gaura, and licked his body. When the herd tasted the immortal Gaṅgā that was Gaurāṅga, they wept in great ecstasy. When he saw this, Gaura said, "Vraja has incomprehensible virtues. And the residents of Vraja have a natural love for Kṛṣṇa," and he touched them all with his lotus hands. The cows danced, almost like the *gopīs* of Vraja, and that sight made Gaura's love surge up, and he danced like a madman and cried "Oh, Oh!"

Meanwhile, Advaita's son Acyutānanda had been frantically missing Gaura. Sometimes he would say, "Where is Gaura?" and let out a roar. He wept ceaselessly as he called out "Gaurāṅga!" Sometimes he would say, "Where is Gauracandra, my life?"

When Gaura learned of his dear devotee's despair, he drew him to himself like a yogi with the words "Come, come, come," and Sītā's son came. The trip from Shantipur to Vraja (normally) takes many days; Acyuta came instantly in the flower-chariot of Gaura's command. Everything is possible for Kṛṣṇa's devotees, who have inconceivable power; there is no marvel in this.

When Acyuta saw Gaurāṅga, he said aloud, "Hey Gaura, you nearly killed me by going so far away. You left the Vraja of devotion and came to the Holy Vraja of the *gopīs*. Do you want to go to the Vraja of devotion, or will you lose yourself in the love of the *gopīs*? Even though the Vraja of the glorious *gopīs* is full of eternal bliss, the Vraja of devotion is more important, because Yaśodā and the other people of Vraja have all been born in Navadvīpa, the Vraja of devotion, for your sake. Completely lost in ecstasy, you came to the now-empty Vraja of the *gopīs*, and when I realized that, I came to get you."

Lord Gaurāṅga said, "You are the best devotee of the lord, and Lord Kṛṣṇa shines through you for the benefit of all beings. Engrossed in love, you always talk with so many crazy people about the eternal activities of Rādhā and Kṛṣṇa."

Acyuta said, "Have Rādhā and Kṛṣṇa both come together now and become one for the sake of some desire? Not even the infinite lord Ananta and the other gods have seen the divine form which by immense fortune appears before me. I said there was nothing in Vṛndāvana, but I have committed a serious error through my own weakness."

Gaura said, "An eternal pure devotee of Kṛṣṇa sees the glorious form of Rādhā-Kṛṣṇa everywhere. Kṛṣṇa considers him dearer than life and never takes his misdeeds seriously. You are Kṛṣṇa's eternal intimate devotee, and you have sparked divine love in me."

Acyuta said, "Your decree is a great Veda, and no living being can stand to be apart from your most pure mercy. Your pure devotee who speaks to you humbly can understand your majesty. I am a miserable creature, I do not understand anything of the truth, but I consider myself most fortunate to be in the shelter of your feet."

Saying, "You have deep attraction for Kṛṣṇa, and anyone who touches you is very blessed," Lord Caitanya grabbed Acyuta and embraced him tightly, crying

"Hari Hari" in divine love. Acyuta, overwhelmed with love of Gaura, sang and danced with the emotions of one of Kṛṣṇa's girlfriends, like a drunkard.

Then, engrossed in love, Lord Caitanya thought of Rādhā Kuṇḍa, Rādhā's pond, and asked everyone, "Where is Rādhā's pond?"

The people of Vraja said, "No one knows that."

Gaura fainted and collapsed. When Acyuta saw Gaurāṅga's deep ecstasy, he called out the name of Rādhā-Kṛṣṇa, his eyes flooding (with tears). Gaura rose up with a roar when he heard Rādhā's name and began to weep, saying, "Where is Rādhā's pond?"

Acyuta said, "O Lord Kṛṣṇa Caitanya, listen to the mysterious truth about Rādhā's pond from me."

Gaura said, "Because you are an eternal companion of Kṛṣṇa's, you can see the long-lost divine sites of his activities and other holy places."

Acyuta said, "I bow to your compassion, which constantly increases the prestige of your devotees. You have decided to recover two great pilgrimage sites, and proclaim the omniscience of your own devotees. Rādhā's pond has inconceivable power, and Śyāma's pond certainly has similar power. If the infinite lord Ananta and the other gods cannot comprehend it, how can I, a contemptible thing, understand it? You know I am like a wooden puppet who dances on the strings of your desire. Your dear Gadādhara Pandit, storehouse of divine love, was my teacher. My father told me that I would find devotion to Kṛṣṇa through the one who has Rādhā's body. He spoke these words out of compassion for me; I hardly know right from wrong. Rādhā's pond is the visible proof of the eternal presence of Kuṇḍeśvarī Rādhā, the goddess of the pond. Who can understand the extent of the greatness of the blessed Rādhā Kuṇḍa, which is present in every sacred place? All holy places cleanse the wicked of their evil and take on those misdeeds themselves. The company of the wise destroys these sins. Scriptures say, 'one should try to get the merit of a holy place.' Rādhā's eternally perfect pond is the embodiment of the power of Kṛṣṇa's mind, and so it is the great refuge of all divine powers. Contemplation on Rādhā's pond destroys all wickedness, according to the eternal dharma. The sight of that blessed pond produces a sprout of devotion; merely touching it gives rise to loving devotion, and bathing in its waters will certainly bring one to Kṛṣṇa. One who dies on its bank becomes Kṛṣṇa's servant. Who can recount the countless virtues of the glorious pond?

Now hear some of its secondary virtues. All the perfected souls sit on the bank of the pond and hear the names of Rādhā and Kṛṣṇa, and weep. The mere sight of that blessed pond destroys suffering, causing the mind to forget the world and causing mental delight to increase. The water itself is like a sweet medicine, prolonging life and destroying disease in those who bathe in it and drink it. Further, Śyāma's pond is connected to Rādhā's pond. Rādhā Kuṇḍa is like Kṛṣṇa's divine beloved. It is established in Lord Nandanandana's eternal form, and when one sees it, Kṛṣṇa's form shines forth. Not even the eternal lord

Ananta can understand its greatness. One who drinks and bathes in it finds Rādhā-Kṛṣṇa."

Saying this, Acyuta bowed to Gaura. Engrossed in love, Gaura held him tightly, saying, "Today I have heard the greatness of the blessed pond. I consider myself blessed in body, soul, and mind." And he left for Rādhā Kuṇḍa, which was nearly invisible, in a great ecstatic trance.

Lord Kṛṣṇa Caitanya said to the master's son, "Here is Rādhā's Pond, look at the evidence. Even though this great holy place is nearly invisible, my mental anguish was destroyed when I saw it. Why else has my great delight suddenly increased?"

Saying that, he shouted out, "Rādhā!" When all the birds and the beasts heard Rādhā's name, they cried like the best of Kṛṣṇa's devotees, engrossed in divine love. Rādhā's name always produces bliss; when it fell on them from Gaura's mouth, it filled them with true divine love. In whom does love not blossom when they hear this sound? Animate and inanimate beings flow with tears in the bliss of divine love.

Lord Gaurāṅga said, "Look, Acyuta, divine love dawns in all creatures just through Rādhā's name. There is no doubt that this is really Rādhā Kuṇḍa and the pond connected to it is Śyāma Kuṇḍa. How fortunate I am! I got to see the holy pond. Association with the wise has this virtue, incomprehensible (even) to the gods."

When he said that, the omniscient lord was overwhelmed with the nectar of divine love and dove into the water. He plunged into Rādhā's pond and swam to Śyāma's pond. He bathed in Śyāma's pond and swam back to Rādhā's pond. When Gaura had finished bathing, he took some mud from the pond and smeared it all over his body, lost in divine love. Gaurahari prostrated himself one hundred times in deep devotion and sang many kinds of praises to the pond. That sight intoxicated Acyuta with divine love, and he walked around this divine pond, roaring. Then, in the emotion of Rādhā, goddess of the pond, Mahāprabhu cried out, "Where is the lord of my life?" Sometimes motionless, sometimes trembling, sometimes laughing aloud, sometimes roaring, sometimes dancing, sometimes speaking humbly; gradually a great wave of the ocean of divine love surged up. Lord Caitanya fainted and fell to the ground.

When Acyuta saw Gaura's motionless body, he cried repeatedly, "Oh no, Gaura, my life!" After some time Sītā's son became a bit calmer and loudly called out "Hari, Hari." Six hours later Gaura regained consciousness and began to dance, crying, "I have found Rādhā's Pond." He had mercifully found the divine couple's two ponds, and revealed them in the Kali Age.

Then Gauracandra took Acyuta's hands and circumambulated the pond, reciting the great mantra. Again and again they prostrated themselves, hundreds of times. Acyuta, engrossed in divine love, bathed in the pond. When Gaura, who was sitting at the base of a tree, heard his humble words of eager devotion, he recovered somewhat, and Gaura said, "Acyuta, Rādhā Kuṇḍa has mercifully been revealed because of your virtues."

Acyuta said, "Why are you doing such a terrible thing? I have taken eternal shelter at your feet. In every age you perform your supernatural activities, and you have recovered the hidden holy places to rescue living beings. The hidden love and the hidden pond were very ancient. By your mercy, we found Rādhā's pond."

Hearing that, Mahāprabhu said, "This is excessive praise. I have no love for this ancestor worship of yours. In the first place, Kṛṣṇa is lord of all, and all are his servants. Īśvara can completely destroy living beings with a thought."

Acyuta said, "Your actions speak humbly, concealing spiritual truth. Just as the sun cannot be hidden by a cloud, so Kṛṣṇa's activities reveal his secrets," (and) called out "Hari." Gaura said, "There is truly no other word but the Name."

"By great good fortune I have found the bearer of the Name," Acyuta cried, and clutched Gaura's feet. Then Gaura, the ocean of compassion, demonstrated that compassion and revealed himself as a pair of perfect images: the image of the king of *rasa*, the most complete manifestation of Lord Kṛṣṇa, with Rādhā, the embodiment of pure love, at his left. When Acyuta saw these two eternal truths he was overwhelmed with divine love and prostrated himself. He composed verses praising Caitanya in many ways, but Gaura asked, "Why are you praising me?"

Acyuta saw Gaura now as a renunciate and answered, "It is good that you have hidden your own form in Rādhā's body, for in serving you, one serves the divine couple," and placed Gaura's lotus feet on his head.

Gaura said, "You are the emperor of love of Kṛṣṇa. Rādhā-Kṛṣṇa appear wherever you are," and embraced him. Acyuta began to dance in the bliss of divine love. Everyone heard about the ponds and were purified by bathing, drinking, and seeing them.

Then Mahāprabhu went to Mount Govardhana. When he saw the mountain where Kṛṣṇa had played, he fainted with divine love. When he regained consciousness, he said, "O, best of mountains, you are wasting away without Kṛṣṇa." And he continued, "How amazing! I see—Oh, my!—the smell of Kṛṣṇa's body is still on your surface." He went and embraced it, and quenched his burning soul. Then, "I will go; maybe I will find the lord of my life," Lord Caitanya said, and extended his arms and ran around Mt. Govardhana to embrace it. Sometimes falling, sometimes rising, finding no refuge anywhere, he circled the mountain, always singing the Name of Hari. The incomprehensible play of Gaura's love, not of this world, spread the nectar of his compassion and rescued living beings. Ever weeping, ever dancing, ever rolling on the ground, Acyutānanda was filled with divine love.

Then Gaurāṅga wandered to all the forest holy places. When he saw the site of the full moon dance, a wave of love surged up. In great ecstasy he marked the spot where Kṛṣṇa had disappeared. Reciting the *Gopī Gītā*, Gaura wept and wandered, sometimes enacting the play of Rādhā-Kṛṣṇa, sometimes singing songs, sometimes dancing. Gaurāṅga's divine love was a great ocean; not even the infinite lord Ananta could describe it.

I am a fool, a wretch, a worm, and cannot understand anything. I merely recount the gist of the words of the Vaiṣṇava holy men. Although Gaura had no desire to leave Vraja, he left Vraja because of his devotees' wishes, (his eyes) streaming with tears.

Īśāna Nāgara, whose hopes are at the feet of Lord Caitanya and Lord Advaita, narrates the *Advaita Prakāśa*.

Chapter 17

Further Pilgrimage Adventures

Caitanya Meets Rūpa and Sanātana; Acyuta Converts the Monist

Victory, victory to Lord Caitanya, victory to Sītā's lord,
Victory to Nityānanda Rāma, and their followers.

Mahāprabhu proceeded to the holy city of Prayāga, where he stayed at the home of a Vaiṣṇava brahmin. He bathed in the confluence of the three rivers and saw the Mādhava image, and danced and chanted the lord's name in the bliss of pure divine love. Lost in ecstasy, the glorious Caitanya prostrated himself one hundred times, singing Mādhava's endless praises, spreading the Name and divine love. That Vaiṣṇava (who hosted him) was so very fortunate!

One day the great scholar Rūpa Gosvāmī came and presented himself at the holy place at Prayāga. A Rāmakeli resident who had been a royal minister, by Caitanya's mercy he had given up his interest in worldly affairs. His most noble brother Anupama, the best of God's devotees, came with him. I cannot describe the bliss present at the meeting of Rūpa with Lord Gaurāṅga! When Rūpa saw Gaurāṅga he melted with love and fell at his feet over and over again and praised him greatly. Then when Anupama saw Gaura, love swelled up in him, too. He covered his head with his garment and prostrated himself and praised him. Lord Caitanya embraced the two men, but they announced, "We are vile untouchables."

Gaura said, "Kṛṣṇa's devotees are the best of all people, and contact with just a taste of devotion transforms a base person into a brahmin. It says in the scriptures that brahmins possess twelve virtues. All those virtues are secondary to devotion, as my lord's servants who accompany him when he travels are secondary to him.

Rūpa Gosvāmī said, "This is true. Tell me where I will most certainly find devotion."

Acyuta said, "Devotion lies on the banks of the Mandākinī River, (yet) some people living there die of thirst."

Rūpa said, "The cātaka bird has such good fortune, yet he is not satisfied except by the cloud of Kṛṣṇa's mercy."

Mahāprabhu said, "Devotion is a priceless jewel, attainable by the mercy of the holy men, scriptures say. The lucky person who happens to get some kindness from holy men forsakes worldly illusion. When the goddess of devotion appears, Māyā-illusion disappears, just as an elephant leaves when a lion approaches."

Rūpa said, "I do not know who is a holy man, I just know that you have attracted me here, the same way iron does not understand the power of a magnet, but just goes when it is pulled."

Mahāprabhu said, "Why are you behaving so humbly? Has some idea arisen in your hearts? I deduce that you are Kṛṣṇa's eternal companions. All the holy men have described signs of the natural behavior of a servant of Kṛṣṇa: compassion for living beings, association with holy men, self-deprecating speech."

Then he eagerly asked for news of Sanātana. Rūpa replied, "He has been imprisoned. Please, free our kinsman. I throw myself at your feet."

Gaura said, "Kṛṣṇa's devotees cannot be bound. You will see him very shortly."

Rūpa said, "Your words are certainly infallible."

Acyuta said, "This is the greatest Veda."

Then Gaura taught both Rūpa and Anupama the practice which would lead to a devotee's realization.

Rūpa Gosvāmī was a great poet. By Caitanya's mercy, he became an ocean of devotion. One day Gaura said to Rūpa and Anupama, "You two go to Holy Vṛndāvana." Rūpa joined his hands in supplication and said, "Listen, Gauracandra. We will find no joy in leaving you to go to Vraja."

Gaura continued, "Vraja is the holy site of the source of cognition and bliss, the site of the eternal activities of Svayaṃ Bhagavān. Over time those sites have been lost. Recovering them is the duty and responsibility of the wise. Spreading devotion, composing devotional scriptures, recovering lost holy sites are our three primary needs. For these reasons, go immediately to Vṛndāvana. Your desires will be fulfilled through Kṛṣṇa's mercy."

Rūpa said, "It is my responsibility to accept your divine command. This is a very serious order that you have given me, the most wretched of men. A dog can even ignore a lion—everything is possible through your great compassion," and he bowed to Lord Kṛṣṇa Caitanya. Rūpa and Anupama set out for Vraja without further ado.

Then Gaura went from Prayāga to Vārāṇāsī. When Candraśekhara saw him, he took him to his house. Candraśekhara said, "Today, by virtue of great good fortune, you have blessed me and shown yourself in a dream."

Gaura said, "Kṛṣṇa's devotees have inconceivable greatness. Engrossed in ecstasy they understand the reality of past, present, and future."

Candraśekhara said, "I am a mean rascal."

Lord Caitanya countered, "You are the ultimate devotee."

He met Tapana Miśra there, who with his friends served Gaurāṅga. Thus over a period of several days Kṛṣṇa Caitanya conferred the Name on many people in holy Kāśī, blessing them.

One day Acyuta was bathing in the Gaṅgā, when a naked renunciate came to bathe at the Maṇikarṇikā landing. Acyuta climbed out onto the bank, calling the name of Lord Kṛṣṇa Caitanya. When the renunciate saw him, he said, "You are from Bengal. You mistakenly attribute divinity to Gaurāṅga. Is it true that he became a renunciate but has forsaken the renunciate creed to sing the name of Hari? I heard that he tricked the Oriya scholar Sarvabhauma with his knowledge of magic. He always works counter to the Vedas and does not consider associating with Muslims to be polluting. If a barbarian says the name of Hari as a joke, he embraces him, without considering his religion. He has influenced many people by this most depraved behavior. What can its basis be but magic?"

When Acyuta heard this slanderous talk about the glorious Caitanya, he responded politely but his heart ached. "O renunciate, listen to what I say: a god-realized being with the thirty-two marks of Īśvara is considered to be Īśvara, and Gaura has all these marks, but we consider them unimportant. All these properties and marks are apparent to one who has the eyes of devotion, but an (ordinary) person cannot see them even after ten million good deeds."

The renunciate said, "Parabrahmā is formless. The idea of his having form is just something holy men say."

Acyuta said, "If people are worshiping a figment of their imaginations, then how can they actually reach Parabrahmā?"

The renunciate said, "The eternal Brāhman is present in every form. Liberation comes only through the realization of this essential monism."

Acyuta said, "So is there a difference between the world and Brāhman?"

The renunciate said, "The whole world is nondifferent from Brāhman."

Acyuta said, "Then the world is a part of Brāhman."

The renunciate said, "Yes, he is apparent in all forms."

Acyuta said, "Brāhman is Bhagavān Himself, full of truth, consciousness, and bliss; the proof is in the Vedas. He takes on many forms through the power of his desire, but he has one essential eternal form whose splendor is all-pervading. All creatures and objects starting with Brāhman, whether animate or inanimate, are partial incarnations of Īśvara. That being the case, how is there a problem with Īśvara's being complete in each of his parts? For nothing can divide the Almighty in two. A leech can contract and expand its body in an instant through the power of illusion; the forms of God are similarly full of the six supernatural powers. There is no doubt that the cause of this power is its pervasion. Svayaṃ Bhagavān has revealed Himself to establish righteousness, out of kindness to humanity." And thus he refuted the renunciate's false assertions with many such arguments from scripture.

The renunciate was amazed and said, "I will admit that Īśvara incarnates for the sake of living beings, but what evidence is there that Īśvara has incarnated in the Kali Age?"

Acyuta said, "Very well, listen carefully. The Vedas, *purāṇas*, and other scriptures proclaim that the Lord's incarnations are countless. Kṛṣṇa has four incarnations, one in each of the four ages. It was proclaimed that he would adopt white, red, black, and yellow forms. In the Kali Age he has incarnated in the form of a devotee; this glorious Kṛṣṇa Caitanya is the yellow-colored one. By his mercy his auspicious birth took place in Navadvīpa. He instructs living beings by practicing his own dharma. Nondevotees see the lord of Māyā as a (ordinary) living being, the way a conch looks yellow through bilious eyes."

The renunciate said, "What proof is there that he is the one?"

Acyuta said, "The form, the virtues, the Name are the evidence. Call 'Gaurāṅga, Gaurāṅga' one time, and your hair will stand on end; it is most wonderful."

So the renunciate shouted Lord Gaurāṅga's name. The moonlight of Gaura's mercy spread through his disciple's words. The inconceivable virtue of discussion with a devotee of Kṛṣṇa made him quiver like the leaves on a kadamba tree.

Amazed, the renunciate proclaimed, "Lord Caitanya is beyond natural law, there is no doubt! Lord Gaurāṅga's name is full of the essence of pure divine love. Dependence on the perfect name of Hari is the greatest sweetness, so I am going wherever Gaura is, and when I see him, I will join him, body, heart, and soul."

Acyuta said, "Come with me, and when you see Lord Gaurāṅga your life will be fulfilled. But if Gauracandra sees you naked, he will be embarrassed and very upset."

The renunciate said, "Who will give clothes to a desireless one?"

Acyuta said, "I will," and tore his garment and gave him half. The renunciate dressed properly, and then the two proceeded to Lord Kṛṣṇa Caitanya. Acyuta prostrated himself at Gaura's feet, but the renunciate took one look at Gaurāṅga and happened to see the universal form in Gaura's body. The sight of that exceedingly marvelous divine majesty made the renunciate's eyes flow with a stream of the Gaṅgā of divine love. With palms joined in supplication he praised Lord Caitanya, "You are the dear lord of Vraja, the lord of all, incarnate. You came as a devotee to instruct people. I, a miserable wretch, cannot understand your greatness, and so I surrender completely to your pure mercy. Drunk with my own egotism, I maligned you terribly. Please, wipe away my sin. I take refuge at your feet." And with this humble praise, the renunciate fell at Gaura's feet.

Gaura touched him, saying "*Namo Nārāyaṇāya*," and infused his soul with divine power. At the touch of the catalyst Gaura, divine love arose in him, and the renunciate raised his arms and began to dance. His fierce roars terrified people. Over and over he cried, "Lord Caitanya is the Lord of all!"

Acyuta danced, and the other disciples danced, saying, "This Kali Age is blessed," and they sang the lord's name, and by the grace of those wise men the renunciate was rescued. Ten million bows at the feet of the holy men! I cannot begin to describe the activities of the wise men, but by the grace of the Vaiṣṇavas I have managed to write a little.

Gaura's influence pervaded Kāśī and led many to become Vaiṣṇavas. Among the renunciates in that place was a Bṛhaspati in knowledge known as Prabodhānanda Sarasvatī. Well-versed in many scriptures, that crest-jewel of scholars was egotistical and spoke ill of Gaurāṅga. That ocean of compassion Lord Caitanya revealed his compassion and brought the logic of many scriptures to support his own opinion, refuting all of Prabodhānanda's doubts. (Finally) Prabodhānanda understood, and said, "Īśvara is in Gaurāṅga." Gaura was very merciful toward Lord Prabodhānanda and awakened his divine power and gave him devotion and divine love. Prabodhānanda became an exemplary Vaiṣṇava and a wise disciple of Gaura. He renounced his false logic and attained the bliss of divine love. Night and day he asserted, "Kṛṣṇa is clearly revealed in this yellow form," and streams of tears flowed from his eyes when he sang the lord's name. He kept running in circles, finding no refuge anywhere. He was always dancing with arms upraised in love, always crying out, "I reviled you." He composed verses praising Lord Gaurāṅga, and people's hair stood on end when they heard his extraordinary descriptions. His students and others among the scholars also took shelter at Gaurāṅga's lotus feet.

There is no end to Gauracandra's extraordinary divine play. I am a miserable creature; what can I do; not even the infinite lord Ananta can do him justice. The glorious Kṛṣṇa Caitanya is a storehouse of pure compassion.

He taught Sanātana the essence of the principle of devotion. Sanātana met Gaura in Kāśī, and went to Vṛndāvana at Mahāprabhu's request. Sanātana, Rūpa's elder brother, supreme in dispassion, was conversant in all the scriptures.

Rūpa established an image of Govinda in Vraja. Sanātana revealed Madana Gopāla. These two brothers were great compassionate holy men. They produced devotional texts and presented them to the devotees. Their nephew was Jiva Gosvāmī, and no devotional text compares to his in terms of proper theory. Gopāla Bhaṭṭa and Raghunātha Bhaṭṭa, great scholars, and Raghunātha Dāsa; all these are free of envy, leaders in devotional scripture, recoverers of lost holy places; they are known as the "*gosvāmīs*."

Mahāprabhu and the two lords revealed the path of devotion and the scriptures of devotion. My lord Advaita praised the virtues of these six *Gosvāmīs*, saying they were *mañjarīs* of Kṛṣṇa's eternal female companions. Lord Caitanya was the one and only Mahāprabhu; he considered both Nityānanda and Advaita to be "*prabhus*." Gadādhara Pandit and Śrīvāsa, the twelve *Gopālas* and the sixty-four *mahantas*, told the truth.

I have written what I heard from the holy men, but I am incapable of understanding the magnitude of Gaurāṅga's countless virtues.

Then Mahāprabhu again set out on the road from Holy Vārāṇāsī to Jhārikhaṇḍa and came to Purī. When they saw Mahāprabhu, the disciples, engrossed in divine love, shed tears of bliss. Rāya Rāmānanda and the others prostrated themselves. Gaura spread out his arms to embrace them all, and a wave of the ocean of the nectar of chanting the lord's name grew in the moonlight of that king of brahmins, the glorious Kṛṣṇa Caitanya. All the devotees together chanted the lord's name. Humanity is so contemptible, yet it attracts the gods.

Īśāna Nāgara, whose hopes are at the feet of Lord Caitanya and Lord Advaita, narrates the *Advaita Prakāśa*.

Chapter 18

Caitanya Revives Gopāla Dāsa; Sītā's Great Feast

Victory, victory to Lord Caitanya, victory to Sītā's lord,
Victory to Nityānanda Rāma, and their followers.

One day Sītā said to her husband Advaita, "The door of my heart has been thrown open, but how long has it been since we last saw Gauracandra? My heart and soul are always crying for him. When will my good fortune yield its fruit, and I again see Gaura's face? When will I offer Gaura his favorite dishes? When will I be able to soothe my heart burned in this conflagration of separation from Gaura? When will I drink the nectar of Gaura's words again? When will I cast off these disturbing worldly longings? If you love me, please heal this mental anguish," and she wept, engrossed in divine love.

My lord said, "Your life is indeed blessed!" and as soon as he spoke, was intoxicated with divine love. "Gaura, Gaura," he roared loudly, and continued, "Whoever surrenders his life to Lord Caitanya will truly know great good fortune. I would consider a person who shivers when he hears Gaura's name, his ultimate disciple. The person who sheds tears when he says 'Gaurāṅga' is an eternally perfected divine embodiment in the form of a disciple," and he roared deeply, and raising his arms, danced and sang the lord's name. After some time Sītānātha recovered from his trance and consoled his wife with talk of Gaura's virtues.

Just then a Vaiṣṇava bowed to the lord and announced news from Śivānanda Sena. "O Lord Sītānātha, listen carefully. Śivānanda sent me to you. He wants to take all of Gaura's associates and go to Purī for the Ratha Yātrā, the Chariot Festival. The lord Nityānanda, Śrīvāsa, Pandit Gadādhara, and all the others have gathered."

When Advaita heard this good news from that glorious Vaiṣṇava, he and Sītā prepared to set out. The very virtuous Sītā Devī delightedly packed all of Gaura's favorite dishes with care. Gopāla Dāsa, eternally surrendered to Gaura, also went to see Gaurāṅga. By the grace of guru and the Vaiṣṇavas, I, miserable wretch, went along with them as a servant. When my lord met Lord Gaurāṅga's other associates, he fell at their feet and embraced them, and bliss surged up. They all set off together, blissfully chanting the lord's name, visiting holy places along the way until they reached Purī.

When Gauracandra heard that his friends had arrived safely, he was very pleased and ran out to greet them. His followers saw Lord Gaurāṅga from a distance and proceeded, engrossed in love, loudly singing the lord's name. The joy in that meeting between Lord Kṛṣṇa Caitanya and his followers cannot be described. Engrossed in love, the Vaiṣṇavas encircled Gaura, and danced and sang the lord's name. Mahāprabhu sank beneath a wave of the ocean of love, oblivious to all his followers. Eventually they were all swimming in it themselves, streams of Suradhunī-Gaṅgā flowing from their eyes. Nityānanda was drunk on pure divine love and raised his arms, shouting "Hare Kṛṣṇa," and danced. The lord Advaita's divine love cannot be described! "We will subdue the wicked," he roared.

Just then he climbed up onto Jagannātha's chariot. When Gaura saw that, he sang a verse in the mood of a *gopī*: "After a long time I have found you, Kṛṣṇa; I will keep you in my heart and never let go of your feet," and then Mahāprabhu was stricken with ecstasy. The two lords replied with the song's refrain. Gradually a wave of the ocean of ecstasy swelled up.

Then great ecstasy arose in Lord Gaurāṅga, and he fainted, chanting the lord's name. Caitanya awoke singing that same verse again. He stretched out his arms and took Nityānanda to his breast. Nitāi held Gaura's hands in his, and they danced a very sweet dance around Advaita. My lord said, "It is difficult to understand the activities of these two." Gaura and Nitāi said, "You alone are the instigator of these activities." Then they all embraced each other tightly and cried "Hari!" and the three lords wept, repeating, "Come! People are no longer afraid! Singing 'Hari,' dancing, singing, we will be delivered."

The followers danced when they heard that. Some wept with divine love, some roared. Just then, Advaita's son Gopāla raised his two hands and danced, charming the whole world. While he was dancing, Gopāla fainted, and no amount of chanting the lord's name could revive him. Sītānātha thought Gopāla Dāsa was dead, and grieved, saying, "Alas Kṛṣṇa, what have you done!"

Then Śacī's son Mahāprabhu called out repeatedly, "Get up, Gopāla!" How could he remain unconscious at the order of Caitanya (consciousness) by whose mercy the world became conscious? By a fraction of Lord Caitanya's mercy, Gopāla Dāsa awoke and said, "I am Caitanya's servant," and roared out, "Lord Kṛṣṇa Caitanya!"

The disciples proclaimed, "He is the divine embodiment in the form of a disciple." Gaura melted with affection and held Gopāla and embraced him, sprinkling him with tears of love. Lord Advaita embraced his son in the bliss of divine love and danced around, saying "Hari, Hari." Nityānanda rubbed his glorious body in love. All the followers took the dust of Gopāla's feet. The greatness of the lord Gopāla Dāsa is unequaled, and I, a miserable creature, cannot begin to describe it.

When they saw Lord Jagannātha's great chariot procession, everyone cried "Hari, Hari." There was more bliss than can be put into words. All of Gaura's associates rolled in the dust in love, and at the end of the festival they bought and ate consecrated food. They got acquainted with others in their guru's lineage, and went home.

Listen to another excellent tale. One day while they were there, Sītānātha was talking to Sītā Devī. "I cannot make Gaurāṅga eat as much as I would like, and this frustration is keeping my mind awake day and night. Whenever we invite Gaura to our place, many renunciates always come with him. Gaura gives all the food to the renunciates, and my desires are thwarted." Sītā listened and said, "That is true. Our hearts will ache until we can get Gaura alone. If I could make him eat all his favorite dishes then my eternal heart's desire would be fulfilled."

Listen to something extraordinary that happened just then: the day darkened and clouds began to gather. A huge storm developed as they watched. Hailstones fell, and people were terrified. No one understood Lord Caitanya's desire in this. Not a soul could leave their house. Just then the omniscient lord Gaurāṅga set out to fulfill his disciples' wishes, and he arrived, by himself, at Advaita's house. Sītā and Advaita, those two mines of the nectar of love of Gaura, floated on the ocean of love when they saw Gaurāṅga. They have such faith, I know they are eternally perfected. When they saw Gaurāṅga they both rose quickly. "Come in, come in, Gaura, my life," they invited. "You are the omniscient bee in the lotus of the hearts of your disciples. Your body is an ocean of the nectar of pure compassion," they said, and seated Gaura on the seat of honor. They had made many preparations for serving him.

I, a worm, went to wash Gaura's feet. He said, "Stop, stop, brahmin, O son of Viṣṇu."

I said, "Alas, alas; why do I have such misfortune! I am not fit to worship Lord Gaurāṅga's feet." And further, "For me to reach those feet which are worthy of the worship of Ananta and the other gods, would be as impossible as for a child to touch the moon." Then I remembered that Kṛṣṇa is an ocean of compassion. He is the incarnation to rescue the fallen wicked people. Since I am fallen, how can he not be compassionate to me? I fell at his feet weeping; he must show compassion. Well, this sacred thread is an enemy of service, and naturally causes conceit to arise. That is why the Vaiṣṇavas no longer wear it, I thought, (and) then cut my sacred thread.

When my lord saw that, he laughed and said, "Īśāna, why have you corrupted brahmin religion? The sacred thread of the twice-born purifies the mind, for it keeps drawing the heart to Parabrahmā," and he gave me another sacred thread.

"I am sorry. What use is this sacred thread if it keeps me from serving Gaura? Do not deceive me," I said, (and) began to cry. Advaita told Gaura repeatedly about my wailing. "You have made a disciple suffer; this is unfair."

At my lord's words, Mahāprabhu became silent. Advaita said, "Īśāna, go serve those glorious feet." When I heard that, I drowned in an ocean of bliss. The guru kindly requested me to serve Gaura. Even someone with the good deeds of ten million births cannot reach him, but by the grace of the guru, I reached him easily.

The mercy of the glorious guru and the Vaiṣṇavas has endless greatness. I am some wretch; I cannot describe the limits of Brahmā.

Then Mahāprabhu went to the temple dining hall, where he was joyously seated on the holy seat. Gaura said, "Come sit, Ācārya Gosvāmī."

My lord said, "Gaura, quit this chicanery. Today you will eat all these things." Then Mahāprabhu laughed and said, "I will make your word come true," and sat for the feast. Mother Sītā began to serve; she offered food and various dishes one after the other. I cannot describe all the cakes and sweet drinks she presented, but Gaurāṅga joyfully ate all of his favorite dishes which Sītā lovingly offered. Gaura said, "Master, I cannot say when I have eaten so much in my life!"

The lord smiled and said, "Listen, Nimāi. There is no concealing your cleverness in my house. The three great goddesses: praise of your followers, words to the wise, and humble speech, are always on your tongue." Mahāprabhu heard, and thought of Viṣṇu. He rinsed his mouth and was offered pan. The master eagerly put him to bed.

Then the hailstorm stopped. The lord Kṛṣṇa Caitanya had enacted a drama not of this world. He descended to give eternal bliss to his followers. Kṛṣṇa is full of great compassion; there is no one like him. Mahāviṣṇu and the others cannot come close to him. "There is no difference between Kṛṣṇa and Kṛṣṇa's pure disciples, this is in all the Vedas," he proclaimed, with arms raised. The desires of Kṛṣṇa's disciples have self-fulfilling power, so when they have a desire, that same desire also arises in Kṛṣṇa.

When will I ever again have such good fortune that the Vaiṣṇava gurus will kindly give me the shelter of their feet? When will I drown in the water of the ocean of the nectar of love of Gaura, and the misdeeds of my body and all my senses be driven out? Nārada and other important devotees of the past worshiped Rādhā or Kṛṣṇa and got salvation, and some, worshiping the image of the couple with an eternal body, went to eternal Vṛndāvana. No one has ever seen such beauty as Rasarājā (Kṛṣṇa) united with the great ecstasy which is Rādhā. The spread of this form in this blessed Kali Age as Gaurāṅga saved living beings. Whoever sees, serves, worships this form, effortlessly attains that treasure of love which is difficult to obtain. I have never heard of such a compassionate incarnation. All the manifestations of Kṛṣṇa contain the primary source.

Even dogs were saved by the Name of Hari. The virtues of the Vaiṣṇavas' leftovers were revealed. One great follower of the lord named Śivānanda Sen had a dog as a pet. When it ate the Vaiṣṇavas' leftovers, its mind was purified. That dog happened to go along with Śivānanda to Purī, and by Caitanya's mercy his karmic bonds were broken, and shouting "Hare Kṛṣṇa" he got an eternal body. Vaiṣṇavas' leftovers are certainly purifying substances; one becomes devoted to Kṛṣṇa by eating a morsel of them. The dust of the feet of the Vaiṣṇavas has unparalleled majesty, and the touch of one mote of it confers deliverance from earthly life. To see a Vaiṣṇava is to see Viṣṇu. To serve a Vaiṣṇava is to worship Kṛṣṇa. Kṛṣṇa said, "My followers are greater than I. They are firmly devoted and refute their misdeeds. Those who mistreat Vaiṣṇavas have no absolution; Kṛṣṇa cannot commute that sin. But if compassion happens to arise in a Vaiṣṇava, any misdeed of his is certainly erased. By Kṛṣṇa's desire his pure devotee has an abundance of divine power. Kṛṣṇa himself accepts that disciple."

Kṛṣṇadāsa instructed people naturally by his own conduct, always rescuing them.

Rādhā-Kṛṣṇa together have now become one disciple, and their wondrous beauty has kindly blessed living beings.

By Gaura's mercy, Śivānanda Sena's son learned all the scriptures at a very young age. He became known by the name Kavi Karṇapūra (and through his writings,) and amazed the world with Śacī's son's activities.

Now I will describe the way Mahāprabhu taught us to worship, the mere thought of which liberates living beings. By the mercy of the lion Lord Advaita, this wretch performed a very difficult-to-attain service at the confluence of the Gaṅgā with the ocean. Gaura's red lotus feet were very soft, so very soft hands were needed to massage them. Then I, a worm, happily said to Caitanya, "Please teach me something, since I have no devotion."

With a great smile and sweet language Gaurāṅga said, "Listen Īśāna, the scriptures which were revealed to the sages will instruct (you) in true religion. Singing the name of Hari is the best of all religions. The Name is far greater than austerity and recitation. All your misdeeds will be driven away if you take up the name. [The desire for constantly pronouncing the name grows and worldly attachment is driven away naturally.] Familiarity with the natural world ruins an ascetic's calling. The various gods and goddesses do not believe in Kṛṣṇa." Whoever hears and studies these words from the lotus-face of Lord Kṛṣṇa Caitanya is considered very fortunate. My endless bows to the feet of Gaurāṅga. He taught the world through his dear disciples' renunciation.

The singer Haridāsa sang like an angel. That supreme disciple of the lord was utterly devoted to Gaura. He traded some begged rice for some good rice to serve Gaura. When Gaura saw the good-quality rice, he asked, "Haridāsa, where did you get this rice?"

Haridāsa said, "From Mother Mādhavī. I traded this and brought it carefully."

Gaura said, "Haridāsa, what have you done! You have corrupted the eternally pure calling of an ascetic. Even though Mādhavī is very virtuous, devoted to religion, attached to guru and Vaiṣṇavas, a pure Kṛṣṇa-worshiper, she is still female, and how can an ascetic's calling be properly preserved in conversing with her? For that reason I disown you."

Haridāsa wept profusely. He bowed to Gaura and left. All the disciples were shocked. Oh, Lord Gaurāṅga's drama has secret meaning and one cannot understand it but through Gaura's followers.

Then Lord Advaita and the others returned to Bengal, but they were all very sad to leave Gaurāṅga.

There is nothing like the activities of Gaura and Gaura's associates. I am a wretch, preaching just the gist of it.

Īśāna Nāgara, whose hopes are at the feet of Lord Caitanya and Lord Advaita, narrates the *Advaita Prakāśa*.

Chapter 19

Rūpa's Dramas; Caitanya Destroys His *Bhāgavata Purāṇa* Commentary; Haridāsa's Liberation

Victory, victory to Lord Caitanya, victory to Sītā's lord,
Victory to Nityānanda Rāma, and their followers.

One night, Mahāprabhu appeared to Rūpa in a dream and very kindly said, "Rūpa, the wonderful drama you have written reveals the divine play of Rādhā and Kṛṣṇa, and the longing in my heart increased with each moment as I listened to that whole beautiful drama."

Lord Caitanya vanished and Rūpa awoke, lost in love, and fainted, but soon that great devotee Rūpa regained consciousness. "Where is Lord Gaurāṅga?" he asked, and wept. After a while he added, "It is difficult to understand your divine play. You have taken birth to expand the hearts of your devotees, and you had the compassion to reveal yourself to your disciples, so you came to me in a dream and commanded me," (and) Rūpa began to dance, jumping up and down like a stick.

Just then Sanātana Gosvāmī arrived. He said, "Rūpa, tell me the good news. I can tell you have been preaching love of Gaura today."

Rūpa said, "Lord, you are absolutely correct. Gaura allowed me to see him in a dream, and spoke to me."

Sanātana said, "This is a tremendously auspicious omen! If you have seen Gaurāṅga (in a dream), you'll certainly see him again."

Rūpa said, "Your word is (absolutely true) like the Vedas. I am going to Purī to see Gaurāṅga," and he prostrated completely before Sanātana. Engrossed in love for Gaura all the way to Purī, he enjoyed the trip, and when he saw Gaurāṅga his eyes flowed with streams of love. He prostrated himself hundreds of times at Caitanya's feet, and Gaura embraced Rūpa warmly.

Rūpa said, "I am the vilest untouchable. Why are you committing the sin of touching me?"

Mahāprabhu said, "You are the best disciple! Your body is like the heavenly Gaṅgā."

Rūpa said, "You are an ocean of compassion. A fraction of your compassion is a mine of everything auspicious. Whoever is lucky enough to touch the

Gaṅgā-nectar of your feet becomes a blessed Vaiṣṇava, like a well of stagnant water upon contact with a *śalagrāma*; you destroy all evil—which is difficult even for the gods."

Mahāprabhu said, "Such flattery!"

Rūpa said, "There was no flattery in what I said."

Gaura told Rāya Rāmānanda and the others of Rūpa's pure dispassion. [Rūpa danced and praised all of Gaura's associates. The Vaiṣṇavas delighted Rūpa.] The bliss of Gaura's associates grew in Rūpa's company. They encircled Lord Gaurāṅga and began to sing the lord's name. In great bliss some sang, some danced, some cried "Gaura!" and wept, intoxicated with divine love. A wave of the ocean of love of Gaura surged forth, and they began to dance and shout "Hare Kṛṣṇa." Sometimes joyous, sometimes transfixed, sometimes breaking out in perspiration, sometimes saying "Lord of my life!" they wept, and thus Lord Kṛṣṇa Caitanya and the devotees blessed the world with a cloud of the nectar of divine love.

After a while they stopped singing the name of Hari, and with Gaura's permission, they all returned to their respective duties.

One day Lord Gaurāṅga and his disciples were sitting and blissfully discussing spiritual topics, when Rūpa Gosvāmī arrived. He prostrated himself completely before Gauracandra, who embraced him and asked him to sit down. He bowed with devotion and sat a bit apart from the group. The great lord Caitanya was omniscient and told Rūpa, "I know what you are thinking. I have heard from the holy men that you have composed a play about Lord Kṛṣṇa. Please present it to the Vaiṣṇavas; I have been eager to hear it."

Rūpa said, "Wherever I am is the lowest place of all; wherever Kṛṣṇa's drama occurs is the highest of all. This fool is as able to disseminate scripture as a wingless bird is able to fly. I would be shy and embarrassed to show what I wrote just for fun, (but) since no one can resist a request from your glorious mouth, please forgive all my faults," and Rūpa recited the play.

Hearing it, the devotees' delight in divine love grew. Sunk in love, they said things like "Rāma, Rāma." "Hearing this play has purified us." "Nowhere has a composition like this been heard, for such is the majesty of the very charming Name of Kṛṣṇa."

In the bliss of divine love Mahāprabhu suggested to Rūpa, "You should divide this play into two parts: *Vidagdha-Mādhava* and *Lalitā-Mādhava*. The mind rejoices at these two names."

The Vaiṣṇavas heard that and cried out "Hari!" The plays came to be known to the world by these two names. By the inconceivable virtues of Lord Gaurāṅga and his friends and associates, the drum of Rūpa's fame was played everywhere, yet Rūpa Gosvāmī's great humility is boundless. Gaurāṅga and his associates were filled with the bliss of divine love.

Rūpa spent several days there. When he saw Jagannātha his delight in divine love increased. Then Mahāprabhu asked him to go to Holy Vraja. He agreed, and left. Brahmā and the other gods cannot describe the limits of the glory of Lord Gaurāṅga and his devotees. When I listened to the holy men my mind was not calm, and so I have remembered only these (few) verses with any certainty.

One day Mahāprabhu was explaining his devotional commentary to the *Bhāgavata (Purāṇa)* to Acyuta, who said, "This commentary is the best of all. There is no need for any other commentary because this one is the essence of all commentaries and provides the most important explanation."

Lord Kṛṣṇa Caitanya responded, "Please heed my command and keep this one secret, since it will undermine the status of many wise men."

Acyuta listened and said with amazement, "I hear what you are asking, but it breaks my heaṛt. The commentary you wrote is the lord of kings of devotion, and every foot of every verse contains a storehouse of love. And yet you have forbidden the dissemination of such a devotional commentary! You have revealed today that the Name is truly an ocean of compassion." He said this, and wept in the bliss of divine love. Gaura sprinkled him with tears of love. Oh! Lord Caitanya's compassion is an extraordinary ocean, the end of which not even the infinite lord Ananta can find. Gaura set aside his own pride to confer happiness on living beings. Kṛṣṇa never took on such humility.

Previously, when Gaura was studying scripture, he had composed a commentary on the treatises on logic. He was crossing the Gaṅgā with that commentary when a brahmin asked him, "Tell me, Sir, have you written any books?"

Lord Gaurāṅga showed him his commentary on logic, and when the brahmin saw it, he wailed, "Alas, alas! My work has all gone to ruin! Once people see this, they will ignore my commentary."

Lord Gaurāṅga responded, "Fear not, O best of brahmins," and compassion rose up from that storehouse of compassion, and he threw his own commentary into the middle of the Gaṅgā. The brahmin reacted joyfully, "No living being could renounce his own interests like that, so you must be an embodiment of Viṣṇu himself. Ten million bows at your feet," and the brahmin departed happily. The earth was filled with the moonlight of Gauracandra's fame.

I know the songs of Lord Caitanya's drama are incomprehensible. I, a worm, am enumerating only a tiny particle of his activities.

Then Śacī's son said to Acyuta, "My right eye is twitching."[27] Acyuta said, "You are full of auspiciousness, and propitious events always occur around you. Probably one of your dear disciples is about to appear, and that is why your eye is twitching."

Just then Sanātana, best of devotees, arrived from Vraja and fell at Gaura's feet. When he saw him, Lord Gaurāṅga said, in the bliss of divine love, "The words of Kṛṣṇa's eternal devotees most certainly come true."

Acyuta said, "You control our hearts, and as the Creator, you preserve living beings in the form of cosmic sound."

[27] An indication of the imminent arrival of a loved one.

When Mahāprabhu heard that, he thought of Viṣṇu. When Sanātana saw Gaura he was covered in divine love. He could not move, broke out with perspiration, his hair stood on end, et cetera, and he bathed Gaura's feet with tears of love. When Gaura stretched out his arms to embrace him, he said, "You have made me a great evildoer. I am a great vile untouchable whose body is a mass of sores and repugnance."

Mahāprabhu said, "Where do you have sores? The body I see is as unblemished as the glow of the sun."

When Sanātana looked down at his own body, he was amazed to see it was disease-free. Acknowledging Lord Kṛṣṇa Caitanya's inconceivable mercy, he raised his arms and began to dance. All the disciples roared with delight, and Mahāprabhu began to sing the lord's name. Some played drums and some played finger cymbals, some laughed and cried with divine love like drunkards. Gradually their chanting the lord's name grew like a wave in the ocean, and Lord Gaurāṅga, engrossed in love, floated on it, sometimes in tears, sometimes trembling, sometimes unconscious, sometimes saying "Hari" and crying, sometimes very humble.

Eventually they stopped singing the lord's name, and Gaura took his disciples and sat down. Then Sanātana asked Gaura, in a soft voice, "Tell me how the eternal dharma compares to (other) religions."

Mahāprabhu said, "You are the greatest of devotees of the lord, conversant in all the scriptures, expert in all knowledge, yet you have asked about spiritual practice. The desires of the wise are not realized (simply) by discussions in good company. The religion of the glorious Vaiṣṇavas is called *sanātana dharma*, the eternal religion. Other religions are secondary religions. The Vedas say that the religion of the glorious Vaiṣṇavas is ever perfect. Śiva preached a secondary religion at Kṛṣṇa's request, and his request was not in vain, but just as traveling along a winding mountain road is difficult, so it took a little while to accomplish Kṛṣṇa's purpose. When one gets Viṣṇu's mantra after many births, as a result of worshiping other gods, his heart becomes purified. Viṣṇu is like a wishing tree with regard to the desires of his disciples, and he gives the gifts of liberation, et cetera, which are very difficult to obtain."

Sanātana said, "I understand your general meaning. The glorious Vaiṣṇava religion is without beginning, most perfect."

Mahāprabhu said, "The glorious Vaiṣṇava religion is the best. Wise men say attachment to the name of Hari is very important." As he revealed many such devotional theories, he delighted Sanātana and the other devotees tremendously.

Shortly thereafter pilgrims began assembling from different areas for Lord Jagannātha's chariot procession. Mahāprabhu's associates—Nityānanda, Advaita, and the other devotees—had traveled from Gauḍa. Gaura was delighted to find his countrymen and asked after each devotee's health. They all bowed to Gaura and blessed him, and Lord Caitanya embraced them all in turn. Then Mahāprabhu bathed in the ocean, king of holy places, with all his devotees, with great delight. He saw the Jagannātha image with his associates, and they all ate consecrated food together. Words cannot describe how much joy there was! I was fortunate enough to see it.

Then the devotees listened as Mahāprabhu described the mood of the *gopīs* of Vraja as best. His stories intoxicated his followers, and they began singing the lord's name with Gaura. Many played drum and hand cymbals; some raised their arms and danced sweetly. Advaita danced well, and they put him in front, and Gaura and Nityānanda were in the middle, dancing as they paraded. The others danced behind them, their hair standing on end. They were so intoxicated with love, their bodies were twitching. They danced so extraordinarily, people were amazed. Everyone sang Hari's virtues like celestial musicians. The disciple-cakoras drank the nectar of the lord's name. Some wept, engrossed in love, some embraced each other; some, maddened and engrossed in ecstasy, laughed wildly. Some were completely overwhelmed with love and collapsed in a faint. The gods were attracted by the extraordinary bliss of their chanting of the lord's name, and so many evil-doers were rescued by the raft of the Name.

On the day of the chariot procession there was a huge festival. I cannot begin to describe it. Mother Subhadrā's chariot went first with Balarāma's chariot right behind it. Thousands and thousands of people were pulling Jagannātha's chariot, but they could not make it budge. All those pilgrims were amazed at this. Mahāprabhu smiled and pulled on a thin rope, and as soon as he touched it, the chariot moved easily. Everyone cried "Hari" with great joy.

Jagannātha Hari performs an extraordinary drama, and whoever sees it is delivered from earthly life. Hari is so kind as to reveal Himself in whatever form one conceives as the true form of Jagannātha, so some see the form of Kṛṣṇa, some see Vāmana, but the Vedas say such a person will not be born again. (On the other hand,) if a person is thinking about illusory matters, he will look right at Kṛṣṇa and not be able to see Him.

There is no end to the divine drama of Lord Jagannātha, and the power of consecrated food is beyond the scope of the gods. If a low-caste person brings food and a brahmin eats it, two kinds of horrible diseases arise immediately. But if even a dog eats consecrated food, the crumbs that fall from its mouth are fit for divine consumption. The virtues of eating consecrated food are inconceivable and indestructible. Not even the infinite Lord Ananta realizes the extent of this. The person who eats only a tiny bit of consecrated food is liberated from all his misdeeds and goes to Vaikuṇṭha. I have heard of no consecrated food as great as that at Purī.

I am such a wretched worm I have no talent; I have just written the tiniest bit.

After the chariot procession, Gaura called his followers together and said, "You have suffered a great deal for my sake, and you keep coming here to Purī; what is the point? You were all born to spread the eternal religion, so stay home and keep disseminating the Name. Spread dharma and fulfill your lives. I have been worshiping for a long time in a secluded place, and all my desires have been fulfilled."

He ordered Nityānanda to get married, and with Gaura's permission, his friends set out for home. Gaura went to a secluded place and remained immersed in love, chanting Hari's name. When he saw his dear disciples he told them the essence of Hari's name. A living being has no other recourse than Hari's name. "Say the Name, think the Name, make the Name your sole recourse. Hari plays with the Name. The Name is Hari Himself; there is no difference, as the Vedas, Purāṇas, et cetera, testify."

Now listen to a story about Brahmā Haridāsa, who recited the Name three hundred thousand times daily. He enjoyed the Name of Hari so much he could see nothing else. This struck all the disciples' minds as wonderful.

Haridāsa knew he was about to be liberated. While he was singing the lord's name, he collapsed. He placed Mahāprabhu's lotus feet on his chest, then gave up his life saying, "Lord Kṛṣṇa Caitanya!"

When Lord Gaurāṅga realized what had happened, he cried "Hari!" loudly. The disciples said, "He was the crest-jewel of holy men." Hari's Name went up in all directions like the breeze, and the chanting of the lord's name began to grow like a wave. Lord Caitanya floated on that ocean of the bliss of divine love, and all the disciples swam in it. Then Gaura constructed Haridāsa's tomb, and he joyously held a great funeral festival. Lord Caitanya Mahāprabhu is an ocean of compassion; I have never heard of such a compassionate embodiment. Gaura is the omnipotent source of all incarnations. The ultimate purpose of his activities is to rescue people. Pure divine love and the Name are difficult even for Brahmā to reach; please do not differentiate between the two.

Ten million bows at the feet of my illustrious guru, Gaurāṅga, by a fraction of whose mercy this beggar has been rescued.

Īśāna Nāgara, whose hopes are at the feet of Lord Caitanya and Lord Advaita, narrates the *Advaita Prakāśa*.

Chapter 20

Nityānanda's Marriage; Advaita's Preaching

Victory, victory to Lord Caitanya, victory to Sītā's lord,
Victory to Nityānanda Rāma, and their followers.

Now hear about the deeds of the lord Nityānanda. He went back to Bengal at Mahāprabhu's request and in due course reached Ambikanagar, where Uddhāraṇa Datta, a favorite of his, served him day and night. He assumed a lovely form which charmed all hearts and astonished even the gods, and everyone insisted, "This is some king's son."

Sūryadāsa Pandit arrived around the same time. He was amazed to see how beautiful Nityānanda was. Sūryadāsa said to him, respectfully, "Where is your home? Tell me your name."

Uddhāraṇa announced, "This is an excellent brahmin, most senior in all the scriptures, from the community of RāṚha. He has the title 'crest-jewel of logicians.' His name is Nityānanda, and he is fully established in the bliss of divine love."

The wise Sūryadāsa heard that (and) said, happily, "Come to my place to rest." Nityānanda heard and smiled, and went to his house, where the brahmin fed him attentively.

The beautiful women of the village came in swarms. Everyone saw how handsome Nityānanda was and admired him. The women said to Suryadāsa's wife, "He would be a suitable groom for your daughters." Sūryadāsa had two Lakṣmī-like daughters, Vasudhā and Jāhnavī, who were unrivaled in beauty and virtue. That revered Kākudmī Sūryadāsa Pandit was adorned by a wife who was chaste and virtuous. She said, "You people bless us. Who would not want to give his daughters to a good groom? But I do not know if that is the pandit's desire. If he consents, then I will agree."

Then when the great scholar Sūryadāsa approached them, the women said, "He will be pleased about this. The two daughters in your house are ready for marriage, and God has kindly sent a groom. Look and listen and tell us what you think."

The scholar said, "I will consider all your opinions," (and) went outside. He brought his kinsmen to his house and addressed them all respectfully. "Tell me what you think about giving my daughters to the visitor."

Everyone said, "We do not know where his home is, and no intelligent person would pay attention to a person of unknown lineage and character. It is not easy to find a groom worth giving one's daughter to. Dakṣa gave his daughter to Śiva and got a goat's head." They discussed various matters in this way. Nityānanda understood that, and left.

My lord Nityānanda set out for the bank of the Gaṅgā. Gaurīdāsa recognized him, even lost in ecstasy. He bowed to Nityānanda and said, "Your drama has countless millions of scenes." When he heard that, the lord roared with laughter and continued on to the bank of the Gaṅgā, but Gaurīdāsa was concerned about how despondent he was.

Gaurīdāsa Pandit, counted among Kṛṣṇa's dear companions in Vraja, was no ordinary man. My lord Advaita said that he had been the cowherd Subala who knew all of Rādhā-Kṛṣṇa's secret activities. Now Rādhā and Kṛṣṇa have taken birth in Nadīyā, and the female associates have come as supporting actors in the drama.

Mahāprabhu's intimate devotee Gaurīdāsa always used to enjoy chanting the lord's name with Gaura and would never stay at home unless Gaura and Nitāi were there. His friends told Mahāprabhu, "Tell this boy to get married. Everyone is happy if he stays in his own house."

Mahāprabhu said, "Good, I will do that. If he is happy and can stay home, no one will worry."

But that evening Pandit Gaurīdāsa brought a flower garland to Mahāprabhu and put the garland around Lord Gaurāṅga's neck. Stammering with love, he prostrated himself. This aroused Gaura's pure emotions of Vraja, and he took him in his arms, saying, "Come, my dearest friend." Gaurīdāsa wiped the tears flowing ceaselessly from Gaura's eyes with his own garment. Lord Gauracandra sank in the deep ocean of Rādhā's emotions and did not emerge for three hours, when he regained consciousness and took Gaurīdāsa's hands and danced. Nityānanda and the others roared with love, and all the devotees sang the lord's name together. A great outpouring of song and dance ensued; I cannot describe one bit of it.

After the chanting Gaura and Nitāi sat down and summoned Gaurīdāsa privately. Mahāprabhu said, "Listen, Dearer-than-life. Get married and stay at home."

Gaurīdāsa said, "Your order is the essence of the Vedas, and a person would be most wicked to ignore it. But I cannot live without you; I would feel like a fish without water."

Gaura listened and smiled and looked at Nityānanda, who said, "Construct an image of Gaura."

Gaura said, "One image by itself is not very beautiful. Set up an image of Nityānanda too, and then you will always be able to see us both. But don't tell anyone else these secret utterances of mine."

When Gaurīdāsa heard, he was filled with the bliss of divine love and bowed at the feet of Gaura and Nityānanda. Gaurīdāsa was a most skillful artisan. The best artisans among the gods do not know such craftsmanship. He placed Gaura and Nityānanda before him and joyfully constructed the wooden images of the two brahmins. The bliss of divine love lights up the living being who merely looks at those perfect images of Gaura and Nityānanda.

Then Gaura and Nitāi embraced Gaurīdāsa and went elsewhere to spread the Name and the love. Gaurīdāsa went to consult with my lord Advaita about consecrating those two images. He bowed at the feet of Sītānātha, who earnestly asked him the news. "Child, why have you come here?"

Gaurīdāsa told him the story from beginning to end.

The lord said, "Child, you are most blessed! You have constructed images of Gaura and Nityānanda. I will consecrate them—that is my good fortune. You prepare the necessary materials."

Acyuta heard him and said, with hands joined in supplication, "Father, please permit me to go to Ambikanagar. Which mantra should I use for the worship? Please tell me the truth, do not hide it."

Sītānātha smiled and said, "If you do not know that, then know this: Kṛṣṇa Himself has taken birth in Nadīyā. He has covered his entire body with Rādhā's physical beauty, so that his form would look different because of the covering of that clothing. I have discovered that Mahāprabhu will be worshiped with the ten-syllable Gopāla mantra.[28] Worship Rādhā because she is the covering over Kṛṣṇa and your worship will be successful, there is no doubt. Nityānanda will be worshiped with the Nārāyaṇa mantra,[29] and this worship will succeed and we will find joy."

Acyuta listened and politely said, "I will certainly do as you request. But Narahari Sarakāra Ṭhākura, the great scholar who lives in Khanda, who is a vessel of divine love, counted as an intimate devotee of Lord Caitanya, whom the holy men call an eternal handmaiden of Kṛṣṇa, told me something different about worshiping Gaura. Tell me the reason for this, my lord."

The lord said, "In the ocean of love which is Lord Kṛṣṇa Caitanya all worship according to devotion is possible. Kṛṣṇa's firm promise to his followers is that Kṛṣṇa worships them in the way they worship him."

When he heard that, Acyuta became intoxicated with bliss and went to Ambikanagar with Gaurīdāsa. The two images were consecrated with great pomp, and Gaurīdāsa held a great festival in the bliss of divine love. Gaurīdāsa was very dear to all the worshipers whose love for Mahāprabhu and the two lords was intense.

I am a miserable creature; how can I understand this mystery? I just write the gist of it because Acyuta asked me to.

Now Lord Nityānanda was sitting on the bank of the Gaṅgā laughing and talking with Uddhāraṇa, when a desolate Sūryadāsa came to the bank of the Gaṅgā carrying Vasudhā's dead body. People were about to cremate her, when the lord Nityānanda approached and said to Sūryadāsa, "Promise me you will give me this girl if I can revive her."

When Sūryadāsa heard, he said to his friends, "If he revives the girl, I promise I will give her to him."

Nityānanda's heart rejoiced when he heard that, and he whispered the Name which restores the dead to life in her ear. As soon as she drank the nectar of Hari's Name, Vasudhā stood up. Everyone was amazed at this supernatural business. Sūryadāsa happily took his daughter and went home, and all the people cried "Hari" in great bliss. Some said of Nityānanda, "He is a great sage," but some said "I think he is a god in disguise." Sūryadāsa recognized the signs in Lord Nityānanda (and) took him home, overwhelmed with divine love. Considering himself most fortunate, he joyfully gave Nityānandacandra his daughter, with great pomp, so the lord Nityānanda married Vasudhā Devī and took Jāhnavī with her as dowry. Then he went and settled in Khaḍadaha village and revealed the worship of the Śyāmasundara (form of Kṛṣṇa).

At an auspicious time after Mahāprabhu disappeared, Mother Vasudhā gave birth to a son. This son of Nityānanda's was always happy and was known to the

[28] *Gopījana vallabhāya svaha.*

[29] *Om namo Nārāyaṇāya.*

world as Vīracandra. People were enchanted as soon as they saw the beauty of him whom my lord called Saṁkarṣaṇa. I heard this from the holy men, and also saw a few things. I am just revealing a little bit of the gist of it.

Meanwhile, Lord Advaita was crying, "Where is the lord of my life?" and weeping at separation from Gaurāṅga. Gradually a wave of the ocean of love of Gaura grew, and Sītānātha, wish-fulfilling tree of the devotees, floated on it. Three hours later the lord floated up out of it, wanting to see Gaurāṅga. "O Gaurāṅga! You have effortlessly burned the hearts and souls of your disciples in the fire of eternal separation. You appeared to spread devotion, but I caused you mental anguish by disseminating intellectual knowledge. I got to see you once by expounding intellectual scholarship (over devotion), so now I will teach dry scholarship again to everyone, and let's see how you react to that. If I do not get to see your feet, I will destroy the world."

With that thought he called his students and gave them a lecture on intellectual yoga, in gentle words. "Scholars say that intellectual knowledge is greater than devotion, and that intellectual knowledge arises after the last stage of devotion. Those who worship God according to intellectual knowledge are liberated from worldly existence in a divine flower chariot. The ancient sages obtained liberation and devotion according to their respective desires through the yoga that comes through intellectual activity."

He gave many such sermons on scholarship, and his students accepted their guru's words. But even though my lord was preaching scholarship with his mouth, he was worshiping Kṛṣṇa twice as much as required. With deep devotion he offered Kṛṣṇa tulasī and placed various kinds of sweets and foods before him, and he closed his eyes and thought of Gaurāṅga. Gaura's associates could not understand what he was doing, and surrounded him, weeping.

Śacī's son was omniscient and understood what was in his followers' hearts, so he knew Advaita was teaching (the supremacy of) monistic liberation and rushed to Advaita's house from Purī to fulfill the desires of his disciple.

When Sītānātha caught the fragrance of Gaura's body, he looked up and saw before him the shining feet of the living Jagannātha, lord of the universe. When he saw Caitanya's incomprehensible mercy to his followers, the glorious Advaita praised him humbly, with great love. He prostrated one hundred times at Gaurāṅga's feet and said, "No one in the three worlds is as fortunate as I."

Gaura said, "You are the eternal-devotee-embodiment. You heralded me (into this world) with your pure devotion, so your work is actually greater than mine. I have appeared before you to satisfy your desire." Then in accord with the master's desire, Gaura joyfully ate the various offerings. After the feast he chewed *pan* and scolded Lord Advaita in a gentle voice, "You were teaching the path of intellectual scholarship in order to see me, but you did not consider the future distress of these people (whom you have misled). If you feel like seeing me, just think of me and I will appear. No more talk of scholarship is to come from your mouth! You teach pure devotion and rescue living beings."

Lord Advaita said, "I have been blessed as I had wished. Now please forgive me."

Mahāprabhu said, "Disciples have ten million misdeeds, yet Kṛṣṇa bestows his grace by showing mercy and forgiving them."

Just then Mother Sītā arrived, and when she saw Gaura, she drowned in the amazing bliss of divine love and burst out crying and took Gaura in her arms. Gaura said, "Mother, I am very thirsty." When she heard that, Sītā brought milk and Gaṅgā water and lovingly put them in Gaurāṅga's mouth. He joyfully drank all that ambrosia, et cetera. Gaura consoled the couple and then disappeared. Sītā and Advaita both meditated on Gaura's compassion and remained intoxicated on divine love all day.

Then at twilight, my lord restrained his love and summoned his students and said, "Listen, everyone. Before, I said that intellectual knowledge is best, but now I have thought about it and changed my mind, and realize devotion has no equal. I know Īśvara is to be found through scholarship, and we can find him through devotion; devotion is better than intellectual scholarship; many scriptures proclaim this. You surely know that liberation is the final step of scholarship; egoism arises from intellectual knowledge of liberation. A liberated egoist does not worship Kṛṣṇa, and because of his offense he will drown repeatedly in the cycle of *saṃsāra*. So the yoga of devotion is the best of all, and one who sets out on the path of devotion cannot fall. Not even the infinite lord Ananta can understand the extent of the glory of devotion. Scriptures prove that the maidservant of the goddess of devotion is liberation. Worship Lord Kṛṣṇa through faithful devotion, and your worldly ties will effortlessly be cut."

He gave many such sermons on devotion. They all, except for three students, took up the devotional path. Kāmadeva Nāgara, Agala Pāgala, and one other did not accept the master's words and said, "Listen, Master, there is no end to your sermons. Sometimes you say scholarship is greater, sometimes devotion is greater. We have firmly decided on the path of intellectual scholarship."

My lord said, "If you do not heed my request I will renounce you and never see you again." When he said that, they went east, and Advaita Ācārya let them go.

Ten million bows to the participants in Gaura's activities. They saw Gaura's activities, which were not of this world, because of their devotion. Lord Gaurāṅga performed his eternal drama among his followers, and it appeared only to those most fortunate who could see with the eyes of pure devotion. The Lord Advaita blessed me profusely, and I have proclaimed just a bit of his divine drama.

Īśāna Nāgara, whose hopes are at the feet of Lord Caitanya and Lord Advaita, narrates the *Advaita Prakāśa*.

Chapter 21

Caitanya's Disappearance; Advaita's Will

Victory, victory to Lord Caitanya, victory to Sītā's lord,
Victory to Nityānanda Rāma, and their followers.

One day Mahāprabhu was sitting in an isolated place talking with his dear friend Jagadānanda. "Please go quickly to Bengal. First, go to my birthplace in Nadīyā and convey ten million bows to my mother's feet. Wherever I may be, I am her slave. I am her son but I cannot carry out my filial obligations, so I have become a great sinner as far as she is concerned. I will not be able to repay my debt to her for ten million ages unless by the nectar of her own compassion she forgives me. Only then will I be saved; otherwise I am lost. I have taken refuge at her lotus feet. (And) give my regards to Kṛṣṇa's devotees, especially to Master Advaita."

Jagadānanda complied with Mahāprabhu's request and, bowing to Gauracandra, set out for Bengal and soon arrived in blessed Navadvīpa. He went to Mother Śacī and prostrated himself at her feet and presented Lord Gaurāṅga's humble message. When Śacī heard (the message), she blessed him again and again. Lord Jagadānanda, a jewel among Gaura's followers, attended on Mother Śacī in various ways.

He gave the disciples Lord Gaurāṅga's report, and those pure men became intoxicated with love when they heard the news. Some said, "Alas, Gaurāṅga, why did you become a renunciate? Why did you grant us the shelter of your feet and then (leave us and) make us drown in sorrow?" (But) some said, "I have been greatly blessed for in his mercy beloved Gaura has remembered me."

Their sorrow saddened Jagadānanda, and he departed for Shantipur, where he bowed at Advaita's feet. Advaita embraced him lovingly and had him sit in a place of honor, and lovingly asked after Gaurāṅga's health.

Then Jagadānanda told him about Gaura: "Lord Kṛṣṇa Caitanya is always drunk on love. Sometimes he calls out 'Rādhā, Rādhā' and is despondent, and sometimes he shouts thunderously 'Where is the lord of my life?' At that sound everyone's hearts melt." When he heard (that report), my lord became intoxicated on pure divine love.

Alas, there is no other topic of conversation but Lord Gaurāṅga. Advaita remained in a trance for three hours and then roared loudly for another three hours. Sometimes he would laugh aloud, sometimes he would weep, and he would just keep saying "revealed; concealed." Many other similar emotions arose, but I am just a miserable creature who cannot describe them. I have just written what I saw; I am just like a parrot who sings what it is taught; I do not understand what it means.

Advaita treated the scholar with respectful hospitality. They spent the night discussing Gaura's virtues, and at dawn, Jagadānanda politely took his leave of

Lord Advaita. Advaita Ācārya recited a riddle with clues that no one but Gaura could understand and said, "Lord Gaurāṅga is the treasure of my life. This is dedicated to his reddened feet:

> Tell the madman that people have become mad,
> Tell the madman they do not sell rice in the market.
> Tell the madman there is no anxiety about the work;
> And tell the madman this is what the madman has said."[30]

When he heard the riddle, my lord Jagadānanda smiled slightly. Advaita saluted him, and he set out for Purī, reaching there a few days later.

When Jagadānanda saw Gaura, his eyes flowed with love. He prostrated himself completely before Lord Caitanya, who lifted Jagadānanda up and embraced him.

After some time, Jagadānanda joined his palms in supplication and said, "Your disciples in Nadīyā are well. Mother Śacī's affection is unequaled. She is worshiping the gods for your welfare and asks blessings from the holy men and blesses them herself with raised arms. And what more can I tell you about Mother Viṣṇupriyā? I was amazed when I saw her faith and devotion. She serves Mother Śacī in many ways; one thousand and one people could not do as well. Every day at dawn she and Mother Śacī bathe in the Gaṅgā and return home, and they never go out at night. Neither the sun nor the moon can see their faces. All your followers go to your house for consecrated food and cannot see them, except for their feet. No one can hear the sounds of their voices, but tears are always flowing on their sad lotus faces. Viṣṇupriyā eats only the remnants left in Śacī's cooking pot; she remains alive only to take care of her. When she finishes serving Śacī she sits in a secluded place ceaselessly reciting the Name. That crest-jewel of virtuous women whose body was full of pure love has a great affection for the nectar of the Name of Hari. She has deep faith in your feet, and by her mercy I learned her news. She has painted a picture of you and installed it with the great mantra of love and devotion. She worships that image in private, offering herself to your lotus feet. Not even the infinite lord Ananta could recite her virtues, and I only have one mouth, so how can I tell you anything?"

Mahāprabhu said, "Say nothing more about this. Tell me the news of the master in Shantipur."

Jagadānanda told him that Advaita Ācārya was well and then recited the allegorical riddle. Lord Caitanya listened to the riddle and smiled and said, "I am supposed to consider that my dismissal," and became motionless. Rūpa and the other devotees asked him, "Mahāprabhu, tell us the meaning of this riddle, for none of us can understand it."

[30] Translation Dimock's, 981.

Lord Gaurāṅga said, "That Advaita Ācārya has realized Kṛṣṇa; that is a superhuman feat. He has bound Svayaṃ Bhavagān with the rope of his love. The unmanifest Kṛṣṇa appeared because of Advaita's desire. Who can understand the meaning of his riddle? He understands its meaning; no one else does."

He told the wise men, "He is the best of gods, the wishing-tree of devotion, and is worthy of the world's worship."

When Caitanya's followers heard this, they marveled. From that day on, Gaura's demeanor changed. He burned with Rādhā's divine intoxication and wept, crying, "O Lord, O Kṛṣṇa." Lost in great ecstasy, he did not know day from night. His followers became alarmed.

One day Gaura went to see Jagannātha and entered the temple crying out "O Lord!" As soon as he entered, the doors closed by themselves. A serious apprehension arose in the minds of the followers. A little later the gates opened by themselves, and everyone realized that Gaurāṅga had disappeared. Caitanya had vanished and was not among the worshipers, and the realized souls among them made a great lamentation that burned the bodies, hearts, and souls of all living beings like Rudra's mighty radiant fire. Lord Gaurāṅga's activities are a vast ocean, and not even Ananta can describe a single current of it. I am far viler than the vilest worm and in my divine bliss am just presenting a tiny bit of its meaning.

Now, Advaita Ācārya, lost in an ecstasy not of this world, realized that Mahāprabhu had disappeared. Advaita fell into a state of divine madness and had no external awareness. He called out "Nimāi, Nimāi!" Sometimes he would say, "Oh, Nimāi, you have brought your book. I have household responsibilities, I am sweeping, I have already taught (class)." Sometimes he would say, "I know your tricks. Whose mood have you taken on, Gaura? Tell me what you have seen and heard." Sometimes he would say, "Nimāi, you stay at my house. Mother Śacī will be sad if you go away." Sometimes he would say, "Gaura, you are the Creator's creator. In this Kali Age you have become the instigator of chanting the Name of the Lord." Sometimes he would say, "You have hidden the essence of Vraja in Vraja. I cannot find it. What is this trick you are playing?"

He raved incoherently like this and after quite a while regained consciousness. He cried out "Hari, Hari!" and everyone said, "Now he is heartsick."

Who can understand this pure ecstasy? Only pure devotees understand, in their hearts. I, the vilest worm, do not have a glimmer of understanding and have only managed to reveal the gist of what I saw.

One day Sītānātha was sitting outside calling the names "Hare Kṛṣṇa" with joy in his heart. A devotee from Purī approached, and when Advaita saw him, he seated him respectfully. People say he shed tears and very eagerly asked after Gaurāṅga's health. The Vaiṣṇava said, "You should know the news about Caitanya. Rumor has it that he has disappeared."

When he heard that, Advaita was completely at a loss. "I knew it, I knew it," he said, and fainted. Much later he regained consciousness. Advaita experienced so many emotions, they cannot be described. Sometimes in a stupor, sometimes roaring, sometimes going in circles, sometimes saying "Gaura, Gaura," he shouted and wept. Mother Sītā came when she heard the sobbing, and when she heard the reason for it, she fainted. Much later Sītā Devī regained consciousness and wailed "Caitanya!" and wept profusely.

Acyuta wept and Kṛṣṇadāsa wept; the despondent Gopāladāsa wept. These three were intimate with Gaura and so were the purest disciples among Sītā's sons.

No one could possibly describe everyone's distress. I am just describing a tiny particle of the meaning.

Advaita was unaware of the passage of day and night, and he and his entire family abstained from eating. The next day Advaita held a great feast and served many brahmins and Vaiṣṇavas. He fed hundreds and hundreds of poor people and gave away a mountain of clothing. A pure stream of Hari *saṅkīrtana* floated away on the waters of the Gaṅgā that was Shantipur toward the ocean of divine love. How many villagers and their families bathed in its waves!

From that day on, Advaita Ācārya, the great lord of yoga, meditated ceaselessly on the form of Lord Gaurāṅga. Mahāprabhu came in a dream and said to Advaita, "Nāḍha, don't be sad about our separation. Your love has drawn me to come back to your house, so you will see me as Kṛṣṇa Miśra's son. Some time later you will find Lord Nityānanda in your own house as the (second) son of your dearest son Kṛṣṇadāsa. I will appear again to satisfy the desire of your dearest son, that eternal disciple engaged in serving me, who always delights in me in his heart."

My lord marveled at such an amazing dream. That day Kṛṣṇa Miśra's son was born, the image of Lord Gaurāṅga, charmer of the world. When Advaita saw his beauty he became intoxicated with divine love. An embodiment of love whose eyes filled with tears when he heard Gaura's virtues, his name was Raghunātha. Then, in due course, on Kṛṣṇa's *dola-pūrṇimā*, the day of the Swing Festival, Kṛṣṇa Miśra's second son was born: the image of Nityānanda, ocean of compassion, who spoke endlessly of Gaurāṅga's glory. My lord named him Dola Govinda. When the disciples heard, they cried out the sound "Hari" with love.

One day Lord Advaita called his sons together. He spoke to them privately with very sweet words. "Sons, all of you must resolve firmly to remember the essence of the obligations of a householder, the evening prayers and the five obligatory sacrifices. The person who always does these is very wise. Do not covet another's wife or property, or you will suffer in the next life. Be compassionate to every creature, do not harm them. Do not malign holy men, (but) praise them. Install the sacred tulasī plant in the courtyard of the house. A house without tulasī is like a cremation ground. Daily singing of the name of Hari is most important. By atoning for one's misdeeds, one escapes Yama the god of death, so refute wickedness and always associate with holy men. One should certainly strive for devotion to Kṛṣṇa. And remember one more thing: do not do anything (solely) for your own pleasure. If you manage your life for the sake of serving Kṛṣṇa, you will accrue neither sin nor merit for your actions. The desire for acting according to one's desires increases steadily; that is how an embodied soul comes and goes in the world, so you should always avoid acting according to your desires. If you make Kṛṣṇa your goal, he will fulfill your desires."

He gave many similar sermons. Acyuta and the others delighted in hearing them. Acyuta, Kṛṣṇa Miśra, and Gopāladāsa: these three always have their delight in serving Kṛṣṇa. Acyuta always has a deep attachment to Kṛṣṇa and the Vaiṣṇavas and is completely indifferent to the world.

My lord began to worship Kṛṣṇa with various offerings, and a wave swelled up on the Gaṅgā of love. Even though the hearts of (all) three are absorbed in Kṛṣṇa, my lord decided to bequeath the (official) worship to Kṛṣṇa Miśra.

"The ascetic Kṛṣṇa Miśra is full of pure devotion, so I think he is a suitable candidate for Kṛṣṇa's service."

Lābhā's son said to Acyuta, "Listen, Acyuta, my son, to what I say. You are my eldest son, first among the Vaiṣṇavas. I have been blessed to have gotten a son like you, for you are most pious, a Bṛhaspati with respect to scripture, crest-jewel of the righteous, very pure-minded. You have been indifferent to the world from childhood, only interested in the great treasure of dispassion, so you rejected marriage. You have attached no importance to the pleasures of the senses, which most people love. Thus I cannot take you away from worship and service of the holy image; I realize that. Kṛṣṇa Miśra, your junior, attached to gods and brahmins, is a great Vaiṣṇava; a good scholar, wise, a storehouse of devotion, crest-jewel of lovers, always conducting himself properly, always accepting my opinion, obedient to me. His heart is with Gaura, so he is a favorite of Gaura's. He got married and is in that (householder) stage of life, and I think he is suitable for serving Kṛṣṇa. Moreover, Kṛṣṇadāsa has two very righteous sons who are attached to Lord Gaurāṅga. Both the elder, Raghunātha, and the younger, Dola Govinda, delight tremendously in serving Kṛṣṇa. One day Raghunātha said to me, 'How can Veda Vyāsa's words be true? The eighty-four hells are full in this Kali Age. Lord Kṛṣṇa Caitanya has blocked that path by rescuing living beings with the great mantra of Hari's Name. Listen and tell me how many souls it takes to fill hell.'

"Dola Govinda heard that, and smiled and said, 'It will be filled with all those wicked people who hate Gaura.'

"When I heard such words I marveled, and from that moment I knew that these two are divine embodiments. My Kṛṣṇadāsa is blessed, blessed are his sons. A relative of mine who worships Gaurāṅga is authorized to serve Madana Gopāla, my life's treasure, and therefore I want to offer the responsibility for this worship to Kṛṣṇa Miśra; what is your desire?"

Acyuta happily joined his palms in prayer and replied, "My heart will accept whatever you command."

Then Lord Advaita said to Kṛṣṇa Miśra, "Madana Gopāla is the lord of my life. Always serve Him with devotion and do not neglect Him; worship Him daily. I know the atheists and wicked people are opposed; renunciates, nondualists, yogis, and intellectuals; enjoyers of sense pleasures and liberation have no desire for devotion. We consider those who have turned away from Kṛṣṇa to be non-Vaiṣṇavas. I will tell you what I mean by 'turned away from Kṛṣṇa': those Vaiṣṇavas who have no sectarian affiliation (and members of) those sects who do not respect Gaurāṅga. Listen to one more thing, Kṛṣṇadāsa. Those among our own people whose hearts are hard ignore my requests and do not respect Gaura. Gaurāṅga is my lord, I am his servant. My five senses are the dust of his feet. Gaura is the lord of my life, Gaura is the object of my worship. Those who do not respect Gaurāṅga are objects of my contempt. No vile-hearted people who have turned away from Kṛṣṇa are ever fit to serve the image of Lord Kṛṣṇa. A proper son preserves the true religion of his ancestors, according to the Vedas."

And after he said that, he eagerly offered the image of Lord Madana Gopāla to Kṛṣṇa Miśra. Kṛṣṇa Miśra was overjoyed to accept Kṛṣṇa's service and prostrated himself at Advaita's lotus feet. With humble praise he bowed at his mother's feet, and Sītā and Advaita both blessed him. Then he humbly bowed to Acyuta.

Acyuta said, "I am dumbfounded by your good fortune. Kṛṣṇa wanted to give you his mercy. He revealed that desire through his own followers, just as Kṛṣṇa revealed the Vedas through Brahmā," and he embraced Kṛṣṇa Miśra.

Gopāla said, "Kṛṣṇa is full of great compassion. By his mercy you will make our lineage prosper, in the same way that the branches, leaves, et cetera, benefit when you water the base of a tree, et cetera." Saying "Oh, such luck!" he bowed to Kṛṣṇa Miśra.

Kṛṣṇa Miśra embraced him warmly, and then the master's very zealous sons Balarāma and Jagadīśa consulted their own companions, and very defiantly had an image of Kṛṣṇa brought. They consecrated and installed that glorious image and held a great festival with their own associates.

Lord Advaita's drama is an ocean difficult to cross; I have disseminated only a drop of its meaning.

Īśāna Nāgara, whose hopes are at the feet of Lord Caitanya and Lord Advaita, narrates the *Advaita Prakāśa*.

Chapter 22

Nityānanda's Disappearance and Advaita's Disappearance; Īśāna Nāgara's Story

Victory, victory to Lord Caitanya, victory to Sītā's lord,
Victory to Nityānanda Rāma, and their followers.

The two lords were deeply distraught and missed Mahāprabhu after he had disappeared, and they wept. I saw the whole situation with my own eyes. I am a contemptible worm, powerless to write about it. These two were constantly in the same state as the *gopīs* of Vraja, deprived of Kṛṣṇa. They always stayed at home and never ate anything, crying for days at a time. Inconsolable in the anguish of separation, they were unaware of anything else. They constantly called out "Alas Gaurāṅga!" One day felt like one hundred aeons. My heart melted when I saw the condition of these two, whose only inner joy was in the name of Gaurāṅga. Eight years passed like this.

One day when Lord Advaita was in Shantipur lovingly recounting Gaura's virtues, he started to become agitated, when a letter arrived from Khaḍadaha. Lord Nityānanda had written asking the scholar to come. As soon as Advaita got the letter, he set out and presented himself immediately at Nityānanda's house. Nityānanda and Advaita embraced each other with great joy when they met. They drowned in love, shouting "Gaura" and weeping. After a while they both regained their senses and went to sit together in a secluded place, where they remained alone for seven consecutive nights. No one knows whether they conversed or not, but on the eighth day, Lord Advaita emerged in a wonderful mood and sang the name of Gaura with the disciples. Nityānanda danced in their midst and fainted from love, meditating on Lord Gaurāṅga's lotus feet. These great ones were so deep in divine love that they forgot the outside world, and Nityānanda disappeared unseen. When they recovered consciousness, none of the great ones could see Nityānanda, and they looked for him.

My lord Advaita, knower of all truth, realized that Nityānanda was beyond their reach. He cried out "Alas" like a drunkard and said, "Why have you brought about such a calamity? Here I am, practically dead from the terrible separation from Gauracandra, I am so depressed. I am still alive, and I want to see you. If you leave me, then where can I go?" My lord babbled on like this. I cannot write a drop of it.

The disciples found out about Nityānanda's disappearance and cried, "Where is Nityānanda?" Lord Vīrabhadra wept and rolled in the dust. Lord Advaitacandra consoled everyone and made preparations for a great funeral feast, sending word to their followers everywhere. All the prominent Vaiṣṇavas came at the appointed time, and delight was again kindled in Khaḍadaha. On the day of the great festival Advaita Ācārya bathed, and everyone began to sing the name of the Lord together. Members of the seven schools[31] played fourteen drums; hundreds and hundreds played finger cymbals very sweetly. One by one the people in each group danced, and Kubera's son danced with each group. I saw that sublime singing of the Lord's

[31] Gauḍīya Vaiṣṇavism had already become factionalized under the separate leadership of Acyuta, Vīracandra, Gaurīdāsa, Narihari Sarakāra, Kṛṣṇa Miśra, Gopāla Ṭhākura, and Dāmodara Pandit. These seven will come with their disciples to the great festival Advaita will convene, later in the text.

name with my own eyes, but I dare not write about it for fear of being charged with exaggeration. After the chanting, all the Vaiṣṇavas reminisced about Gaurāṅga's activities. Then Vīrabhadra carefully arranged three seats side by side and brought three feasts and placed them there.

Then he began to speak to Lord Advaita: "I have one wish of you," he said. "Gosvāmī, please fulfill this boy's desire. Please eat at my house today just like Mahāprabhu and you two lords used to sit together to eat; these miserable eyes would be satisfied by seeing that."

All the leaders agreed that this was a good idea. Then my lord went to set out the feast. First he set out Lord Mahāprabhu's food, and then he fed Nityānanda on Mahāprabhu's right. My lord himself sat at Gaurāṅga's left, and when the Vaiṣṇavas saw that, they cried "Hari!"

Vīracandra performed the *ārati* for the meal. He lit incense and lamps and gazed upon the moon of his face. All the Vaiṣṇava leaders, who displayed the nine types of dispassion, worshiped Gaurāṅga and sang the name of the lord. Whether this extraordinary beauty was the cause of the bliss, how could a dimwit like me describe it all?

Vīracandra raised his arms in the midst of the assembly and said, "Listen to one word of mine, all you Vaiṣṇavas. Whenever anyone holds a great feast, he should place food before the three lords like this. Afterward, carefully take that consecrated food and offer it to holy men, brahmins, and Vaiṣṇavas. Feeding the three lords is like performing a great sacrifice, and a home is blessed when the three lords are fed. Lord Caitanya, Nityānanda, Advaita Gosvāmī; in the three is one; all three are in one; there is no difference or separation. The person who differentiates among the three will never reach the feet of Caitanya. One cannot get love and devotion without Gaura's mercy, and this difficult-to-obtain birth will have been in vain. The sacrifices of anyone who does not feed the three lords at a feast will be like Dakṣa's sacrifice and will not succeed. He will not be able to profit from distributing food, and his sacrifice will be completely ruined and will go to the dogs. He will live in hell in his next life, and as long as the sun and moon remain, he will not be released."

I heard everything just as Vīracandra said it. All the Vaiṣṇavas said, "So be it, so be it." Then my lord ate and got up to rinse his mouth and offer *pan* to the others. Vīracandra happily transformed the offering into consecrated food and presented it (to those gathered). The brahmins, Vaiṣṇavas, holy men, and all the leaders, et cetera, who got that consecrated food considered themselves to have accomplished their life's goals. After the feast, Vīracandra got my lord's permission and happily made preparations to worship him. He mixed turmeric with milk in a new pot and decorated it with young mango leaves, then covered it with new clothes and set it before Advaita. At my lord's request he honored Lord Acyutānanda and sang the lord's name. All of Gaura's associates blessed the milk and danced in the mood of the Gokula *gopīs*. I could not see the end of the joy that occurred, but I am just writing a fraction of its meaning, to purify my soul.

After the feast everyone went home, and my lord Advaita took us all back to Shantipur. But after he came home, Advaita became depressed and would say nothing but "Hare Kṛṣṇa." One day, Advaita Ācārya asked me, a worm, to go find out the news from Navadvīpa and return to Shantipur. When I returned I prostrated myself at his feet and he said, "Īśāna Dāsa, tell me the news."

I told him, "The residents of Navadvīpa are all very depressed about Gaurāṅga's disappearance. Fortunately, I got to see Pandit Dāmodara, who asked, 'Where is he? Has he come? When he disappeared, Mother Viṣṇupriyā's and Śacī Devī's doors closed of their own accord, because of their devotion. She has taken on such a strict vow, no one can see her without her permission. She bathes at dawn, after performing her daily prayers. She says Hari's name, and with each repetition she takes one grain of rice from the earthen pot. In this way she takes the name in the third three-hour period of the day. After reciting the Name she eats only that amount of rice. Then she wraps a cloth over her mouth and cooks carefully. She eats only unsalted uncooked food, but she feeds Mahāprabhu and pleads with him. Wailing in various ways, she rinses his mouth, and she herself eats only a handful of consecrated food. She distributes the rest of it to his followers. Who could undertake such a harsh vow?'

"These words struck me like a thunderbolt, and I thought about how I might be able to see Mother. Just then Gadādhara Dāsa, Rāma Pandit, and the other excellent disciples came. They all went inside with Dāmodara to take consecrated food, with tears in their eyes. Then, at Mother Viṣṇupriyā's request, the scholar took me inside. When I went in, I saw Mother's body hidden by the curtain; by great good fortune I was able to see only her blessed feet. By the disciples' grace I got a little consecrated food. I considered my life's purpose accomplished, and my depression lifted. What further can I say about the hardships Mother suffered? Who could have endured them without divine powers?"

When my lord heard that, he wept. Considering it Kṛṣṇa's wish, he restrained his grief. It breaks my heart to describe Mother Viṣṇupriyā's condition, which I saw with my own eyes; I cannot write about her.

A few days later, Sītānātha was sitting in the courtyard reading the *Bhāgavata Purāṇa*, when a pure Vaiṣṇava came and prostrated himself before my lord. Advaita said to him, "Now, where have you come from?"

He said, "Lord Vīracandra sent me. He is now twenty years old and is uninitiated and lacks a suitable guru. He hopes to get a mantra from you so he is coming in a boat, bent on true knowledge."

Advaita Ācārya said, "This idea of Vīra's is not right. It is counter to the sanctions of his own people. You have understood what I am saying; go tell Vīra to get his mantra from his mother Jāhnavī."

The Vaiṣṇava heard that and went to Khaḍadaha and told Jāhnavī about my lord's request. When Jāhnavī heard, she sent for a holy man, and when he was brought, he initiated Vīra.

Now hear about the disappearance of Lord Advaita. It breaks my heart to write about it. One day Advaita was enrapt in great ecstasy, wandering around asking, "Where is Nimāi?" The master's trance lasted for quite a while, and then he summoned his dear sons and said, "Children, listen to my sorrows. My mischievous followers are slandering Gaurāṅga, and my heart cannot bear it. I must die in expiation, so tell Lord Gaurāṅga's dear followers my request, now," and with that my lord was struck dumb.

Acyuta immediately spread the word. Vīracandra received his written request and brought his disciples to Shantipur. Gaurīdāsa came from Ambikanagar. All the Navadvīpa disciples came to my lord: Narahari Sarakāra came with his followers, and that great scholar Kavi Karṇapūra came. Śyāmadāsa, Viṣṇudāsa, Jadunandana, and all of Advaita's dear disciples came to Shantipur and prostrated themselves at his feet and praised him.

Advaita Ācārya said, "You are all very dear to me. Please comply with my one request. My motivation is to disseminate Lord Caitanya Mahāprabhu's virtues and teachings as far as possible. You must abandon the company of all those wild heretics who hate Lord Gaurāṅga, and you all should sing the name of Gaura, and fulfill my lifelong desire."

When they heard that, love arose in all the disciples, and they began to sing Gaura's name and virtues. All seven—Acyuta, Kṛṣṇa Miśra, Gopāla Ṭhākura, Vīracandra, Narahari the stream of *rasa*, Gaurīdāsa Pandit, and Dāmodara Pandit—all seven danced most charmingly. When Advaita heard Gaura's virtues, love surged up in him, and he began to dance in their midst as they sang. Gradually their chanting the lord's name swelled up like a wave in the ocean and Lord Advaita floated on it in great ecstasy. He first was struck dumb, and then that jewel-lord collapsed. He began to cry, "Where is Gaura, my life?"

Advaita's extraordinary emotions are not possible for a normal person. All his disciples surrounded Advaita and wept. Then my lord said, "I've found Gaurāṅga!" His body trembled like a kadamba flower.

Suddenly he ran into the temple of Madana Gopāla and passed beyond the grasp of ordinary mortals. His followers ran here and there looking for my lord and could not find him, and wept, rolling in the dust.

Acyuta realized that Lord Advaita had disappeared. He wailed and told all of Gaura's people, "He was the one branch of the wishing tree of Gaura's love in which Gaura had not completely demanifested, but today Gaurāṅga's activities are finished."

When everyone heard that, they all wept uncontrollably. "Alas Gaurāṅga, alas Gaurāṅga, alas Nityānanda. Alas also devotee-embodiment my lord Advaitacandra." No other words than those were on everyone's lips. Stony hearts actually melted in this lamentation. Day and night passed with no one's awareness, and then on the second day, everyone bathed in the Gaṅgā.

Lord Acyuta held a great celebration. Everyone got consecrated food and went home. Advaita Ācārya had dwelled on earth for 125 years, playing out countless millions of dramas. Those activities are an ocean of nectar, difficult to reach and difficult to cross. The infinite lord Ananta could not reach it, let alone a contemptible finite person like me. I have behaved so boldly to purify my soul, but I cannot touch a drop of the ocean of his drama. I have neither knowledge nor understanding; how can I write a book? What to write? Dharma is the witness to what I have written.

Reading Laudiya Kṛṣṇadāsa's *Bālya-Līlā-Sūtra* will purify the earth. I have written this book at my lord's order, according to what I have read, or what I heard from Kṛṣṇadāsa, or what Padmanābha or Śyāmadāsa told me, or what I saw with my own sinful eyes. I finished this book in 1568 in Lauḍa.

I will briefly tell the holy men the deep secret of why I went to Lauḍa.

One day, Advaita Ācārya spoke to me in private. "I cannot live apart from Gaurāṅga. I will soon vanish from the world of the living. Recite Gaura's name and Gaura's virtues constantly. I will say one more thing; listen carefully. You are my dear disciple, you are like my son, but do not be depressed about my death. Preach Gaura's name in my birthplace. Please heed my request," my lord said, and stopped speaking. I thought that if I carried out the guru's request, the purpose of my birth would surely be fulfilled.

Then after Advaita Ācārya disappeared, Sītā Ṭhākurānī gave me this order. I did not know what to think! "O Īśānadāsa, I love you very much, and I would be happy if you got married."

I said, "Mother, I understand that you are commanding me, but it's not within my power to comply with this request. I am almost seventy years old, and no brahmin will offer me his daughter now!"

Mother said, "Kṛṣṇa always fulfills his worshipers' wishes. That is why he is called the wishing tree of his devotees' wishes. Go east with Jagadānanda; he will arrange your marriage properly. Preach about Gaura and his religion there, and many living beings will be saved. Your descendants will be great devotees of the lord and will liberate living beings with the name of Hari."

I accepted this command of Mother Sītā's and came east with Jagadānanda Raya. I started my family to comply with my lord's request, and I came straight to blessed Lauḍa. I wrote this book here; I have just abided by the guru's request. I have written just a hint, at his request. It has some faults, and any good points cannot be due to me. This beggar beseeches the feet of his Vaiṣṇava audience please to forgive the faults of this wretch, by your own virtues. I am so old and have no understanding. I offer this book at the feet of Lord Caitanya. I have written as best I could; please, holy men, correct it. The blessed feet of the guru, Kṛṣṇa, and the Vaiṣṇavas are my sole object. My countless bows to all their feet. These three share a single essence. Only their bodies are separate. Just as living beings can see different shapes of earrings and necklaces made of the same gold, so these three have manifested in various forms to rescue living beings. These three are the embodiment of an ocean of mercy, and their feet are the boat on which I will cross beyond earthly existence. I make this offering to the feet of these three. No one can reckon how great a sinner I am, so by your own virtues, please forgive my misdeeds and wipe them out. Reveal the name of the savior of the fallen. In the three worlds no one is as fallen as I; I will remain at his feet until I die.

Īśāna Nāgara, whose hopes are at the feet of Lord Caitanya and Lord Advaita, recites the *Advaita Prakāśa*.

Mahāprabhu Lord Gaura Govinda, the son of Śacī; his generals Lord Advaita and Lord Nityānanda: these three are a single soul, my life's treasure. My heart rests eternally at the feet of these three.

Salutations to the glorious moons Caitanya, Nityānanda, and Advaita.

Appendix 1

ADVAITA ĀCĀRYA'S THEOLOGICAL IDENTITIES

I. In Kavi Karṇapūra's *Gauragaṇoddeśadīpikā*
Sadāśiva

II. In the *Bālya-Līlā-Sūtra*
Sadāśiva; Vāsudeva; Nārāyaṇa; Mahāviṣṇu + Gopeśvara + Ādiśiva

III. In the *Advaita Prakāśa*
Hari; Śiva; Śiva-Vedapañcānana; Sadāśiva; Mahāviṣṇu; Hari-Hara; Kṛṣṇa; Īśvara; Gopeśvara

IV. In the *Advaita Maṅgala*
Kṛṣṇa Pūrṇatama; Vāsudeva; Brahmā; Kṛṣṇa; Nārāyaṇa; Mahāviṣṇu; Īśvara; Śrīdhara Viṣṇu; Rādhā-Kṛṣṇa; Ujjvala; Sampūrṇa Mañjarī; Sadāśiva

Appendix 2

THE BENGALI CALENDAR

Bengali Month	English Equivalent
Vaiśākha	April-May
Jyaiṣṭha	May-June
Āṣāḍha	June-July
Śravaṇa	July-August
Bhādra	August-September
Āśvina	September-October
Kārtika	October-November
Agrahāyaṇa	November-December
Pauṣa	December-January
Māgha	January-February
Phālguna	February-March
Caitra	March-April

GLOSSARY OF NAMES, EPITHETS, AND TERMS

ācārya. "Master," the title given to a scholar who has mastered a particular large body of knowledge. In modern India the title connotes a person who has a Ph.D.

alaṃkāra. The study of rhetorical and literary ornamentation.

Ananta. "Infinite," the name of the many-headed cosmic serpent who serves as Viṣṇu's bed in the cosmic ocean between cycles of creation. Ananta is Viṣṇu's elder brother who precedes him into each earthly appearance, and so is Balarāma and also Nityānanda.

Ananta Saṃhitā. A text Īśāna Nāgara says Mādhavendra Purī gave to Advaita Ācārya during Advaita's pilgrimage tour of India. No one outside the Advaita Ācārya lineage mentions it.

āpsarasa. Exquisitely beautiful heavenly nymph, often sent by the gods to distract sages whose severe practices are threatening the gods' sovereignty.

Arjuna. Third of the five heroic Pāṇḍava brothers of the epic *Mahābhārata* and best friend of Kṛṣṇa in adulthood.

avadhūta. A Śaiva sect whose members are noted for outrageous behavior.

avatāra. "Descent," of a god from heaven to earth.

Badshah. A local ruler under the Mughal system.

Bahulā. A cow whose honesty in the face of danger, and devotion to her calf, so impressed Kṛṣṇa that in her next birth she became one of his wives.

bhajana. A devotional hymn, usually in the form of names of the chosen deity.

bhakta. Devotee; worshiper.

bhakti. Devotion.

bhāva. The underlying emotion of a devotional situation.

Bhīma. One of the five Pāṇḍava brothers, heroes of the epic *Mahābhārata*; Bhīma was particularly noted for his physical strength.

Brahmā. Creator god. In standard iconography Brahma often has four faces, one looking in each cardinal direction, to demonstrate his omniscience. He emerges from a lotus in Viṣṇu's navel at the dawn of each cycle of creation.

brahmacārī. Young man in the first of four stages of life, the *varṇāśrama*-dharma; this is the (celibate) student phase of life.

cākora. A mythological bird whose sole sustenance is moonbeams.

candra. "Moon," added to any name to indicate beauty, or affection on the part of the speaker for the person so named.

cātaka. mythological bird that lives on raindrops and so relies on clouds for its sustenance.

Dantavakra. Demon slain by Kṛṣṇa as a child.

darśana. "Seeing," the ritual act of seeing and being seen by a god or saintly person so as to receive spiritual blessings.

Devakī. Kṛṣṇa's biological mother, who had been imprisoned by her brother Kaṃśa.

devī. "Goddess," used as an honorific for any woman.

dīkṣā. Initiation, usually by a guru, into a particular practice, mantra, or stage of life.

Dīvālī. The autumn festival which elsewhere in India celebrates Prince Rāma's return to his kingdom of Āyodhyā after fourteen years of exile. In Bengal this time is observed as Kālī Pūjā in honor of the fierce warrior goddess Kālī. Īśāna's use of the term may be an attempt to make his account reach beyond Bengal.

Dola Yātrā. Spring festival celebrated on the fourteenth day, the full moon, of the month of Phālguṇa in which Kṛṣṇa and Rādhā are placed on swings; this is also Caitanya's birthday.

Durvāsa. Irascible sage of the epics and *purāṇas*, noted for cursing (with dire consequences) anyone who ignores him or does not treat him well.

Dvāpara Yuga. The third of the four ages in the cycle of creation, when Kṛṣṇa and the eternal *līlā* touched the earth in Vraja.

Dvarakā. Kingdom in western India where Kṛṣṇa lived with his thousands of wives after leaving the Vraja-Mathurā region.

Ekādaśī. Eleventh day of both the dark and the light lunar fortnight, on which pious Vaiṣṇavas fast.

gandharva. Semidivine celestial musician.

Gaṅgā. The Ganges River, most sacred (for "Hindus") of all waterways in South Asia. Also called the Bhāgīrathī, for the mythological sage Bhagīratha, who summoned the river to earth from heaven so that he could properly perform the funeral rites for his ancestors.

Garuḍa. Viṣṇu's eagle mount.

Gauracandra. "The fair moon," epithet of Caitanya.

Gaurahari. "Golden Hari," epithet of Caitanya.

Gaurāṅga. "The golden-bodied one," epithet of Caitanya.

Gayā. City in what is now the state of Bihar housing the important pilgrimage site of the Viṣṇupada Temple. Pilgrims often perform rituals for their recently deceased relatives here.

Goloka. Literally "cow world," Kṛṣṇa's heaven.

Gopāla. "Cow protector," the young cowherd Kṛṣṇa.

Govardhana. Hill in Vraja. Legend has it that Indra once sent a fierce storm to get rid of Kṛṣṇa, who simply lifted Mt. Govardhana and held it aloft to provide shelter for himself and all his companions.

Govinda. the young cowherd Kṛṣṇa.

Haladhara. Epithet of Balarāma, meaning "plow bearer"; Balarāma's origins trace to early agricultural settlements in North India.

Hari. Kṛṣṇa; any form of Viṣṇu.

Hari-Hara. Joint form of Viṣṇu and Śiva.

Icchāśakti. Kṛṣṇa's Power of Desire, who always precedes him into the world.

Indra. In the Vedic pantheon, king of the gods; displaced, according to Vaiṣṇavas, by Kṛṣṇa.

Īśvara. Literally "Mighty Lord," the term most often connnotes Śiva.

Jāhnu. The ancient sage who drank the Gaṅgā after becoming annoyed with it for flowing through his hermitage. The *Mahābhārata* version of the story has Jāhnu later expel the river from his ear. One epithet of the Gaṅgā is Jāhnavī, derived from Jāhnu's name.

Jarāsandha. An evil king and lifelong enemy of Kṛṣṇa who was finally slain, in the epic *Mahābhārata*, by the mighty warrior hero Bhīma.

Jaṭilā. Rādhā's mother-in-law, always suspicious of her daughter-in-law's activities.

kadamba. Nauclea Cadamba, a tree with orange blossoms whose leaves quiver, giving rise to the simile "to tremble like a kadamba."

Kālapā grammar. The Sanskrit grammar most commonly taught in Bengal during Advaita's student days.

Kali Yuga. The fourth and hence most degenerate age in the four-age cycle of creation.

Kaṃśa. Devakī's brother who usurped the throne of Mathurā from Vasudeva, Kṛṣṇa's father.

Kānu. Nickname of Kṛṣṇa.

Kāśī. Also known as Vārāṇāsī and Benares, an important pilgrimage city along the Gaṅgā.

kāyastha. Bengali caste originally formed by brahmin-*śūdra* marriages.

Keśava Bhāratī. A *sannyāsī* in the Bhāratī order of renunciates, he initiated Viśvambhara Miśra into that order and conferred upon him the name Kṛṣṇa Caitanya.

kīrtana. A style of devotional singing involving repetition of the names and epithets of the deity.

Kīrtīdā. Rādhā's mother.

kṣatriya. The broad caste grouping of rulers and military officers.

Kubjā. An ugly woman whose devotion to Kṛṣṇa ultimately rendered her beautiful.

kulīna. The highest-ranking among Bengali brahmins.

līlā. "Play," or "activities," usually in reference to Kṛṣṇa.

liṅgam. "Phallus," the symbol most often used to symbolize the god Śiva.

Mādhava. Kṛṣṇa.

Madhva Ācārya. Putative founder of the dualistic school of Vaiṣṇavism with which the Gauḍīyas formally affiliated in the eighteenth century, though the two have little in common. This marriage of convenience, which legitimated the Gauḍīyas and gave them access to a particular temple in Jaipur, was probably prompted by the similarity of the names of Madhva and Mādhavendra Purī.

mahanta. "Great one," a Gauḍīya Vaiṣṇava term referring to any of the sixty-four community leaders who recognized Caitanya's divinity during his lifetime. Elsewhere, the abbot of a monastery.

Mahāprabhu. "Great lord," the most common epithet for Caitanya.

mahāprasada. "Great grace," specifically food that has been offered to the Jagannātha deity at the temple in Puri and then distributed to devotees.

Mahāviṣṇu. The form of Viṣṇu who reposes on the cosmic serpent Ananta in the ocean of milk between ages of creation. Outside of the Bengali Vaiṣṇava tradition this form is the source of all forms of Viṣṇu. Mahāviṣṇu always carries four items by which his various forms can be recognized: conch, lotus, discus, and mace.

Mahāyogeśvara. Great Lord of the Yogis; epithet of Śiva and hence also of Advaita Ācārya.

Mandākinī. Tributary of the River Gaṅgā originating at Kedarnath in the mountains of northern Uttar Pradesh; sacred to Śiva.

Māndhātā. An ancient mythological king.

mañjarīs. "Buds," the prepubescent girls who assisted Rādhā and Kṛṣṇa during their romantic trysts, and so were very close to the divine couple.

Māyā. "Illusion" or "magic," personified as Kṛṣṇa's feminine counterpart, the magic of creation, who always precedes him into the world.

Nāḍha. Nickname for Advaita based on the home of one of his ancestors in Nadiyala, but also a variant on an old word meaning "bald."

Nadiyala. Nickname for a man from the village of Nadiyala, here applied to Advaita Ācārya's paternal grandfather Narasiṃha.

Nanda. Kṛṣṇa. Also proper name of Kṛṣṇa's foster father.

Nandīśvara. Epithet of Śiva; literally, "Nandi (Śiva's bull-vehicle)'s lord."

Nārada. Divine sage and friend of Kṛṣṇa who travels frequently between heaven and earth and usually appears carrying a stringed instrument.

Narasiṃha. Patronymic indicating the son of Nrisiṃha.

Nārāyaṇa. Distant and majestic form of Viṣṇu that predates the notion of avatāra by which Viṣṇu descends to earth in times of crisis to restore righteousness.

Navagrāma. Advaita's birthplace on the Surma River, upriver from the present-day town of Sunamgunj in Sylhet District of Bangladesh.

Nīlācala. Old name for the city of Purī.

Nitāi. Nickname for Nityānanda.

nityasiddha. "Eternally perfected," refers to an individual who through assiduous practice has entered a state so pure that he or she will undergo no further rebirth.

pandit. A scholar.

parakīyā. Literally "another's woman," the doctrine propagated by some of the Gauḍīyas that worship of Kṛṣṇa should follow the model of an illicit love affair in which the partners are willing to risk everything for that love, and in which each union may well be the last.

paratattva. The doctrine (*tattva*) centered on worship in the erotic mood, through sexual ritual with another's (*para*) woman or man.

prabhu. "Lord," used as a title of respect for any man, but specifically in Gauḍīya theology to refer to both Nityānanda and Advaita.

Pradyumna. One of Kṛṣṇa's sons by Rukmiṇī; the third evolute of Vāsudeva in the *caturvyūha* theological scheme.

prasāda. "Grace," usually in reference to food or other substance which has been offered to a deity and then its remnants, to assembled devotees.

Prayāga. Present-day city of Allahabad in the state of Uttar Pradesh, at the confluence of the rivers Gaṅgā, Yamunā, and the mythological Sarasvatī.

pūjā. Ritual worship; a festival devoted to a particular deity.

Purī. Important pilgrimage city on the Bay of Bengal in what is now the state of Orissa. The enormous Jagannātha Temple complex where Caitanya spent much of his life is in Purī.

Pūrṇamāsī/Paurṇamāsī. Old woman ally of Rādhā and Kṛṣṇa in Vraja who acts as their go-between and helps arrange their clandestine trysts.

pūrvarāga. The "preceding emotion," the feeling of anticipation of a love affair that has yet to occur.

Pūtanā. Demoness who tried to kill the infant Kṛṣṇa by smearing poison on her breasts and posing as a wet nurse; Kṛṣṇa killed her instead by sucking her life force out through her breasts.

Rādhā. Kṛṣṇa's favorite among the gopīs of Braja. Also called Rai and Rādhikā.

rajas. One of the qualities of nature, rajas is the quality of energy and activity.

rasa. Literally, "juice" or "sap," rasa is the flavor, the emotional experience, of devotional activity.

rāsa līlā. The episode most famously told in Book X of the *Bhāgavata Purāṇa* in which Kṛṣṇa and the cowherd maidens of Vraja dance in the moonlight; Kṛṣṇa replicates himself thousands of times so that each woman thinks she and she alone is dancing with Kṛṣṇa.

Rohiṇī. Devakī's co-wife married to Vasudeva; mother of Balarāma.

sacrifice. Brahmin householders perform five "sacrifices" daily, which are understood to cultivate compassion and repay creation for their very existence. These are scriptural study, ritual worship, offering water to the ancestors, providing hospitality to guests, and giving food to other creatures.

sādhu. Holy, virtuous, wise man; a renunciate.

sakha. One of Kṛṣṇa's young male friends in Vraja.

sakhī. One of the young women associated with Rādhā and Kṛṣṇa in Vraja.

śālagrāma. A black geode worshiped as representative of Viṣṇu.

Saṃkarṣaṇa. See Ananta. The first evolute of Kṛṣṇa in the *catur vyūha* theory of the *Pāñcarātra* tradition.

saṅkīrtana. Congregational singing of devotional songs.

sannyāsin, sannyāsī. One who has taken formal renunciation in one of the ten orthodox monastic orders whose founding is attributed to the eighth-century Śaṅkara. *Sannyāsīs* cut all ties with their past, including their family and caste affiliations.

Śantanu. Ancient mythological king whose first wife was the River Gaṅgā, who made his son (later known as Bhīṣma) give up his rights to the throne in favor of his stepmother's sons.

sattva. One of the three qualities of nature, *sattva* is the quality of purity and goodness.

Setubandhu. In the far south, where Hanuman and his monkey army built a bridge to take Rāma to Lanka to rescue his wife Sītā from the demon King Rāvana, who had kidnapped her.

Śeṣa. See Ananta.

Sītānātha. Sītā's "lord," or husband; epithet of Advaita Ācārya.

Śrī. "Glorious," a title roughly equivalent to Lord or Lady.

Śrīdhara. "Holder of [the Goddess] Śrī," an epithet of Viṣṇu, whose iconography often depicts his consort goddess seated on his lap.

Subala. One of Kṛṣṇa's closest boyhood friends in Vraja.

śūdra. Lowest of the four large caste groupings, still within the caste system; the servant class.

sukta. A favorite Bengali dish of bitter vegetables.

svarūpa. Literally, one's "own form"; the innate form, or essence, of a god.

Svayaṃ Bhagavān. The Lord Himself, the most complete form of divinity.

Śyāma. "The dark one," Kṛṣṇa, so named because his complexion is very dark.

tamas. One of the three qualities of nature, *tamas* is inertia.

ṭhākura. Title for a brahmin man.

ṭhākurānī. Title for a married brahmin woman.

tīrtha. Pilgrimage site, usually located on a river.

Treta Yuga. Second of the four ages of creation; Rāma was the *avatāra* of the Treta Yuga.

tulasī. Sacred basil (*Ocimum sanctum*), a plant that adorns many Vaiṣṇava homes. No meal is served unless it has first been offered to Kṛṣṇa topped with a tulasī leaf. Initiated Vaiṣṇavas wear a choker of small tulasī beads and use a string of 108 tulasī beads to count their prayers.

Ujjvala. One of Kṛṣṇa's closest boyhood friends.

Vaikuṇṭha. Viṣṇu's heaven.

vaiśya. A member of the merchant class, the third of the large caste groupings.

Vasudeva. Kṛṣṇa's biological father, imprisoned by the evil King Kaṃśa.

Vāsudeva. Patronymic for Vasudeva, and so an epithet of Kṛṣṇa.

Veda-Pañcānana. Śiva (the five-faced) who knows the Vedas; epithet of Advaita Ācārya.

Vedāṅgas. Literally, "limbs" of the Vedas, a body of texts considered auxiliary to the four Vedas. These limbs usually number six and include phonetics, metrics, grammar, etymology, astrology, and ritual.

Viṣṇupada Temple. An important site for performing final funeral rites, built on a spot where Vaiṣṇavas believe Viṣṇu himself once stepped. The temple is located in the modern city of Gayā in the state of Bihar.

Viśvambhara Miśra. Given name of Kṛṣṇa Caitanya.

vrata. Vow. Ritual fast undertaken, usually by women for the health and longevity of their husbands and/or sons; each vrata has its own tale explaining how it came about.

Vṛkabhānu. Rādhā's father.

Yadu. Kṛṣṇa's clan name.

Yaśodā. Kṛṣṇa's foster mother in the pastoral community of Vṛndāvana.

Yogamāyā. Kṛṣṇa's magical power of illusion which always precedes him into birth on earth.

BIBLIOGRAPHY

Bhattacharjee, Jatindramohan. *Catalogus Catalogorum of Bengali Manuscripts*. Calcutta: Asiatic Society of Bengal, 1978.

Bhattacharya, Narendra Nath. *History of the Śākta Religion*. Delhi: Munshiram Manoharlal, 1974.

Brzezinski, Jan. "Women Saints in Gauḍīya Vaiṣṇavism." *Journal of Vaiṣṇava Studies* 3.4 (1995): 57–83.

Callewaert, Winand, and Rupert Snell, eds. *According to Tradition: Hagiographical Writing in India*. Wiesbaden: Harrassowitz, 1996.

Caudhurī, Acyutacaraṇa Tattvanidhi. "Īśāna Nāgarera *Advaita Prakāśa*." *Baṅgīya Sāhitya Pariṣat Patrikā* 3.4 (1303 B.E.): 249–254.

Chakrabarty, Ramakanta. *Vaiṣṇavism in Bengal 1486–1900*. Calcutta: Sanskrit Pustak Bhandar, 1985.

Chandidas, Baru. *Singing the Glory of Lord Krishna: The Śrīkṛṣṇakīrtan*. Translated and annotated by Mimi Klaiman. Chico: Scholars Press, 1984.

Chatterjee, Rama. *Religion in Bengal during the Pala and the Sena Times*. Calcutta: Punthi Pustak, 1985.

Cleverly, Barbara. *The Last Kashmiri Rose*. New York: Dell, 2001.

Das Gupta, Bepin Vihari. *Govinda's Kadcha: A Black Forgery*. Dacca: Dasgupta, 1937.

Dāsa, Haridāsa. *Gauḍīya Vaiṣṇava Abhidhāna*. Navadvīpa: Haribol Kutir, n.d.

De, Sushil Kumar. *Early History of the Vaishnava Faith and Movement in Bengal*. Calcutta: KLM, 1986 (1961).

Dimock, Edward C., Jr. *Place of the Hidden Moon: Erotic Mysticism in the Vaiṣṇava-sahajiyā Cult of Bengal*. Chicago: University of Chicago Press, 1989 (1966).

Dimock, Edward C., Jr., and Denise Levertov, translators. *In Praise of Krishna: Songs from the Bengali*. Chicago: University of Chicago Press, 1967.

Dimock, Edward C., Jr., and Tony K. Stewart. *Caitanya Caritāmṛta of Kṛṣṇadāsa Kavirāja*. Cambridge: Department of Sanskrit and Indian Studies, Harvard University, 1999.

Eaton, Richard M. *The Rise of Islam and the Bengal Frontier 1204–1760*. Delhi: Oxford University Press, 1994.

Entwistle, Alan W. *Braj: Centre of Krishna Pilgrimage*. Groningen: Egbert Forsten, 1987.

Ghoṣa, Mṛṇālakānti, ed. *Īśāna Nāgarara Advaita Prakāśa*. 3rd ed. Calcutta: Amṛta Bājāra Patrikā, 1339.

Gold, Daniel. *Aesthetics and Analysis in Writing on Religion: Modern Fascinations*. Berkeley: University of California Press, 2003.

Haberman, David L. *Acting as a Way of Salvation: A Study of Raganuga Bhakti Sadhana*. New York: Oxford University Press, 1988.

———, translator. *The Bhaktirasāmṛtasindhu of Rūpa Gosvāmin*. New Delhi: Indira Gandhi National Centre for the Arts, 2003.

Hardy, Friedhelm. "Madhavendra Puri: A Link between Bengal Vaiṣṇavism and South Indian Bhakti." *Journal of the Royal Asiatic Society of Great Britain and Ireland* 1 (1974): 23–41.

Hawley, John Stratton, ed. *Saints and Virtues*. Berkeley: University of California Press, 1987.

Hobsbawm, Eric, and Ranger, Terence, eds., *The Invention of Tradition*. Cambridge: Cambridge University Press, 2000 (1983).

Inden, Ronald. *Marriage and Rank in Bengali Culture: A History of Caste and Clan in Middle Period Bengal*. Berkeley: University of California Press, 1976.

Kar, Sibir. *Acyutacaraṇa Tattvanidhi: Jīvana o Sāhitya 1272–1360*. Karimganj, Assam: Yugaśakti Prakāśanālaya, 1991.

Karve, Irawati. *Hindu Society: An Interpretation*. Poona: Deccan College, 1961.

Kermode, Frank. *The Genesis of Secrecy: On the Interpretation of Narrative*. Cambridge: Harvard University Press, 1979.

Kieckhefer, Richard, and George D. Bond, eds. *Sainthood: Its Manifestation in World Religions*. Berkeley: University of California Press, 1990.

Klaiman, M. H. *Baru Caṇḍīdāsa: Singing the Glory of Lord Krishna: The Śrīkṛṣṇakīrtan*. Translated and annotated by Mimi Klaiman. Chico: Scholars Press, 1984.

Kṛṣṇadāsa, Lauḍīya. *Bālyalīlāsūtra*. Ed. and trans. Acyutacaraṇa Tattvanidhi Caudhurī. Caritamālikā Series No. 2. Karimgañja: Śrīdhara Library, 1915.

LaCapra, Dominick. *Rethinking Intellectual History*. Ithaca, NY: Cornell University Press, 1983.

Lakoff, George, and Mark Johnson. *Metaphors We Live By*. Chicago: University of Chicago Press, 1980.

Maiti, Ravindranātha, ed. *Haricaraṇa Dāsera Advaita Maṅgala*. Bardhaman: Bardhaman University, 1966.

Majumdar, Bimanbihari. "Śrī Caitanyacaritera Upādāna." Ph.D. diss., Calcutta University, 1939.

Majumdar, R. C., ed. *History of Bengal*. Vol. 1. Dacca: University of Dacca, 1943.

Mannheim, Karl. *Essays on the Sociology of Culture*. London: Routledge, 1992 (1956).

Manring, Rebecca J. "At Home in the World: The Lives of Sītādevī." *International Journal of Hindu Studies* Vol. 2, No. 1 (1998): 21–42.

——— *Reconstructing Tradition: Advaita Ācārya and the Gauḍīya Vaiṣṇava Tradition at the Cusp of the Twentieth Century*. New York: Columbia University Press, 2005.

———. "Sītā Devī: An Early Vaiṣṇava Guru." In *The Graceful Guru: Hindu Female Gurus in India and the United States*, ed. Karen Pechilis-Prentiss, 51–64. Oxford University Press, 2004.

Manring, Rebecca J., and Stewart, Tony K. "In the Name of Devotion: The Hagiographies of Advaitācārya." *Journal of Vaiṣṇava Studies* 5. no.1 (1997): 103–126.

Matsobara, Mitsonori. *Pāñcarātra Saṃhitās and Early Vaishnava Theology*. Delhi: Motilal Banarsidass, 1994.

McDermott, Rachel Fell. *Mother of My Heart, Daughter of My Dreams: Kālī and Ūmā in the Devotional Poetry of Bengal*. New York: Oxford University Press, 2001.

Nāgara, Īśāna. *Advaita Prakāśa*. Ed. Keśavalāla Rāya, Kolkata: Keśavalāla Rāya, 1898.

———. *Advaita Prakāśa*. 2nd ed. Ed. Mṛṇālakānti Ghoṣa, N.P., n.d.

———. *Advaita Prakāśa*. New edition. Ed. Satīśacandra Mitra, Kolkata: Ashutosh Library, 1926.

———. *Advaita Prakāśa*. 3rd ed. Ed. Mṛṇālakānti Ghoṣa, Kolkata: Viśvakoṣa Press, 1933.

Rasmussen, David M. *Mythic-Symbolic Language and Philosophic Anthropology: A Constructive Interpretation of the Thought of Paul Ricoeur*. The Hague: Martinus Nijhoff, 1971.

Ray, Ratnalekha. *Change in Bengal Agrarian Society c. 1760–1850*. New Delhi: Manohar, 1979.

Raychaudhuri, Tapan. *Perceptions, Emotions, Sensibilities: Essays on India's Colonial and Post-colonial Experiences*. New Delhi: Oxford University Press, 1999.

Ricoeur, Paul. *Time and Narrative*. 3 Vols. Chicago: University of Chicago Press, 1990.

Said, Edward. *The World, the Text, and the Critic*. Cambridge, MA: Harvard University Press, 1983.

Sartori, Andrew. *Bengal in Global Concept History: Culturalism in the Age of Capital*. Chicago: University of Chicago Press, 2008.

Sen, Dinesh Chandra. "The Karcha by Govindadas." *Calcutta Review* 14, no.3 (1925): 567–578.

Sengupta, Nitish. *History of the Bengali-speaking People*. New Delhi: UBSPD, 2001.

Smith, Jonathan Z. *Drudgery Divine: On the Comparison of Early Christianities and the Religions of Late Antiquity*. Chicago: University of Chicago Press, 1990.

———. *Imagining Religion: From Babylon to Jonestown*. Chicago: University of Chicago Press, 1982.

Smith, William L. *The One-Eyed Goddess: A Study of the Manasā Maṅgala*. Stockholm: Almqvist and Wiksell International, 1980.

Spiegel, Gabrielle. *The Past as Text*. Baltimore: Johns Hopkins, 1997.

Stewart, Tony K. *The Final Word: The Caitanya Caritāmṛta and the Grammar of Religious Tradition*. New York: Oxford University Press, 2010.

———. "One Text from Many: The *Caitanya Caritāmṛta* as 'Classic' and 'Commentary.'" In *According to Tradition: Hagiographical Writing in India*, ed. Winand M. Callewaert and Rupert Snell, 317–56. Wiesbaden: Harrassowitz, 1994.

Talbot, Cynthia. "The Story of Prataparudra: Hindu Historiography on the Deccan Frontier." In *Beyond Turk and Hindu: Rethinking Religious Identities in Islamicate South Asia* ed. David Gilmartin and Bruce B. Lawrence, Gainesville: University Press of Florida, 2000.

Tarafdar, Momtazur Rahman. *Husain Shahi Bengal 1494–1538 AD: A Socio-Political Study*. Dacca: Asiatic Society of Pakistan, 1965.

Van Schendel, Willem. *A History of Bangladesh*. Cambridge: Cambridge University Press, 2009.

Vasu. *Vaṅgera Jātīya Itihāsa*. Calcutta: Viśvakoṣa Press, 1911–33.

White, Hayden. *Tropics of Discourse: Essays in Cultural Criticism*. Baltimore: Johns Hopkins University Press, 1978.

Worthen, Thomas D. *The Myth of Replacement: Stars, Gods and Order in the Universe*. Tucson: University of Arizona Press, 1991.

INDEX